NUMBER TWO HUNDRED AND TWENTY-FOUR

The Old Farmer's Almanac

CALCULATED ON A NEW AND IMPROVED PLAN FOR THE YEAR OF OUR LORD

2016

BEING LEAP YEAR AND (UNTIL JULY 4) 240TH YEAR OF AMERICAN INDEPENDENCE

Fitted for Boston and the New England states, with special corrections and calculations to answer for all the United States.

Containing, besides the large number of Astronomical Calculations and the Farmer's Calendar for every month in the year, a variety of

NEW, USEFUL, & ENTERTAINING MATTER.

Established in 1792 by Robert B. Thomas (1766–1846)

Each morning sees some task begin, Each evening sees it close;
Something attempted, something done, Has earned a night's repose.
–Henry Wadsworth Longfellow, American poet (1807–82)

Cover T.M. registered in U.S. Patent Office

Copyright © 2015 by Yankee Publishing Incorporated
ISSN 0078-4516

Library of Congress Card No. 56-29681

Original wood engraving by Randy Miller

THE OLD FARMER'S ALMANAC • DUBLIN, NH 03444 • 603-563-8111 • ALMANAC.COM

Contents

(continued on page 4)

Contents

(continued from page 2)

There's more of everything at Almanac.com.

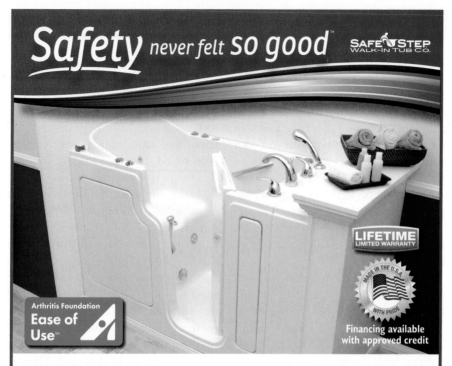

Weather Proof

Readers consistently tell us that "weather" is the #1 reason they read this Almanac. It has been this way for centuries, possibly due in part to a weather forecast that we made (or maybe *didn't* make) 200 years ago.

Nobody expected what actually happened.

Snow fell during July and August of 1816 in New England and parts of Canada.

The diary of Rev. Thomas Robbins of East Windsor, Connecticut, tells of a foot of snow in the Berkshires in June.

In July, heavy frosts and ice storms occurred. On the 4th, Caleb Emery of Lyman, New Hampshire, visited a well that was completely frozen over 8 feet belowground; it remained that way until July 25.

The region's corn crop, except where near ponds or the ocean, failed.

So many birds froze that few were seen in New England for 3 years.

In the history books, the period is referred to as "the year without a summer" and "the cold summer of 1816." Its cause was eventually shown to have been an 1815 volcanic eruption of Mount Tambora in what was then the Dutch East Indies. This event had left volcanic dust circling the globe, lowering temperatures as much as several degrees and resulting in snow. Such an eruption would explain the appearance of the Sun in 1816 as "in a cloud of smoke," as described in the *American Magazine of History*.

But did the Almanac predict this weather? We still get questions about this, and we've had an eye out for copies of that 1816 edition. Several have been found, but none has a snow prediction for that summer.

As the story goes, the printer inserted a "snow" prediction into the 1816 edition as a joke while Almanac founder Robert B. Thomas was sick in bed with the flu. When Thomas discovered the "error," he destroyed all—or maybe most of—the "snow" copies and had the 1816 Almanac reprinted with the more conventional forecast. It's said that word got out anyway, and during the early months of that year, Thomas repeatedly had to deny making such a ridiculous forecast. Then, when it really did snow in July, he changed his tune and took full credit. "Told you so!" he allegedly said.

If the story is true, it's a good example of what this Almanac's 11th editor, Robb Sagendorph, always referred to as "almanacsmanship." Today, our meteorologist, not the printer, makes the weather predictions. Almanacsmanship goes into all of the *other* pages.

–J. S., June 2015

However, it is by our works and not our words that we would be judged. These, we hope, will sustain us in the humble though proud station we have so long held in the name of

Your obedient servant,

Robt. B. Thomas.

OUR PROFESSIONAL PERFORMANCE
YOUR COUNTRY VALUES

Life in the country is a conscious choice.
And, for generations, your family has relied on the best, most dependable equipment available to work the land you love. Today, more and more farmers are using dependable, professional-grade equipment to maintain their yards, too.

And for that, they're turning to Exmark. For more than 30 years, Exmark has set the standard in professional equipment. Today, they're the first choice of landscape professionals — purchased two-to-one over the next best-selling brand.

Get a better cut, faster — from Exmark. Professional performance. Superior productivity. Legendary durability. And, the first choice of everyone who makes a living from the land.

www.exmark.com

ON THE FARM

Healthy soils are a key advantage for farmers dealing with increasingly unpredictable weather. The better they manage the soil, the less they need to spend on fertilizers, pesticides, and fuel.
–*Helen Husher, spokesperson, Northeast Sustainable Agriculture Research and Education*

COMING SOON

● robot "bees" that pollinate crops

● audio pest control: Plants "hear" the man-made sound of insects chewing vibrations and release chemicals to protect themselves.

● drones to detect where crops may need replanting or pesticide application

● plants with leaves that grow at an angle: They absorb less sunlight and offset climate change.

HIGH TECH, HERE NOW

● DNA analysis to help ranchers learn which cattle will produce large numbers of the tastiest steaks

● nutrient-dense varieties of veggies (data suggest that plants will become less nutritious with rising CO_2 levels)

● light, electric, four-wheel vehicles to help farmers carry a ton of cargo

FORWARD-THINKING FARMERS ARE . . .

● using no-till cover crops and diverse rotations to improve soil quality and control erosion

● converting abandoned urban factories into state-of-the-art greenhouses

● connecting with grocery shoppers by doing in-store cooking demos

BY THE NUMBERS

42% of organic farms sell directly to consumers (compared to **7%** of all U.S. farms)

2,398: number of greenhouse acres now in production in Ontario

17.3 million: number of Christmas trees harvested annually

WORD FOR THE WISE
"Grocerant": a place that serves as both grocery and restaurant

- sitting at communal tables for face-to-face interaction
- sharing tastes from companions' plates

GOOD EATS

Specialty food stores and supermarkets are becoming the new community centers.
–Denise Purcell, senior director, Specialty Food Association

PEOPLE ARE TALKING ABOUT . . .

- airline food delivered to the home
- frozen yogurt in edible dried-fruit wrappers (to reduce packaging waste)
- smaller portions (for better health)

- butter tastings as appetizers, to sample flavors and types

EATING IS MORE SOCIAL: WE'RE . . .

- meeting and dining at food halls (not courts)
–Darcy Lenz, assistant food editor, Cooking Light

APP-SOLUTELY APPETIZING!

Restaurants want to give diners reason to post photos of meals on social media: "Look for architectonic creations on plates that beg to be photographed and shared. Chefs are realizing that the look of food is as important as taste."
–Daniel Levine, director, The Avant-Guide Institute

BY THE NUMBERS

12% of Americans eat dessert after supper

1,128: number of snacks the average adult eats each year

91% of us snack daily

205: number of weekday breakfasts eaten at home per person per year, on average, as this becomes the family meal

FLAVORS WE'RE CRAVING

- "smoke" in butter, vegetables, and cocktails
- heritage breeds of chicken (firmer and stronger-flavored)

(continued)

The New York Botanical Garden

GARDENING

People are seeing public parks, botanical gardens, and arboreta as the cultural hearts of their cities—places for serenity, learning, and great local food.

–Casey Sclar, executive director, American Public Gardens Association

BY THE NUMBERS

42 million: number of U.S. households that grow food in a home or community garden

3 million: number of community gardens in the United States

$3.5 billion: amount Americans spend on food gardening

NUMBER OF HOUSEHOLDS GROWING . . .

Vegetables: **32 million**

Herbs: **20 million**

Fruit trees: **14 million**

Berries: **12 million**

–National Gardening Association

PEOPLE ARE TALKING ABOUT . . .

• "tablescaping," with pansy and petunia centerpieces and candelabras

• planting new, adaptable tree varieties

• *Tamarixia radiata*, natural predator of the "yellow dragon" fly that is ravaging orange groves

APP-SOLUTELY AMAZING!

• apps that alert when fruit and veggies are ripe
• Internet-connected indoor hydroponic crops tracked remotely by growers

in Florida and southern California

• small, lightweight, greenhouse "community gardens" in vacant urban areas

• backyard "pub-sheds"

SPACE-SAVERS

• Park Seeds' picks: 'Mega Bite' tomatoes, 'Spacemaster 80' cukes, 'Norli' snow peas, 'Bull Dog' okra

HARDWORKING PLANTS

• multipellet seeds that produce several varieties of plants

• 'EnduraScape', a new verbena that tolerates

temperatures from the teens to more than 100°F

• mildew-resistant impatiens and basil

INCREDIBLE EDIBLES

• drinks flavored with homegrown herbs: lemonade with thyme or lavender; water with cucumber and mint; hot teas sweetened with stevia leaves

• Asian greens: bok choy for crunchy stems and cabbagelike taste; mizuna for a peppery, spicy

Photo: John Peden/New York Botanical Garden

Mother Nature's Solutions

flavor; Chinese kale, which tastes similar to broccoli, to be steamed or blanched

–Dave Forehand, VP, Dallas Arboretum and Botanical Garden

TOP CROPS

• W. Atlee Burpee's choices: 'Caracas' carrot, 'Fresh Pickles' cucumber, 'Cherry Stuffer' red pepper, 'Tweety' yellow pepper, 'Baby Boomer' tomato, 'Baby Bubba' okra

• Ball Horticultural Company's best picks: 'Honeynut' squash, 'Patio Baby' eggplant,

SMALL IS BIG!

Containers and small plots burst with compact and dwarf plants that yield full-size fruit and harvests.

'Cute Stuff' red pepper, 'Patio Snacker' cucumber

• Dallas Arboretum and Botanical Garden's favorite varieties: 'Babybeat' beet; 'Fairy Tale' purple and white mini-eggplant; 'Pattypan' summer squash in white, yellow, and green

COMEBACK KIDS

• four-season 'Emerald Triumph' and 'HomeFree' viburnum: white flowers in spring, glossy leaves in summer, red fall color, and dark blue fruit in winter; also 'Cardinal' and 'Isanti' red twig dogwoods

–Tom Brinda, horticultural manager, Minnesota Landscape Arboretum

• in the South: 'Endless Summer' hydrangea and twice-blooming azaleas

• in the North: weigela that blooms in late spring and early fall

(continued)

AROUND THE HOUSE

The ability to age in place, through in-home accessibility, continues to influence home design trends.
–*Matt Tinder, spokesperson, The American Institute of Architects*

PEOPLE ARE TALKING ABOUT . . .

• historical homes restored to their original state, including candlelit chandeliers and century-old toilets

• architectural firms helping folks to move from large, costly houses and build tiny, low-energy homes

"IN" TOUCHES

• textured wallpaper embedded with recycled glass or beads

• computer-scanned paintings printed as custom wallpaper

BY THE NUMBERS

63% of new homes completed in 2013 had porches

Less than **1%** of households are full-service smart homes

HOME IMPROVEMENTS

• neutral gray in the kitchen: walls, cabinets, and furniture

• brass, copper, and rose-gold metals for lamps and cabinet and furniture hardware

EVERYTHING OLD . . .

We love tractor parts, rusty wheelbarrows, and plows in yards; artful antique doors; and old wooden tables for plants.
–*Randy Schultz, content editor, www.homegardenandhomestead.com*

WORDS FOR THE WISE

The *"conscious home"*: a living space that is aware of and responds to residents' habits and needs

• worn/weathered wood in tables, paneling, and floors, and the look of it in ceramic tiles and wallpaper
–*Amy Panos, senior editor, Better Homes & Gardens*

BRIGHT IDEAS

• homes that float in floods

• storage under floorboards and in crawl spaces for out-of-season clothing and extra linens

• sensors in pots that self-water indoor plants

IN DEMAND . . .

• ramps, elevators, and on-grade entries

• home offices, fitness and mud rooms

DATA DETECTORS

• wind sensors gauge neighborhood pollution (so that folks can choose the healthiest walking routes)

• research cameras identify light bulb choices and "lights out" times in urban homes

(continued)

OUR PASSION FOR FASHION

Fashion is finally ready to let go of retro, revival, and revamp trends. Space and science will lead the way.

–Amanda Hallay, fashion merchandising professor, LIM College

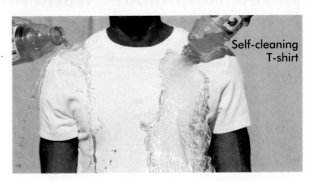

Self-cleaning T-shirt

TECH-SAVVY TEXTILES AND BLING

- tiny, invisible nano-wires in fabric will trap body heat
- small tubes in fabric will air-condition wearers
- jackets will charge cellphones
- jewelry will light up for calls or texts
- textiles will emit mood-indicative scents
- necklaces will release perfume

- sock sensors will audibly advise joggers on gait and stride

WEATHER-OR-NOT WEAR

- For women, the look is whites, icy blues, frosty pinks, and muted pistachio greens, with plastic and glass buttons, heels, and hair accessories: "The overall feeling is of a cold and ethereal Nordic landscape."

- For men, expect jackets and pants in cracked and ripped fabrics that appear worn and weathered (think deserts and dust storms) and natural landscape colors—muddy browns, red russets, burnt siennas. "Colors and fabrics will appear to have withstood the test of time and environmental extremes."

- We'll also find both men and women in acid greens, deep purples, midnight blues, turquoise, and matte black, colors that evoke celestial galaxies and the northern lights.

–Steven Faerm, associate professor of fashion, Parsons The New School for Design

GUYS AND GALS ARE SUITING UP

For women, "There's a return to modern classics from the not-so-distant past, including the fitted menswear jacket as a core wardrobe staple."

–Sharon Haver, founder, FocusOnStyle.com

For men, "Black has traditionally not been acceptable for business suits, but there has been a gain in its popularity."

–Andy Gilchrist, author, The Encyclopedia of Men's Clothes

FOR MEN ONLY

- cashmere baseball caps (think diamond and square patterns)

(continued)

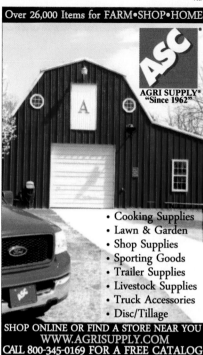

Over 26,000 Items for FARM•SHOP•HOME

ASC

AGRI SUPPLY®
"Since 1962"

- Cooking Supplies
- Lawn & Garden
- Shop Supplies
- Sporting Goods
- Trailer Supplies
- Livestock Supplies
- Truck Accessories
- Disc/Tillage

SHOP ONLINE OR FIND A STORE NEAR YOU
WWW.AGRISUPPLY.COM
CALL 800-345-0169 FOR A FREE CATALOG

at home in nature™

From seaside getaways to mountain retreats, the Pacific Yurt goes where you want to be.

Call today for a brochure:
1.800.944.0240
www.yurts.com

pacific
yurts® Inc.
WORLD'S LEADING MANUFACTURER

http://remedies.net

The Essiac Handbook

Learn about the Famous Ojibway Herbal Healing Remedy

For Your <u>FREE</u> *Copy:*

Call Toll Free: **1-888-568-3036**

or Write: **PO Box 640, Crestone, CO 81131**

ENERGY • DETOX • VITALITY

- athletic-inspired knits
- plaid and checkered suits and sports jackets
- foreign-language words, in script, on T-shirts and jackets

ALL TOGETHER NOW

Watch for both men and women in . . .

- fedoras and other broad-brim hats
- motorcycle jackets in faux leather and denim
- fringed suede jackets
- snug, sweatshirt-y slacks and jeans

BY THE NUMBERS

1,000: kilowatt-hours of electricity used monthly by one home, on average

1,000: kilowatt-hours saved yearly by one person wearing nanowire thermal textiles that both create and trap heat

OUR ANIMAL FRIENDS

As people increasingly look for all-natural, chemical-free, organic products for themselves, so, too, are they seeking the same for their pets.
–*Bob Vetere, president and CEO, American Pet Products Association*

BY THE NUMBERS

32% of dog owners take pooches on car trips when traveling at least 2 nights

9% of dog owners have financially provided for their pets in their wills

TO KEEP PETS HEALTHY

- get disposable patches of grass delivered to apartment-dwelling cats and dogs
- use aromatherapy beds with lavender inserts to soothe pets to sleep
- use sunscreens for doggy noses and ears

UBER-PAMPERED PETS

- Christmas card photos

will feature special holiday outfits for rabbits, guinea pigs, ferrets, and turtles.

PEOPLE ARE TALKING ABOUT . . .

- dating services that let dogs in on first dates, to see if the owners' pooches are compatible

APP-SOLUTELY AMAZING!

- devices that count dogs' steps
- pet video cameras that film life from the animal's point of view
- collars that track pets' vital signs

(continued)

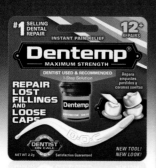
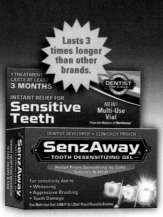

Wearable wristband
and shoe sensors

HEALTH AND WELLNESS

Simple wristband
activity trackers will
be replaced by much
more informative
wearable sensors.
*–Dr. Steven Steinhubl, director of
digital medicine, Scripps Health*

ALWAYS ON

• Doctors will remotely
monitor our stress levels,
blood pressure, pulse
rate, body position, and
sleep quality.

**GET HAPPY!
THIS WORKS:**

• Walk fast, upright, with
arms swinging. (Sitting,
slumped, makes us sad.)

• Talk with strangers
in trains, buses,
and waiting rooms.

• Be a matchmaker
for friends, especially
unlikely pairings.

• Be optimistic: It
doubles the likelihood
of ideal heart health and
increases the likelihood
of lower blood sugar
and cholesterol.

**PEOPLE ARE TALKING
ABOUT . . .**

• devices to measure
breath bacteria
and hydration levels

• showerheads infused
with vitamin C

• ultraviolet lights
in ducts to sterilize
incoming air

(continued)

Photo: courtesy of Amiigo.com

• nontraditional cross-training: flipping tractor tires and pushing pickup trucks instead of visiting a gym

RUN FOR YOUR LIFE

• 6.2 is the average increase in longevity, in years, for men who jog

• 5.6 is the average increase in longevity, in years, for women who jog

NEW HEALTH HABITS

• evaluating sweat patterns in hot rooms

while covered in red powder (powdered body parts that don't turn purple indicate a need for treatment)

• using human as well as bee bacteria to treat infections

• not being skinny (because it does not necessarily equate with being healthy)

FUTURE FACTORS

• molecular-level X rays that allow doctors to assess our genetic makeup

• bloodstream nanosensors to monitor organ health

BY THE NUMBERS

69% of U.S. adults use apps to track a health indicator

47% of folks want toothbrushes to advise how to clean teeth

17% of doctor visits in the United States and Canada were electronic (not in person) in 2014

(continued)

OUR CULTURAL LANDSCAPE

Web sites are rating doctors, professors, restaurant servers, boyfriends, and more. Even housecleaners and taxicab drivers are rating you, their customers.
–*Daniel Levine, director, The Avant-Guide Institute*

PEOPLE ARE TALKING ABOUT . . .

• traveling uphill on skis for a better workout

• luminescent trees replacing streetlights

• basketballs that "coach," encouraging players to move faster and play better

• backyard bird sightings: as part of Cornell University's Ornithology Lab FeederWatch and NestWatch programs, "citizen scientists" report and compare data

SAFETY FIRST

• for female cyclists: reflective accents on ballet flats, scarves, sequin tops, and headbands

• for male cyclists: reflective accents on blazers, shirts, and trousers

PEDAL POWER UP

• bike pedals with GPS (so that if a bike's stolen, it's still not "lost")

• wheel sensors that warn cyclists of potholes

• stationary bikes to produce backup power for homes and brewing beer

BY THE NUMBERS

75% of Americans think that it's fine for women to propose marriage (5% actually do so)

400,000: projected sales of drones

TRAVEL TRENDS

• Battery stations will enable electric scooters to swap out expended batteries for fully charged ones.

• Drivers will swivel and converse face-to-face with passengers.

• Rear auto windows will project digital landscapes over boring real ones, for passengers' amusement.

BACK TO THE FUTURE

• Vintage airplanes are being renovated and used as hotels.

• Groups of people at coffeehouses, bars, and bookstores are keying together on manual typewriters.

(continued on page 30)

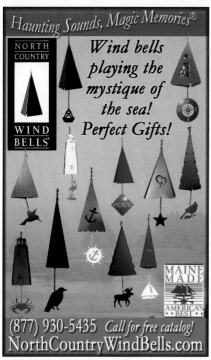

Haunting Sounds, Magic Memories®

NORTH COUNTRY WIND BELLS®

Wind bells playing the mystique of the sea! Perfect Gifts!

MAINE MADE · AMERICA'S BEST

(877) 930-5435 *Call for free catalog!*
NorthCountryWindBells.com

Davis Hill Weather Stick®
"the original"

802-533-2400

davishillco@hotmail.com

PO Box 38, East Hardwick, VT 05836
Wholesale Inquiries Welcome

$5 Each plus S&H
Min. order 2

DROLL YANKEES®
The World's Best Bird Feeders®

A-6F
Classic Sunflower/ Mixed Seed Feeder

The ORIGINAL Droll Yankees Bird Feeder is back!

If one of your childhood memories is feeding and watching birds at home, chances are your family owned a Droll Yankees bird feeder!

Droll Yankees Inc.
Find a store or shop - drollyankees.com
(800) 352-9164 • drollbird@drollyankees.com

MONEY MATTERS

There is a whole range of companies offering you the ability to share, usually for a price, anything from a meal to your bicycle to your clothes.
–Kaushik Ramakrishnan, business development manager, Ericsson

PEOPLE ARE TALKING ABOUT . . .

- gardeners providing for their plants' care in their wills

- wired piggy banks with an app that tracks balances and sends alerts when the bank is moved

- crowdfunding sites raising money to send a drone to scour the woods for Sasquatch (Big Foot)

- hobbies that become successful businesses

WE'RE MAKING ENDS MEET BY . . .

- giving away unwanted stuff on Web sites, earning credits to get other people's stuff at no cost

- undertaking inexpensive leisure-time activities: reading, gardening, cooking

- renting or owning in communal settings, getting a room and bath, with group kitchens, living area, workspaces, and recreational facilities

- offering the public use of our (urban) toilet for a fee

NEW HABITS

- buying merchandise with an eye toward reselling after using, thus being sure to keep the manuals, packaging, and receipts: "Online selling has opened up the door to . . . temporary ownership."

- valuing multipurpose items: "Consumers want food with a medicinal component, products with a charity tie-in, and clothing that serves a technological need."

BY THE NUMBERS

$3.40: average amount children receive for each lost tooth

58% of U.S. taxpayers say that completing a federal tax return is easy

7% of Americans would pay more taxes if returns were easier to fill out

4,900: tons of worn-out bills recycled by the U.S. Federal Reserve annually

- becoming "mini-entrepreneurs": "Having lots of ways of supple-menting income gives people a sense of freedom and empowerment."

- going cashless yet spending faster: "Apps are making it painless to pay—until you get the bill."
–Emerita Kit Yarrow, professor of psychology and marketing, Golden Gate University

(continued)

COLLECTORS' CORNER

The market will see stronger and renewed interest in items relating to great triumphs in freedom throughout history.
–Gary Piattoni, appraiser, Evanston, Illinois

HEATING UP

• UFO memorabilia: photographs, posters, and souvenirs produced for shops in Roswell, New Mexico

• Wheaties boxes autographed by the featured athlete

• toys: 1960s Japanese-made space toys; '70s Star Wars toys; '80s electronics, video games

HOT STUFF

• *Where the Wild Things Are*, 1st edition, by Maurice Sendak: $20,000

• a salesman's sample hay rake in its original carrying case: $20,145

WANTED TO BUY

Items relating to the American Revolution, Declaration of Independence and Constitution signers, the 1876 Centennial, the Bill of Rights, women's suffrage, the fall of the Berlin Wall, India's independence, and the Magna Carta
–Piattoni

• glass signage from Aetna Insurance Company, with mother-of-pearl inlay: $51,300

• Superman's debut comic book: $3.2 million

FINDING FAVOR

• agricultural artifacts: "The more moving parts and the better the quality of craftsmanship, the better they do."
–Andrew P. Truman, head of the antique advertising, toy, and doll division, James D. Julia, Auctioneers

• old scientific gadgets: "Science and technology auctions are now at most major auction houses."
–Antoinette Rahn, online editor, Antique Trader

• early explorers' chronicles: "Some journals and diaries of women settlers heading west have sold for a lot of money."
–Piattoni

COLLECT 'EM FOR LOVE, NOT MONEY

• Hummel, Roseville, cut glass, china, and linens

• Art & Crafts decor
–Timothy Gordon, Missoula, Montana-based appraiser ■

Stacey Kusterbeck, a frequent contributor to *The Old Farmer's Almanac,* writes about popular culture from New York State.

Thanks to BetterWOMAN, I'm winning the battle for

Bladder Control.

All Natural
Clinically-Tested Herbal Supplement

- Reduces Bladder Leaks
- Reduces Urinary Frequency
- Safe and Effective – No Known Side Effects
- Costs Less than Traditional Bladder Control Options
- Sleep Better All Night
- **Live Free of Worry, Embarrassment, and Inconvenience**

You don't have to let bladder control problems control you.
Call now!

Frequent nighttime trips to the bathroom, embarrassing leaks and the inconvenience of constantly searching for rest rooms in public – for years, I struggled with bladder control problems. After trying expensive medications with horrible side effects, ineffective exercises and undignified pads and diapers, I was ready to resign myself to a life of bladder leaks, isolation and depression. But then I tried **BetterWOMAN**.

When I first saw the ad for BetterWOMAN, I was skeptical. So many products claim they can set you free from leaks, frequency and worry, only to deliver disappointment. When I finally tried BetterWOMAN, I found that it actually works! It changed my life. Even my friends have noticed that I'm a new person. And because it's all natural, I can enjoy the results without the worry of dangerous side effects. Thanks to BetterWOMAN, I finally fought bladder control problems and I won!

Also Available: **BetterMAN**®
The 3-in-1 Formula Every Man Needs –
Better **BLADDER**, Better **PROSTATE**, and Better **STAMINA!**
Order online at www.BetterMANnow.com.

Limited Time Offer

Call Now & Ask How To Get A
FREE BONUS BOTTLE
CALL TOLL-FREE 1-888-643-7437
or order online: www.BetterWOMANnow.com

These statements have not been evaluated by the FDA. This product is not intended to diagnose, treat, cure or prevent any disease. *Use as directed. Individual results may vary.*
BetterMAN and BetterWOMAN are the trademarks of Interceuticals, Inc. ©2015 Interceuticals, Inc.

A BREWER'S BOUNTY

in Bloom

The popularity of home brewing has spawned interest in home brew-gardens.

BY GEORGE HOMSY

A

LMOST AS SOON AS COLONISTS STARTED FARMING IN THE NEW WORLD, THEY STARTED BREWING BEER. IN THE LATE 1500S, THOMAS HERIOT, ONE OF THE FIRST VIRGINIA SETTLERS, WROTE IN HIS JOURNAL THAT "WE MADE OF THE SAME IN THE COUNTRY SOME MAULT, WHEREOF WAS BREWED AS GOOD ALE AS WAS TO BE DESIRED. SO LIKEWISE BY THE HELPE OF HOPS, THEREOF MAY BE MADE AS GOOD BEERE."

THE QUEST FOR GOOD BEER AND ALE PERSEVERES IN THE GROWING RANKS OF HOME BREWERS WHO RAISE THEIR OWN HOPS, GRAINS, AND HERBS. THE GOAL, OFTEN, IS TO BREW BEER OF A PARTICULAR FLAVOR.

IN THE TRADITIONAL MANNER, A CULTIVATED HOP PLANT GROWS UP A HOP-POLE.

The most common plant in a brewer's garden, hops have an intoxicating effect even before being brewed into alcohol. The plant contains an oil that acts as a mild sedative. This was supposedly discovered when ancient harvesters dozed off during their labors. Hops-filled pillows are said to help cure insomnia and enhance the lucidity of dreams.

GROWING HOPS

But the plants certainly aren't sleepers. Known by the scientific name *Humulus lupulus* (the second word means "small wolf" and honors its hardiness and tenacity), hops are vigorous growers that can soar up to a foot a day, topping out at 15 to 20 feet in height if conditions are right. The perennial vines love to climb and can shade porches or cover ugly utility poles. A simple string trellis provides enough support to guide the vines up the sides of a house, since they climb without digging into walls for support.

Dozens of varieties of hops are available in North America and used in different combinations by brewers seeking

Precision Cultivator!

Mantis Does It All!
- *Speed Weeds In Minutes*
- *Tills New Garden Beds*
- *Digs Planting Holes*
- *And Much More...*

90 Day RISK-FREE Trial

Easy-to-Use Tiller! | Busts Tough Sod!

This 20 lb Wonder Will Cut Your Garden Chores...*In-Half!*

Discover The Mantis Difference...In Your Own Garden!

The Mantis Tiller is the lightest weight, easy-to-use gardening powerhouse that makes back-breaking hand tools...*OBSOLETE!* From sod busting a new garden, to weeding around delicate plants, or digging a hole for a new shrub...the **Mantis can do it all!**

- Powerful enough for big gardens... nimble enough for small.
- Turns even tough, hard clay soil into rich, crumbly loam.
- So lightweight that it's a breeze to handle in the garden.

- Cuts through tough soil and roots like a chainsaw through wood!
- Create and maintain beautiful planting beds all season long.
- Power weeds the average garden in under 20 minutes!

SAVE $40
ON ALL OUR MODELS!

Call Toll-Free For Your FREE Catalog and DVD...TODAY!

1-888-240-4556 Dept. MT151136

YES! Please rush my FREE Catalog and DVD plus details on your 90 day NO-RISK Trial, $40 Savings (on all models) and other special offers.

NAME_____

ADDRESS_____

CITY_____STATE_____ZIP_____

Mail to: Mantis, 1028 Street Rd, Dept. MT151136, Southampton, PA 18966

Easy-to-Handle Weighs Just...20 lbs ...and It's All Muscle!

Mantis
We Make Gardening Easier®
www.mantistiller.com

© 2015, Schiller Grounds Care, Inc.

AMARANTH (LEFT) AND SORGHUM IN AUTUMN AT SUNSET (RIGHT)

to find the right flavor. 'Cascade', developed by Oregon State University and best for brewing American-style ale, is a favorite because of its hardiness across the country. 'Perle', another backyard variety, is popular for flavoring German-style lagers and pilsners.

GROWING GRAINS

Grain, another important beer component, is often overlooked by gardeners because some beer recipes demand more than can be grown easily in a backyard. (Think barley, rye, and wheat.) Also, the crop requires threshing and mashing to produce the extract needed for beer. (If it's these grains that you seek, contact a home-brewer supplier.) Some people committed to backyard brew-gardens develop recipes using smaller amounts of grain for flavoring.

From a gardener's perspective, the

more important role for grains is visual. Many are tall, dramatic plants that can hold up well in a lush green garden dominated by hops. Amaranth adds a nutty flavor to a beer's taste, while its large, towering, bronze-to-burgundy seed heads make a bold statement to the eye. Sorghum, popular in South African beer, has spectacular orange/red or black and white seed heads. The kernels of 'Black Aztec' corn mature to a blue/black color and are used to make "chicha," a Peruvian corn beer.

HERBS AND FRUIT

The other major components of a brewer's garden are the herbs and/or fruit used to flavor beers. Many are readily familiar to gardeners: Thyme, licorice, ginger, and Saint-John's-wort are common. Brewers often experiment with herbs, although caution here is advised. Some traditional brewing herbs such as tansy

36

Photos, from left: age fotostock/SuperStock; Lisa Kyle Young/Media Bakery

New England Bells

Handcrafted in New Hampshire using the finest leather and solid brass sleigh bells

Heirloom Collection
Designer Door Chimes
Dog Collar Bells • Custom Work

603-863-3800
NewEnglandBells.com

HANDMADE on Cape Cod

made in USA
Since 1988

SANDWICH LANTERN

ONION LIGHTS
ANCHOR LIGHTS
CHANDELIERS • SCONCES

Available in:

SOLID COPPER *or* SOLID BRASS

17 Jan Sebastian Dr., Ste #1, Sandwich, MA 02563

508-833-0515

sandwichlantern.com

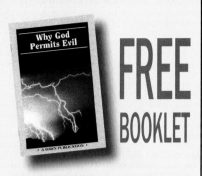

FREE BOOKLET

WHY GOD PERMITS EVIL

Send for this
FREE BOOKLET
Read why evil seems to prosper. We know that death plagues us all, but the Bible says that it will not always be so.

The Bible has details of all the world's current ills along with the ultimate cure.

Phone or write for your
***FREE* 32-page copy**
1-800-234-DAWN

DAWN PUBLISHING
199 RAILROAD AVENUE
EAST RUTHERFORD NJ 07073

or from **our website**
www.dawnbible.com

Gardening

and wormwood are mildly toxic. Other historic recipes will not taste right to modern beer drinkers. Often these beers do not include hops, and the results can be too strong for modern tastes.

More palatable recipes are provided in *The Homebrewer's Garden* (Storey Publishing, 1998), written by brothers Joe and Dennis Fisher. The ingredients include pumpkin, blackberries, and raspberries, as well as dandelions for use in both a bitter and a stout. "We really like horehound beer and heather ale as well," says Dennis. "But," finishes Joe, "our favorite beer is the one that is in front of us."

THE BREWER'S GARDEN

If you're thinking of growing the ingredients for a batch or merely for the pleasure of the plants, consider this advice.

■ A beer garden can be grown almost everywhere in the United States and southern Canada. Various hop varieties are hardy from Zones 3 to 8, and the herbs can be selected to fit your local climate.

(continued)

Get started with an easy DIY kit!

mr.L
micro+drip
Irrigation

Conserves Water

No gluing.
No digging.
And no more
handwatering.
All you need is an outdoor faucet!

Available at select Lowe's Stores
www.misterlandscaper.com

Mobile Website

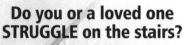

Gardening

■ Hop plants sprout from rootstock called rhizomes that are planted horizontally, keeping the shoots 2 inches from the surface. Patience is important. Do not expect a high yield of hops the first year.

■ Cones on female hop plants contain a yellowish powder called lupulin that gives beer its flavor and aroma.

IF YOU DRINK BEER WHILE EATING WATERMELON, IT WILL TURN TO STONE IN YOUR STOMACH.
—FOLKLORE

■ If you grow hops in a container, use a very rich soil mix. They are voracious feeders.

■ Keep hops away from the favorite foods of Japanese beetles, such as roses, grapevines, and raspberry bushes.

■ Hops are typically dried before storage. They can be stored in a vacuum-sealed bag in a freezer for up to a year without a loss of quality.

■ You need at least 800 square feet of grain to harvest a bushel, which is enough for 25 gallons of an all-grain beer.

■ Beware of some "traditional" brewing herbs such as mugwort, pennyroyal, and thorn apple. Despite their history in brewing, they are poisonous.

■ Do not use herbicides or pesticides on your lawn if you hope to harvest the dandelions for beer. *(continued)*

BURN SAFELY

with the
Stainless Steel

Portable
BurnCage™

PERFECT FOR:

- Sensitive financial documents
- All burnable household waste*
- Old leaves and branches

STAINLESS STEEL CONSTRUCTION is lightweight, durable, and portable (it folds for easy storage).

PERFORATED LID and sidewalls maximize airflow and trap embers.

1600° TEMPERATURES mean more thorough burning with less ash.

* Always check with local ordinances before burning.

No more **UNSAFE** and **UNSIGHTLY** rusty barrel!

88689X © 2015

BurnCage.com

The *Original* Trimmer-on-Wheels
Just Got BETTER!

NEW LOW PRICE!

The *NEW* DR® TRIMMER/MOWER

TRIMS, MOWS waist-high grass and weeds.

CUTS BRUSH, SAPLINGS up to 3" thick with exclusive accessories.

THICKEST, LONGEST-LASTING CORD available anywhere (225 mil Sawtooth™).

NEW TOW-BEHIND MODELS TOO!

88688X © 2015

The *ONLY* Trimmer Guaranteed Not To Wrap!

DRtrimmers.com

FREE SHIPPING
6 MONTH TRIAL

SOME LIMITATIONS APPLY
Call or go online for details.

Call for a FREE DVD and Catalog!
Includes product specifications and factory-direct offers.

TOLL FREE 800-731-0493

NO FREE SHIPPING, 6 MONTH TRIAL OR DVD FOR BURNCAGE

PROFESSIONAL POWER
DR
DONE RIGHT

A CHEAP BEER RECIPE

TAKE 2 OUNCES OF GOOD HOPS AND BOIL THEM 3 OR 4 HOURS IN THREE TO FOUR PAILFULS OF WATER. THEN SCALD 2 QUARTS OF MOLASSES IN THE LIQUOR AND TURN IT INTO A CLEAN HALF-BARREL, BOILING HOT. THEN FILL IT UP WITH COLD WATER. BEFORE IT IS QUITE FULL, PUT IN YOUR YEAST TO WORK IT. THE NEXT DAY YOU WILL HAVE AGREEABLE, WHOLESOME SMALL BEER THAT WILL NOT FILL WITH WIND AS THAT WHICH IS BREWED WITH MALT OR BRAN, AND IT WILL KEEP GOOD TILL IT IS ALL DRANK OUT.

–THE OLD FARMER'S ALMANAC, 1815

A BREWER'S PLOT PLAN

This design *(opposite)* for a fenced garden in full sun measures approximately 16x12 feet and uses a total of 16 different kinds of plants and four 5x3-foot raised beds. Amaranth grows in three half-barrel planters. At the entrance, big pots contain hops that clamber over a trellis. A second trellis, the wall of a house, or a high fence contains the garden on the opposite side.

1. 'Cascade' hops *(Humulus lupulus)*, 2 plants
2. 'Perle' hops *(H. lupulus)*, 4 plants
3. 'Excelsior' barley *(Hordeum vulgare)*, ½ pound of seeds
4. Amaranth *(Amaranthus caudatus)*, 6 plants
5. Blueberries *(Vaccinium corymbosum)*, 2 plants
6. Blackberries *(Rubus spp.)*, 6 plants
7. Horehound *(Marrubium vulgare)*, 3 plants
8. Basil *(Ocimum basilicum)*, 6 plants
9. Cilantro *(Coriandrum sativum)*, 4 plants
10. Anise hyssop *(Agastache foeniculum)*, 4 plants
11. Sage *(Salvia officinalis)*, 4 plants
12. Heather *(Calluna vulgaris)*, 4 plants
13. Thyme *(Thymus vulgaris)*, 6 plants
14. Bee balm *(Monarda didyma)*, 4 plants
15. 'Black Aztec' corn *(Zea mays)*, 9 plants
16. 'Bloody Butcher' corn *(Z. mays)*, 9 plants ∎

George Homsy is an assistant professor in the Department of Public Administration at Binghamton (N.Y.) University. Through embarking on semi-organized beer-tasting excursions, he frequents the growing number of breweries and brewpubs sprouting up throughout New York State.

TRELLIS, WALL OF HOUSE, OR HIGH FENCE

'CASCADE' HOPS   'PERLE' HOPS

 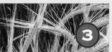

AMARANTH 'EXCELSIOR' BARLEY AMARANTH 'EXCELSIOR' BARLEY AMARANTH

BLUEBERRIES   BLACKBERRIES

RAISED BEDS

HOREHOUND   BASIL   CILANTRO   ANISE HYSSOP

SAGE   HEATHER   THYME   BEE BALM

NOT TO SCALE

 **TRELLIS ENTRANCE**

'PERLE' HOPS   'PERLE' HOPS

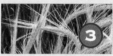

'BLACK AZTEC' CORN   'BLOODY BUTCHER' CORN

Photos: 1, 2, 7, 9, 11, 13: H. Zell/Wikimedia; 3: USDA/ARS; 4: age fotostock/SuperStock; 5: Thinkstock; 6: Biberi/Wikimedia; 8: Mikrolit/Wikimedia; 10: Kurt Stüber/Wikimedia; 12: Willow/Wikimedia; 14: Karelj/Wikimedia; 15: Wikimedia; 16: courtesy of Seed Savers Exchange

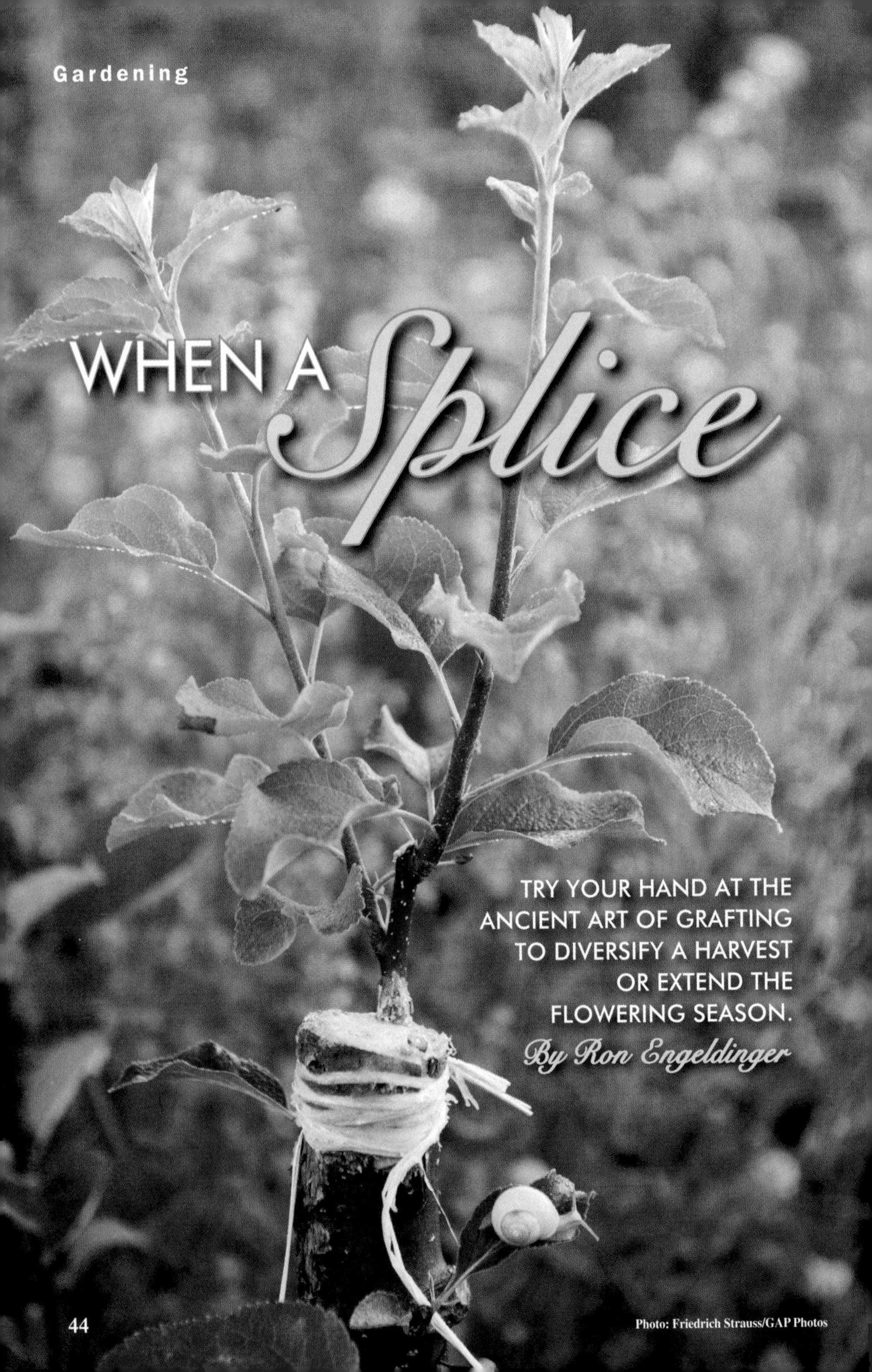

WHEN A *Splice*

TRY YOUR HAND AT THE ANCIENT ART OF GRAFTING TO DIVERSIFY A HARVEST OR EXTEND THE FLOWERING SEASON.

By Ron Engeldinger

Photo: Friedrich Strauss/GAP Photos

IS *Nice*

ELSTAR AND GOLDEN DELICIOUS
ARE TWO HEALTHY APPLE VARIETIES
GRAFTED ONTO ONE ROOTSTOCK.

ONE LILAC BUSH WITH TWO DIFFERENT BLOOM COLORS

*T*he idea of harvesting Golden Delicious, Jonathan, and Granny Smith apples from the same tree seems exotic. Similarly, having long-lived blooms on your lilac or camellia bush in the spring might seem like a daydream. But you can have both! You can achieve these effects by grafting the plants: A single apple tree can have several different varieties on separate branches. A lilac bush can have both early and midseason blooms or one bush with a variety of colors.

Grafting has been practiced for centuries (the ancient Greeks did it!), and the methods have not changed much. The parts from two or more plants are joined so that they grow to become one plant: A woody twig or branch from the new addition, called a scion, is securely spliced to a compatible host plant, called the stock or rootstock. The practice enables you to develop unique and varied plants for your garden or orchard, and it's a boon for small-space gardeners.

Most fruit and nut trees and many flowering shrubs can be grafted successfully. The process is simple even if you are a novice gardener, and the results can be fun.

Just remember that the stock plant must be healthy and compatible with the scion. Generally, this means that you want to graft matching plants—in this case, an apple scion to an apple stock or a lilac scion to a lilac stock.

A TEMPTING APPLE

Many gardeners start by grafting apples. Apples graft easily, and the many varieties available can provide satisfying results. In a small space, a dwarf or semidwarf stock works well. The cleft graft *(see page 48)* works best for older established apple trees, while the whip graft is good for small trees or small branches on larger trees.

LILACS TO LOVE

Lilac blooming season is short, so you can extend it by grafting early-season

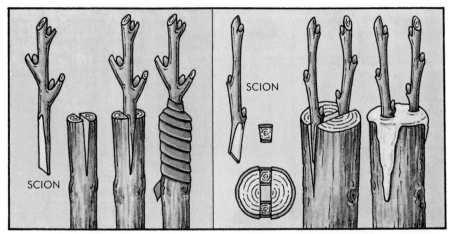

CLEFT GRAFTING   CLEFT GRAFTING ON LARGE BRANCHES

and midseason varieties onto one bush. Lilacs are a bit harder to graft than apples because they grow more slowly. However, many folks have been very successful with a little work and some patience, and you can be, too.

Lilacs respond well to cleft grafting. Grafting a lilac scion onto an already healthy lilac stock works best. While some gardeners have successfully grafted lilac scions to privet stock (a shrub generally used for hedges), grafting a lilac to any other tree or bush, such as a camellia or magnolia, will not work.

DIY: BASIC CLEFT GRAFTING

The best time to graft is early spring—April and May in northern regions—when the plants are still dormant but getting ready to grow. Scions should be young and healthy. New growth from last season usually works best. Since the scion is a living plant, harvest it carefully. Use a clean, sharp knife or shears.

While there are many types of grafts,

the cleft graft is one of the most popular. The stock should be 1 to 4 inches in diameter. It can be the main stem of the stock or a large branch. The scion (usually two are used) should be about ¼ inch in diameter and have at least three or four leaf buds. Usually a straight branch about 6 to 8 inches long works well.

1. Using a sharp saw, remove a piece of the stem or branch of the stock, leaving a clean cut.

2. Make a cut (the cleft) in the stock 1 to 2 inches deep, perpendicular to the sawn end.

3. Taper the end of one or two scions into a long wedge shape. Gently pry apart the cleft and insert the tapered end of the scion into the cleft. A clefting tool, sold at many garden centers, works best, but you can use any flat tool to pry apart the cleft.

4. Insert the scion so that the cambium layer of the scion comes into contact with the cambium layer of the stock. Pay attention to the position of the scions. The cambium layer that lies just under the bark is the actively growing part of

Visit Almanac.com/Shop to buy Almanacs, calendars, cookbooks, and gifts for all occasions.

Gardening

the tree or twig. It is where the scion and stock will fuse to become one plant.

5. After the scions are inserted and positioned properly, remove the tool and allow the cleft to close around the scions.

6. Seal the entire grafted area with grafting wax or grafting paint. You want to keep water and pests out and also protect the area from drying out. Grafting paints or paintlike sealants that are painted onto the graft union are more popular these days because they are much easier to use than waxes.

7. You may need to bind the scion to the stock to keep it in place. Most nurseries sell grafting tape that is designed to hold the grafted sections, but common electrical tape or even strips of rubber also work. Remember to remove the tape or

TRY THEM ALL
As you gain experience and confidence in the grafting process, there are a number of different grafting techniques that you may want to try:

■ Bark grafts, where the scion is inserted under a flap of bark on the stock, are used with large-diameter stocks.

■ Splice grafts join a scion and stock of the same diameter.

■ In a whip graft (also called a whip-and-tongue graft), an interlocking tongue from the scion is inserted into a groove in the stock.

■ Saddle grafts are used to form a bridge over the damaged area of a stock.

binding once the graft takes hold (usually after 3 to 4 weeks) so that it does not restrict the growth of the grafted section.

A BIT ABOUT BUD GRAFTING

Budding is a special form of grafting in which the scion is simply a single mature leaf bud. Budding is often used in nurseries for fruit tree propagation. Apples and lilacs both respond well to budding. The advantage to budding is that it can be done in the summer because the buds are cut from shoots of the current season's growth. The scion bud is inserted under a bark flap cut on the stock.

SCION SOURCES

There are many ways to get clippings to use as scions. Check with friends or relatives who are gardeners. Perhaps you can trade a cutting from one of your plants for a cutting from one of theirs. Establish connections with your local nursery or garden center manager, who may allow you to take cuttings. Check with local orchards or farms to see about collecting cuttings when they prune. In some areas, nurseries or garden clubs sponsor scion exchange events.

You will rarely achieve 100 percent success with grafting. Some grafts will fail even when you have done everything right, but do not despair. If your first attempts do not produce the results that you want, keep trying. With practice and persistence, you can soon become a proficient grafter and enjoy the fruit of your labor. ∎

Ron Engeldinger has been gardening in Oregon for about 35 years, growing mainly apples, pears, berries, and vegetables.

Granddaughter, I Love You Always
Personalized Heirloom Music Box

Plays the melody
"You Are My Sunshine"

FREE
Personalization!

Shown smaller
than actual
size of about
6" x 4"

Personalized Gift ... Exceptional Value!

Act now to acquire your exclusive *Personalized Heirloom Music Box*. The limited edition includes a heart-shaped charm you can personalize with your granddaughter's name for just $59.99*, payable in three installments of $19.99. Our 365-day money-back guarantee assures your 100% satisfaction. Send no money now. Just return the attached coupon today, and indicate the name for personalization on the charm.

www.bradfordexchange.com/musicbox

Heirloom quality ...
limited availability!

♥ Loving sentiment and roses adorn the silver-plated filigree frame glass lid

♥ Hand-crafted music box is beautifully finished in mahogany

♥ Includes a poem card

©2014 BGE   01-19109-001-DDM1UP

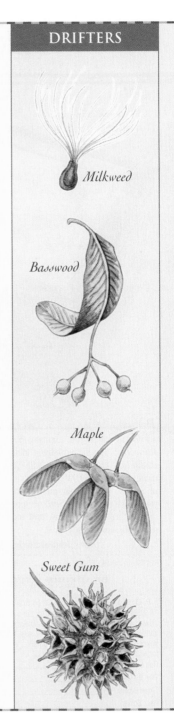

DRIFTERS

Milkweed

Basswood

Maple

Sweet Gum

MARVELOUS JOURNEYS MADE BY SEEDS

Some fly on the wind, some hitch a ride, some float, and a few become enflamed.

BY CYNTHIA VAN HAZINGA

ILLUSTRATIONS BY KIM KURKI

Many plants, even those that we consider invasive, must set seed to survive as a species. How plants disperse their seeds is one of nature's most fascinating adventure stories. Come along for the ride and discover a few of the means and methods.

THE DRIFTERS

W ind, with the help of gravity, is the most common means of seed dispersal, especially for small, light seeds. Witchweed *(Striga asiatica)* produces one of the smallest seeds in nature, and it is easily transported by wind (or water). Orchid seeds, so minute that they resemble dust, and the graceful, plumed achenes of the common dandelion *(Taraxacum officinale)* also float in the air. If conditions are right, dandy achenes may fly as far as 500 miles. Some plumed seeds, like those of milkweed *(Asclepias syriaca)*—which bears its brood in banana-shape pods that split to release their tufts—fly farther than winged ones (think of

FLOATERS	HITCHHIKERS	EXPLODERS

Yellow Flag

Burdock

Jewelweed

Sycamore

Berries

Witch Hazel

Willow

Violet

Mistletoe

Coconut

Horse Chestnut

Bur-reed

55

maple trees). Tumbleweed can produce up to 250,000 seeds. These are dispersed as weed tumbles, driven by the wind.

Many plants that produce large seeds hold them in aerodynamically designed pods or vessels. Seeds with only one terminal wing, such as those of lime and ash trees, fall like spinning torpedoes. Seeds with two wings glide: Maple tree seeds, or samaras, spin like helicopter blades; basswood seeds are carried in bracts with "parachutes"; tree-of-heaven pods have "propeller" wings; and sweet gum stores its winged seeds in a ball. (Get it? "Gum ball.") True yams *(Dioscorea)* are climbers with thin, papery seeds with wings.

Did You Know?
The invasive tree of heaven
(Ailanthus altissima) was
introduced in North America
as an ornamental in
Pennsylvania in 1784. Turbulent
winds have been known to
carry its seeds over 1,475 feet.

The speed at which any of these travels depends on the height of its parent and the wind velocity, among other things.

THE FLOATERS

Water dispersal is most effective at dispersing seeds when a body of water, whether a rivulet or an ocean, is moving and the seed is buoyant. Coconuts (remember, these are fruit with seeds), mangroves, and seeds of other tropical trees commonly float on sea tides. Sea beans *(Entada gigas)* have been known to travel on water from Africa, Australia, or South America to land in Europe!

Freshwater travelers include yellow flag *(Iris pseudacorus),* water mint (the calyx also clings to animal fur), tiny foxglove, willow (in capsules), cottonwood, and sycamore, which all produce fluffy and buoyant seeds. These can travel great distances before they wash ashore and germinate—or not. For example, water lily seeds sink immediately and settle on the bottom, where they sprout. Sedge and rush seeds also sink, but float to the surface when they become small plants. Some floating fruit, especially legumes, have seeded pods made super-buoyant with trapped air; eventually, the pods decay to release the seeds or are rubbed open as they tumble along in a brook or river.

Many of the light, corky, seedlike fruit of the carrot family float easily on streams, some for several months. Seeds of some of the gourd family, which owe their buoyancy to their light, corky structure, have a similar habit.   *(continued)*

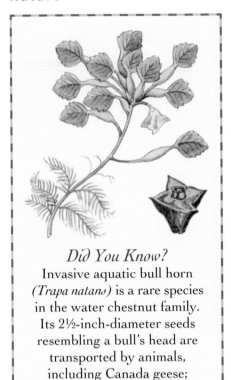

Did You Know?

Invasive aquatic bull horn (*Trapa natans*) is a rare species in the water chestnut family. Its 2½-inch-diameter seeds resembling a bull's head are transported by animals, including Canada geese; fishing nets; wooden boats; and other vehicles.

The seeds of the sea rocket *(Cakile maritima),* a member of the mustard family, reside in twin pods resembling a two-stage missile. One pod remains attached to the parent and produces a new plant in place. The other breaks off and gets carried away on a wave.

Unlike most palms, the coco de mer palm *(Lodoicea maldivica),* the largest seed-bearing plant in the world, seems doomed to stay in its home, the Seychelles Islands: Its seed, at up to 40 pounds or more, is too heavy to float, but it has been transported by men and replanted. (Its archaic name, *Lodoicea callypige,* comes from the Greek words meaning "beautiful rump" because ancient sailors who came upon it on the beach believed it to be a woman's disembodied buttocks.)

THE HITCHHIKERS

Merely by going about their business, birds and animals serve as agents of seed distribution; seeds, by design or attraction, become hitchhikers. For example, burdock (*Arctium* sp.) seeds have hooked bracts, and cleavers (*Galium aparine;* a member of the Madder family), aka "Velcro plant," have hooked hairs, or bristles, that cling to animal skins.

The seeds of both Pittosporum, named from the Greek for "pitch-seed" because of their characteristic stickiness, and mistletoe are tacky enough when mature to fix onto a bird's wing or beak.

More frequently, hungry birds and other animals—especially bats and rodents, but also reptiles and other mammals—transport, hoard, eat, and excrete seeds. Birds swallow seeds while feeding on fleshy fruit and berries, which are often alluringly bright red, black, blue, or purple. Protective coatings prevent such seeds from disintegration during digestion. Cherry pits, for example, pass through a bird's system undigested. In the northern forests of South America's Patagonia, the mousy

I have great faith in a seed. Convince me that you have a seed there, and I am prepared to expect wonders.
—Henry David Thoreau, American writer (1817–62)

Save up to 50% or more on heating costs*

envi™
wall-mounted room heater

energy saving   heats room for as little as 4 cents per hour*

ultra-safe   leave unattended 24/7; cool to the touch

healthy   fanless - doesn't blow dust
& allergens or dry the air

effective   100% Pure Stack Convection;
gentle whole room warmth!

silent   fanless design, auto dimming power light

easy install   installs in minutes, no drill;
hardwired & plug-in models

stylish   slim space saving design,
19" wide x 22" tall x 2" thin!

eheat.com 1-800-807-0107

(*visit website for details) | Free Shipping* | 10% OFF Coupon: OFA1510 | 2 or more 15% OFF Coupon: OFA1515
on Dehydrators within Continental USA.

LOWEST PRICE EVER
on DR® Leaf and Lawn Vacuums!

NEW Models
Starting at
$**1,299**⁹⁹

Unload with just one hand!

Doubles as a utility trailer!

88042X © 2015

The **NEW DR® Leaf Vacuum** is designed from the top down to make yard clean up easier, faster, and more thorough than ever before. And for a limited time we are offering them at incredible low introductory prices!

☑ **Rated #1 in Vacuum Power**   ☑ **Stores Flat in Minutes**
☑ **Easy, 1-Hand Dumping**   ☑ **Converts to a Utility Trailer**

FREE SHIPPING
6 MONTH TRIAL
SOME LIMITATIONS APPLY
Call or go online for details.

Call for FREE DVD and Catalog!
TOLL FREE **800-731-0493**
DRleafvac.com

PROFESSIONAL POWER
DR
DONE RIGHT

marsupial *monito del monte* (Spanish for "monkey of the mountain") ingests the seeds of the mistletoe species *Tristerix corymbosus* and later eliminates them onto the bark of host trees.

Plants do not typically produce food-source seeds in great quantities because these seeds tend to be relatively large, heavy, and thus energetically expensive to produce.

Seed dispersal is not the domain of terrestrial creatures alone. Aquatic plants—for example, invasive bur-reed *(Sparganium),* the common name of which refers to its spiky flower head, and water crow-foot *(Ranunculus aquatilis),* an aquatic buttercup whose family name derives from the Latin for

"little frog" because it prefers moist habitats—have seeds that stick to the plumage and feet of waterbirds.

THE EXPLODERS

Some seedpods and ripe flowers have the energy and structure to scatter themselves, even shooting seeds a good distance. Many are legumes, laburnum, or gorse; others include knotgrass, lady's slippers, violets, and vetches. The seed cases of jewelweed (aka touch-me-not, *Impatiens* spp.) and Chinese wisteria dry so thoroughly that the slightest pressure, even a light wind, causes them to burst and broadcast their seeds through the air—the former, a couple of meters; the latter, according to one source, as far as 80 feet. The cranesbill geranium's seed capsule has a beaklike column, hence the name. When ripe, oxalis's small, cylindrical capsule suddenly explodes, sowing its seeds up to 13 feet away.

With specially shaped flowers, splash-cup plants such as Chrysosplenium and Mazus actually flip their seeds—sometimes more than 3 feet—in response to the force of raindrops falling on their petals. "Bird's nest" fungi (which reproduce with spores, not seeds) also use this method, as do some kalanchoes, which can shoot their seeds as far as 5 feet.   *(continued)*

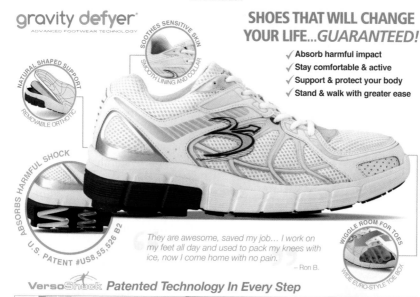

Nature

Witch hazel's two-chambered capsules announce the expulsion of their two shiny black seeds with an audible "snap" (hence its other common name: the snapping hazelnut) before projecting them 20 to 30 feet. Black walnuts' spongy hulls bounce and roll when they hit the ground, while horse chestnuts' hulls split when they crash on terra firma, allowing the seeds to roll away. Dry poppy seed heads have little holes around the top that allow the small seeds to be thrown out (think of a salt shaker) when the wind blows.

The largest plant with an explosive dispersal method is probably the tropical evergreen sandbox tree *(Hura crepitans)*. It's orange-size fruit burst with a popping sound (hence the nickname "monkey's dinner bell") and throw their seeds at speeds of up to 230 feet per second.

The smallest plant in this category may

Did You Know?
You can eat the tasty seeds popped from a jewelweed seedpod!

> ### Did You Know?
> Some scientists split the
> mechanics of seed dispersal into
> autochory (dispersal by
> the plant's own means) and
> allochory (dispersal by external
> means), although the
> combinations and adaptations
> are endlessly exceptional.

be the ground-hugging squirting cucumber *(Ecballium elaterium).* When the pressure from water absorption peaks, it pushes its seeds through its stopper-like stem with a thrust that can carry them as far as 20 feet.

THE FIRE NEEDERS

Fire, although often destructive, is also an agent of dispersal for some seeds. The ashen remains of a fire may create ideal conditions for growth to recur. Fire-dispersed seeds do not move, and they must be able to stay dormant for long periods of time.

Lodgepole pine trees, which stand 70 feet tall, on average, need a blaze to melt the resin that coats the tree's cones and release the winged seeds to fall to the forest floor. Thousands of them: Years after a fire, as many as 50,000 lodgepole seedlings may have sprouted on 1 acre. Much smaller 4- to 6-foot-tall fireweed *(Chamerion angustifolium)* is so called for its propensity to sprout in areas cleared by wildfires. One plant can produce up to 80,000 seeds. ■

Cynthia Van Hazinga drifts, floats, hitchhikes, and explodes between New York City and New Hampshire.

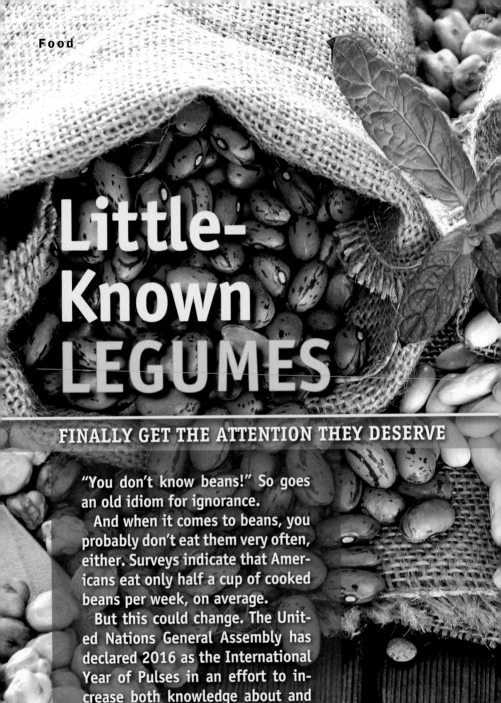

Little-Known LEGUMES

FINALLY GET THE ATTENTION THEY DESERVE

"You don't know beans!" So goes an old idiom for ignorance.

And when it comes to beans, you probably don't eat them very often, either. Surveys indicate that Americans eat only half a cup of cooked beans per week, on average.

But this could change. The United Nations General Assembly has declared 2016 as the International Year of Pulses in an effort to increase both knowledge about and consumption of beans and their botanical relatives, known collectively as the pulse crops. *(continued)*

Photo: Media Bakery

Clinical research has shown that pulse foods may help to prevent heart disease and other chronic diseases.

BY MARGARET BOYLES

Food

You probably already know the pulses, crops in the bean and pea family (the legumes) grown for their mature, dry seeds. In North America, the term generally applies to dry beans and peas, lentils, and chickpeas. The name derives from an ancient Greek word for thick soup or porridge.

"I'm bullish on chickpeas," says George Vandemark, a USDA geneticist engaged in conventional breeding efforts to improve the mineral and fatty-acid profiles of chickpeas. He could be speaking for pulse breeders, farmers, and processors when he adds, "They're fantastic crops to work with—ancient crops that are going to play a big role in the future of the global food supply."

Soil Loves Pulses

Pulse crops use about half the nonrenewable energy inputs of other agricultural crops and a fraction of the water.

"Their sustainability has largely to do with their ability to 'fix' nitrogen gas from the air into plant-specific forms," says Hans Kandel, an agronomist with North Dakota State University Cooperative Extension.

Pulses include (left to right) brown lentils, chickpeas, French green lentils, kidney beans, black-eyed peas, red lentils, and pinto beans.

TOP PULSE PRODUCERS

■ North Dakota leads in U.S. pulse production; other state sources are Idaho, Michigan, Minnesota, Montana, Nebraska, and Washington.

■ Canada dominates global lentil and dry pea production, with most of it centered in Saskatchewan and Alberta.

■ India leads in chickpeas.

■ Brazil grows the most dry beans.

"Nitrogen is the common limiting factor in most cultivated crops, and nitrogen fertilizers are a high-energy input."

"You have to have the right species of bacteria in the soil for the crop to fix nitrogen," he adds, noting that most North American farmers who include pulses in their crop rotations "inoculate" the seeds with the appropriate bacterial strain before planting to ensure optimum nitrogen fixation.

Besides tolerating drought well, pulses

COOKING METHODS

■ Pressure cookers, which are enjoying a comeback, are ideal for cooking pulses. They save hours, reducing cooking time to minutes. Plus, many say that pressure-cooked pulses have better taste and texture than stove top and slow cooker methods. Dry or presoaked beans can be put under pressure; follow the manufacturer's instructions.

■ Hot-soak dry beans, chickpeas (*above*), and whole dry peas: Boil them in water for 3 minutes, then let them soak for up to 24 hours. Pour off the soaking water, rinse, and cook in fresh water as directed, or until tender (tenderness time varies with the age of the dried seed and other factors). Lentils and split peas do not require soaking.

People Should Love Pulses

"Pulse foods are low in fat and sodium, low-glycemic, and gluten-free," says Julie Garden-Robinson, a nutrition specialist with North Dakota State University Extension. "All pulses provide an excellent source of protein, fiber, potassium, and folate, as well as many essential minerals.

"Clinical research has shown that pulse foods help to manage blood glucose levels and lower both total and LDL ['bad'] cholesterol, and may help to prevent heart disease, obesity, asthma, some types of cancer, and other chronic diseases."

Gram for gram, pulses are the least expensive proteins. "Although pulse foods lack certain essential amino acids that humans need to make 'complete proteins,' eating a wide diversity of foods each day that include whole grains, nuts, and vegetables, as well as pulses, will supply adequate protein," she adds.

Cooked pulses are the only food group to qualify by USDA standards as either a protein or a vegetable (e.g., with chicken, lentils "count" as a veggie; with a vegetarian meal, they count as a protein).

benefit growers in other ways, too, such as by . . .

■ improving the soil, e.g., through releasing compounds that "feed" beneficial soil microorganisms or that make nutrients more available to other crops

■ increasing soil biodiversity

■ breaking the cycles of plant disease, weeds, and insect pests

■ increasing the yields of nonlegume crops planted the following season

Gardeners Can Love Pulses

Green beans and fresh peas are popular home garden crops. Growing dry beans or peas is another story. Gardeners face a long season, weeds, animal and insect pests, and plant diseases. If all goes well, a 25-foot row of dry beans or peas will yield only 2 to 3 pounds of seeds. However, if you have time and space, dry beans can be satisfying to grow; plus, you can try varieties not available in stores. *(continued)*

Mrs. Nelson's
CANDY HOUSE
"Your house for all occasions"

Candies! For over 50 years we have
used only the finest ingredients in
our candies—cream, butter, honey,
and special blends of chocolates.
Call for a FREE brochure. Long famous
for quality candies mailed all over the
world. Treat yourself or someone
special today.

Come visit us today!

292 Chelmsford Street
Chelmsford, MA 01824
For Free Brochure Call:

978-256-4061

Finally, a civilized
way to polish
your silver!

CAPE COD®
METAL
POLISHING CLOTHS

...and your brass, copper, & nickel too!

before   *after*

Economy Size Tin
contents:
12 polishing Cloths
1 buffing cloth
1 pair of gloves

800-682-4246

www.capecodpolish.com

Mortise & Tenon Red Cedar
Quality Wood Shutters

Interior & Exterior
Painted or Unfinished

Made in USA

Shuttercraft
QUALITY WOOD SHUTTERS
INTERIOR & EXTERIOR
EST. 1986

Family owned 25 years
Colonial Craftsmanship

Madison, CT - (203) 245-2608 - www.shuttercraft.com

Home Cooks Love Pulses

These versatile legumes can be as quick or complicated to prepare as you want, depending on the dish. Here are a few recipes; find more at Almanac.com.

Cranberry Bean Soup

If desired, add 1 to 2 cups of chopped kale or cabbage and an additional 1 cup of water.

2 cups dry cranberry beans

1 cup whole dry peas

1 meaty ham bone

2 bay leaves

1 onion, peeled and stuck with 4 cloves

5 potatoes, peeled and chopped

2 carrots, peeled and chopped

4 leeks, white parts only, chopped, or 3 onions, peeled and chopped

3 cloves garlic, minced

grated Parmesan cheese

■ Soak the beans and peas overnight in water to cover. Drain and place in a soup pot with 3 quarts of water, ham bone, bay leaves, and onion. Bring to a boil, reduce the heat, cover, and simmer for 2 hours, or until the beans and peas are tender.

■ Remove the bone, chop the meat into small bits, discard the bone, and return the meat to the pot. Add the potatoes, carrots, leeks, and garlic. Simmer, partially covered, for 30 minutes, or until the vegetables are tender. Remove the bay leaves and clove-stuck onion.

■ Garnish with grated Parmesan cheese.

Makes 6 to 8 servings. *(continued)*

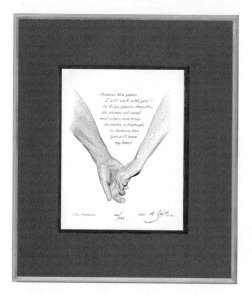

A Most Unusual Gift of Love

THE POEM READS:

"Across the years I will walk with you—
in deep, green forests; on shores of sand:
and when our time on earth is through,
in heaven, too, you will have my hand."

Dear Reader,

The drawing you see above is called *The Promise*. It is completely composed of dots of ink. After writing the poem, I worked with a quill pen and placed thousands of these dots, one at a time, to create this gift in honor of my youngest brother and his wife.

Now, I have decided to offer *The Promise* to those who share and value its sentiment. Each litho is numbered and signed by hand and precisely captures the detail of the drawing. As a wedding, anniversary or Valentine's gift or simply as a standard for your own home, I believe you will find it most appropriate.

Measuring 14" by 16", it is available either fully-framed in a subtle copper tone with hand-cut double mats of pewter and rust at $135*, or in the mats alone at $95*. Please add $14.50 for insured shipping and packaging. Your satisfaction is completely guaranteed.

My best wishes are with you.

The Art of Robert Sexton • P.O. Box 581 • Rutherford, CA 94573

All major credit cards are welcomed. Please send card name, card number, address and expiration date, or phone **(415) 989-1630** between 10 a.m.-6 P.M. PST, Monday through Saturday. Checks are also accepted.

*Please allow up to 2 weeks for delivery. *California residents- please include 8.0% tax*

Please visit my Web site at

www.robertsexton.com

I love a warm or cold lentil salad, marinated in my choice of dressing and surrounded by roasted vegetables: winter squash, brussels sprouts or cabbage wedges, red onions, and maybe sweet potatoes in fall and winter; asparagus, onions, zucchini strips, and peppers in spring and summer. Cheese is optional, but whole-grain flatbread, for me, is not.

Another favorite is split-pea salad. Cook the peas (green and yellow mixed look pretty) in water with a bay leaf until soft. Drain and remove bay leaf. Add salt and pepper, to taste. Dress the cooled peas with a slightly thinned basil pesto or a garlicky vinaigrette with honey mustard. Serve on a bed of salad greens. This preparation would work well with any of the cooked pulses, including any of the dozens of different beans.

—*M. B.*

Hummus

Use as a dip or spread it on bread.

1 can (20 ounces) chickpeas or 2½ cups cooked

¼ cup fresh lemon juice

2 cloves garlic, minced or roasted

2 tablespoons olive oil, divided

4 tablespoons tahini

salt and freshly ground black pepper, to taste

fresh minced parsley, for garnish

■ Drain the chickpeas and reserve the liquid.

■ In a blender or food processor, combine the chickpeas, lemon juice, garlic, 1 tablespoon of olive oil, and tahini. Blend until smooth. Add enough reserved liquid to make a creamy consistency. Taste and add salt and pepper, if desired.

■ Transfer to a bowl, drizzle with the remaining olive oil, and garnish with parsley. Refrigerate until ready to serve.

Makes 2 cups. *(continued)*

Photo: Becky Luigart-Stayner; food styling, Ana Kelly; prop styling, Jan Gautro

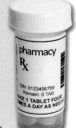

Peg's Black Bean Brownies

*Black beans add about 24 grams of protein and 20 grams of fiber
to a conventional brownie recipe — and nobody will know!*

1 can (15 ounces) black beans, drained and rinsed, or 2 cups cooked

3 eggs

¼ cup unsweetened cocoa powder

¾ cup sugar

3 tablespoons vegetable oil, or 1½ tablespoons olive oil and 1½ tablespoons butter

½ teaspoon baking powder

pinch of salt

½ cup dark chocolate chips

½ cup chopped walnuts

■ Preheat the oven to 350°F and grease an 8x8-inch baking pan.

■ Put the first seven ingredients into a blender or food processor and blend until smooth.

■ Transfer to a bowl and stir in the chocolate chips and walnuts. Pour into the prepared pan.

■ Bake for 35 minutes, or until a toothpick inserted into the center comes out clean.   *–M. B.* ■

Margaret Boyles lives in a wood-heated house in central New Hampshire, where she grows vegetables, eats pulse crops, and keeps chickens.

          Photo: Becky Luigart-Stayner; food styling, Ana Kelly; prop styling, Jan Gautro

Home Resource

HOME • GARDEN • FOOD

Shop the Online Marketplace at
Almanac.com for more
unique products and services.

All Seasons Log Home Care

Since 1994, I Wood Care has
provided quality log home
preservation products to manu-
facturers, dealers, contractors
and log home owners alike.

Sashco, Sikkens, ABR-X100,
Perma-Chink, Continental-
WeatherSeal, Lifetime and more!

1-800-721-7715

www.iwoodc.com • E: info@iwoodc.com

Old Village Paint

Top quality
historic paint for
*200 years,
since 1816.*

800-498-7687
www.old-village.com

The New Litter Robot "Open Air"

The highest rated
automatic self-cleaning
litter box just got
better. Say goodbye to
the litter box smell
and enjoy the freedom
from scooping litter.
Great for kittens and
cats of ALL sizes.

1-888-227-8650 • www.litter-robot.com

HARD-TO-FIND Traditional Moveable Louver Shutters

Quality hardwoods
custom made to
your size!

Shuttercraft.com

203-245-2608

Madison, CT

Shelves That Slide
*Custom pullout shelves
for your cabinets*

Sliding trash and
recycle centers, tip out
trays, lazy susans and
wire pullouts. Order
online, call or email
for a free catalog.

ShelvesThatSlide.com
1-800-598-7390

Millie's PIEROGI

Homemade Pierogi
We make and ship fully-
cooked pierogi with these
popular fillings: cabbage,
potato & cheese, prune,
blueberry, potato & onion,
farmer's cheese, or potato
& cheese w/kielbasa.
Box of 6 trays $45.00
Box of 10 trays $68.00
Polish Party Pack $69.00
Plus S&H. One dozen pierogi/tray.

129 Broadway • Chicopee Falls, MA 01020
milliespierogi.com • 800-743-7641

GOAT MILK SOAP

Cranberry Ridge Farm
A goat milk soapery
Take care of your body with hand-
made goat milk soap. Always made
with vegetable oils and therapeutic
grade essential oils. Cranberry
Ridge Farm has been crafting fine
skin care products since 1999.
There is always a good excuse to
use pure goat milk soap.
118 Nichols Road
Williamstown, NY 13493

315-964-9900 • cranberryridgefarmny.com

Winners in the 2015
Dips and Spreads Recipe Contest

Thanks to the hundreds of entrants who made choosing the
prize recipients another delicious dilemma. Try these recipes and tell us
at Almanac.com/Feedback if *you* think that they're winners.

FIRST PRIZE: $250
Florentine Spinach Dip

16 ounces cream cheese, softened

1 cup Alfredo sauce

1 box (10 ounces) frozen spinach, thawed and squeezed dry

½ cup chopped artichoke hearts

¼ cup diced sun-dried tomatoes

¼ cup diced roasted red peppers

2 cups shredded Italian-blend cheese

½ cup grated Parmesan cheese

¼ teaspoon Italian seasoning

1 dash hot sauce

■ Preheat the oven to 350°F.

■ In a large bowl, stir together all of the ingredients until combined. Spoon into a lightly greased 2-quart casserole.

■ Bake for 25 to 30 minutes, or until golden brown.

Makes 25 servings.

–Crystal Schlueter, Northglenn, Colorado

Pesto Strata

PESTO:

2 cups Italian parsley without stems

¾ cup grated Parmesan cheese

1 clove garlic

3 tablespoons olive oil

1 slice bread

½ teaspoon salt

¼ teaspoon freshly ground black pepper

FILLING:

16 ounces cream cheese, softened

½ cup (1 stick) unsalted butter, softened

FOR PESTO:

■ Combine pesto ingredients in a food processor or blender and process until smooth. Add additional oil as necessary to create a smooth paste.

FOR FILLING:

■ Mix cream cheese and butter and set aside.

■ Line a deep bowl or container with plastic wrap. Put one-third of the filling on the bottom, followed by one-third of the pesto. Repeat the layers two more times.

■ Cover and place in refrigerator. When ready to serve, invert onto a serving dish.

Makes 10 to 12 servings.

–Nancy Vargas, Sierra Madre, California

(continued)

Photos: Becky Luigart-Stayner; food styling, Ana Kelly; prop styling, Jan Gautro

Dressed-Up Crab Rangoon Dip

12 ounces cream cheese, softened

2 cans (6 ounces each) crabmeat,
well drained and picked over for shells

3 scallions, chopped

2 tablespoons chopped roasted red peppers

¾ cup shredded Swiss cheese

⅓ cup grated Parmesan cheese

1 teaspoon prepared horseradish

1 tablespoon Worcestershire sauce

1 tablespoon milk

¼ teaspoon garlic powder

¼ teaspoon salt

⅛ teaspoon freshly ground black pepper

2 tablespoons chopped slivered almonds

1 scallion, green part only, chopped,
for garnish

■ Preheat the oven to 375°F. Spray an 8x8-inch baking dish with nonstick cooking spray; set aside.

■ In a bowl, mix together the cream cheese, crabmeat, scallions, red peppers, Swiss cheese, Parmesan, horseradish, Worcestershire sauce, milk, garlic powder, salt, and black pepper.

■ Place crab mixture into prepared baking dish and bake for 20 to 25 minutes, or until bubbly around the edges.

■ Top with almonds and cook for 5 minutes more.

■ Garnish with chopped green scallions.
Makes 25 servings.

–Debbie Reid, Clearwater, Florida

■

ENTER THE 2016 RECIPE CONTEST: SAVORY PIES
Got a great savory pie recipe that your family and friends love? It could win!
See contest rules on page 271.

You're a Gem!

Semiprecious facts and folklore about birthstones

BY MARTIE MAJOROS • ILLUSTRATIONS BY TIM ROBINSON

JANUARY
GARNET

History: The word "garnet" comes from the Latin word *granatum,* meaning pomegranate. In Asia, bullets were made from garnets because it was believed that they would cause enemies to bleed more.

Source: Garnets form in layers of rock deep underground, where they withstand extreme temperature variations. Geologists study garnets to understand the effects of temperature and pressure on surrounding rocks.

Lore: Garnets prevent nightmares, guarantee safe travel, and bring friendship. If you dream of losing a garnet necklace, unexpected good fortune is in your future.

FEBRUARY
AMETHYST

History: Italian Renaissance artist and scientist Leonardo da Vinci (1452–1519) believed that wearing an amethyst could increase intelligence.

Source: Amethysts are a type of quartz often found in geodes amidst cooled lava.

Lore: Wearing an amethyst will give you courage and help to prevent insomnia. A dream of receiving an amethyst as a gift brings good luck. A dream of giving one means you forgive the recipient.

MARCH
AQUAMARINE

History: In Latin, *aqua* means water and *mare* means sea. Sailors once wore aquamarine stones carved with the image of Neptune, the Roman god of the seas, to protect them during their travels.

Source: Aquamarine is a type of beryl, a mineral that forms from cooling magma deep inside Earth. Beryl can be found in many colors, ranging from blue-green to yellow to red.

Lore: Wearing an aquamarine is believed to alleviate illness. If you dream of an aquamarine, you will soon make new friends.

Centuries ago, people believed that certain gemstones had special healing powers, such as being able to cure mental and physical ills at certain times of the year. Today, these amulets are used as ornaments, and every month has associated with it a gem that is the "birthstone" of those born in that month.

APRIL DIAMOND	MAY EMERALD	JUNE PEARL

APRIL — DIAMOND

History: It is believed that the first engagement ring that contained a diamond was given in 1477 by Archduke Maximilian of Austria to his fiancée, Mary of Burgundy. Today, diamonds are the most popular choice of stone for an engagement ring.

Source: Diamond contains tightly formed carbon crystals, making it the hardest mineral on Earth.

Lore: Wearing a diamond will protect you from negative energies and bring you peace. If you dream of wearing diamond earrings, you will receive good financial advice.

MAY — EMERALD

History: In the 1700s, powdered emeralds were sold by chemists to help relieve pain. Emeralds were favorite gems of Egypt's Cleopatra and Russia's Catherine the Great.

Source: Emeralds, like aquamarine, are a form of the mineral beryl.

Lore: Wearing an emerald may help to strengthen your memory. If you dream of buying an emerald, someone you trust may deceive you.

JUNE — PEARL

History: English philosopher Sir Francis Bacon (1561–1626) is believed to have eaten a paste of ground pearls and lemon juice to cure illness.

Source: Natural pearls are formed inside the shell of oysters when a grain of sand or other particle gets inside the shell and causes an irritation. Because it can't get rid of the irritating particle, the oyster covers it with a smooth, crystalline substance called nacre, forming a pearl.

Lore: Pearls are associated with purity, honesty, and calmness. If you dream of a pearl ring, expect romance.

(continued)

Stones: diamond, emerald, and pearl, Thinkstock

JULY
RUBY

History: One of the largest rubies in the world is called the "Peace" ruby because it was found in 1919 shortly after World War I ended.

Source: Rubies are a form of corundum (aluminum oxide); their color may range from deep blood red to paler rose red.

Lore: If you own a ruby, you will live in harmony with all people and be protected from danger. If you dream of a ruby, you will have good luck.

AUGUST
PERIDOT

History: The largest peridot ever found weighs 319 carats. It is in the Smithsonian Institution in Washington, D.C.

Source: Peridot has been found in volcanic lava in Hawaii and in meteorites that have fallen to Earth. In the 1700s, a meteorite that landed in Siberia contained many peridot crystals that were large enough to be used in pieces of jewelry.

Lore: Peridot is believed to help depression. If you dream that you find a peridot while digging in the garden, you will have an unexpected visitor.

SEPTEMBER
SAPPHIRE

History: In the 15th century, it was thought that holding a sapphire near a spider would kill it. In the 17th century, it was believed that holding or wearing sapphires helped you to foretell the future.

Source: Sapphires, like rubies, are a form of corundum, the second-hardest mineral. Ranging in color from light to dark blue, they are found chiefly in placer deposits.

Lore: Sapphires are thought to ease pain and reduce stress. If you dream that you are wearing a sapphire, be warned: You should be less impulsive.

(continued)

OCTOBER
OPAL

History: The word "opal" comes from the Greek word *opallios,* meaning to see a change in color. Australian aboriginal tribes believed that opals were the Creator's footprints on Earth.

Source: Opals are a type of quartz that forms tiny spheres. When light hits the spheres, the colors of the spectrum become visible.

Lore: Opals help to control temper and calm nerves. A dream of an opal means that good luck will come.

NOVEMBER
TOPAZ

History: In the Middle Ages (500–1500), topaz was ground into a powder and mixed with wine to guarantee a good night's sleep.

Source: Topaz is found in igneous rocks and sometimes hydrothermal veins.

Lore: It is believed that topaz will help to balance emotions. If you dream of topaz, a problem with which you have been struggling will soon be solved.

DECEMBER
TURQUOISE

History: In ancient Turkey, Tibet, and Persia, turquoise stones were attached to horses' bridles. It was thought that the stones protected the animals from the ill effects of drinking cold water when they were overheated from exertion.

Source: Turquoise is found most often in very dry areas where volcanic activity has occurred.

Lore: Wearing turquoise will calm and balance emotions. A dream of turquoise means victory and success. ∎

Martie Majoros, whose birthstone is turquoise, writes from the shores of Lake Champlain in Burlington, Vermont.

JET STREAMS:

HOT CURVES AND COLD WEATHER

BY EVELYN BROWNING GARRISS
AND JAMES J. GARRISS III

ILLUSTRATIONS BY ROB SCHUSTER

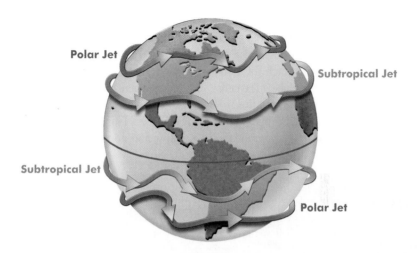

Polar Jet

Subtropical Jet

Subtropical Jet

Polar Jet

IF THERE'S ONE THING THAT THE HEADLINES HAVE TAUGHT US, IT'S THAT THE POLAR VORTEX HAS BECOME A WEATHER CELEBRITY. NEARLY EVERY POLAR JET STREAM WIGGLE DURING RECENT YEARS HAS BEEN CALLED A "POLAR VORTEX" BECAUSE THIS SOUNDS MUCH SCARIER THAN "CURVY JET STREAM."

The polar jet stream has been very active for a number of years and since 2012 has allowed large masses of northern air to flow south.

What is the jet stream, and why is it doing this to us?

A jet stream is a strong, fast, narrow wind that forms when two air masses touch in the stratosphere at about 33,000 feet, or 6 miles above sea level. The greater the difference between the air mass temperatures, the stronger, straighter, and faster the jet stream winds.

There are numerous jet streams forming all around the world, from the giant African easterly jet that spits tropical depressions toward us in hurricane season to smaller barrier jets that zip beside differ-

ent mountain ranges. There is even a jet stream that occasionally dips down to the peak of Mt. Everest, allowing the bravest of mountain climbers to feel its chill.

The most important jet streams are the high-altitude winds that form between the five major global air masses:

■ the tropical air mass around the equator

■ the two subtropical air masses, one north and one south of the tropics

■ the two polar air masses, one over the Arctic and the other over the Antarctic

The strongest of these are the polar jets, which form between the frigid polar and warm subtropical air masses *(page 88).* These travel at 200 miles per hour, from 4

Illustration sources: opposite, NASA; above, NOAA

to 7½ miles above sea level. The weaker subtropical jets, which form between warm subtropical and hot tropical air masses, soar at 6 to 10 miles. Both types tend to be long and narrow (roughly 100 to 200 miles in width) and stretch for thousands of miles around the globe. (The cells shown are patterns of air circulation.)

Most North Americans hear only about the polar jet stream that circles around the

page 90). They discovered that when its winds circling the Arctic are very strong (or "positive"), polar air gets trapped in the high latitudes. The Arctic air grows colder and the area south of the polar air mass grows warmer. This happened in 2012, when the AO had one of the most positive readings ever measured. Alaska froze, Fairbanks received 29 feet of snow, and northern Canada recorded

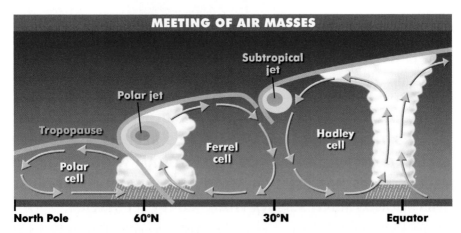

MEETING OF AIR MASSES

Subtropical jet · Polar jet · Tropopause · Hadley cell · Ferrel cell · Polar cell

North Pole · **60°N** · **30°N** · **Equator**

Arctic air mass. When it dips south, cold polar air pours southward with it. The notorious "polar vortex" is usually just the jet stream veering southeast of the Rocky Mountains, allowing the polar air mass to flow south and freeze everyone from Chicago to New Orleans. When the cold air crashes into warmer, wetter air from the Gulf of Mexico and the Atlantic, powerful storms slam the coastlines.

Because the southern surge of the polar jet stream can be disastrous, scientists are trying to learn how to predict it. Here's some of what they are learning.

■ Scientists call the behavior of the polar jet stream the **Arctic Oscillation** (AO;

record low temperatures. Meanwhile, winter never seemed to arrive in the lower 48 states and spring temperatures and planting arrived 6 weeks early.

■ With a weaker jet stream circling the pole (or "negative" AO; *page 90*), Arctic air can escape. As the cold air expands south, it and the winds around it interact, reinforcing each other. Both dip south and spread across the Canadian Prairies and the U.S. Midwest. This is not just a North American event. When air pressure and temperatures weaken the jet stream, it becomes curvy, pushed south by the Arctic air and north by the warmer subtropical air. As it veers south,

AO: ARCTIC OSCILLATION

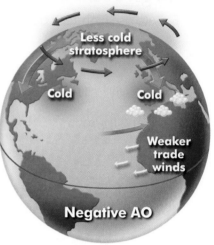

then north, then south again, cold air slams Canada and the central and eastern United States and then is pushed back by warm air from the Gulf of Mexico. This causes the jet stream to continue to ripple, as it moves east around the Northern Hemisphere. Where the cold and warm air masses collide, enormous storms bury people in blizzards and floods. Indeed, many scientists now claim that most of the recent extreme weather is at least partially due to the curvy, downright loopy, behavior of the polar jet stream.

■ Because the celebrated polar vortex weather is created by a weak and wavering jet stream, meteorologists are trying to understand what shapes the wind circling the Arctic. They have discovered that the combination of different air pressures and temperatures (particularly the contrast between the polar and subtropical air mass temperatures), combined with Earth's rotation, determines the strength of the jet stream.

CURRENT NEWS

Scientists have found two observable patterns that cause the jet stream to plunge into the eastern United States. These patterns are largely shaped by semipermanent low-pressure areas in the northern oceans. Scientists can use their measurements of these air pressures to predict the weather for a few days at a time.

PACIFIC NORTH AMERICAN PATTERN (PNA):

This pattern is shaped by the strength of the Aleutian Low (south of Alaska's Aleutian Islands) and the West Coast High *(page 92)*.

When the air pressures in both of these air masses are strong (or positive), the jet stream veers north over western North America. The West Coast becomes warm and dry, sometimes as far north as western Canada and Alaska. Then the jet stream slams deep into the center and eastern parts of the continent, bringing Arctic air. Typically, the Rocky Mountains, which interrupt the flow of Pacific air, divide

Illustration source: NASA

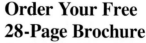

PNA: PACIFIC NORTH AMERICAN PATTERN

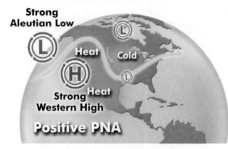

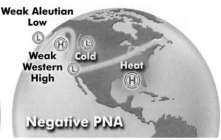

Illustration source: The Weather Centre

western warmth and eastern chill.

When the two air pressures are weak (or negative), the jet stream and cool air drift into the West and the rest of North America is heated by marine air from the Gulf of Mexico and remains relatively warm.

NORTH ATLANTIC OSCILLATION (NAO): The Icelandic Low and the mid-Atlantic Azores High control the strength and direction of winds around the Atlantic Ocean *(below)*.

When there is a strong "positive" difference between the air pressure areas, the prevailing winds and the polar jet stream blast across the Atlantic. They trap cold Arctic air, forcing it to stay north.

When the areas' pressure is similar, or "negative," the jet stream and Atlantic winds are weaker and wander north and south. Cold Arctic air can slam the U.S. South in the winter, and hot tropical air can invade the northern latitudes during summer. The eastern regions of North America suffer stormier winters and summer heat waves. Rainfall patterns shift by hundreds, even thousands, of miles.

THE POWER OF THREE— OR EVEN TWO

Three patterns—the negative AO, positive PNA, and negative NAO—individually create curvy polar jet streams that allow Arctic air to flow south. When two or three of them happen at the same time, cries of "polar vortex" or "Snowmageddon" go up! The effects are critical for U.S. and Canadian weather. *(continued)*

NAO: NORTH ATLANTIC OSCILLATION

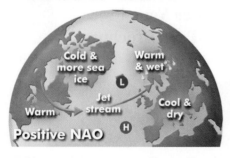

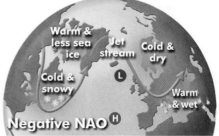

Illustration source: NOAA

Weather

THE REALLY LONG VIEW

Are we going to experience more frigid winters in the East and droughts in the West?

The answer, according to some recent scientific studies, is yes.

Scientists have been examining glaciers to find a record of past weather. Water temperatures shape water chemistry, and by studying the oxygen in water, researchers can learn what weather conditions were present when the ice formed. By examining the chemistry of all of the layers in a glacier, they have a year-to-year history of the weather in that area. By examining and comparing the history of glaciers in different parts of North America, they can reconstruct the changing climate, including whether the polar jet streams were curvy or straight.

Using these techniques, one international study headed by Chinese scientist Zhongfang Liu showed how the behavior of the polar jet stream has been changing:

■ Jet streams started to get curvier around 4,000 years ago.

■ This curving process started to speed up in 1850, and the effects are becoming more extreme.

■ The North American West is getting warmer, while the East is getting the concentrated wintertime cold.

■ This tends to go in cycles of 20+ years, and we are in the middle of a cold cycle. ■

Evelyn Browning Garriss and **James J. Garriss III** blog about jet streams and historical climatology at Almanac.com/Weather.

WINTER 2015–16

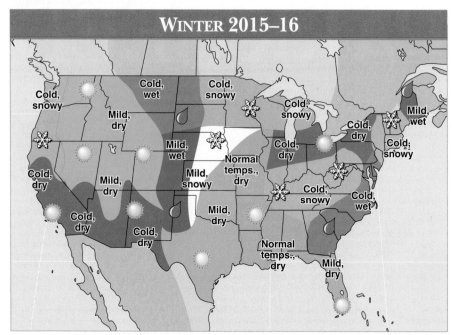

These weather maps correspond to the winter (November through March) and summer (June through August) predictions in the General Weather Forecast (opposite). Forecast terms here represent deviations from the normals; learn more on page 189.

SUMMER 2016

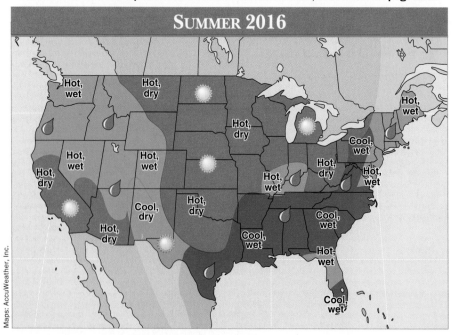

Maps: AccuWeather, Inc.

The General Weather Report and Forecast

For regional forecasts, see pages 192–209.

What's shaping the weather? Solar Cycle 24 is now in its declining phase after reaching double peaks in 2011 and 2014. Despite having two maxima, this cycle is the smallest in over 100 years; as solar activity continues to decline from these low peaks, we expect temperatures in much of the nation to be below normal this winter and above normal in the coming summer. The winter of 2015–16 will be another snowy one in much of the northeast quarter of the country, with areas in the Pacific Northwest also relatively snowy.

Other important factors in the coming weather patterns include a continued warm phase in the Atlantic Multidecadal Oscillation (AMO), a near-neutral phase in the North Atlantic Oscillation (NAO) in most of the winter, and the long-term cool phase of the Pacific Decadal Oscillation (PDO) likely nearing its end. Oscillations are linked ocean–atmosphere patterns that influence the weather over periods of weeks to years.

One of the keys to the upcoming winter will again be the El Niño Southern Oscillation (ENSO), which many are forecasting to be in its warm El Niño phase this winter. If they are correct, then winter will likely be rainier than we are forecasting in California and the Southwest. Unfortunately, we believe that it is more likely that El Niño will be in a weak to neutral phase.

Winter will be cold again in much of the nation, with below-normal temperatures along most of the Atlantic seaboard and in the Ohio Valley, Great Lakes, Pacific Northwest, and southwestern states and above-normal temperatures in Florida and Maine, from the Gulf coast into the Heartland, and in the Rockies states. Snowfall will be above normal in most of the Northeast and the Ohio Valley, northern Plains, and Pacific Northwest but below normal in most other areas. Most of the states from the Gulf of Mexico into the Heartland will have below-normal precipitation. We expect above-normal rainfall from the mid-Atlantic into the Southeast and from the Texas Panhandle into Montana. Most other areas, including most of California, should have below-normal precipitation.

Spring will be warmer than normal from Texas to Minnesota, but cooler than normal in most other areas. Spring precipitation will be below normal in most states in the eastern and central parts of the nation, but above normal in most spots in the West.

Summer temperatures will be above normal in most of the nation, the main exceptions being the Southeast and along the spine of the Appalachians. Rainfall will be below normal in most of the nation's midsection, which may reduce yields of corn, wheat, soybeans, and other crops grown within this area. The drought in much of California will likely continue as well, putting additional stress on our food supply.

Hurricane season will be more active than it was last year, with threats along the Atlantic and Gulf shores. The best chance for a major hurricane strike is in early July in Florida and from late August to mid-September along the Texas and Louisiana Gulf coasts.

Autumn temperatures will be much warmer than normal in most of the eastern two-thirds of the nation and below normal in the West. Precipitation will be below normal in most of New England, in Georgia, and in parts of the Great Lakes and Tennessee Valley states and above normal elsewhere.

To learn how we make our weather predictions, turn to page 189 and to get a summary of the results of our forecast for last winter, turn to page 190.

The Old Farmer's Almanac

Established in 1792 and published every year thereafter
ROBERT B. THOMAS, *founder* (1766–1846)

YANKEE PUBLISHING INC.

EDITORIAL AND PUBLISHING OFFICES
P.O. Box 520, 1121 Main Street, Dublin, NH 03444
Phone: 603-563-8111 • Fax: 603-563-8252

EDITOR *(13th since 1792):* Janice Stillman
ART DIRECTOR: Colleen Quinnell
MANAGING EDITOR: Jack Burnett
SENIOR RESEARCH EDITOR: Mare-Anne Jarvela
SENIOR EDITORS: Sarah Perreault, Heidi Stonehill
EDITORIAL ASSISTANCE: Tim Clark
INTERN: Sarah Drory
WEATHER GRAPHICS AND CONSULTATION:
AccuWeather, Inc.

V.P., NEW MEDIA AND PRODUCTION:
Paul Belliveau
PRODUCTION DIRECTORS:
Susan Gross, David Ziarnowski
SENIOR PRODUCTION ARTISTS:
Rachel Kipka, Jennifer Freeman

WEB SITE: ALMANAC.COM
NEW MEDIA EDITOR: Catherine Boeckmann
NEW MEDIA DESIGNERS: Lou S. Eastman, Amy O'Brien
E-COMMERCE MANAGER: Alan Henning
PROGRAMMING: Reinvented, Inc.

CONTACT US
We welcome your questions and comments about articles in and topics for this Almanac. Mail all editorial correspondence to Editor, The Old Farmer's Almanac, P.O. Box 520, Dublin, NH 03444-0520; fax us at 603-563-8252; or contact us through Almanac.com/Feedback. *The Old Farmer's Almanac* can not accept responsibility for unsolicited manuscripts and will not acknowledge any hard-copy queries or manuscripts that do not include a stamped and addressed return envelope.

All printing inks used in this edition of *The Old Farmer's Almanac* are soy-based. This product is recyclable. Consult local recycling regulations for the right way to do it.

Thank you for buying this Almanac! We hope that you find it "useful, with a pleasant degree of humor." Thanks, too, to everyone who had a hand in it, including advertisers, distributors, printers, and sales and delivery people.

OUR CONTRIBUTORS

Bob Berman, our astronomy editor, is the director of Overlook Observatory in Woodstock and Storm King Observatory in Cornwall, both in New York. In 1976, he founded the Catskill Astronomical Society. Bob has led many aurora and eclipse expeditions, venturing as far as the Arctic and Antarctic.

Tim Clark, a retired high school English teacher from New Hampshire, wrote the Farmer's Calendar essays that appear in this edition. His recordings of them are available free at Almanac.com/Multimedia. He has composed the weather doggerel on the Calendar Pages since 1980.

Bethany E. Cobb, our astronomer, earned a Ph.D. in astronomy at Yale University and is an Assistant Professor of Honors and Physics at George Washington University. She also conducts research on gamma-ray bursts and follows numerous astronomy pursuits, including teaching astronomy to adults at the Osher Lifelong Learning Institute at UC Berkeley. When she is not scanning the sky, she enjoys playing the violin, figure skating, and reading science fiction.

Celeste Longacre, our astrologer, often refers to astrology as "a study of timing, and timing is everything." A New Hampshire native, she has been a practicing astrologer for more than 25 years. Her book, *Love Signs* (Sweet Fern Publications, 1999), is available for sale on her Web site, www.yourlovesigns.com.

Michael Steinberg, our meteorologist, has been forecasting weather for the Almanac since 1996. In addition to college degrees in atmospheric science and meteorology, he brings a lifetime of experience to the task: He began predicting weather when he attended the only high school in the world with weather Teletypes and radar.

"To you, it's the perfect lift chair. To me, it's the best sleep chair I've ever had."

Easy-to-use remotes for massage/heat and recline/lift

— J. Fitzgerald, VA

Complete with battery backup in case of power outage

Sit up, lie down — and anywhere in between!

Our Perfect Sleep Chair® is just the chair to do it all. It's a chair, true – the finest of lift chairs – but this chair is so much more! It's designed to provide total comfort and relaxation not found in other chairs. It can't be beat for comfortable, long-term sitting, TV viewing, relaxed reclining and – yes! – peaceful sleep. Our chair's recline technology allows you to pause the chair in an infinite number of positions, including the Trendelenburg position and the zero gravity position where your body experiences a minimum of internal and external stresses. You'll love the other benefits, too: It helps with correct spinal alignment, promotes back pressure relief, and encourages better posture to prevent back and muscle pain.

And there's more! The overstuffed, oversized biscuit style back and unique seat design will cradle you in comfort. Generously filled, wide armrests provide enhanced arm support when sitting or reclining. The high and low heat settings along with the dozens of massage settings, can provide a soothing relaxation you might get at a spa – just imagine getting all that in a lift chair! Shipping charge includes white glove delivery. Professionals will deliver the chair to the exact spot in your home where you want it, unpack it, inspect it, test it, position it, and even carry the packaging away! Includes one year service warranty and your choice of fabrics and colors. If you're not 100% satisfied simply return the chair within 30 days for a refund of the product purchase price. – Call now!

The Perfect Sleep Chair®

Call now toll free for our lowest price.

Please mention code 100188 when ordering.

1-888-317-9118

© 2015 *firstSTREET* for Boomers and Beyond, Inc.

This lift chair puts you safely on your feet!

46383

THE 2016 EDITION OF

The Old Farmer's Almanac
Established in 1792 and published every year thereafter

ROBERT B. THOMAS, *founder* (1766–1846)

YANKEE PUBLISHING INC.
P.O. Box 520, 1121 Main Street, Dublin, NH 03444
Phone: 603-563-8111 • Fax: 603-563-8252

PUBLISHER *(23rd since 1792):* Sherin Pierce
EDITOR IN CHIEF: Judson D. Hale Sr.

FOR DISPLAY ADVERTISING RATES
Go to Almanac.com/AdvertisingInfo or
Call 800-895-9265, ext. 149

Stephanie Bernbach-Crowe • 914-827-0015
Steve Hall • 800-736-1100, ext. 320
Susan Lyman • 646-221-4169

FOR CLASSIFIED ADVERTISING
Call Gallagher Group • 203-263-7171

AD PRODUCTION COORDINATOR: Janet Grant

PUBLIC RELATIONS
Quinn/Brein • 206-842-8922
ginger@quinnbrein.com

CONSUMER MAIL ORDERS
Call 800-ALMANAC (800-256-2622)
or go to Almanac.com/Shop

CONSUMER MARKETING MANAGER:
Kate McPherson • 800-895-9265, ext. 188

RETAIL SALES
Stacey Korpi, 800-895-9265, ext. 160

ALMANAC FUND-RAISING
ofafundraising@yankeepub.com
Carlene McCarty • vtbooklady@gmail.com

DISTRIBUTORS
NATIONAL: Curtis Circulation Company
New Milford, NJ
BOOKSTORE: Houghton Mifflin Harcourt
Boston, MA

The Old Farmer's Almanac publications are available for sales promotions or premiums. Contact Beacon Promotions, info@beaconpromotions.com.

YANKEE PUBLISHING INCORPORATED
Jamie Trowbridge, *President;* Judson D. Hale Sr., *Senior Vice President;* Paul Belliveau, Jody Bugbee, Judson D. Hale Jr., Brook Holmberg, Sherin Pierce, *Vice Presidents.*

The Old Farmer's Almanac/Yankee Publishing Inc. assumes no responsibility for claims made by advertisers or failure by its advertisers to deliver any goods or services advertised herein. Publication of any advertisement by The Old Farmer's Almanac/Yankee Publishing Inc. is not an endorsement of the product or service advertised therein.

PRINTED IN U.S.A.

Talk Show Doctor Reveals Digestion Remedy That Works Instantly!

Television host and best selling author explains how a new aloe-vera extract can make bouts of heartburn, acid-reflux, constipation, gas, bloating, diarrhea, and other stomach nightmares disappear!

Doctor recommended AloeCure® may be the most important application ever discovered for digestive health!

Recently, medical professionals and alternative medicine experts have taken to the airways to reveal a simple secret that amazed millions who suffer with digestion nightmares. People haven't stopped talking about it since.

FDA WARNS ABOUT POPULAR ANTACIDS

A recent FDA warning explained that excessive use of antacids could lead to an increased risk of hip, wrist, and spine fractures. Especially in people over the age of 50.

So when AloeCure® was presented on National TV, you can imagine how thrilled people were to find out they could finally get relief without having to rely on pharmaceutical proton pump inhibitors. But now, according to Dr. Liza Leal, M.D & Chief Medical Officer at Meridian Medical, your stomach problems could be over by simply drinking a small amount of a tasty Aloe Vera extract every day. It's as simple as that!

FINALLY THERE'S HOPE...

At first, the thought of drinking aloe vera might make some people back away. But in fact, this delicious "digestion cocktail" is doing amazing things for people who suffer with digestive problems --- even if they've had them for years. Here's how it works...

STOP STOMACH INDIGESTION

Your stomach naturally produces acid so strong, it can dissolve an aluminum spoon in just 30 minutes! And when excess acid escapes into your esophagus, throat and stomach lining, it unleashes the discomfort of Acid-Reflux, heartburn, ulcers and more misery. Add the problems of stress, and "all hell breaks loose."

Dr. Liza Leal, a well known expert on chronic pain management explains... "AloeCure® can work genuine miracles. It buffers high acid levels with amazing speed, so your stomach feels completely at ease just moments after drinking it." In fact, it could wipe out stomach discomfort, and frantic runs to the bathroom.

"I'm always in 'indigestion hell'. Doctors put me on all sorts of antacid remedies. Nothing worked. A friend said, "Why don't you try AloeCure®. I was shocked! It worked! I stopped taking the PPIs altogether and replaced it with a daily diet of AloeCure®. I didn't feel even the slightest hint of indigestion! For the first time in 40 years I didn't need pills or tablets to avoid indigestion. Thank you AloeCure®! - *Ralph Burns*

UNTIL NOW, LITTLE COULD BE DONE...

But "AloeCure® can help virtually anyone. Even people with chronic stomach discomfort can feel better right away," says Dr. Leal. And what's really exciting is AloeCure® aids in keeping your digestive tract healthy, so with regular use intestinal distress stops coming back.

Digestion Defender #1: Balances Stomach Acid: Your first line of defense is calcium malate. This natural acid buffer instantly sends stomach acid levels plunging. And holds acid levels down so they are not likely to return!

Digestion Defender #2: Instant, Soothing Relief: AloeCure® is brimming with polysaccharides, a "wonder" compound that gently coats the throat, esophagus and stomach, carrying instant relief to cells scorched by excess acid.

WHAT DOCTORS SAY...

AloeCure® is backed by important scientific studies that confirm... aloe calms stomach acid and allows your body to heal itself.

Dr. Liza Leal, M.D & Chief Medical Officer at Meridian Medical. says, "That's why I recommend it to patients who suffer from bouts of heartburn, Acid-Reflux, ulcers, and irritable bowel syndrome..."

Dr. Santiago Rodriguez agrees. "Just two ounces of AloeCure® reduces the acids in your stomach by ten times."

AloeCure® may be the most important application ever discovered for digestive health!

SAFE AND EASY TO USE

With no sugar, no stimulants, and zero calories, AloeCure® is safe, all-natural and has absolutely no side effects. Just drink two ounces, once in the morning, and once at night, and start enjoying immediate life-changing relief!

TRY IT 100% RISK-FREE!

The makers of AloeCure® have agreed to send you up to 6 FREE bottles PLUS 2 free bonus gifts with your order— they're yours to keep no matter what. That's enough AloeCure® for 30 days of powerful digestive relief, absolutely free!

But hurry! This is a special introductory offer, reserved for our readers only. But you must call now!

CALL NOW, TOLL-FREE!
1-855-468-8410

THESE STATEMENTS HAVE NOT BEEN EVALUATED BY THE FDA. THESE PRODUCTS ARE NOT INTENDED TO DIAGNOSE, TREAT, CURE OR PREVENT ANY DISEASE. RESULTS MAY VARY.

Eclipses

■ There will be four eclipses in 2016, two of the Sun and two of the Moon. Solar eclipses are visible only in certain areas and require eye protection to be viewed safely. Lunar eclipses are technically visible from the entire night side of Earth, but during a penumbral eclipse, the dimming of the Moon's illumination is slight.

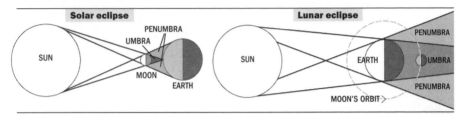

March 8–9: Total eclipse of the Sun. This eclipse will not be visible from North America but will be visible from southern and eastern Asia, northern and eastern Australia, and the Pacific Ocean.

March 23: Penumbral eclipse of the Moon. This eclipse will be visible from North America. In eastern regions, the Moon will be very close to the horizon, and only the beginning of the eclipse will be visible before the Moon sets. The Moon will be entering the penumbra at 5:37 A.M. EDT and leaving the penumbra at 9:57 A.M. Western regions will be able to see the entire eclipse.

September 1: Annular eclipse of the Sun. This eclipse will not be visible from North America but will be visible from Africa, the Indian Ocean, and Antarctica.

September 16: Penumbral eclipse of the Moon. This eclipse will not be visible from North America but will be visible from Australia, Asia, Africa, Europe, and South America.

Full-Moon Dates (Eastern Time)				
	2016	**2017**	**2018**	**2019**	**2020**
Jan.	23	12	1 & 31	21	10
Feb.	22	10	–	19	9
Mar.	23	12	1 & 31	20	9
Apr.	22	11	29	19	7
May	21	10	29	18	7
June	20	9	28	17	5
July	19	9	27	16	5
Aug.	18	7	26	15	3
Sept.	16	6	24	14	2
Oct.	16	5	24	13	1 & 31
Nov.	14	4	23	12	30
Dec.	13	3	22	12	29

The Moon's Path

The Moon's path across the sky changes with the seasons. Full Moons are very high in the sky (at midnight) between November and February and very low in the sky between May and July.

Next Total Eclipses of the Sun

August 21, 2017: visible from most locations in North America.

July 2, 2019: visible from South America and the South Pacific Ocean.

December 14, 2020: visible from South America and Antarctica.

Bright Stars

Transit Times

■ This table shows the time (EST or EDT) and altitude of a star as it transits the meridian (i.e., reaches its highest elevation while passing over the horizon's south point) at Boston on the dates shown. The transit time on any other date differs from that of the nearest date listed by approximately 4 minutes per day. To find the time of a star's transit for your location, convert its time at Boston using Key Letter C (see Time Corrections, page 250).

–Beth Krommes

| Star | Constellation | Magnitude | Time of Transit (EST/EDT) Bold = P.M. Light = A.M. ||||||Altitude (degrees) |
			Jan. 1	Mar. 1	May 1	July 1	Sept. 1	Nov. 1	
Altair	Aquila	0.8	**12:52**	8:57	5:57	1:57	**9:49**	**5:49**	56.3
Deneb	Cygnus	1.3	**1:43**	9:47	6:47	2:47	**10:40**	**6:40**	92.8
Fomalhaut	Psc. Aus.	1.2	**3:59**	**12:03**	9:03	5:03	1:00	**8:56**	17.8
Algol	Perseus	2.2	**8:09**	**4:13**	**1:13**	9:13	5:10	1:10	88.5
Aldebaran	Taurus	0.9	**9:36**	**5:40**	**2:41**	10:41	6:37	2:37	64.1
Rigel	Orion	0.1	**10:15**	**6:19**	**3:19**	11:19	7:15	3:16	39.4
Capella	Auriga	0.1	**10:17**	**6:21**	**3:21**	11:22	7:18	3:18	93.6
Bellatrix	Orion	1.6	**10:25**	**6:29**	**3:30**	11:30	7:26	3:26	54.0
Betelgeuse	Orion	var. 0.4	**10:55**	**6:59**	**4:00**	**12:00**	7:56	3:56	55.0
Sirius	Can. Maj.	−1.4	**11:45**	7:49	**4:49**	**12:49**	8:46	4:46	31.0
Procyon	Can. Min.	0.4	12:43	8:43	5:43	**1:44**	9:40	5:40	52.9
Pollux	Gemini	1.2	12:49	8:49	5:50	**1:50**	9:46	5:46	75.7
Regulus	Leo	1.4	3:12	**11:12**	**8:12**	**4:12**	**12:08**	8:09	59.7
Spica	Virgo	var. 1.0	6:28	2:32	**11:28**	**7:29**	**3:25**	11:25	36.6
Arcturus	Boötes	−0.1	7:18	3:22	**12:23**	**8:19**	**4:15**	**12:15**	66.9
Antares	Scorpius	var. 0.9	9:32	5:36	2:36	**10:32**	6:29	**2:29**	21.3
Vega	Lyra	0	11:39	7:43	4:43	12:43	**8:35**	**4:35**	86.4

Rise and Set Times

■ To find the time of a star's rising at Boston on any date, subtract the interval shown at right from the star's transit time on that date; add the interval to find the star's setting time. To find the rising and setting times for your city, convert the Boston transit times above using the Key Letter shown at right before applying the interval (see Time Corrections, page 250). The directions in which the stars rise and set, shown for Boston, are generally useful throughout the United States. Deneb, Algol, Capella, and Vega are circumpolar stars—they never set but appear to circle the celestial north pole.

Star	Interval (h. m.)	Rising Key	Dir.*	Setting Key	Dir.*
Altair	6 36	B	EbN	E	WbN
Fomalhaut	3 59	E	SE	D	SW
Aldebaran	7 06	B	ENE	D	WNW
Rigel	5 33	D	EbS	B	WbS
Bellatrix	6 27	B	EbN	D	WbN
Betelgeuse	6 31	B	EbN	D	WbN
Sirius	5 00	D	ESE	B	WSW
Procyon	6 23	B	EbN	D	WbN
Pollux	8 01	A	NE	E	NW
Regulus	6 49	B	EbN	D	WbN
Spica	5 23	D	EbS	B	WbS
Arcturus	7 19	A	ENE	E	WNW
Antares	4 17	E	SEbE	A	SWbW

*b = "by"

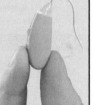

The Twilight Zone

Twilight is the time when the sky is partially illuminated preceding sunrise and again following sunset. The ranges of twilight are defined according to the Sun's position below the horizon. **Civil twilight** occurs when the Sun's center is between the horizon and 6 degrees below the horizon (visually, the horizon is clearly defined). **Nautical twilight** occurs when the center is between 6 and 12 degrees below the horizon (the horizon is distinct). **Astronomical twilight** occurs when the center is between 12 and 18 degrees below the horizon (sky illumination is imperceptible). When the center is at 18 degrees (**dawn** or **dark**) or below, there is no illumination.

Length of Astronomical Twilight (hours and minutes)

LATITUDE	Jan. 1 to Apr. 10	Apr. 11 to May 2	May 3 to May 14	May 15 to May 25	May 26 to July 22	July 23 to Aug. 3	Aug. 4 to Aug. 14	Aug. 15 to Sept. 5	Sept. 6 to Dec. 31
25°N to 30°N	1 20	1 23	1 26	1 29	1 32	1 29	1 26	1 23	1 20
31°N to 36°N	1 26	1 28	1 34	1 38	1 43	1 38	1 34	1 28	1 26
37°N to 42°N	1 33	1 39	1 47	1 52	1 59	1 52	1 47	1 39	1 33
43°N to 47°N	1 42	1 51	2 02	2 13	2 27	2 13	2 02	1 51	1 42
48°N to 49°N	1 50	2 04	2 22	2 42	—	2 42	2 22	2 04	1 50

TO DETERMINE THE LENGTH OF TWILIGHT: The length of twilight changes with latitude and the time of year. See the **Time Corrections, page 250,** to find the latitude of your city or the city nearest you. Use that figure in the chart above with the appropriate date to calculate the length of twilight in your area.

TO DETERMINE WHEN DAWN OR DARK WILL OCCUR: Calculate the sunrise/sunset times for your locality using the instructions in **How to Use This Almanac, page 120.** Subtract the length of twilight from the time of sunrise to determine when dawn breaks. Add the length of twilight to the time of sunset to determine when dark descends.

EXAMPLE:

Boston, Mass. (latitude 42°22')

Sunrise, August 1	5:37 A.M. EDT
Length of twilight	− 1 52
Dawn breaks	3:45 A.M.
Sunset, August 1	8:03 P.M. EDT
Length of twilight	+ 1 52
Dark descends	9:55 P.M.

Principal Meteor Showers

SHOWER	BEST VIEWING	POINT OF ORIGIN	DATE OF MAXIMUM*	NO. PER HOUR**	ASSOCIATED COMET
Quadrantid	**Predawn**	N	**Jan. 4**	25	—
Lyrid	Predawn	S	Apr. 22	10	Thatcher
Eta Aquarid	Predawn	SE	May 4	10	Halley
Delta Aquarid	Predawn	S	July 30	10	—
Perseid	**Predawn**	NE	**Aug. 11–13**	50	**Swift-Tuttle**
Draconid	Late evening	NW	Oct. 9	6	Giacobini-Zinner
Orionid	Predawn	S	Oct. 21–22	15	Halley
Taurid	Late evening	S	Nov. 9	3	Encke
Leonid	Predawn	S	Nov. 17–18	10	Tempel-Tuttle
Andromedid	Late evening	S	Nov. 25–27	5	Biela
Geminid	**All night**	NE	**Dec. 13–14**	75	—
Ursid	Predawn	N	Dec. 22	5	Tuttle

*May vary by one or two days   **Moonless, rural sky   **Bold** = most prominent

Created with one thing in mind —
Simplicity.

NEW!

877-600-0770

CALL?

NO CONTRACT!

We created the Jitterbug with one thing in mind—to offer people a cell phone that's easy to see and hear, simple to use and affordable. Now, we've made the cell phone experience even better with the Jitterbug5.

It features a lightweight, comfortable design with a backlit keypad and big, legible numbers. There is even a dial tone so you know the phone is ready to use. You can also increase the volume with one touch, and the speaker's been improved so you get great audio quality and can hear every word. The battery has been improved too—it's one of the longest-lasting on the market—so you won't have to charge it as often. The phone comes to you with your account already set up and is easy to activate!

Don't pay for minutes you'll never use! The rate plans are simple too. There are a variety of affordable plans to choose from. The U.S.-based customer service is knowledgeable and helpful, and the phone gets service virtually anywhere in the continental U.S.

Try the Jitterbug5 for yourself for 30 days and if you don't love it, just return it for a refund of the product purchase price!

Available in
Red and Blue!

100% U.S. Based Customer Service

12:36 Mon Sep 14 jitterbug **NEW!** 12:36 Mon Sep 14 jitterbug

Call now and receive
a **FREE** Car Charger
a $25⁰⁰ value!

VISA MasterCard American Express DISCOVER

jitterbug5

Call now!

**Helpful Jitterbug experts are
ready to answer your questions.**

Please mention promotional code 100189.

1-877-600-0770
www.JitterbugDirect.com

47633

The Visible Planets

■ Listed here for Boston are viewing suggestions for and the rise and set times (EST/EDT) of Venus, Mars, Jupiter, and Saturn on specific days each month, as well as when it is best to view Mercury. Approximate rise and set times for other days can be found by interpolation. Use the Key Letters at the right of each listing to convert the times for other localities **(see pages 120 and 250)**. *For all planet rise and set times by zip code, visit* Almanac.com/Astronomy.

Venus

♀ **Venus has a poor 2016 until late autumn. The year opens** with it in Scorpius, quite low in the east at dawn and nearly at its minimum brightness. It meets the crescent Moon on January 7 and has twilight conjunctions with Saturn on the following two mornings. Venus plummets even lower and is lost in solar glare on the far side of its orbit throughout the spring. It reaches superior conjunction on June 6, when it is occulted by the Sun. Venus visibly returns in September as an evening star, in Virgo, when it is glimpsed very low in western twilight. Thereafter it gradually inches higher, becoming obvious at nightfall in November and much higher and brighter in December.

Jan. 1	rise	4:14	E	Apr. 1	rise	5:56	C	July 1	set	8:54	E
Jan. 11	rise	4:36	E	Apr. 11	rise	5:44	C	July 11	set	8:59	E
Jan. 21	rise	4:54	E	Apr. 21	rise	5:32	C	July 21	set	8:58	E
Feb. 1	rise	5:10	E	May 1	rise	5:21	B	Aug. 1	set	8:51	D
Feb. 11	rise	5:19	E	May 11	rise	5:13	B	Aug. 11	set	8:41	D
Feb. 21	rise	5:23	E	May 21	rise	5:08	B	Aug. 21	set	8:29	D
Mar. 1	rise	5:22	D	June 1	rise	5:07	A	Sept. 1	set	8:14	C
Mar. 11	rise	5:16	D	June 11	set	8:27	E	Sept. 11	set	8:00	C
Mar. 21	rise	6:08	D	June 21	set	8:43	E	Sept. 21	set	7:48	B

Oct. 1	set	7:37	B
Oct. 11	set	7:29	B
Oct. 21	set	7:26	A
Nov. 1	set	7:28	A
Nov. 11	set	6:37	A
Nov. 21	set	6:52	A
Dec. 1	set	7:11	A
Dec. 11	set	7:32	A
Dec. 21	set	7:54	B
Dec. 31	set	8:14	B

Mars

♂ **This is a good year for Mars, which achieves its biggest** and brightest appearance in over a decade. The year opens with the Orange Planet a magnitude 1 "star" in Virgo, rising at around 1:30 A.M. By March, it breaks the zero-magnitude threshold, in Scorpius. April finds it brightening explosively, retrograding in Ophiuchus, and rising before midnight. Mars reaches opposition on May 22 at a brilliant magnitude –2, when it rises at sunset and is out all night. It stays brilliant in June, then slowly fades for the rest of the year. It remains easily visible through the year's end.

Jan. 1	rise	1:24	D	Apr. 1	**rise**	**11:41**	E	July 1	set	2:06	A
Jan. 11	rise	1:13	D	Apr. 11	**rise**	**11:09**	E	July 11	set	1:29	A
Jan. 21	rise	1:01	D	Apr. 21	**rise**	**10:31**	E	July 21	set	12:55	A
Feb. 1	rise	12:46	D	May 1	**rise**	**9:47**	E	Aug. 1	set	12:23	A
Feb. 11	rise	12:31	E	May 11	**rise**	**8:58**	E	Aug. 11	set	11:54	A
Feb. 21	rise	12:15	E	May 21	set	5:24	A	Aug. 21	set	11:32	A
Mar. 1	**rise**	**11:57**	E	June 1	set	4:26	A	Sept. 1	set	11:11	A
Mar. 11	**rise**	**11:36**	E	June 11	set	3:35	A	Sept. 11	set	10:55	A
Mar. 21	rise	12:15	E	June 21	set	2:48	A	Sept. 21	set	10:42	A

Oct. 1	**set**	**10:32**	A
Oct. 11	**set**	**10:25**	A
Oct. 21	**set**	**10:21**	A
Nov. 1	**set**	**10:18**	A
Nov. 11	**set**	**9:16**	A
Nov. 21	**set**	**9:16**	B
Dec. 1	**set**	**9:16**	B
Dec. 11	**set**	**9:17**	B
Dec. 21	**set**	**9:17**	B
Dec. 31	**set**	**9:17**	B

☞ **Bold = P.M.**   ☞ Light = A.M.

–illustrations, Beth Krommes

Jupiter

♃ Jupiter opens the year on the Leo/Virgo border, rising before midnight. By mid-February, brilliant Jupiter has retrograded into Leo and clears the eastern horizon by 7:00 P.M. It reaches opposition on March 8, when it is out all night as the sky's brightest "star." Jupiter remains conspicuous through the spring and early summer but sinks lower into dusk's glare during August. It closely meets Venus on August 27, but is then quite low and disappears soon after. Jupiter reappears as a morning star, low in the eastern dawn, in mid-October, where it closely meets Mercury on October 11.

Jan. 1	rise	**10:19**	C	Apr. 1	set	5:41	D	July 1	set	**11:42**	D
Jan. 11	rise	**9:40**	C	Apr. 11	set	5:00	D	July 11	set	**11:06**	D
Jan. 21	rise	**8:59**	C	Apr. 21	set	4:19	D	July 21	set	**10:30**	D
Feb. 1	rise	**8:12**	C	May 1	set	3:38	D	Aug. 1	set	**9:51**	D
Feb. 11	rise	**7:28**	C	May 11	set	2:59	D	Aug. 11	set	**9:16**	C
Feb. 21	rise	**6:43**	C	May 21	set	2:20	D	Aug. 21	set	**8:41**	C
Mar. 1	rise	**6:02**	C	June 1	set	1:37	D	Sept. 1	set	**8:03**	C
Mar. 11	rise	**5:16**	C	June 11	set	1:00	D	Sept. 11	set	**7:28**	C
Mar. 21	set	6:27	D	June 21	set	12:23	D	Sept. 21	set	**6:54**	C

Oct. 1	rise	6:21	C
Oct. 11	rise	5:53	C
Oct. 21	rise	5:24	C
Nov. 1	rise	4:53	C
Nov. 11	rise	3:23	C
Nov. 21	rise	2:54	C
Dec. 1	rise	2:23	D
Dec. 11	rise	1:52	D
Dec. 21	rise	1:20	D
Dec. 31	rise	12:46	D

Saturn

♄ The Ringed Planet starts the year low in the east at dawn, in Ophiuchus. Its rings are now angled wide open and appear gorgeous through any telescope using more than 30×. Made of icy boulders, the highly reflective rings boost Saturn to its brightest showing in more than a decade, at nearly magnitude zero. The planet rises before midnight starting in April. Saturn reaches opposition and its nearest approach to Earth on June 3, when it rises at sunset and is out all night. Remaining in Ophiuchus, it is well placed all summer, although it never ascends very high. Sinking lower in the autumn, it falls into twilight in November and vanishes until next year.

Jan. 1	rise	4:58	E	Apr. 1	rise	12:24	E	July 1	set	3:29	A
Jan. 11	rise	4:24	E	Apr. 11	rise	**11:40**	E	July 11	set	2:47	A
Jan. 21	rise	3:49	E	Apr. 21	rise	**10:59**	E	July 21	set	2:06	A
Feb. 1	rise	3:10	E	May 1	rise	**10:17**	E	Aug. 1	set	1:22	A
Feb. 11	rise	2:34	E	May 11	rise	**9:35**	E	Aug. 11	set	12:42	A
Feb. 21	rise	1:58	E	May 21	rise	**8:52**	E	Aug. 21	set	**11:59**	A
Mar. 1	rise	1:24	E	June 1	set	5:35	A	Sept. 1	set	**11:16**	A
Mar. 11	rise	12:46	E	June 11	set	4:53	A	Sept. 11	set	**10:38**	A
Mar. 21	rise	1:08	E	June 21	set	4:11	A	Sept. 21	set	**10:01**	A

Oct. 1	set	**9:24**	A
Oct. 11	set	**8:47**	A
Oct. 21	set	**8:11**	A
Nov. 1	set	**7:32**	A
Nov. 11	set	**5:56**	A
Nov. 21	set	**5:21**	A
Dec. 1	set	**4:46**	A
Dec. 11	rise	6:56	E
Dec. 21	rise	6:22	E
Dec. 31	rise	5:48	E

Mercury

☿ Mercury alternately dashes from the morning to the evening sky every few months. The planet is best observed when it is at least 5 degrees above the horizon 40 minutes after sunset or before sunrise. This year, favorable "evening star" conditions occur in twilight during the first few evenings of January and again in early April, with a lesser showing in the first 3 weeks of December. In the predawn eastern sky, Mercury is an observable morning star at the end of June and optimally seen from September 24 to October 11.

DO NOT CONFUSE ■ *Mars with Saturn in the southeast during April and May. Mars is orange and brighter.* ■ *Jupiter with Venus on August 27, very low in the west after sunset. Venus is brighter.* ■ *Jupiter with Mercury on October 11, in morning twilight. Mercury is slightly orange.*

Astronomical Glossary

Aphelion (Aph.): The point in a planet's orbit that is farthest from the Sun.

Apogee (Apo.): The point in the Moon's orbit that is farthest from Earth.

Celestial Equator (Eq.): The imaginary circle around the celestial sphere that can be thought of as the plane of Earth's equator projected out onto the sphere.

Celestial Sphere: An imaginary sphere projected into space that represents the entire sky, with an observer on Earth at its center. All celestial bodies other than Earth are imagined as being on its inside surface.

Circumpolar: Always visible above the horizon, such as a circumpolar star.

Conjunction: The time at which two or more celestial bodies appear closest in the sky. **Inferior (Inf.):** Mercury or Venus is between the Sun and Earth. **Superior (Sup.):** The Sun is between a planet and Earth. Actual dates for conjunctions are given on the **Right-Hand Calendar Pages, 125–151;** the best times for viewing the closely aligned bodies are given in **Sky Watch** on the **Left-Hand Calendar Pages, 124–150.**

Declination: The celestial latitude of an object in the sky, measured in degrees north or south of the celestial equator; analogous to latitude on Earth. This Almanac gives the Sun's declination at noon.

Eclipse, Lunar: The full Moon enters the shadow of Earth, which cuts off all or part of the sunlight reflected off the Moon. **Total:** The Moon passes completely through the **umbra** (central dark part) of Earth's shadow. **Partial:** Only part of the Moon passes through the umbra. **Penumbral:** The Moon passes through only the **penumbra** (area of partial darkness surrounding the umbra). **See page 102** for more information about eclipses.

Eclipse, Solar: Earth enters the shadow of the new Moon, which cuts off all or part of the Sun's light. **Total:** Earth passes through the umbra (central dark part) of the Moon's shadow, resulting in totality for observers within a narrow band on Earth. **Annular:** The Moon appears silhouetted against the Sun, with a ring of sunlight showing around it. **Partial:** The Moon blocks only part of the Sun.

Ecliptic: The apparent annual path of the Sun around the celestial sphere. The plane of the ecliptic is tipped 23½° from the celestial equator.

Elongation: The difference in degrees between the celestial longitudes of a planet and the Sun. **Greatest Elongation (Gr. Elong.):** The greatest apparent distance of a planet from the Sun, as seen from Earth.

Epact: A number from 1 to 30 that indicates the Moon's age on January 1 at Greenwich, England; used in calculations for determining the date of Easter.

Equinox: When the Sun crosses the celestial equator. This event occurs two times each year: **Vernal** is around March 20 and **Autumnal** is around September 22.

Evening Star: A planet that is above the western horizon at sunset and less than 180° east of the Sun in right ascension.

Golden Number: A number in the 19-year cycle of the Moon, used in calculations for determining the date of Easter. (Approximately every 19 years, the Moon's phases occur on the same dates.) Add 1 to any given year and divide by 19; the remainder is the Golden Number. If there is no remainder, use 19.

Greatest Illuminated Extent (Gr. Illum. Ext.): When the maximum surface area of a planet is illuminated as seen from Earth.

Magnitude: A measure of a celestial object's brightness. **Apparent** magnitude measures the brightness of an object as seen from Earth.

Objects with an apparent magnitude of 6 or less are observable to the naked eye. The lower the magnitude, the greater the brightness. An object with a magnitude of –1, for example, is brighter than an object with a magnitude of +1.

Midnight: Astronomically, the time when the Sun is opposite its highest point in the sky. Both 12 hours before and after noon (so, technically, both A.M. and P.M.), midnight in civil time is usually treated as the beginning of the day, rather than the end. It is typically displayed as 12:00 A.M. on 12-hour digital clocks. On a 24-hour time cycle, 00:00, rather than 24:00, usually indicates midnight.

Moon on Equator: The Moon is on the celestial equator.

Moon Rides High/Runs Low: The Moon is highest above or farthest below the celestial equator.

Moonrise/Moonset: When the Moon rises above or sets below the horizon.

Moon's Phases: The changing appearance of the Moon, caused by the different angles at which it is illuminated by the Sun. **First Quarter:** Right half of the Moon is illuminated. **Full:** The Sun and the Moon are in opposition; the entire disk of the Moon is illuminated. **Last Quarter:** Left half of the Moon is illuminated. **New:** The Sun and the Moon are in conjunction; the Moon is darkened because it lines up between Earth and the Sun.

Moon's Place, Astronomical: The position of the Moon within the constellations on the celestial sphere at midnight. **Astrological:** The position of the Moon within the tropical zodiac, whose twelve 30° segments (signs) along the ecliptic were named more than 2,000 years ago after constellations within each area. Because of precession and other factors, the zodiac signs no longer match actual constellation positions.

Morning Star: A planet that is above the eastern horizon at sunrise and less than 180° west of the Sun in right ascension.

Node: Either of the two points where a celestial

body's orbit intersects the ecliptic. **Ascending:** When the body is moving from south to north of the ecliptic. **Descending:** When the body is moving from north to south of the ecliptic.

Occultation (Occn.): The eclipse of a star or planet by the Moon or another celestial object.

Opposition: The Moon or a planet appears on the opposite side of the sky from the Sun (elongation 180°).

Perigee (Perig.): The point in the Moon's orbit that is closest to Earth.

Perihelion (Perih.): The point in a planet's orbit that is closest to the Sun.

Precession: The slowly changing position of the stars and equinoxes in the sky caused by a slight wobble as Earth rotates around its axis.

Right Ascension (R.A.): The celestial longitude of an object in the sky, measured eastward along the celestial equator in hours of time from the vernal equinox; analogous to longitude on Earth.

Solar Cycle: In the Julian calendar, a period of 28 years, at the end of which the days of the month return to the same days of the week.

Solstice, Summer: When the Sun reaches its greatest declination (23½°) north of the celestial equator, around June 21. **Winter:** When the Sun reaches its greatest declination (23½°) south of the celestial equator, around December 21.

Stationary (Stat.): The brief period of apparent halted movement of a planet against the background of the stars shortly before it appears to move backward/westward (retrograde motion) or forward/eastward (direct motion).

Sun Fast/Slow: When a sundial reading is ahead of (fast) or behind (slow) clock time.

Sunrise/Sunset: The visible rising and setting of the upper edge of the Sun's disk across the unobstructed horizon of an observer whose eyes are 15 feet above ground level.

Twilight: For definitions of civil, nautical, and astronomical twilight, see page 106. ∎

THE BIGGEST MOON
OF OUR LIVES

THIS COULD BE YOUR
ONCE-IN-A-LIFETIME "SUPERMOON"!

BY BOB BERMAN

If you don't see this Supermoon, you won't have another opportunity until November 25, 2034. So put the 2016 event on your calendar and hope for clear skies!

THE TERM "Supermoon" is newly coined. You're not likely to find it in any early astronomy textbook; it originated with an astrologer in 1979, and in recent years, the media and even NASA have started using it. "Supermoon" is easily defined: It's a big full Moon, one that occurs on days when the Moon comes closest to Earth.

Yes, closest. The Moon's orbit around Earth is not circular like the paths of Jupiter's four large satellites or Neptune's big moon, Triton. Our Moon travels in an oval, or elliptical, path, moving closer and then farther away and then again closer to Earth.

As the Moon carves its elongated path through space, it does not simply travel around Earth; its orbit changes compass direction, taking about 9 years to complete all of the sweeps in the pattern. Think of it this way: Every month, after the Moon reaches its closest approach to Earth, or perigee, the perigee point advances a bit. So perigees gradually unfold in new positions in space, continually changing the dates when we can expect a "big Moon." During a 9-year cycle, these occur in every season. (See the Right-Hand Calendar Pages, 125–151, for perigee dates.)

What's more, the shape of the Moon's orbit changes. Sometimes it's rounder, sometimes more oval. When more oval, its near-point gets unusually close to us. So the Moon's perigee distance varies. The distance becomes more extreme when a perigee coincides with a new or full Moon because the Moon and Sun are then in a straight line and exert their greatest gravitational tug. If this alignment occurs within a few months of Earth being closest to the Sun (from November to February), the Moon comes closer still. That's when we may get an "extreme perigee"— precisely what will happen this year.

ON NOVEMBER 14, 2016, the celestial clockwork gears mesh to bring the Moon only 217,000 miles from Earth, surface to surface. Closer than ever!

Well, almost ever. The last time the Moon came this close was on January 26, 1948. The world population back then was less than a third of what it is now, which means that most people

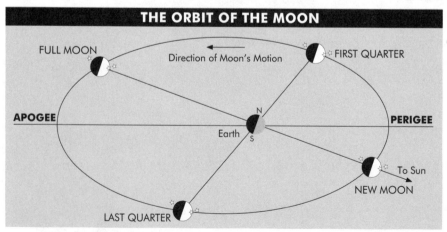

THE ORBIT OF THE MOON

FULL MOON

Direction of Moon's Motion

FIRST QUARTER

APOGEE

Earth

PERIGEE

To Sun

NEW MOON

LAST QUARTER

Perfect Choice HD™ is simple to use, hard to see and easy to afford...

Invention of the Year

PERSONAL SOUND AMPLIFICATION PRODUCTS (PSAPs)

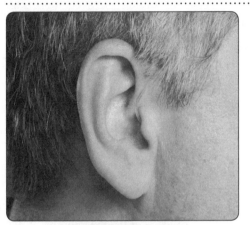

THEY'RE NOT HEARING AIDS

Personal Sound Amplification Products use advanced digital processing to amplify the frequencies of human speech. Thanks to the efforts of a doctor who leads a renowned hearing institute, this product is manufactured in an efficient production process that enables us to make it available at an affordable price.

The unit is small and lightweight enough to hide behind your ear... only you'll know you have it on. It's comfortable and won't make you feel like you have something stuck in your ear. It provides high quality audio so soft sounds and distant conversations will be easier to understand.

Need an extra volume boost? Try Perfect Choice HD™ for yourself with our exclusive home trial.

Call now toll free for the lowest price ever.

1-866-428-5030

Please mention
promotional code
100190.

1998 Ruffin Mill Road,
Colonial Heights, VA 23834

WEIGHT	Less than 1 ounce
SOUND QUALITY	Excellent: Optimized for speech
FITTING REQUIRED?	No
ONE-ON-ONE SETUP	Free
RETURN POLICY	60 Days

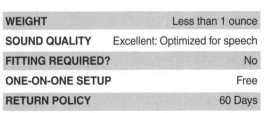

81016

now alive have never witnessed a Moon as big, bright, and close as the November 2016 full Supermoon.

The Moon will appear most impressive soon after rising, in the evening's fading twilight. The difference in apparent size between this Moon and a more-distant full Moon (on March 23, for example) will be about 14 percent. The difference in brightness will be an increase of about 30 percent. Add the famous Moon illusion, and the effect will be dramatic, indeed. The illusion is a psycho-optical effect: Celestial objects low in the sky are perceived as much larger. (Even constellations such as the Big Dipper or Orion look enormous when they're low.) So on November 14, at around 6:00 P.M. local time everywhere, an uncommonly large lunar body will loom even larger, thanks to the effects of this optical illusion.

The Supermoon's effects will be observed in other ways, too. Tides are very sensitive to changes in the Moon's proximity. Both high and low ocean tides, as well as those in rivers connected to the sea (e.g., the Hudson River), will be accompanied by a disproportionate tidal enhancement, especially on November 15. (Tides typically require a day to maximally catch up with the Moon's influence.) While the Moon will be 14 percent larger, the tides will be significantly higher—25 to 30 percent or more can be expected. But there won't be flooding, unless a storm brings strong onshore winds at the same time *(see box)*.

One place where tides will be especially sensitive to the Moon's presence is Atlantic Canada's Bay of Fundy, where one of the best viewing spots is Minas Basin. Fundy strangely ignores typical full and new Moon tidal enhancement and puts on a show when the Moon hits a perigee. ∎

BE READY FOR SUPER TIDES, TOO

Items 1, 2, and 3 below will all occur with this year's Supermoon; beachfront residents should hope that items 4 and 5 do not. Note that enhancement is expressed as a vertical change. Because beach slope varies, even a 1-foot vertical tidal rise can spread water 200 feet beyond normal high tide levels! At the Bay of Fundy, tides can come in a half-mile; however, the vertical rise is only 50 feet, not 2,600 feet.

1. Because the Sun and Moon will be aligned with Earth, tides at the full and new Moons (called "spring" tides because they ride so high) will rise 2 to 3 vertical feet above neap tides, which occur at the first and third quarter Moon phases.

2. Lunar perigee will coincide with the spring tide. Tides will rise an additional several inches or more, depending on location and topography.

3. An extreme lunar perigee creates "proxigean tides," which can rise yet another foot higher than most years' perigean spring tides.

4. Strong onshore winds can make tides several feet higher still.

5. A major low-pressure system can cause a 1-inch drop in atmospheric pressure, pulling tides upward yet another foot.

Bob Berman, *Old Farmer's Almanac* astronomy editor, is the director of Overlook Observatory in Woodstock and Storm King Observatory in Cornwall, both in New York.

Teach Your Brain How to Remember Again – with Just a Simple Pill

Are you tired of feeling "foggy"... absent-minded... or confused? Find out how some people stay sharp and mentally focused - even at age 90!

By Steven Wuzubia, Health Correspondent;

Clearwater, Florida:

Nothing's more frustrating than when you forget names... misplace your keys... or just feel "a little confused". And even though your foggy memory gets laughed off as just another "senior moment", it's not very funny when it keeps happening to you. Like gray hair and reading glasses... some people accept their memory loss as just a part of getting older. But it doesn't have to be that way.

Today, people in their 70's, 80's even their 90's... are staying mentally fit, focused and "fog-free". So what do they know that you don't?

THE SECRET TO UNLOCK YOUR BRAIN

A tiny pill called Lipogen PS Plus, made exclusively in Israel, is an incredible supplement that feeds your brain the nutrients it needs to stay healthy. Developed by Dr. Meir Shinitzky, Ph.D., former visiting professor at Duke University, and recipient of the prestigious J.F. Kennedy Prize.

Dr. Shinitzky explains: "Science has shown, when your brain nutrient levels drop, you can start to experience memory problems. Your ability to concentrate and stay focused becomes compromised. And gradually, a "mental fog" sets in. It can damage every aspect of your life".

In recent years, researchers identified the importance of a remarkable compound called phosphatidylserine (PS). It's the key ingredient in Lipogen. And crucial to your ability to learn and remember things as you age.

OFFICIALLY REVIEWED BY THE U.S. FOOD AND DRUG ADMINISTRATION:

Lipogen safety has been reviewed by the Food & Drug Administration. Lipogen is the **ONLY** Health Supplement that has a "Qualified Health Claim for both **Cognitive Dysfunction** and **Dementia**".

SIGNIFICANT IMPROVEMENTS

In 1992, doctors tested phosphatidylserine on a select group of people aged 60-80 years old. Their test scores showed impressive memory

MY MEMORY WAS STARTING TO FAIL ME.

I'd forget all kinds of things and my memory was becoming pretty unreliable. Something I just said would completely slip my mind and I was worried about it. I read about Lipogen and wanted to try it. After a few weeks, I noticed I wasn't forgetting things anymore. It's great! I have actual recall, which is super! Thanks Lipogen for giving me my memory back.

- Ethel Macagnoney

improvement. Test subjects could remember more and were more mentally alert. But doctors noticed something else. The group taking phosphatidylserine, not only enjoyed sharper memory, but were also more upbeat and remarkably happy.

YOUR MEMORY UNLEASHED!

Lipogen is an impressive fusion of the most powerful, natural memory compounds on Earth. It produces amazing results, especially for people who have tried everything to improve their memory before, but failed. Lipogen gives your brain the vital boost it needs to jump-start your focus and mental clarity. "It truly is a godsend!" says Shinitzky.

"SEE FOR YOURSELF" RISK-FREE SUPPLY

We've made special arrangements with the distributor of Lipogen PS Plus to offer you a "Readers Only Discount". This trial is 100% Risk-Free. It's a terrific deal. If Lipogen PS Plus doesn't help you think better, remember more, and improve your mind, clarity and mood – you won't pay a penny! (less S&H).

So don't wait. Now you can join the thousands of people who think better, remember more, and enjoy clear, "fog-free" memory. Think of it as making a "wake-up call" to your brain.

Call Now, Toll-Free!
1-800-609-3558

CALENDAR

2015

January
S	M	T	W	T	F	S
				1	2	3
4	5	6	7	8	9	10
11	12	13	14	15	16	17
18	19	20	21	22	23	24
25	26	27	28	29	30	31

February
S	M	T	W	T	F	S
1	2	3	4	5	6	7
8	9	10	11	12	13	14
15	16	17	18	19	20	21
22	23	24	25	26	27	28

March
S	M	T	W	T	F	S
1	2	3	4	5	6	7
8	9	10	11	12	13	14
15	16	17	18	19	20	21
22	23	24	25	26	27	28
29	30	31				

April
S	M	T	W	T	F	S
			1	2	3	4
5	6	7	8	9	10	11
12	13	14	15	16	17	18
19	20	21	22	23	24	25
26	27	28	29	30		

May
S	M	T	W	T	F	S
					1	2
3	4	5	6	7	8	9
10	11	12	13	14	15	16
17	18	19	20	21	22	23
24	25	26	27	28	29	30
31						

June
S	M	T	W	T	F	S
	1	2	3	4	5	6
7	8	9	10	11	12	13
14	15	16	17	18	19	20
21	22	23	24	25	26	27
28	29	30				

July
S	M	T	W	T	F	S
			1	2	3	4
5	6	7	8	9	10	11
12	13	14	15	16	17	18
19	20	21	22	23	24	25
26	27	28	29	30	31	

August
S	M	T	W	T	F	S
						1
2	3	4	5	6	7	8
9	10	11	12	13	14	15
16	17	18	19	20	21	22
23	24	25	26	27	28	29
30	31					

September
S	M	T	W	T	F	S
		1	2	3	4	5
6	7	8	9	10	11	12
13	14	15	16	17	18	19
20	21	22	23	24	25	26
27	28	29	30			

October
S	M	T	W	T	F	S
				1	2	3
4	5	6	7	8	9	10
11	12	13	14	15	16	17
18	19	20	21	22	23	24
25	26	27	28	29	30	31

November
S	M	T	W	T	F	S
1	2	3	4	5	6	7
8	9	10	11	12	13	14
15	16	17	18	19	20	21
22	23	24	25	26	27	28
29	30					

December
S	M	T	W	T	F	S
		1	2	3	4	5
6	7	8	9	10	11	12
13	14	15	16	17	18	19
20	21	22	23	24	25	26
27	28	29	30	31		

2016

January
S	M	T	W	T	F	S
					1	2
3	4	5	6	7	8	9
10	11	12	13	14	15	16
17	18	19	20	21	22	23
24	25	26	27	28	29	30
31						

February
S	M	T	W	T	F	S
	1	2	3	4	5	6
7	8	9	10	11	12	13
14	15	16	17	18	19	20
21	22	23	24	25	26	27
28	29					

March
S	M	T	W	T	F	S
		1	2	3	4	5
6	7	8	9	10	11	12
13	14	15	16	17	18	19
20	21	22	23	24	25	26
27	28	29	30	31		

April
S	M	T	W	T	F	S
					1	2
3	4	5	6	7	8	9
10	11	12	13	14	15	16
17	18	19	20	21	22	23
24	25	26	27	28	29	30

May
S	M	T	W	T	F	S
1	2	3	4	5	6	7
8	9	10	11	12	13	14
15	16	17	18	19	20	21
22	23	24	25	26	27	28
29	30	31				

June
S	M	T	W	T	F	S
			1	2	3	4
5	6	7	8	9	10	11
12	13	14	15	16	17	18
19	20	21	22	23	24	25
26	27	28	29	30		

July
S	M	T	W	T	F	S
					1	2
3	4	5	6	7	8	9
10	11	12	13	14	15	16
17	18	19	20	21	22	23
24	25	26	27	28	29	30
31						

August
S	M	T	W	T	F	S
	1	2	3	4	5	6
7	8	9	10	11	12	13
14	15	16	17	18	19	20
21	22	23	24	25	26	27
28	29	30	31			

September
S	M	T	W	T	F	S
				1	2	3
4	5	6	7	8	9	10
11	12	13	14	15	16	17
18	19	20	21	22	23	24
25	26	27	28	29	30	

October
S	M	T	W	T	F	S
						1
2	3	4	5	6	7	8
9	10	11	12	13	14	15
16	17	18	19	20	21	22
23	24	25	26	27	28	29
30	31					

November
S	M	T	W	T	F	S
		1	2	3	4	5
6	7	8	9	10	11	12
13	14	15	16	17	18	19
20	21	22	23	24	25	26
27	28	29	30			

December
S	M	T	W	T	F	S
				1	2	3
4	5	6	7	8	9	10
11	12	13	14	15	16	17
18	19	20	21	22	23	24
25	26	27	28	29	30	31

2017

January
S	M	T	W	T	F	S
1	2	3	4	5	6	7
8	9	10	11	12	13	14
15	16	17	18	19	20	21
22	23	24	25	26	27	28
29	30	31				

February
S	M	T	W	T	F	S
			1	2	3	4
5	6	7	8	9	10	11
12	13	14	15	16	17	18
19	20	21	22	23	24	25
26	27	28				

March
S	M	T	W	T	F	S
			1	2	3	4
5	6	7	8	9	10	11
12	13	14	15	16	17	18
19	20	21	22	23	24	25
26	27	28	29	30	31	

April
S	M	T	W	T	F	S
						1
2	3	4	5	6	7	8
9	10	11	12	13	14	15
16	17	18	19	20	21	22
23	24	25	26	27	28	29
30						

May
S	M	T	W	T	F	S
	1	2	3	4	5	6
7	8	9	10	11	12	13
14	15	16	17	18	19	20
21	22	23	24	25	26	27
28	29	30	31			

June
S	M	T	W	T	F	S
				1	2	3
4	5	6	7	8	9	10
11	12	13	14	15	16	17
18	19	20	21	22	23	24
25	26	27	28	29	30	

July
S	M	T	W	T	F	S
						1
2	3	4	5	6	7	8
9	10	11	12	13	14	15
16	17	18	19	20	21	22
23	24	25	26	27	28	29
30	31					

August
S	M	T	W	T	F	S
		1	2	3	4	5
6	7	8	9	10	11	12
13	14	15	16	17	18	19
20	21	22	23	24	25	26
27	28	29	30	31		

September
S	M	T	W	T	F	S
					1	2
3	4	5	6	7	8	9
10	11	12	13	14	15	16
17	18	19	20	21	22	23
24	25	26	27	28	29	30

October
S	M	T	W	T	F	S
1	2	3	4	5	6	7
8	9	10	11	12	13	14
15	16	17	18	19	20	21
22	23	24	25	26	27	28
29	30	31				

November
S	M	T	W	T	F	S
			1	2	3	4
5	6	7	8	9	10	11
12	13	14	15	16	17	18
19	20	21	22	23	24	25
26	27	28	29	30		

December
S	M	T	W	T	F	S
					1	2
3	4	5	6	7	8	9
10	11	12	13	14	15	16
17	18	19	20	21	22	23
24	25	26	27	28	29	30
31						

Love calendar lore? Find more at Almanac.com.

How to Use This Almanac

–Beth Krommes

The Calendar Pages (124–151) are the heart of *The Old Farmer's Almanac*. They present sky sightings and astronomical data for the entire year and are what make this book a true almanac, a "calendar of the heavens." In essence, these pages are unchanged since 1792, when Robert B. Thomas published his first edition. The long columns of numbers and symbols reveal all of nature's precision, rhythm, and glory, providing an astronomical look at the year 2016.

Why We Have Seasons

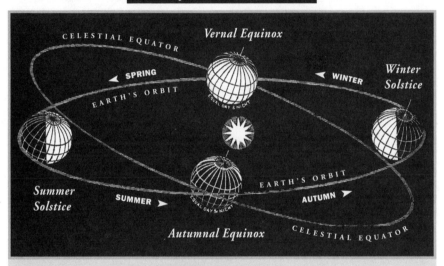

THE SEASONS OF 2016

Vernal equinox... March 20, 12:30 A.M. EDT	Autumnal equinox..Sept. 22, 10:21 A.M. EDT
Summer solstice..... June 20, 6:34 P.M. EDT	Winter solstice....... Dec. 21, 5:44 A.M. EST

■ The seasons occur because as Earth revolves around the Sun, its axis remains tilted at 23.5 degrees from the perpendicular. This tilt causes different latitudes on Earth to receive varying amounts of sunlight throughout the year.

In the Northern Hemisphere, the summer solstice marks the beginning of summer and occurs when the North Pole is tilted toward the Sun. The winter solstice marks the beginning of winter and occurs when the North Pole is tilted away from the Sun.

The equinoxes occur when the hemispheres equally face the Sun. At this time, the Sun rises due east and sets due west. The vernal equinox marks the beginning of spring; the autumnal equinox marks the beginning of autumn.

In the Southern Hemisphere, the seasons are the reverse of those in the Northern Hemisphere. **(continued)**

The Left-Hand Calendar Pages • 124–150

C A L E N D A R

The **Left-Hand Calendar Pages** contain sky highlights, daily Sun and Moon rise and set times, the length of day, high tide times, the Moon's astronomical place and age, and more for Boston. Examples of how to calculate astronomical times for your location are shown below.

A   S A M P L E   M O N T H

SKY WATCH ☆ *The box at the top of each Left-Hand Calendar Page describes the best times to view celestial highlights, including conjunctions, meteor showers, and planets. The dates on which select astronomical events occur appear on the Right-Hand Calendar Pages.*

1 2 3 4 5 6 7 8

Get these pages with times set to your zip code at Almanac.com/Access.

Day of Year	Day of Month	Day of Week	☼ Rises h. m.	Rise Key	☼ Sets h. m.	Set Key	Length of Day h. m.	Sun Fast m.	Declination of Sun ° '	High Tide Times Boston	☾ Rises h. m.	Rise Key	☾ Sets h. m.	Set Key	☾ Astron. Place	☾ Age
1	1	Fr.	7:13	E	4:22	A	9 09	12	23 s.00	4 4¼	11:52	D	11:15	D	VIR	21
2	2	Sa.	7:13	E	4:23	A	9 10	12	22 55	4¾ 5	—	–	11:43	C	VIR	22
3	3	C	7:13	E	4:24	A	9 11	11	22 49	5¾ 6	12:49	E	12:12	C	VIR	23

1 To calculate the sunrise time for your locale: Note the Sun Rise Key Letter on the chosen day. In the **Time Corrections** table on **page 250**, find your city or the city nearest you. Add or subtract the minutes that correspond to the Sun Rise Key Letter to/from the sunrise time given for Boston.

E X A M P L E :

■ To calculate the time of sunrise in Denver, Colorado, on the first day of the month:

Sunrise, Boston, with Key Letter E (above)	7:13 A.M. EST
Value of Key Letter E for Denver (p. 250)	+ 7 minutes
Sunrise, Denver	7:20 A.M. MST

Use the same procedure with Boston's sunset time and the Sun Set Key Letter value to calculate the time of sunset in your locale.

2 To calculate the length of day for your locale: Note the Sun Rise and Sun Set Key Letters on the chosen day. In the **Time Corrections** table on **page 250**, find your city. Add or subtract the minutes that correspond to the Sun Set Key Letter to/from Boston's length of day. *Reverse* the sign (minus to plus, or plus to

minus) of the Sun Rise Key Letter minutes. Add or subtract it to/from the first result.

E X A M P L E :

■ To calculate the length of day in Richmond, Virginia, on the first day of the month:

Length of day, Boston (above)	9h. 09m.
Sunset Key Letter A for Richmond (p. 254)	+ 41m.
	9h. 50m.
Reverse sunrise Key Letter E for Richmond (p. 254, +11 to −11)	− 11m.
Length of day, Richmond	9h. 39m.

3 Use the Sun Fast column to change sundial time to clock time. A sundial reads natural, or Sun, time, which is neither Standard nor Daylight time. To calculate clock time on a sundial in Boston, subtract the minutes given in this column; add the minutes when preceded by an asterisk [*]. To convert the time to your city, use Key Letter C in the table on **page 250**.

ATTENTION, READERS: *All times given in this edition of the Almanac are for Boston, Massachusetts, and are in Eastern Standard Time (EST), except from 2:00 A.M., March 13, until 2:00 A.M., November 6, when Eastern Daylight Time (EDT) is given.*

E X A M P L E :

■ To change sundial time to clock time in Boston, or, for example, in Salem, Oregon:

Sundial reading	
(Boston or Salem)	12:00 noon
Subtract Sun Fast (p. 120)	− 12 minutes
Clock time, Boston	11:48 A.M. EST
Use Key Letter C for Salem	
(p. 253)	+ 27 minutes
Clock time, Salem	12:15 P.M. PST

4 This column gives the degrees and minutes of the Sun from the celestial equator at noon EST or EDT.

5 This column gives the approximate times of high tides in Boston. For example, the first high tide occurs at 4:00 A.M. and the second occurs at 4:15 P.M. the same day. (A dash indicates that high tide occurs on or after midnight and is recorded on the next day.) Figures for calculating high tide times and heights for localities other than Boston are given in the **Tide Corrections** table on **page 248**.

6 To calculate the moonrise time for your locale: Note the Moon Rise Key Letter on the chosen day. Find your city on **page 250**. Add or subtract the minutes that correspond to the Moon Rise Key Letter to/from the moonrise time given for Boston. (A dash indicates that the moonrise occurs on or after midnight and is recorded on the next day.) Find the longitude of your city on **page 250**. Add a correction in minutes for your city's longitude (see table, above right).

–Beth Krommes

➡ Get the Left-Hand Calendar Pages with times set to your zip code at **Almanac.com/Access**.

Longitude of city	Correction minutes
58°–76°	0
77°–89°	+1
90°–102°	+2
103°–115°	+3
116°–127°	+4
128°–141°	+5
142°–155°	+6

Use the same procedure with Boston's moonset time and the Moon Set Key Letter value to calculate the time of moonset in your locale.

E X A M P L E :

■ To calculate the time of moonset in Lansing, Michigan, on the first day of the month:

Moonset, Boston,	
with Key Letter D (p. 120)	11:15 A.M. EST
Value of Key Letter D	
for Lansing (p. 252)	+ 54 minutes
Correction for Lansing	
longitude, 84° 33'	+ 1 minute
Moonset, Lansing	12:10 P.M. EST

7 The Moon's Place is its *astronomical* position among the constellations (not the zodiac) at midnight. For *astrological* data, see **pages 242–244**.

Constellations have irregular borders; on successive nights, the midnight Moon may enter one, cross into another, then move to a new area of the previous. It visits the 12 zodiacal constellations, as well as Auriga **(AUR)**, a northern constellation between Perseus and Gemini; Cetus **(CET)**, which lies south of the zodiac, just south of Pisces and Aries; Ophiuchus **(OPH)**, a constellation primarily north of the zodiac but with a small corner between Scorpius and Sagittarius; Orion **(ORI)**, a constellation whose northern limit first reaches the zodiac between Taurus and Gemini; and Sextans **(SEX)**, which lies south of the zodiac except for a corner that just touches it near Leo.

8 The last column gives the Moon's Age, which is the number of days since the previous new Moon. (The average length of the lunar month is 29.53 days.) **(continued)**

The Right-Hand Calendar Pages • 125–151

A SAMPLE MONTH

- Weather prediction rhyme.
- Religious feasts generally appear in this font. A ᵀ indicates a major feast that the church has this year temporarily transferred to a date other than its usual one.
- Symbols for notable celestial events. (See opposite page for explanations.)
- The bold letter is the Dominical Letter (from A to G), a traditional ecclesiastical designation for Sunday determined by the date on which the first Sunday falls. For 2016, a leap year, the Dominical Letter is **C** through February. It then reverts to **B** for the rest of the year.
- Proverbs, poems, and adages generally appear in this font.
- Sundays and special holy days generally appear in this font.
- Noteworthy historical events, folklore, and legends appear in this font.
- Civil holidays and astronomical events appear in this font.
- High tide heights, in feet, at Boston, Massachusetts.

Day of Month	Day of Week	Dates, Feasts, Fasts, Aspects, Tide Heights	Weather
1	B	Rogation S. • Orthodox Easter • May Day • { 9.8 / 9.6	Blessed
2	M.	St. Athanasius • ℂ AT ☍ • ♂♇ℂ • Tides { 10.0 / 10.1	blossoms
3	Tu.	Sts. Philip & Jamesᵀ • ℂ ON EQ. • 39°F, Phoenix, Ariz., 1899 • { 10.4 / 10.8	banish
4	W.	♂♂ℂ • First Freedom Ride began, 1961 • { 10.8 / 11.4	sadness;
5	Th.	Ascension • Cinco de Mayo • ♂♀ℂ • Tides { 11.1 / 12.0	all
6	Fr.	New ● • ℂ AT PERIG. • ♂♀ℂ • Baseball player Willie Mays born, 1931	is
7	Sa.	14-pound pearl reportedly collected at Palawan Island, Philippines, 1934 • Tides { 11.4 / —	gladness!
8	B	1st S. af. Asc. • Mother's Day • Pianist Rudolf Serkin died, 1991	Birds
9	M.	St. Gregory of Nazianzus • ℂ RIDES HIGH • ♀ TRANSIT OVER ☉ • ♀ IN INF. • ♂ • ♃ STAT.	return
10	Tu.	Union Pacific and Central Pacific railroads linked with golden spike, Promontory Point, Utah, 1869 • { 11.9 / 10.5	with
11	W.	St. Mamertus, St. Pancras, and St. Gervais do not pass without a frost. • Three • { 11.3 / 10.1	joyous
12	Th.	Flag of Manitoba officially adopted, 1966 • Chilly • { 10.7 / 9.7	chorus
13	Fr.	♂♀ℂ • Cranberries in bud now. • Saints • Tides { 10.1 / 9.4	for
14	Sa.	34 cavalry camels disembarked at Indianola, Tex., 1856 • { 9.6 / 9.3	us.
15	B	Whit. S. • Pentecost • ℂ AT ☍ • ♂♃ℂ	Showers
16	M.	ℂ ON EQ. • U.S. Congress gave authorization to mint the nickel, 1866 • Tides { 9.2 / 9.4	fill
17	Tu.	Joliet-Marquette Mississippi River expedition began, 1673	each
18	W.	Ember Day • ℂ AT APO. • Mount St. Helens, Wash., 1980 • Deadly eruption, { 9.2 / 9.8	rill
19	Th.	St. Dunstan • For what thou canst do thyself, rely not on another. • Tides { 9.2 / 10.0	with
20	Fr.	Ember Day • The Saturday Evening Post published its first cover with Norman Rockwell painting, 1916	liquid
21	Sa.	Ember Day • Vesak • Full Flower ○ • ♂♂ℂ • ♀ STAT. • { 9.4 / —	trill,
22	B	Trinity • ♂♄ℂ • ♂ AT ☍ • Wrights' "Flying Machine" patented, 1906	echoed
23	M.	Victoria Day (Canada) • North-West Mounted Police authorized (now Royal Canadian Mounted Police), 1873	back
24	Tu.	ℂ RUNS LOW • 6- to 8-inch-deep hail, near Ada, Okla., 1940 • Tides { 10.3 / —	from
25	W.	St. Bede • ♂♇ℂ • Andrew Moyer patented method for mass production of penicillin, 1948 • { 10.3 / 9.3	hill
26	Th.	Radio and television personality Art Linkletter died, 2010 • { 10.2 / 9.3	to

☞ **For explanations of Almanac terms, see the glossaries on pages 110, 153, and 154.**

Predicting Earthquakes

Note the dates in the **Right-Hand Calendar Pages** when the Moon rides high or runs low. The date of the high begins the most likely 5-day period of earthquakes in the Northern Hemisphere; the date of the low indicates a similar 5-day period in the Southern Hemisphere. Also noted are the 2 days each month when the Moon is on the celestial equator, indicating the most likely time for earthquakes in either hemisphere.

–Beth Krommes

Find more heavenly details at Almanac.com.

■ Throughout the **Right-Hand Calendar Pages** are groups of symbols that represent notable celestial events. The symbols and names of the principal planets and aspects are:

☉	**Sun**	♆	**Neptune**
○●☾	**Moon**	♇	**Pluto**
☿	**Mercury**	☌	**Conjunction (on the**
♀	**Venus**		**same celestial**
⊕	**Earth**		**longitude)**
♂	**Mars**	☊	**Ascending node**
♃	**Jupiter**	☋	**Descending node**
♄	**Saturn**	☍	**Opposition (180**
♅	**Uranus**		**degrees from Sun)**

E X A M P L E :

♂♀☾ on the 5th day of the month (see opposite page) means that on that date a conjunction (☌) of Venus (♀) and the Moon (☾) occurs: They are aligned along the same celestial longitude and appear to be closest together in the sky.

EARTH AT PERIHELION AND APHELION

■ Perihelion: January 2, 2016. Earth will be 91,403,891 miles from the Sun. Aphelion: July 4, 2016. Earth will be 94,512,986 miles from the Sun.

2016 Calendar Highlights

MOVABLE RELIGIOUS OBSERVANCES

Septuagesima Sunday.	**January 24**
Shrove Tuesday.	**February 9**
Ash Wednesday.	**February 10**
Palm Sunday	**March 20**
Good Friday.	**March 25**
Easter	**March 27**
Passover begins at sundown.	**April 22**
Orthodox Easter.	**May 1**
Rogation Sunday.	**May 1**
Ascension Day.	**May 5**
Whitsunday–Pentecost.	**May 15**
Trinity Sunday.	**May 22**
Corpus Christi	**May 29**
Ramadan begins at sundown	**June 5**
Rosh Hashanah begins at sundown. .	**October 2**
Yom Kippur begins at sundown . .	**October 11**
First Sunday of Advent	**November 27**
Chanukah begins at sundown . .	**December 24**

CHRONOLOGICAL CYCLES

Dominical Letter.	**C/B**
Epact.	**21**
Golden Number (Lunar Cycle).	**3**
Roman Indiction	**9**
Solar Cycle	**9**
Year of Julian Period	**6729**

–Beth Krommes

ERAS

Era	Year	Begins
Byzantine	**7525**	September 14
Jewish (A.M.)*	**5777**	October 2
Chinese (Lunar) [Year of the Monkey]	**4714**	February 8
Roman (A.U.C.)	**2769**	January 14
Nabonassar	**2765**	April 20
Japanese	**2676**	January 1
Grecian (Seleucidae)	**2328**	September 14 (or October 14)
Indian (Saka)	**1938**	March 22
Diocletian	**1733**	September 11
Islamic (Hegira)*	**1438**	October 1

Year begins at sundown.

C A L E N D A R

SKY WATCH ☆ *Venus stands very near Mars from the 1st to the 3rd, just before dawn in the east, with Jupiter closely above them. The crescent Moon passes to the right of Jupiter on the 6th and to the right of Venus on the 7th, with nearby Mars just above them both. This planet group forms a nice little triangle, although the Martian "point," at magnitude 1.7, is so dim that it might easily be overlooked; Venus is 200 times brighter! Look at the crescent Moon to see earthshine—a faint glow on its dark portion caused by reflection of sunlight from Earth. Saturn passes behind the Sun in a conjunction on the 29th, ending its evening star role.*

◑	**Last Quarter**	3rd day	7th hour	24th minute
●	**New Moon**	11th day	12th hour	47th minute
◐	**First Quarter**	19th day	1st hour	27th minute
○	**Full Moon**	25th day	17th hour	44th minute

After 2:00 A.M. on November 1, Eastern Standard Time is given.

Get these pages with times set to your zip code at Almanac.com/Access.

Day of Year	Day of Month	Day of Week	☼ Rises h. m.	Rise Key	☼ Sets h. m.	Set Key	Length of Day h. m.	Sun Fast m.	Declination of Sun ° ′	High Tide Times Boston		☾ Rises h. m.	Rise Key	☾ Sets h. m.	Set Key	☾ Astron. Place	☾ Age
305	1	D	6:17	D	4:37	B	10 20	32	14 s. 28	2½	2¾	9:32	B	11:20	E	GEM	20
306	2	M.	6:18	D	4:36	B	10 18	32	14 47	3½	3½	10:31	C	12:03	E	GEM	21
307	3	Tu.	6:19	D	4:35	B	10 16	32	15 06	4¼	4½	11:29	C	12:41	E	CAN	22
308	4	W.	6:20	D	4:34	B	10 14	32	15 25	5¼	5½	—	–	1:15	E	LEO	23
309	5	Th.	6:22	E	4:32	B	10 10	32	15 43	6¼	6½	12:27	C	1:45	D	LEO	24
310	6	Fr.	6:23	E	4:31	B	10 08	32	16 01	7¼	7½	1:24	D	2:14	D	LEO	25
311	7	Sa.	6:24	E	4:30	B	10 06	32	16 19	8	8¼	2:20	D	2:42	C	VIR	26
312	8	D	6:25	E	4:29	B	10 04	32	16 36	8¾	9¼	3:17	D	3:10	C	VIR	27
313	9	M.	6:27	E	4:28	B	10 01	32	16 54	9½	9¾	4:14	E	3:40	C	VIR	28
314	10	Tu.	6:28	E	4:27	B	9 59	32	17 10	10	10½	5:11	E	4:11	C	VIR	29
315	11	W.	6:29	E	4:26	B	9 57	32	17 27	10¾	11¼	6:09	E	4:46	B	LIB	0
316	12	Th.	6:30	E	4:25	B	9 55	32	17 43	11¼	11¾	7:06	E	5:24	B	LIB	1
317	13	Fr.	6:32	E	4:24	B	9 52	32	18 00	12	—	8:03	E	6:08	B	OPH	2
318	14	Sa.	6:33	E	4:23	B	9 50	31	18 15	12½	12½	8:58	E	6:57	B	OPH	3
319	15	D	6:34	E	4:22	B	9 48	31	18 31	1¼	1¼	9:49	E	7:51	B	SAG	4
320	16	M.	6:35	E	4:21	B	9 46	31	18 46	2	2	10:37	E	8:50	C	SAG	5
321	17	Tu.	6:37	E	4:20	B	9 43	31	19 01	2¾	2¾	11:20	E	9:53	C	SAG	6
322	18	W.	6:38	E	4:19	B	9 41	31	19 15	3½	3¾	12:01	E	10:59	C	AQU	7
323	19	Th.	6:39	E	4:19	B	9 40	30	19 29	4½	4¾	12:38	D	—	–	CAP	8
324	20	Fr.	6:40	E	4:18	B	9 38	30	19 43	5½	5¾	1:14	D	12:07	D	AQU	9
325	21	Sa.	6:41	E	4:17	B	9 36	30	19 56	6¼	6¾	1:49	D	1:16	D	PSC	10
326	22	D	6:43	E	4:17	B	9 34	30	20 09	7¼	7¾	2:25	C	2:28	E	CET	11
327	23	M.	6:44	E	4:16	B	9 32	29	20 22	8¼	8¾	3:03	C	3:40	E	PSC	12
328	24	Tu.	6:45	E	4:15	A	9 30	29	20 34	9¼	9¾	3:45	C	4:52	E	ARI	13
329	25	W.	6:46	E	4:15	A	9 29	29	20 46	10	10¾	4:31	B	6:04	E	TAU	14
330	26	Th.	6:47	E	4:14	A	9 27	29	20 57	10¾	11½	5:22	B	7:11	E	TAU	15
331	27	Fr.	6:48	E	4:14	A	9 26	28	21 08	11¾	—	6:17	B	8:13	E	TAU	16
332	28	Sa.	6:50	E	4:13	A	9 23	28	21 19	12¼	12½	7:16	B	9:09	E	GEM	17
333	29	D	6:51	E	4:13	A	9 22	27	21 29	1¼	1¼	8:16	C	9:57	E	GEM	18
334	30	M.	6:52	E	4:13	A	9 21	27	21 s. 39	2	2¼	9:16	C	10:38	C	CAN	19

NOVEMBER HATH 30 DAYS • 2015

The winds are out with loud increasing shout,
Where late before them walked the biting frost. –Jones Very

Day of Month	Day of Week	Dates, Feasts, Fasts, Aspects, Tide Heights	Weather
1	D	All Saints' • Daylight Saving Time ends, 2:00 A.M. • Tides {10.1 / 10.8}	*Clear,*
2	M.	All Souls' • *Thunder in November, a fertile year to come.* • Tides {9.6 / 10.2}	*brittle:*
3	Tu.	Election Day • ☌♀♂ • Actress Mary Martin died, 1990 • {9.2 / 9.6}	*Rains*
4	W.	Computational wizard Shakuntala Devi born, 1929 • {9.0 / 9.3}	*a*
5	Th.	Cartoonist Al Capp died, 1979 • 2" snow, Salisbury, Mo., 1995 • Tides {9.0 / 9.1}	*little,*
6	Fr.	☌♃☾ • Talking headlight installed on locomotive, Schenectady, N.Y., 1934 • {9.1 / 9.1}	*but*
7	Sa.	☾ ON EQ. • ☾ AT ☊ • ☾ AT APO. • ☌♀☾ • ☌♂☾	*warmish.*
8	D	24th S. af. P. • Black bears head to winter dens now. • {9.6 / 9.3}	*Stormish!*
9	M.	Peak of multiday storm that caused 12 major shipwrecks on Great Lakes, U.S./Ont., 1913 • {9.9 / 9.4}	*Snow*
10	Tu.	*Luna 17* spacecraft launched, 1970 • Tides {10.1 / 9.4}	*north,*
11	W.	St. Martin of Tours • Veterans Day • New ● • ☌☿☾ • {10.2 / 9.5}	*rain*
12	Th.	Indian Summer • ☌♄☾ • Social reformer Elizabeth Cady Stanton born, 1815 • {10.4 / 9.4}	*south.*
13	Fr.	Lobsters move to offshore waters now. • Tides {10.4 / —}	*Wetter*
14	Sa.	☾ RUNS LOW • Artist Claude Monet born, 1840 • Tides {9.4 / 10.4}	*and*
15	D	25th S. af. P. • ☌♇☾ • Tennis pro Helen Mersi Kelesi born, 1969	*milder,*
16	M.	Walt Disney announced plans to build Epcot Center, 1965 • Tides {9.3 / 10.2}	*now*
17	Tu.	St. Hugh of Lincoln • ☿ IN SUP. ☌ • Crab apples are ripe now. • {9.2 / 10.1}	*colder*
18	W.	♆ STAT. • Twain's *The Celebrated Jumping Frog of Calaveras County* published, 1865 • {9.3 / 10.0}	*and*
19	Th.	☌♆☾ • Frederick Blaisdell granted patent for paper-wrapped pencil, 1895 • {9.5 / 10.0}	*wilder.*
20	Fr.	*Be slow of giving advice, ready to do a service.* • {9.8 / 10.0}	*Murky—*
21	Sa.	☾ ON EQ. • ☾ AT ☋ • William C. Bullitt became first U.S. ambassador to U.S.S.R., 1933	*turkeys*
22	D	26th S. af. P. • ☌♅☾ • Ferris wheel inventor George W. G. Ferris Jr., died, 1896	*won't*
23	M.	St. Clement • ☾ AT PERIG. • –38°F, Chinook, Mont., 1985 • {11.3 / 10.5}	*be*
24	Tu.	Justus Falckner first Lutheran pastor ordained in America (Philadelphia), 1703 • Tides {11.7 / 10.7}	*hard*
25	W.	Full Beaver ○ • ☌☿♄ • Albert Einstein submitted paper on theory of relativity, 1915	*to*
26	Th.	Thanksgiving Day • *You may believe any thing that is good of a grateful man.* • {12.1 / 10.7}	*track*
27	Fr.	☾ RIDES HIGH • Basketball player Wilt Chamberlain scored 18 baskets in a row, 1963 • Tides {12.0 / —}	*over*
28	Sa.	Ferdinand Magellan first entered Pacific Ocean from Atlantic, through what is now Strait of Magellan, 1520	*the*
29	D	1st S. of Advent • ☌♄☉ • Tides {10.2 / 11.1}	*snow-*
30	M.	St. Andrew • Comedienne Lucille Ball married Desi Arnaz, 1940 • Tides {9.9 / 10.6}	*pack!*

At table, it becomes no one to be bashful. –Plautus

Farmer's Calendar

■ Until she died at the age of 100, my mother-in-law, Betty, was a Thanksgiving magnet. She drew dozens of interesting guests, such as two former Lost Boys of the Sudan, to her table. I should say "tables"—every flat surface in the house had to be set up to entertain the crowd.

Everyone shared the cooking and cleaning while Betty sat in the front parlor, interrogating the guests. She wasn't much interested in talking about herself. The kids made place cards for everyone, or learned to play mah-jongg, or just raced around the 1813 colonial that had a spinning wheel and a cavalry saber in the attic. A favorite tradition was to teach the younger children how to hang spoons off their noses.

Another was to give prospective sons-in-law an antique chair that was guaranteed to collapse under them and then observe their reactions. I got one of these chairs in 1970, my first Thanksgiving there. My son-in-law got one almost three decades later. It was probably the same chair.

When Betty passed away, so did the farmhouse Thanksgivings. It was a natural transition from the crowds and card tables and chaos to less complicated gatherings. The food is just as good, the company equally diverse and stimulating. But I miss Betty, and the spoons, and the collapsing chairs.

SKY WATCH ☆ *It's still a postmidnight party for all of the bright planets. Dawn now finds Jupiter at its highest, in the southeast, with Venus lowest, floating left of Virgo's blue main star Spica. Still faint but brightening Mars hovers in between. The Moon passes just below Jupiter on the 4th and eye-catchingly close to Venus during the wee hours of the 7th, for a major don't-miss conjunction. This year brings a rare second fabulous meteor shower under ideal moonless skies, when the Geminids blaze on the 13th starting at around 8:00* P.M. *These "shooting stars" are strangely slow, at half the speed of summer's Perseids. Winter begins with the solstice on the 21st, at 11:48* P.M.

◑	**Last Quarter**	3rd day	2nd hour	40th minute
●	**New Moon**	11th day	5th hour	29th minute
◐	**First Quarter**	18th day	10th hour	14th minute
○	**Full Moon**	25th day	6th hour	11th minute

All times are given in Eastern Standard Time.

Get these pages with times set to your zip code at Almanac.com/Access.

Day of Year	Day of Month	Day of Week	☼ Rises h. m.	Rise Key	☼ Sets h. m.	Set Key	Length of Day h.	m.	Sun Fast m.	Declination of Sun °	'	High Tide Times Boston		☾ Rises h. m.	Rise Key	☾ Sets h. m.	Set Key	☾ Astron. Place	☾ Age
335	1	Tu.	6:53	E	**4:12**	A	9	19	27	21 s.	49	3	**3**	**10:15**	C	11:15	E	CAN	20
336	2	W.	6:54	E	**4:12**	A	9	18	26	21	58	$3\frac{3}{4}$	**4**	**11:13**	C	11:47	D	LEO	21
337	3	Th.	6:55	E	**4:12**	A	9	17	26	22	06	$4\frac{3}{4}$	**5**	—	–	**12:17**	D	LEO	22
338	4	Fr.	6:56	E	**4:11**	A	9	15	26	22	15	$5\frac{1}{2}$	**$5\frac{3}{4}$**	12:11	D	**12:45**	D	LEO	23
339	5	Sa.	6:57	E	**4:11**	A	9	14	25	22	22	$6\frac{1}{2}$	**$6\frac{3}{4}$**	1:07	D	**1:13**	C	VIR	24
340	6	**D**	6:58	E	**4:11**	A	9	13	25	22	30	$7\frac{1}{4}$	**$7\frac{3}{4}$**	2:04	D	**1:42**	C	VIR	25
341	7	M.	6:59	E	**4:11**	A	9	12	24	22	37	8	**$8\frac{1}{2}$**	3:01	E	**2:12**	C	VIR	26
342	8	Tu.	7:00	E	**4:11**	A	9	11	24	22	43	$8\frac{3}{4}$	**$9\frac{1}{4}$**	3:59	E	**2:45**	C	LIB	27
343	9	W.	7:01	E	**4:11**	A	9	10	23	22	49	$9\frac{1}{2}$	**10**	4:57	E	**3:22**	B	LIB	28
344	10	Th.	7:02	E	**4:11**	A	9	09	23	22	55	$10\frac{1}{4}$	**$10\frac{3}{4}$**	5:55	E	**4:04**	B	SCO	29
345	11	Fr.	7:03	E	**4:11**	A	9	08	23	23	00	$10\frac{3}{4}$	**$11\frac{1}{2}$**	6:51	E	**4:51**	B	OPH	0
346	12	Sa.	7:03	E	**4:11**	A	9	08	22	23	04	$11\frac{1}{2}$	—	7:45	E	**5:44**	B	SAG	1
347	13	**D**	7:04	E	**4:11**	A	9	07	22	23	09	12	**$12\frac{1}{4}$**	8:35	E	**6:43**	C	SAG	2
348	14	M.	7:05	E	**4:12**	A	9	07	21	23	12	$12\frac{3}{4}$	**1**	9:21	E	**7:46**	C	SAG	3
349	15	Tu.	7:06	E	**4:12**	A	9	06	21	23	16	$1\frac{1}{2}$	**$1\frac{3}{4}$**	10:03	E	**8:51**	C	AQU	4
350	16	W.	7:06	E	**4:12**	A	9	06	20	23	18	$2\frac{1}{4}$	**$2\frac{1}{2}$**	10:41	D	**9:58**	C	CAP	5
351	17	Th.	7:07	E	**4:12**	A	9	05	20	23	21	$3\frac{1}{4}$	**$3\frac{1}{2}$**	11:17	D	**11:06**	D	AQU	6
352	18	Fr.	7:08	E	**4:13**	A	9	05	19	23	23	4	**$4\frac{1}{2}$**	11:51	D	—	–	AQU	7
353	19	Sa.	7:08	E	**4:13**	A	9	05	19	23	24	5	**$5\frac{1}{2}$**	**12:25**	C	12:15	D	PSC	8
354	20	**D**	7:09	E	**4:14**	A	9	05	18	23	25	6	**$6\frac{1}{2}$**	**1:01**	C	1:25	E	PSC	9
355	21	M.	7:09	E	**4:14**	A	9	05	18	23	26	7	**$7\frac{1}{2}$**	**1:39**	C	2:35	E	CET	10
356	22	Tu.	7:10	E	**4:15**	A	9	05	17	23	26	8	**$8\frac{1}{2}$**	**2:22**	C	3:44	E	ARI	11
357	23	W.	7:10	E	**4:15**	A	9	05	17	23	25	$8\frac{3}{4}$	**$9\frac{1}{2}$**	**3:09**	B	4:52	E	TAU	12
358	24	Th.	7:11	E	**4:16**	A	9	05	16	23	24	$9\frac{3}{4}$	**$10\frac{1}{2}$**	**4:01**	B	5:56	E	TAU	13
359	25	Fr.	7:11	E	**4:16**	A	9	05	16	23	23	$10\frac{1}{2}$	**$11\frac{1}{4}$**	**4:58**	B	6:55	E	ORI	14
360	26	Sa.	7:12	E	**4:17**	A	9	05	15	23	21	$11\frac{1}{2}$	—	**5:58**	C	7:47	E	GEM	15
361	27	**D**	7:12	E	**4:18**	A	9	06	15	23	18	12	**$12\frac{1}{4}$**	**6:59**	C	8:32	E	GEM	16
362	28	M.	7:12	E	**4:18**	A	9	06	14	23	16	$12\frac{3}{4}$	**1**	**8:00**	C	9:12	E	CAN	17
363	29	Tu.	7:12	E	**4:19**	A	9	07	14	23	12	$1\frac{1}{2}$	**$1\frac{3}{4}$**	**9:00**	C	9:46	D	LEO	18
364	30	W.	7:13	E	**4:20**	A	9	07	13	23	09	$2\frac{1}{4}$	**$2\frac{1}{2}$**	**9:58**	D	10:18	D	LEO	19
365	31	Th.	7:13	E	**4:21**	A	9	08	13	23 s.	04	3	**$3\frac{1}{4}$**	**10:56**	D	10:47	D	LEO	20

 To use this page, see p. 120; for Key Letters, see p. 250. ☞ **Bold = P.M.** ☞ Light = A.M.

DECEMBER HATH 31 DAYS • 2015

Now see stern Winter nearer draw,
Sol's feeble rays refuse to thaw. –William Cole

Day of Month	Day of Week	Dates, Feasts, Fasts, Aspects, Tide Heights	Weather
1	Tu.	Dupree Gardens opened, Land O' Lakes, Fla., 1940	*A million*
2	W.	**St. Viviana** • Statesman Jean-Charles Chapais born, 1811 • Tides { 9.2 / 9.4	*snowflakes*
3	Th.	*Daylight will peep through a small hole.* • Tides { 9.0 / 9.0	*fall to*
4	Fr.	☾ ON EQ. • ☾ AT ☊ • ☌♃☾ • First television appearance of mime Marcel Marceau, 1955	*earth,*
5	Sa.	☾ AT APO. • ☌♂☾ • Electric eels lit Christmas tree, Living Planet Aquarium, Sandy, Utah, 2012	*as*
6	**D**	**2nd S. of Advent** • **St. Nicholas** • **Chanukah begins at sundown**	*from*
7	M.	**St. Ambrose** • **Nat'l Pearl Harbor Remembrance Day** • ☌♀☾ • { 9.4 / 8.7	*a great*
8	Tu.	John McCrae's *In Flanders Fields* poem published, 1915 • Tides { 9.7 / 8.9	*saltshaker.*
9	W.	Winterberry fruit especially showy now. • Tides { 10.0 / 9.1	*A billion*
10	Th.	**St. Eulalia** • ☌♄☾ • Businessman Armand Hammer died, 1990 • Tides { 10.3 / 9.2	*more*
11	Fr.	**New ●** • Bijou Theatre opened, first in U.S. lit by electricity, Boston, 1882 • { 10.5 / 9.3	*arrive*
12	Sa.	**Our Lady of Guadalupe** • ☾ RUNS LOW • ☌☿☾ • Tides { 10.6 / —	*a day*
13	**D**	**3rd S. of Advent** • **St. Lucia** • ☌♇☾ • { 9.5 / 10.7	*or two*
14	M.	Halcyon Days begin. • Capt. Sue Dauser, Navy Nurse Corps, received Distinguished Service Medal, 1945	*later.*
15	Tu.	Sioux chief Sitting Bull died, 1890 • *Echo 1* commemorative stamp issued, D.C., 1960 • { 9.6 / 10.7	*A trillion*
16	W.	Ember Day • *December cold with snow, good for rye.* • { 9.7 / 10.5	*now*
17	Th.	☌♆☾ • France formally recognized American independence, 1777 • Tides { 9.8 / 10.2	*descend*
18	Fr.	Ember Day • ☾ ON EQ. • ☾ AT ☋ • Tides { 10.0 / 10.0	*en masse,*
19	Sa.	Ember Day • ☌☿♇ • ☌♅☾ • Tides { 10.2 / 9.8	*rising*
20	**D**	**4th S. of Advent** • Name "Canadian National Railways" authorized, 1918	*by the*
21	M.	**St. Thomas** • **Winter Solstice** • ☾ AT PERIG. • Tides { 10.7 / 9.7	*meter;*
22	Tu.	Composer Giacomo Puccini born, 1858 • Tides { 11.1 / 9.9	*let's*
23	W.	Home economist Marjorie Child Husted died, 1986 • 9.6" snow, Wilmington, N.C., 1989 • { 11.4 / 10.0	*hope,*
24	Th.	*A happy heart is better than a full purse.* • Tides { 11.5 / 10.1	*whatever*
25	Fr.	**Christmas** • **Full Cold ○** • ☾ RIDES HIGH • Tides { 11.6 / 10.2	*comes*
26	Sa.	**St. Stephen** • **Boxing Day (Canada)** • **First day of Kwanzaa** • ♅ STAT.	*to pass,*
27	**D**	**1st S. af. Ch.** • Beware the Pogonip. • { 10.1 / 11.2	*that*
28	M.	**Holy Innocents** • ☿ GR. ELONG. (20° EAST) • Westminster Abbey consecrated, London, 1065	*'16*
29	Tu.	**St. John[T]** • Morning "silvered by the icicles everywhere shining," New London, Conn., 1747	*will*
30	W.	Writer Rudyard Kipling born, 1865 • Tides { 9.5 / 9.8	*be*
31	Th.	**St. Sylvester** • ☾ AT ☊ • ☌♃☾ • Tides { 9.3 / 9.3	*sweeter!*

Farmer's Calendar

■ *Dec. 1:* Every year, we watch the pond with conflicting hopes. We like snow, but we love black ice, which happens only when the pond freezes before the first snow.

Black ice is perfectly smooth and perfectly transparent. Many years ago, we lived on a pond farther north, where one winter we had a full week of black ice. While we were skating, we could occasionally see beaver swimming beneath our blades.

One night, a powdery snow fell and we went out for a final skate. Even as the inches piled up, we glided along as if we were flying above the clouds. The next morning, the snow had frozen and the skating was done.

Dec. 5: It's been in the 20s every night for the past week, and we had some light snow overnight. There's a little bit of open water at the northwest end of the pond, where a brook tumbles in, but otherwise it's a white sheet, so there'll be no black ice this year.

Dec. 9: Spoke too soon. When we walked past the pond this morning, there was not a shard of ice on it, as if we had been transported back in time to September. Two days of rain and two more of mild temperatures and southern breezes had restored our little pond to a liquid state.

Temporarily.

THE FIRST MONTH • 2016

SKY WATCH ☆ *Mercury is easy to spot on the first few nights of 2016, embedded in twilight. Mars, in Virgo, rises at around 1:30 A.M. and dangles below the Moon on the 3rd. At dawn on the 7th, the waning crescent hovers to the left of Venus and Saturn. These two planets are closest together the following two mornings and best seen 40 minutes before sunrise. The crescent Moon stands just above Mercury on the 10th. In the evening of the 19th, the Moon dramatically occults (blocks) the bright orange star Aldebaran. Jupiter rises before midnight on the Leo/Virgo border and hovers above the Moon on the 27th.*

◑	**Last Quarter**	2nd day	0 hour	31st minute
●	**New Moon**	9th day	20th hour	31st minute
◐	**First Quarter**	16th day	18th hour	27th minute
○	**Full Moon**	23rd day	20th hour	46th minute
◑	**Last Quarter**	31st day	22nd hour	29th minute

All times are given in Eastern Standard Time.

Get these pages with times set to your zip code at Almanac.com/Access.

Day of Year	Day of Month	Day of Week	☼ Rises h. m.	Rise Key	☼ Sets h. m.	Set Key	Length of Day h. m.	Sun Fast m.	Declination of Sun ° ′	High Tide Times Boston		☾ Rises h. m.	Rise Key	☾ Sets h. m.	Set Key	☾ Astron. Place	☾ Age
1	1	Fr.	7:13	E	**4:22**	A	9 09	12	23 s.00	4	**4¼**	**11:52**	D	11:15	D	VIR	21
2	2	Sa.	7:13	E	**4:23**	A	9 10	12	22 55	4¾	**5**	—	–	11:43	C	VIR	22
3	3	**C**	7:13	E	**4:24**	A	9 11	11	22 49	5¾	**6**	12:49	E	**12:12**	C	VIR	23
4	4	M.	7:13	E	**4:25**	A	9 12	11	22 43	6½	**7**	1:46	E	**12:44**	C	VIR	24
5	5	Tu.	7:13	E	**4:26**	A	9 13	11	22 36	7¼	**8**	2:44	E	**1:19**	B	LIB	25
6	6	W.	7:13	E	**4:27**	A	9 14	10	22 29	8¼	**8¾**	3:42	E	**1:58**	B	LIB	26
7	7	Th.	7:13	E	**4:28**	A	9 15	10	22 22	9	**9½**	4:39	E	**2:43**	B	OPH	27
8	8	Fr.	7:13	E	**4:29**	A	9 16	9	22 14	9¾	**10¼**	5:35	E	**3:34**	B	OPH	28
9	9	Sa.	7:13	E	**4:30**	A	9 17	9	22 06	10½	**11**	6:28	E	**4:31**	B	SAG	0
10	10	**C**	7:13	E	**4:31**	A	9 18	8	21 57	11	**11¾**	7:17	E	**5:33**	C	SAG	1
11	11	M.	7:12	E	**4:32**	A	9 20	8	21 48	11¾	—	8:01	E	**6:39**	C	CAP	2
12	12	Tu.	7:12	E	**4:33**	A	9 21	8	21 39	12½	**12½**	8:42	E	**7:48**	C	AQU	3
13	13	W.	7:12	E	**4:34**	A	9 22	7	21 29	1¼	**1½**	9:19	D	**8:57**	D	AQU	4
14	14	Th.	7:11	E	**4:35**	A	9 24	7	21 18	2	**2¼**	9:55	D	**10:07**	D	AQU	5
15	15	Fr.	7:11	E	**4:36**	A	9 25	7	21 07	2¾	**3¼**	10:29	C	**11:16**	E	PSC	6
16	16	Sa.	7:10	E	**4:38**	A	9 28	6	20 56	3¾	**4**	11:04	C	—	–	PSC	7
17	17	**C**	7:10	E	**4:39**	A	9 29	6	20 45	4¾	**5¼**	11:41	C	12:25	E	PSC	8
18	18	M.	7:09	E	**4:40**	A	9 31	6	20 33	5¾	**6¼**	**12:21**	C	1:34	E	ARI	9
19	19	Tu.	7:09	E	**4:41**	B	9 32	5	20 20	6¾	**7¼**	**1:04**	B	2:40	E	TAU	10
20	20	W.	7:08	E	**4:42**	B	9 34	5	20 07	7¾	**8¼**	**1:53**	B	3:44	E	TAU	11
21	21	Th.	7:08	E	**4:44**	B	9 36	5	19 54	8¾	**9¼**	**2:46**	B	4:44	E	TAU	12
22	22	Fr.	7:07	E	**4:45**	B	9 38	4	19 41	9½	**10¼**	**3:44**	B	5:37	E	GEM	13
23	23	Sa.	7:06	E	**4:46**	B	9 40	4	19 27	10½	**11**	**4:44**	C	6:25	E	GEM	14
24	24	**C**	7:05	E	**4:47**	B	9 42	4	19 13	11¼	**11¾**	**5:44**	C	7:07	E	CAN	15
25	25	M.	7:05	E	**4:49**	B	9 44	4	18 58	**12**	—	**6:45**	C	7:44	E	CAN	16
26	26	Tu.	7:04	E	**4:50**	B	9 46	3	18 43	12½	**12¾**	**7:45**	D	8:17	D	LEO	17
27	27	W.	7:03	E	**4:51**	B	9 48	3	18 28	1¼	**1¼**	**8:43**	D	8:48	D	LEO	18
28	28	Th.	7:02	E	**4:52**	B	9 50	3	18 12	1¾	**2**	**9:41**	D	9:17	D	VIR	19
29	29	Fr.	7:01	E	**4:54**	B	9 53	3	17 56	2½	**2¾**	**10:37**	D	9:45	C	VIR	20
30	30	Sa.	7:00	E	**4:55**	B	9 55	3	17 40	3¼	**3½**	**11:34**	E	10:13	C	VIR	21
31	31	**C**	6:59	E	**4:56**	B	9 57	3	17 s.23	4	**4½**	—	–	10:44	C	VIR	22

 To use this page, see p. 120; for Key Letters, see p. 250. ☞ **Bold = P.M.** ☞ Light = A.M.

January hath 31 days • 2016

The years have linings just as goblets do,
The old year is the lining of the new. –Charlotte Fiske Bates

Day of Month	Day of Week	Dates, Feasts, Fasts, Aspects, Tide Heights	Weather
1	Fr.	New Year's Day • **Holy Name** • ☾ ON EQ. • Tides {9.0 8.9	*Snow*
2	Sa.	☾ AT APO. • ⊕ AT PERIHELION • Willis H. Carrier granted patent for air conditioner, 1906	*bursts*
3	C	**2nd S. af. Ch.** • ☌♂☾ • 8" ice accretion after 3 days, northern Idaho, 1961	*at first,*
4	M.	**St. Elizabeth Ann Seton** • Poet T. S. Eliot died, 1965 • Tides {9.0 8.2	*mercury*
5	Tu.	Twelfth Night • ☌♇☉ • ☿ STAT. • Tides {9.2 8.3	*diving:*
6	W.	**Epiphany** • ☌♀☾ • ☌♄☾ • Tides {9.5 8.5	*Snow*
7	Th.	**Orthodox Christmas** • Distaff Day • Emperor Hirohito of Japan died, 1989	*steadier*
8	Fr.	☾ RUNS LOW • ☌♀♄ • ♃ STAT. • *Earth is dearer than gold.* • {10.3 9.1	*now—*
9	Sa.	New ● • ☌♇☾ • NBA's Toronto Raptors first to miss all free throw attempts in game, 1996	*when's*
10	C	**1st S. af. Ep.** • ☌☿☾ • Spindletop oil gusher hit, Beaumont, Tex., 1901	*the*
11	M.	Plough Monday • 75-mph wind gusts, Yankton, S.Dak., 1990 • Tides {11.1 —	*plow*
12	Tu.	Swimmer Melvin Stewart set world record in 200-meter butterfly, 1991 • Tides {10.0 11.2	*arriving?*
13	W.	**St. Hilary** • ☌♆☾ • Hippopotamus Blackie died at approx. age 59, 2014 • {10.2 11.1	*Wintry*
14	Th.	☾ AT ☋ • ☾ AT PERIG. • ☿ IN INF. ☌ • "U.S." general Benedict Arnold born, 1741	*mix*
15	Fr.	☾ ON EQ. • Philip Livingston, signer of Declaration of Independence, born, 1716 • {10.4 10.5	*leaves*
16	Sa.	☌♅☾ • Last day of "Great Snowstorm" from Ga. to Maine, 1831 • {10.4 10.1	*roadways*
17	C	**2nd S. af. Ep.** • U.S. statesman Benjamin Franklin born, 1706 • {10.4 9.7	*slick.*
18	M.	**Martin Luther King Jr.'s Birthday (observed)** • {10.4 9.4	*Milder*
19	Tu.	*If the grass grows in Janiveer, It grows the worse for 't all the year.* • Tides {10.5 9.3	*for a*
20	W.	First Canadian Chief Engineer of Public Works, Samuel Keefer, born, 1811 • Tides {10.6 9.3	*spell,*
21	Th.	☾ RIDES HIGH • ☌☿♇ • Tenor Plácido Domingo born, 1941 • Tides {10.8 9.5	*then*
22	Fr.	**St. Vincent** • Uranium atom first split by cyclotron, 1939	*cold*
23	Sa.	**Full Wolf** ○ • January thaw traditionally begins about now. • Tides {11.0 9.8	*as . . .*
24	C	**Septuagesima** • 44°F to –56°F in 24 hours, Browning, Mont., 1916	*Hello!*
25	M.	**Conversion of Paul** • ☿ STAT. • Tides {10.8 —	*Whaddaya*
26	Tu.	**Sts. Timothy & Titus** • Sculptress Elisabet Ney born, 1833	*know?*
27	W.	☾ AT ☊ • ☌♃☾ • Ornithologist John James Audubon died, 1851 • {9.7 10.2	*It's*
28	Th.	**St. Thomas Aquinas** • ☾ ON EQ. • Space shuttle *Challenger* exploded, 1986	*10 below!*
29	Fr.	Baseball Hall of Fame elected first members, 1936 • Raccoons mate now. • {9.4 9.3	*Slop,*
30	Sa.	☾ AT APO. • ☌☿♇ • Avalanche closed Trans-Canada Highway near B.C./Alta. border, 2006	*glop,*
31	C	**Sexagesima** • *The further we go, the further behind.* • Tides {9.0 8.5	*stop!*

Farmer's Calendar

■ We had a big snowstorm recently—a real lollapalooza, about 28 inches. Strong winds accompanied it, so when I went out to shovel afterward, some of the drifts were more than 3 feet deep.

However, the same wind, forced through a narrow opening between the house and the woodpile, had scoured out valleys and arroyos where the ground was almost bare. It occurred to me that while a straight line is the shortest distance between two points, in these circumstances, it might not be the best route.

So I tried contour shoveling, clearing a way to the composter, the propane tank, and the woodpile by taking the path of least resistance; shoveling 20 linear feet of 2-inch-deep snow is easier than lifting 10 linear feet of snow that's 40 inches deep.

Yes, it took longer, but in the end, my back was less sore than it would have been after bulldozing straight through the drifts. It also helped me to see the snowscape better: its voluptuous curves, how it glittered in direct sunlight, its ultramarine gloom in the shadows.

The result was a meandering trail that looped around the highest ridges and mesas, then doubled back toward the target, shoveling in cursive, not block letters. It was what a mathematician might call an elegant solution.

SKY WATCH ☆ *Not a single naked-eye planet appears in the evening sky in the beginning of the month. Night's opening hours are dominated by Orion and the Dog Star, Sirius. On the 6th at dawn, 40 minutes before sunrise, the waning crescent Moon meets Mercury and Venus low in the southeast in Sagittarius. By midmonth, brilliant, creamy Jupiter, retrograding into Leo, starts rising at 7:30 P.M. and is nicely up by 10:00, ruling the rest of the night as the brightest "star" in the sky. February opens the 3-month window for optimally observing Jupiter and its moons through backyard telescopes. The Moon passes very closely below Jupiter on the 23rd. Mars, brightening noticeably in Libra, rises by 1:00 A.M. and is halfway up the southern sky at dawn. On Leap Day (the 29th), it dangles below the Moon.*

● **New Moon**	8th day	9th hour	39th minute
◐ **First Quarter**	15th day	2nd hour	47th minute
○ **Full Moon**	22nd day	13th hour	20th minute

All times are given in Eastern Standard Time.

Get these pages with times set to your zip code at Almanac.com/Access.

Day of Year	Day of Month	Day of Week	☼ Rises h. m.	Rise Key	☼ Sets h. m.	Set Key	Length of Day h. m.	Sun Fast m.	Declination of Sun ° ′	High Tide Times Boston		☾ Rises h. m.	Rise Key	☾ Sets h. m.	Set Key	☾ Astron. Place	☾ Age
32	1	M.	6:58	E	**4:58**	B	10 00	2	17 s.07	4¾	5¼	12:31	E	**11:16**	B	LIB	23
33	2	Tu.	6:57	E	**4:59**	B	10 02	2	16 49	5¾	6¼	1:28	E	**11:53**	B	LIB	24
34	3	W.	6:56	E	**5:00**	B	10 04	2	16 32	6½	7¼	2:24	E	**12:34**	B	OPH	25
35	4	Th.	6:55	E	**5:02**	B	10 07	2	16 14	7½	8	3:20	E	**1:21**	B	OPH	26
36	5	Fr.	6:54	D	**5:03**	B	10 09	2	15 56	8¼	9	4:14	E	**2:15**	B	SAG	27
37	6	Sa.	6:53	D	**5:04**	B	10 11	2	15 38	9¼	9¾	5:05	E	**3:15**	C	SAG	28
38	7	**C**	6:52	D	**5:06**	B	10 14	2	15 19	10	10½	5:53	E	**4:20**	C	SAG	29
39	8	M.	6:50	D	**5:07**	B	10 17	2	15 00	10¾	11¼	6:36	E	**5:29**	C	AQU	0
40	9	Tu.	6:49	D	**5:08**	B	10 19	2	14 41	11½	—	7:16	D	**6:40**	D	AQU	1
41	10	W.	6:48	D	**5:09**	B	10 21	2	14 22	12	12¼	7:54	D	**7:52**	D	AQU	2
42	11	Th.	6:47	D	**5:11**	B	10 24	2	14 02	12¾	1	8:30	D	**9:04**	E	PSC	3
43	12	Fr.	6:45	D	**5:12**	B	10 27	2	13 42	1½	2	9:06	C	**10:15**	E	PSC	4
44	13	Sa.	6:44	D	**5:13**	B	10 29	2	13 22	2½	2¾	9:43	C	**11:25**	E	PSC	5
45	14	**C**	6:43	D	**5:15**	B	10 32	2	13 02	3¼	3¾	10:22	C	—	–	ARI	6
46	15	M.	6:41	D	**5:16**	B	10 35	2	12 41	4¼	4¾	11:04	B	12:33	E	TAU	7
47	16	Tu.	6:40	D	**5:17**	B	10 37	2	12 21	5¼	6	11:51	B	1:37	E	TAU	8
48	17	W.	6:39	D	**5:18**	B	10 39	2	12 00	6½	7	**12:42**	B	2:38	E	TAU	9
49	18	Th.	6:37	D	**5:20**	B	10 43	2	11 39	7½	8¼	**1:37**	B	3:32	E	GEM	10
50	19	Fr.	6:36	D	**5:21**	B	10 45	2	11 18	8½	9¼	**2:35**	C	4:21	E	GEM	11
51	20	Sa.	6:34	D	**5:22**	B	10 48	2	10 56	9½	10	**3:34**	C	5:04	E	CAN	12
52	21	**C**	6:33	D	**5:24**	B	10 51	2	10 35	10¼	10¾	**4:34**	C	5:43	E	CAN	13
53	22	M.	6:31	D	**5:25**	B	10 54	2	10 13	11	11½	**5:33**	C	6:17	E	LEO	14
54	23	Tu.	6:30	D	**5:26**	B	10 56	3	9 51	11½	—	**6:32**	D	6:48	D	LEO	15
55	24	W.	6:28	D	**5:27**	B	10 59	3	9 29	12	12¼	**7:30**	D	7:18	D	LEO	16
56	25	Th.	6:27	D	**5:29**	B	11 02	3	9 07	12¾	1	**8:27**	D	7:46	C	VIR	17
57	26	Fr.	6:25	D	**5:30**	B	11 05	3	8 44	1¼	1½	**9:24**	E	8:15	C	VIR	18
58	27	Sa.	6:24	D	**5:31**	C	11 07	3	8 22	2	2¼	**10:20**	E	8:44	C	VIR	19
59	28	**C**	6:22	D	**5:32**	C	11 10	3	7 59	2½	3	**11:17**	E	9:16	C	LIB	20
60	29	M.	6:20	D	**5:33**	C	11 13	4	7 s.36	3¼	3¾	—	–	9:50	B	LIB	21

FEBRUARY HATH 29 DAYS • 2016

No summer sunset afterglow
Can match the soft rose of the snow. –Anna Boynton Averill

Day of Month	Day of Week	Dates, Feasts, Fasts, Aspects, Tide Heights	Weather
1	M.	**St. Brigid** • ☌♂☾ • First U.S. dental dispensary opened, N.Y.C., 1791	*Groundhog*
2	Tu.	**Candlemas** • Groundhog Day • *On Candlemas Day, The good goose begins to lay.*	*cowers—*
3	W.	☌♄☾ • Fire destroyed Parliament buildings, Ottawa, Ont., 1916 • Tides { 9.1 / 8.1	*powers*
4	Th.	☾ RUNS LOW • United Service Organizations (USO) incorporated, 1941 • Tides { 9.3 / 8.4	*of*
5	Fr.	**St. Agatha** • ☌♀♇ • Religious leader Roger Williams arrived in America [Boston], 1631	*rain,*
6	Sa.	☿ GR. ELONG. (26° WEST) • ☌☿☾ • ☌♀☾ • ☌♇☾ • Tides { 10.2 / 9.2	*snow*
7	**C**	**Quinquagesima** • Manufacturer John Deere born, 1804 • { 10.8 / 9.8	*showers.*
8	M.	**Chinese New Year (Monkey)** • **New** ● • Tides { 11.2 / 10.3	*Flakes*
9	Tu.	**Shrove Tuesday** • ☌♆☾ • Singer Sophie Tucker died, 1966 • { 11.5 / —	*and*
10	W.	**Ash Wednesday** • ☾ AT ☋ • ☾ AT PERIG. • { 10.7 / 11.6	*drops*
11	Th.	☾ ON EQ. • Mount Holyoke Seminary, first U.S. college for women, chartered, South Hadley, Mass., 1836 • { 11.0 / 11.5	*are*
12	Fr.	☌♅☾ • U.S. president Abraham Lincoln born, 1809 • Tides { 11.1 / 11.1	*intermixed,*
13	Sa.	First Barbie dolls went on sale, 1959 • Tides { 11.0 / 10.6	*floating*
14	**C**	**1st S. in Lent** • **Valentine's Day** • *First deserve, and then desire.*	*first,*
15	M.	**Washington's Birthday (observed)** • Susan B. Anthony born, 1820 • Tides { 10.6 / 9.5	*then*
16	Tu.	Winter's back breaks. • Canadian Pacific Railway Company incorporated, 1881 • { 10.4 / 9.1	*falling.*
17	W.	Ember Day • ☾ RIDES HIGH • Tie broken: Thomas Jefferson to be U.S. president; Aaron Burr, V.P., 1801	*While*
18	Th.	England's Queen "Bloody" Mary I born, 1516 • Tides { 10.2 / 9.0	*it's*
19	Fr.	Ember Day • First official U.S. government weather predictions published, 1871 • Tides { 10.2 / 9.2	*mild,*
20	Sa.	Ember Day • Regeneration of *Silene stenophylla* from 30,000-year-old fruit tissue announced, 2012 • { 10.4 / 9.4	*get*
21	**C**	**2nd S. in Lent** • Ballerina Dame Margot Fonteyn died, 1991 • { 10.4 / 9.6	*your*
22	M.	**Full Snow** ○ • 10-lb. 14-oz. 'aweoweo caught, Penguin Bank, O'ahu, Hawaii, 2005 • { 10.5 / 9.7	*furnace*
23	Tu.	☌♃☾ • U.S. rocket mail flight across Greenwood Lake, N.Y. to N.J., 1936 • { 10.4 / —	*fixed.*
24	W.	**St. Matthias** • ☾ ON EQ. • ☾ AT ☊ • Skunks mate now.	*Appalling!*
25	Th.	Painter Pierre-Auguste Renoir born, 1841 • Tides { 9.8 / 10.0	*Do*
26	Fr.	☾ AT APO. • Canada's GEODESIC mission launched into northern lights, Alaska, 2000 • Tides { 9.7 / 9.7	*I*
27	Sa.	Edwin Land granted patent for self-developing film, 1951	*hear*
28	**C**	**3rd S. in Lent** • ☌♆☉ • Territory of Colorado created, 1861 • { 9.4 / 8.9	*Key West*
29	M.	Leap Day • ☌♂☾ • *Leap year was never a good sheep year.* • { 9.2 / 8.6	*calling?*

Be yourself; everyone else is already taken.
–Unknown

Farmer's Calendar

■ Every once in a while, we enjoy an influx of exotic birds, brought here on strong winds or by a shortage of food in their home territories. Ornithologists call it an "irruption." There was a tragic example in late May of 1974 when strong southwesterly winds blew scarlet tanagers all the way north to New Hampshire, where there were no insects for them to eat. I will never forget their flame-red bodies littering a green field.

Over the last two winters, we have been blessed with an abundance of snowy owls coming south in search of prey. In this case, it was not winds but an abundance of lemmings, the owl's favorite snack, that expanded their territory and led to our shock when one of the white phantoms flew through the beam of our headlights.

This being a presidential election year, we can expect a political irruption as candidates from all corners of the nation flock to New Hampshire for the first primary of the season. We can look forward to shaking hands with shivering would-be Chief Executives at diners and factory gates and answering questions from the national reporters who follow. One of those reporters, perhaps disoriented by the cold, once asked me how I liked living in Vermont.

"This is New Hampshire," I said. He wrote it down.

THE THIRD MONTH • 2016

SKY WATCH ☆ *Saturn, in Ophiuchus all year, hovers to the right of the Moon early on the 2nd. Venus floats to the Moon's right on the 7th at dawn but is challengingly low. On the 8th, Jupiter reaches opposition and is at its biggest and brightest of 2016; the Giant Planet is visible all night long. Spring arrives with the equinox on the 20th, a half-hour after midnight. Jupiter floats to the upper left of the Moon on the 21st. The full Moon undergoes a penumbral eclipse before dawn on the 23rd for western United States and Canadian insomniacs. Mars forms a triangle with the Moon and dimmer Saturn on the 29th, a few hours before dawn.*

◑	**Last Quarter**	1st day	18th hour	11th minute
●	**New Moon**	8th day	20th hour	55th minute
◐	**First Quarter**	15th day	13th hour	3rd minute
○	**Full Moon**	23rd day	8th hour	1st minute
◑	**Last Quarter**	31st day	11th hour	17th minute

After 2:00 A.M. on March 13, Eastern Daylight Time is given.

Get these pages with times set to your zip code at Almanac.com/Access.

Day of Year	Day of Month	Day of Week	☼ Rises h. m.	Rise Key	☼ Sets h. m.	Set Key	Length of Day h. m.	Sun Fast m.	Declination of Sun ° '	High Tide Times Boston		☾ Rises h. m.	Rise Key	☾ Sets h. m.	Set Key	☾ Astron. Place	☾ Age
61	1	Tu.	6:19	D	**5:35**	C	11 16	4	7 s.13	4	**4½**	12:13	E	10:29	B	SCO	22
62	2	W.	6:17	D	**5:36**	C	11 19	4	6 51	5	**5½**	1:08	E	11:12	B	OPH	23
63	3	Th.	6:15	D	**5:37**	C	11 22	4	6 27	5¾	**6½**	2:01	E	**12:01**	B	SAG	24
64	4	Fr.	6:14	D	**5:38**	C	11 24	4	6 04	6¾	**7½**	2:53	E	**12:57**	B	SAG	25
65	5	Sa.	6:12	D	**5:40**	C	11 28	5	5 41	7¾	**8¼**	3:41	E	**1:58**	C	SAG	26
66	6	**B**	6:11	C	**5:41**	C	11 30	5	5 18	8½	**9¼**	4:26	E	**3:05**	C	CAP	27
67	7	M.	6:09	C	**5:42**	C	11 33	5	4 54	9½	**10**	5:07	E	**4:15**	C	CAP	28
68	8	Tu.	6:07	C	**5:43**	C	11 36	5	4 31	10¼	**10¾**	5:47	D	**5:28**	D	AQU	0
69	9	W.	6:05	C	**5:44**	C	11 39	6	4 08	11¼	**11½**	6:24	D	**6:42**	D	AQU	1
70	10	Th.	6:04	C	**5:45**	C	11 41	6	3 44	**12**	—	7:01	C	**7:56**	E	PSC	2
71	11	Fr.	6:02	C	**5:47**	C	11 45	6	3 20	12½	**12¾**	7:39	C	**9:09**	E	PSC	3
72	12	Sa.	6:00	C	**5:48**	C	11 48	6	2 57	1¼	**1¾**	8:19	C	**10:20**	E	CET	4
73	13	**B**	6:59	C	**6:49**	C	11 50	7	2 33	3	**3½**	10:02	C	—	–	ARI	5
74	14	M.	6:57	C	**6:50**	C	11 53	7	2 09	4	**4½**	10:48	B	12:28	E	TAU	6
75	15	Tu.	6:55	C	**6:51**	C	11 56	7	1 46	5	**5½**	11:39	B	1:32	E	TAU	7
76	16	W.	6:54	C	**6:52**	C	11 58	7	1 22	6	**6¾**	**12:33**	B	2:29	E	ORI	8
77	17	Th.	6:52	C	**6:54**	C	12 02	8	0 58	7	**7¾**	**1:30**	B	3:19	E	GEM	9
78	18	Fr.	6:50	C	**6:55**	C	12 05	8	0 35	8¼	**9**	**2:28**	C	4:04	E	CAN	10
79	19	Sa.	6:48	C	**6:56**	C	12 08	8	0 s.11	9¼	**9¾**	**3:27**	C	4:43	E	CAN	11
80	20	**B**	6:47	C	**6:57**	C	12 10	9	0 N.12	10	**10¾**	**4:26**	C	5:18	E	LEO	12
81	21	M.	6:45	C	**6:58**	C	12 13	9	0 36	11	**11¼**	**5:24**	D	5:50	D	LEO	13
82	22	Tu.	6:43	C	**6:59**	C	12 16	9	0 59	11½	12	**6:22**	D	6:20	D	LEO	14
83	23	W.	6:41	C	**7:00**	C	12 19	10	1 23	**12¼**	—	**7:19**	D	6:49	D	VIR	15
84	24	Th.	6:40	C	**7:02**	C	12 22	10	1 46	12½	**12¾**	**8:16**	E	7:17	C	VIR	16
85	25	Fr.	6:38	C	**7:03**	C	12 25	10	2 10	1¼	**1½**	**9:13**	E	7:46	C	VIR	17
86	26	Sa.	6:36	C	**7:04**	C	12 28	10	2 33	1¾	**2**	**10:09**	E	8:17	C	VIR	18
87	27	**B**	6:34	C	**7:05**	C	12 31	11	2 57	2¼	**2¾**	**11:05**	E	8:50	B	LIB	19
88	28	M.	6:33	C	**7:06**	D	12 33	11	3 20	3	**3½**	—	–	9:27	B	LIB	20
89	29	Tu.	6:31	C	**7:07**	D	12 36	11	3 44	3¾	**4¼**	12:00	E	10:07	B	OPH	21
90	30	W.	6:29	C	**7:08**	D	12 39	12	4 07	4½	**5**	12:53	E	10:53	B	OPH	22
91	31	Th.	6:28	C	**7:10**	D	12 42	12	4 N.30	5¼	**6**	1:44	E	11:45	B	SAG	23

 To use this page, see p. 120; for Key Letters, see p. 250. ☞ **Bold = P.M.** ☞ Light = A.M.

MARCH HATH 31 DAYS • 2016

Tossing his mane of snows in wildest eddies and tangles,
Lion-like, March cometh in. –William Dean Howells

Day of Month	Day of Week	Dates, Feasts, Fasts, Aspects, Tide Heights	Weather
1	Tu.	St. David • Peace Corps established, 1961 • Tides { 9.1 / 8.3	*Snow*
2	W.	St. Chad • ☌♄☾ • *Anger is often more hurtful than the injury that caused it.*	*spitter,*
3	Th.	☾ RUNS LOW • Dance instructor Arthur Murray died, 1991 • Tides { 9.1 / 8.2	*then*
4	Fr.	☌♇☾ • Vt. became 14th U.S. state, 1791 • Tides { 9.3 / 8.5	*bitter.*
5	Sa.	St. Piran • Football player Robert Patrick "Rocky" Bleier born, 1946 • Tides { 9.8 / 9.0	*You'll*
6	**B**	4th S. in Lent • Nora Stanton Blatch first woman elected to American Society of Civil Engineers, 1906	*need*
7	M.	St. Perpetua • ☌♀☾ • Alexander Graham Bell telephone patented, 1876 • { 10.9 / 10.3	*rain*
8	Tu.	New ● • Eclipse ☉ • ☌☿☾ • ☌♆☾ • ♃ AT ☍	*boots*
9	W.	☾ ON EQ. • ☾ AT ☋ • Hummingbirds migrate north now. • { 11.7 / 11.4	*and*
10	Th.	☾ AT PERIG. • ☌☿♆ • ☌♅☾ • { 11.8 / —	*bumbershoots.*
11	Fr.	Andrew Rotz made 11,123 consecutive Texas skips in 3 hrs., 10 min., Las Vegas, Nev., 2003 • { 11.7 / 11.6	*Whiteout!*
12	Sa.	Automobile manufacturer Clement Studebaker born, 1831	*Now*
13	**B**	5th S. in Lent • **Daylight Saving Time begins, 2:00 A.M.** • Uranus discovered, 1781	*it's*
14	M.	Clean Monday • *Sow beans in the mud and they'll grow like a wood.* • Tides { 11.2 / 10.1	*bright*
15	Tu.	Beware the ides of March. • Trumpet player Harry James born, 1916 • Tides { 10.7 / 9.5	*out.*
16	W.	☾ RIDES HIGH • First docking of 2 spacecraft (*Gemini VIII* and Agena target vehicle), 1966 • { 10.3 / 9.1	*Gather*
17	Th.	**St. Patrick's Day** • National Gallery of Art dedicated, D.C., 1941 • { 9.9 / 9.0	*shamrocks*
18	Fr.	Maude Farris-Luse (age 115 years, 56 days) died, 2002	*and*
19	Sa.	St. Joseph • *Is't on St. Joseph's Day clear, So follows a fertile year.* • { 9.8 / 9.2	*wool socks*
20	**B**	**Palm Sunday** • **Vernal Equinox** • ☌♀♆ • { 9.9 / 9.5	*for the*
21	M.	The Guess Who's "American Woman" released as single, 1970 • Tides { 10.0 / 9.7	*equinox!*
22	Tu.	☾ AT ☊ • ☌♃☾ • Deadly tornado struck Urbana, Ohio, blowing Bible 15 miles, 1830	*Drip*
23	W.	**Full Worm** ○ • **Eclipse** ☾ • ☾ ON EQ. • ☿ IN SUP. ☌ • { 10.1 / —	*the*
24	Th.	Maundy Thursday • Clement Hardy issued patent for rotary disk plow, 1896 • { 9.9 / 10.0	*light*
25	Fr.	**Good Friday** • ☾ AT APO. • ♄ STAT. • { 10.0 / 9.8	*fantastic:*
26	Sa.	Est. 7.4-magnitude earthquake, Owens Valley, Calif., 1872 • Chipmunks emerge from hibernation now.	*Has*
27	**B**	**Easter** • *Do not look upon the vessel, but upon that which it contains.* • { 9.9 / 9.3	*winter*
28	M.	Easter Monday • ☌♂☾ • Singer Reba McEntire born, 1955 • { 9.7 / 9.0	*played*
29	Tu.	☌♄☾ • National Road, first federally funded road, authorized, 1806 • Tides { 9.5 / 8.7	*its*
30	W.	☾ RUNS LOW • Canadian navy stopped issuing rum rations, 1972 • Tides { 9.4 / 8.5	*last*
31	Th.	☌☿♅ • ☌♇☾ • Philosopher René Descartes born, 1596 • { 9.3 / 8.5	*trick?*

Farmer's Calendar

■ For many years, we've had a phoebe nest atop our front porch light fixture. Phoebes are small gray birds with the habit of flicking their tails up and down while perching on a branch or wire. Their call is a harsh, indignant "fee-BEE!"

I don't know why Mama phoebe chose such a public place to raise her young. Every time the door opened, she had to flee to the oak tree across the driveway. No wonder she sounded vexed.

In past years, she used the old nest, but this year it has remained unoccupied. She is trying to build a new one above the front door, on a half-inch-wide piece of molding. It's too narrow. Despite her best efforts, every morning little bits of moss appear on the porch right under the door.

There are two mysteries here. One is why the phoebe doesn't just reoccupy the old nest. My wife thinks that it's because the last brood Mama raised there all died. Perhaps there's some subtle residue of disaster in it, too faint for human senses, that keeps the phoebes away.

The other mystery is why she persists in trying to do the impossible. She has numerous other places to build a nest. Maybe for phoebes, like people, the tug of home is too strong to resist, even when we should.

THE FOURTH MONTH • 2016

SKY WATCH ☆ *Mercury's best 2016 evening star appearance unfolds in the first week of April, 40 minutes after sunset in the west. Orange Aldebaran is occulted by the Moon soon after nightfall on the 10th and is best seen from the eastern United States and Canada. Mars, retrograding, brightens dramatically to magnitude –1.3 and rises before midnight at midmonth. Dangling just below Mars all month is the orange supergiant Antares, whose very name means "The Rival of Mars." Brilliant Jupiter hovers just above the Moon on the 17th. On the 25th, the gibbous Moon forms a dramatic triangle with Mars to its lower right and Saturn to its lower left. All inhabit the constellation of Ophiuchus, the Serpent Bearer.*

●	**New Moon**	7th day	7th hour	24th minute
◐	**First Quarter**	13th day	23rd hour	59th minute
○	**Full Moon**	22nd day	1st hour	24th minute
◑	**Last Quarter**	29th day	23rd hour	29th minute

All times are given in Eastern Daylight Time.

Get these pages with times set to your zip code at Almanac.com/Access.

Day of Year	Day of Month	Day of Week	☼ Rises h. m.	Rise Key	☼ Sets h. m.	Set Key	Length of Day h. m.	Sun Fast m.	Declination of Sun ° ′	High Tide Times Boston		☾ Rises h. m.	Rise Key	☾ Sets h. m.	Set Key	☾ Astron. Place	☾ Age
92	1	Fr.	6:26	C	**7:11**	D	12 45	12	4 N.53	6¼	**7**	2:32	E	**12:42**	B	SAG	24
93	2	Sa.	6:24	C	**7:12**	D	12 48	12	5 16	7¼	**7¾**	3:17	E	**1:44**	C	CAP	25
94	3	**B**	6:22	C	**7:13**	D	12 51	13	5 39	8¼	**8¾**	3:59	E	**2:51**	C	AQU	26
95	4	M.	6:21	C	**7:14**	D	12 53	13	6 02	9	**9¾**	4:38	D	**4:01**	D	AQU	27
96	5	Tu.	6:19	C	**7:15**	D	12 56	13	6 25	10	**10½**	5:16	D	**5:14**	D	AQU	28
97	6	W.	6:17	C	**7:16**	D	12 59	14	6 47	11	**11¼**	5:53	D	**6:28**	E	PSC	29
98	7	Th.	6:16	B	**7:17**	D	13 01	14	7 10	11¾	—	6:31	C	**7:43**	E	PSC	0
99	8	Fr.	6:14	B	**7:19**	D	13 05	14	7 32	12¼	**12¾**	7:10	C	**8:58**	E	PSC	1
100	9	Sa.	6:12	B	**7:20**	D	13 08	14	7 55	1	**1½**	7:53	C	**10:10**	E	ARI	2
101	10	**B**	6:11	B	**7:21**	D	13 10	15	8 17	1¾	**2½**	8:39	B	**11:18**	E	TAU	3
102	11	M.	6:09	B	**7:22**	D	13 13	15	8 39	2¾	**3¼**	9:30	B	—	–	TAU	4
103	12	Tu.	6:07	B	**7:23**	D	13 16	15	9 01	3½	**4¼**	10:25	B	12:20	E	ORI	5
104	13	W.	6:06	B	**7:24**	D	13 18	15	9 22	4½	**5¼**	11:22	B	1:15	E	GEM	6
105	14	Th.	6:04	B	**7:25**	D	13 21	16	9 44	5½	**6¼**	**12:21**	C	2:03	E	GEM	7
106	15	Fr.	6:02	B	**7:26**	D	13 24	16	10 05	6¾	**7½**	**1:21**	C	2:45	E	CAN	8
107	16	Sa.	6:01	B	**7:28**	D	13 27	16	10 26	7¾	**8½**	**2:20**	C	3:21	E	LEO	9
108	17	**B**	5:59	B	**7:29**	D	13 30	16	10 47	8¾	**9¼**	**3:18**	C	3:54	D	LEO	10
109	18	M.	5:58	B	**7:30**	D	13 32	17	11 08	9¾	**10**	**4:16**	D	4:24	D	LEO	11
110	19	Tu.	5:56	B	**7:31**	D	13 35	17	11 29	10½	**10¾**	**5:13**	D	4:52	D	VIR	12
111	20	W.	5:55	B	**7:32**	D	13 37	17	11 49	11¼	**11½**	**6:10**	D	5:20	C	VIR	13
112	21	Th.	5:53	B	**7:33**	D	13 40	17	12 10	11¾	—	**7:07**	E	5:49	C	VIR	14
113	22	Fr.	5:52	B	**7:34**	D	13 42	17	12 30	12	**12½**	**8:03**	E	6:19	C	VIR	15
114	23	Sa.	5:50	B	**7:35**	D	13 45	18	12 50	12½	**1**	**9:00**	E	6:51	B	LIB	16
115	24	**B**	5:49	B	**7:37**	D	13 48	18	13 09	1¼	**1¾**	**9:55**	E	7:26	B	LIB	17
116	25	M.	5:47	B	**7:38**	D	13 51	18	13 29	1¾	**2¼**	**10:49**	E	8:06	B	OPH	18
117	26	Tu.	5:46	B	**7:39**	D	13 53	18	13 48	2½	**3**	**11:41**	E	8:50	B	OPH	19
118	27	W.	5:44	B	**7:40**	D	13 56	18	14 07	3¼	**3¾**	—	–	9:39	B	SAG	20
119	28	Th.	5:43	B	**7:41**	E	13 58	18	14 26	4	**4½**	12:29	E	10:33	B	SAG	21
120	29	Fr.	5:41	B	**7:42**	E	14 01	18	14 44	4¾	**5½**	1:14	E	11:32	C	SAG	22
121	30	Sa.	5:40	B	**7:43**	E	14 03	19	15 N.03	5¾	**6¼**	1:56	E	**12:35**	C	AQU	23

 To use this page, see p. 120; for Key Letters, see p. 250. ☞ **Bold = P.M.** ☞ Light = A.M.

APRIL HATH 30 DAYS • 2016

It is the springtime: April violets glow
In wayside nooks. –Thomas Buchanan Read

Day of Month	Day of Week	Dates, Feasts, Fasts, Aspects, Tide Heights	Weather
1	Fr.	**All Fools'** • *If you want to make a fool of yourself, you'll find a lot of people ready to help you.* • {9.3 / 8.6	*Flakes*
2	Sa.	Tap dancer Charles "Honi" Coles born, 1911 • Tides {9.5 / 9.0	*alive!*
3	**B**	**2nd S. of Easter** • Writer F. Scott Fitzgerald married Zelda Sayre, 1920	*Spring's*
4	M.	**Annunciation**† • ☌♆☾ • *Ben Hur* won 11 Academy Awards, 1960	*arrived!*
5	Tu.	☾ AT ☋ • Blizzard left 27.2" snow, St. John's, Nfld., 1999 • Tides {10.9 / 10.9	*Or is this*
6	W.	☾ ON EQ. • ☌♀☾ • Twin mongoose lemurs born, Busch Gardens, Tampa, Fla., 2012	*warmth*
7	Th.	**New** ● • ☾ AT PERIG. • ☌♅☾ • Circus owner Phineas T. Barnum died, 1891	*illusion?*
8	Fr.	☌☿☾ • Clint Eastwood elected mayor, Carmel, Calif., 1986 • Tides {12.0 / 11.7	*Snow*
9	Sa.	☌♅☉ • England's King Henry I reprimanded in church for long hair, 1105 • {12.2 / 11.5	*and*
10	**B**	**3rd S. of Easter** • American Society for the Prevention of Cruelty to Animals incorporated, 1866	*rain,*
11	M.	2' snow, N.J., 1841 • Circus owner James A. Bailey died, 1906 • Tides {11.8 / 10.7	*then*
12	Tu.	☾ RIDES HIGH • Moose River gold mine collapsed, N.S., 1936	*mild*
13	W.	U.S. president Thomas Jefferson born, 1743 • Astronomer Annie Jump Cannon died, 1941	*again—*
14	Th.	Sky full of unknown moving objects Nuremberg, Germany, 1541 • Tides {10.2 / 9.3	*chaos*
15	Fr.	*If frogs make a noise in the time of cold rain, warm dry weather will follow.* • Tides {9.8 / 9.1	*and*
16	Sa.	♂ STAT. • Roman Emperor Otho died, A.D. 69 • {9.5 / 9.2	*confusion!*
17	**B**	**4th S. of Easter** • Lawyer Samuel Chase born, 1741 • {9.5 / 9.4	*Showers*
18	M.	☾ AT ☊ • ☌♃☾ • ♇ STAT. • ☿ GR. ELONG. (20° EAST) • {9.5 / 9.6	*cool*
19	Tu.	☾ ON EQ. • Women granted suffrage in Alta., 1916 • Tides {9.6 / 9.8	*our*
20	W.	Hot Springs Reservation (now National Park) established, Ark., 1832 • Tides {9.7 / 10.0	*vernal*
21	Th.	☾ AT APO. • Writer Charlotte Brontë born, 1816 • {9.7 / —	*ardor.*
22	Fr.	**Passover begins at sundown** • **Full Pink** ○ • ☌♀♅ • Okla. land rush began, 1899	*Planting*
23	Sa.	**St. George** • U.S. president James Buchanan born, 1791 • Tides {10.2 / 9.6	*peas?*
24	**B**	**5th S. of Easter** • *Old Farmer's Almanac* founder Robert B. Thomas born, 1766	*Just a*
25	M.	**St. Mark** • ☌♂☾ • ☌♄☾ • N.Y. first U.S. state to require auto license plates, 1901	*tease!*
26	Tu.	*A good name is better than riches.* • Tides {10.0 / 9.1	*Raining*
27	W.	☾ RUNS LOW • Steamboat *Sultana* exploded on Mississippi R., near Memphis, Tenn., 1865	*harder!*
28	Th.	☌♇☾ • ☿ STAT. • *25–28:* Large tornado outbreak, eastern U.S./southern Can., 2011	*Mellow—*
29	Fr.	Poplars leaf out about now. • U.S. president Hoover received King and Queen of Siam, 1931	*forsythia's*
30	Sa.	Folklorist Edith Margaret Fowke born, 1913 • Tides {9.7 / 9.2	*yellow.*

Fog is rain that whispers. –Olivia Dresher

Farmer's Calendar

■ It rained last night, and this morning our road was covered with efts (pronounced "eefts" around here). They're juvenile spotted newts, about an inch long, who were born in fresh water, probably the pond across the road, and emerged a month or so later to spend the next 3 or 4 years on land before returning to their wet world.

You can't miss them. They're bright orange-red. Old-timers might call them cunning, which used to mean "cute" or "beguiling." My mother-in-law, a pediatrician, used the word when she held newborn babies: "Isn't she cunning!" When I hold an eft in the palm of my hand, I stare at its tiny toes with the same astonishment and delight.

Efts need moisture to survive; during a dry spell, they crawl under the leaf mold. If they're not quick, we find them on the road. They're no longer cunning as little hardened orange-red commas. Although their bright color warns some predators that they are toxic, most efts don't survive on land. They're eaten by birds and lizards or crushed by cars. Those who make it back to the pond turn olive-green and spend the rest of their lives in water.

Efts, according to biologists, are economically valuable because they eat mosquito larvae. We should give them credit for being cunning, too.

SKY WATCH ☆ *The brilliant winter constellations, now low in the west at nightfall, plunge into twilight at midmonth and disappear until fall. Jupiter, in Leo, sits to the upper left of the Moon on the 14th. The Moon forms a triangle with brilliant Mars and first-magnitude Saturn on the 21st. Mars reaches opposition on the 22nd. Rising at sunset at a brilliant magnitude –2.0, it is out all night long. This is the planet's biggest and brightest appearance in over a decade, although seeing details on the Martian disk can still be challenging with small telescopes. The Moon hovers to the left of Saturn on the 22nd. At dawn, the eastern sky is now empty, with Venus long vanished into the solar glare.*

●	**New Moon**	6th day	15th hour	30th minute
☽	**First Quarter**	13th day	13th hour	3rd minute
○	**Full Moon**	21st day	17th hour	15th minute
☾	**Last Quarter**	29th day	8th hour	12th minute

All times are given in Eastern Daylight Time.

Get these pages with times set to your zip code at Almanac.com/Access.

Day of Year	Day of Month	Day of Week	☼ Rises h. m.	Rise Key	☼ Sets h. m.	Set Key	Length of Day h. m.	Sun Fast m.	Declination of Sun ° ′	High Tide Times Boston		☽ Rises h. m.	Rise Key	☽ Sets h. m.	Set Key	☽ Astron. Place	☽ Age
122	1	**B**	5:39	B	**7:44**	E	14 05	19	15 N.21	6¾	7¼	2:35	E	**1:41**	C	CAP	24
123	2	M.	5:37	B	**7:46**	E	14 09	19	15 38	7¾	8¼	3:11	D	**2:50**	D	AQU	25
124	3	Tu.	5:36	B	**7:47**	E	14 11	19	15 56	8¾	9¼	3:47	D	**4:02**	D	PSC	26
125	4	W.	5:35	B	**7:48**	E	14 13	19	16 13	9½	10	4:23	C	**5:15**	E	CET	27
126	5	Th.	5:34	B	**7:49**	E	14 15	19	16 30	10½	11	5:01	C	**6:30**	E	PSC	28
127	6	Fr.	5:32	B	**7:50**	E	14 18	19	16 47	11½	11¾	5:41	C	**7:44**	E	CET	0
128	7	Sa.	5:31	B	**7:51**	E	14 20	19	17 03	12¼	—	6:26	B	**8:57**	E	TAU	1
129	8	**B**	5:30	B	**7:52**	E	14 22	19	17 20	12½	1¼	7:16	B	**10:04**	E	TAU	2
130	9	M.	5:29	B	**7:53**	E	14 24	19	17 35	1½	2¼	8:10	B	**11:04**	E	TAU	3
131	10	Tu.	5:28	B	**7:54**	E	14 26	19	17 51	2¼	3	9:08	B	**11:57**	E	GEM	4
132	11	W.	5:26	B	**7:55**	E	14 29	19	18 06	3¼	4	10:09	B	—	–	GEM	5
133	12	Th.	5:25	B	**7:56**	E	14 31	19	18 21	4¼	5	11:11	C	12:42	E	CAN	6
134	13	Fr.	5:24	B	**7:57**	E	14 33	19	18 36	5¼	6	**12:11**	C	1:22	E	CAN	7
135	14	Sa.	5:23	B	**7:58**	E	14 35	19	18 50	6¼	7	**1:11**	C	1:56	D	LEO	8
136	15	**B**	5:22	B	**7:59**	E	14 37	19	19 04	7¼	7¾	**2:09**	D	2:27	D	LEO	9
137	16	M.	5:21	B	**8:01**	E	14 40	19	19 18	8¼	8¾	**3:07**	D	2:56	D	VIR	10
138	17	Tu.	5:20	B	**8:02**	E	14 42	19	19 31	9	9½	**4:04**	D	3:24	C	VIR	11
139	18	W.	5:19	B	**8:03**	E	14 44	19	19 44	10	10¼	**5:00**	E	3:52	C	VIR	12
140	19	Th.	5:18	A	**8:03**	E	14 45	19	19 57	10¾	10¾	**5:57**	E	4:22	C	VIR	13
141	20	Fr.	5:18	A	**8:04**	E	14 46	19	20 10	11¼	11½	**6:54**	E	4:53	C	LIB	14
142	21	Sa.	5:17	A	**8:05**	E	14 48	19	20 22	12	—	**7:50**	E	5:27	B	LIB	15
143	22	**B**	5:16	A	**8:06**	E	14 50	19	20 33	12	12¾	**8:45**	E	6:05	B	SCO	16
144	23	M.	5:15	A	**8:07**	E	14 52	19	20 45	12¾	1¼	**9:38**	E	6:47	B	OPH	17
145	24	Tu.	5:14	A	**8:08**	E	14 54	19	20 55	1½	2	**10:28**	E	7:35	B	SAG	18
146	25	W.	5:14	A	**8:09**	E	14 55	19	21 06	2	2¾	**11:14**	E	8:28	B	SAG	19
147	26	Th.	5:13	A	**8:10**	E	14 57	19	21 16	2¾	3½	**11:57**	E	9:25	B	SAG	20
148	27	Fr.	5:12	A	**8:11**	E	14 59	18	21 26	3½	4¼	—	–	10:26	C	CAP	21
149	28	Sa.	5:12	A	**8:12**	E	15 00	18	21 36	4¼	5	12:36	E	11:30	C	CAP	22
150	29	**B**	5:11	A	**8:12**	E	15 01	18	21 45	5¼	6	1:12	D	**12:36**	D	AQU	23
151	30	M.	5:11	A	**8:13**	E	15 02	18	21 54	6¼	6¾	1:47	D	**1:45**	D	AQU	24
152	31	Tu.	5:10	A	**8:14**	E	15 04	18	22 N.02	7¼	7¾	2:21	D	**2:55**	E	PSC	25

May hath 31 days • 2016

Blest power of sunshine! Genial day!
What balm, what life is in thy ray. –Thomas Moore

Day of Month	Day of Week	Dates, Feasts, Fasts, Aspects, Tide Heights	Weather
1	**B**	**Rogation S.** • **Orthodox Easter** • **May Day** • { 9.8 / 9.6	*Blessed*
2	M.	**St. Athanasius** • ☾ at ☋ • ☌♆☾ • Tides { 10.0 / 10.1	*blossoms*
3	Tu.	**Sts. Philip & James**[T] • ☾ on Eq. • 39°F, Phoenix, Ariz., 1899 • { 10.4 / 10.8	*banish*
4	W.	☌♅☾ • First Freedom Ride began, 1961 • { 10.8 / 11.4	*sadness;*
5	Th.	**Ascension** • **Cinco de Mayo** • ☌♀☾ • Tides { 11.1 / 12.0	*all*
6	Fr.	**New** ● • ☾ at perig. • ☌☿☾ • Baseball player Willie Mays born, 1931	*is*
7	Sa.	14-pound pearl reportedly collected at Palawan Island, Philippines, 1934 • Tides { 11.4 / —	*gladness!*
8	**B**	**1st S. af. Asc.** • **Mother's Day** • Pianist Rudolf Serkin died, 1991	*Birds*
9	M.	**St. Gregory of Nazianzus** • ☾ rides high • ☿ transit over ☉ • ☿ in inf. ☌ • ♃ stat.	*return*
10	Tu.	Union Pacific and Central Pacific railroads linked with golden spike, Promontory Point, Utah, 1869 • { 11.9 / 10.5	*with*
11	W.	*St. Mamertus, St. Pancras, and St. Gervais do not pass without a frost.* • **Three** • { 11.3 / 10.1	*joyous*
12	Th.	Flag of Manitoba officially adopted, 1966 • **Chilly** • { 10.7 / 9.7	*chorus*
13	Fr.	☌☿♀ • Cranberries in bud now. • **Saints** • Tides { 10.1 / 9.4	*for*
14	Sa.	34 cavalry camels disembarked at Indianola, Tex., 1856 • { 9.6 / 9.3	*us.*
15	**B**	**Whit. S.** • **Pentecost** • ☾ at ☊ • ☌♃☾	*Showers*
16	M.	☾ on Eq. • U.S. Congress gave authorization to mint the nickel, 1866 • Tides { 9.2 / 9.4	*fill*
17	Tu.	Joliet-Marquette Mississippi River expedition began, 1673	*each*
18	W.	Ember Day • ☾ at apo. • Deadly eruption, Mount St. Helens, Wash., 1980 • { 9.2 / 9.8	*rill*
19	Th.	**St. Dunstan** • *For what thou canst do thyself, rely not on another.* • Tides { 9.2 / 10.0	*with*
20	Fr.	Ember Day • *The Saturday Evening Post* published its first cover with Norman Rockwell painting, 1916	*liquid*
21	Sa.	Ember Day • **Vesak** • **Full Flower** ○ • ☌♂☾ • ☿ stat. • { 9.4 / —	*trill,*
22	**B**	**Trinity** • ☌♄☾ • ♂ at ☍ • Wrights' "Flying Machine" patented, 1906	*echoed*
23	M.	**Victoria Day (Canada)** • North-West Mounted Police authorized (now Royal Canadian Mounted Police), 1873	*back*
24	Tu.	☾ runs low • 6- to 8-inch-deep hail, near Ada, Okla., 1940 • Tides { 10.3 / 9.3	*from*
25	W.	**St. Bede** • ☌♇☾ • Andrew Moyer patented method for mass production of penicillin, 1948 • { 10.3 / 9.3	*hill*
26	Th.	Radio and television personality Art Linkletter died, 2010 • { 10.2 / 9.3	*to*
27	Fr.	German battleship *Bismarck* sunk, WWII, 1941 • Tides { 10.1 / 9.3	*hill*
28	Sa.	French West India Company secured royal grant of all French colonies in America, 1664 • { 10.1 / 9.5	*by every*
29	**B**	**Corpus Christi** • ☌♆☾ • Hockey player Luc Bourdon died, 2008 • { 10.0 / 9.8	*lark*
30	M.	**Memorial Day** • ☾ at ☋ • *Mariner 9* launched, Cape Kennedy, Fla., 1971 • { 10.0 / 10.2	*and*
31	Tu.	**Visit. of Mary** • ☾ on Eq. • *Such a beginning, such an end.*	*whippoorwill!*

Farmer's Calendar

■ Spring has been late this year. We had January, February, March, more March, and then a weird hybrid I'm calling Maypril. When we got up the morning of the Memorial Day parade, the temperature was 37 degrees and it was raining.

We dressed warmly and drove up to the center of town for the procession, one of my favorite events of the year. The police closed Main Street, a tricky business, as it is the main east-west highway in southern New Hampshire, and the whole town marched up to the cemetery, following the veterans, the middle school band, and a gaggle of Cub Scouts, Brownies, and Little Leaguers.

The cemetery looks west across our lake, which was flecked with whitecaps in a stiff breeze. As we assembled among the stones, some going back to Revolutionary times, the drivers waiting for us were released, and they roared by. Between the traffic and the wind, hardly a word of the minister's patriotic speech was audible.

Then the police closed the road again, and we retreated into town for the national anthem and the raising of the flag back to full-staff. All in all, it was a miserable way to spend a morning, but compared to what many of the men with flags on their graves suffered, we could hardly complain.

SKY WATCH ☆ *A fabulous planet month! Saturn, in Ophiuchus, attains opposition on the 3rd. Its icy reflective rings, tilted wide "open," are stunning through telescopes and give Saturn its brightest appearance in more than a decade. On the 6th, Venus reaches its invisible superior conjunction. Its alignment with the Sun and Earth is so perfect that it is actually occulted by the Sun. Mars, still brilliant, retrogrades into Libra; like Saturn, it remains out all night long. Jupiter beats them both in brightness and doesn't set until after midnight. The Moon hovers to the left of Jupiter on the 11th and sits above Saturn on the 18th. Summer begins with the solstice on the 20th, at 6:34 P.M.*

● **New Moon**	4th day	23rd hour	0 minute
◑ **First Quarter**	12th day	4th hour	10th minute
○ **Full Moon**	20th day	7th hour	3rd minute
◐ **Last Quarter**	27th day	14th hour	19th minute

All times are given in Eastern Daylight Time.

Get these pages with times set to your zip code at Almanac.com/Access.

Day of Year	Day of Month	Day of Week	☼ Rises h. m.	Rise Key	☼ Sets h. m.	Set Key	Length of Day h. m.	Sun Fast m.	Declination of Sun ° '	High Tide Times Boston		☾ Rises h. m.	Rise Key	☾ Sets h. m.	Set Key	☾ Astron. Place	☾ Age
153	1	W.	5:10	A	8:15	E	15 05	18	22 N.10	8¼	8¾	2:56	C	4:07	E	PSC	26
154	2	Th.	5:09	A	8:16	E	15 07	18	22 17	9¼	9¾	3:34	C	5:20	E	PSC	27
155	3	Fr.	5:09	A	8:16	E	15 07	17	22 25	10¼	10½	4:15	C	6:32	E	ARI	28
156	4	Sa.	5:08	A	8:17	E	15 09	17	22 31	11¼	11½	5:01	B	7:42	E	TAU	0
157	5	B	5:08	A	8:18	E	15 10	17	22 38	12	—	5:53	B	8:47	E	TAU	1
158	6	M.	5:08	A	8:18	E	15 10	17	22 44	12¼	1	6:50	B	9:45	E	ORI	2
159	7	Tu.	5:08	A	8:19	E	15 11	17	22 50	1¼	1¾	7:51	B	10:35	E	GEM	3
160	8	W.	5:07	A	8:20	E	15 13	16	22 55	2	2¾	8:54	C	11:18	E	CAN	4
161	9	Th.	5:07	A	8:20	E	15 13	16	23 00	3	3½	9:57	C	11:56	E	CAN	5
162	10	Fr.	5:07	A	8:21	E	15 14	16	23 04	3¾	4½	10:59	C	—	-	LEO	6
163	11	Sa.	5:07	A	8:21	E	15 14	16	23 08	4¾	5¼	11:59	D	12:29	D	LEO	7
164	12	B	5:07	A	8:22	E	15 15	16	23 12	5½	6¼	12:58	D	12:59	D	LEO	8
165	13	M.	5:07	A	8:22	E	15 15	15	23 15	6½	7	1:55	D	1:28	D	VIR	9
166	14	Tu.	5:07	A	8:23	E	15 16	15	23 18	7½	8	2:52	D	1:56	C	VIR	10
167	15	W.	5:07	A	8:23	E	15 16	15	23 20	8½	8¾	3:49	E	2:24	C	VIR	11
168	16	Th.	5:07	A	8:23	E	15 16	15	23 22	9¼	9½	4:46	E	2:54	C	LIB	12
169	17	Fr.	5:07	A	8:24	E	15 17	15	23 23	10	10¼	5:42	E	3:27	B	LIB	13
170	18	Sa.	5:07	A	8:24	E	15 17	14	23 25	10¾	11	6:38	E	4:03	B	SCO	14
171	19	B	5:07	A	8:24	E	15 17	14	23 25	11½	11½	7:33	E	4:44	B	OPH	15
172	20	M.	5:07	A	8:25	E	15 18	14	23 26	12¼	—	8:25	E	5:30	B	SAG	16
173	21	Tu.	5:07	A	8:25	E	15 18	14	23 25	12¼	1	9:13	E	6:22	B	SAG	17
174	22	W.	5:08	A	8:25	E	15 17	14	23 25	1	1½	9:58	E	7:19	B	SAG	18
175	23	Th.	5:08	A	8:25	E	15 17	13	23 24	1¾	2¼	10:38	E	8:19	C	CAP	19
176	24	Fr.	5:08	A	8:25	E	15 17	13	23 23	2½	3	11:15	D	9:23	C	AQU	20
177	25	Sa.	5:09	A	8:25	E	15 16	13	23 21	3¼	3¾	11:50	D	10:28	C	AQU	21
178	26	B	5:09	A	8:25	E	15 16	13	23 19	4	4¾	—	-	11:35	D	AQU	22
179	27	M.	5:09	A	8:25	E	15 16	12	23 16	5	5½	12:24	D	12:44	D	PSC	23
180	28	Tu.	5:10	A	8:25	E	15 15	12	23 13	6	6½	12:58	C	1:53	E	PSC	24
181	29	W.	5:10	A	8:25	E	15 15	12	23 10	7	7½	1:33	C	3:03	E	PSC	25
182	30	Th.	5:11	A	8:25	E	15 14	12	23 N.06	8	8¼	2:11	C	4:14	E	ARI	26

JUNE HATH 30 DAYS • 2016

Then flash the wings returning summer calls
Through the deep arches of her forest halls. –Oliver Wendell Holmes

Day of Month	Day of Week	Dates, Feasts, Fasts, Aspects, Tide Heights	Weather
1	W.	☌♅☾ • Lake appeared this month in Salton Sink, Colorado Desert, Calif., 1891 • Tides {10.2 11.1	*Stay*
2	Th.	*Surveyor I* made first U.S. soft landing on Moon, 1966	*inside.*
3	Fr.	☾ AT PERIG. • ☌☿☾ • ♄ AT ☍ • Sally Jane Priesand ordained as rabbi, 1972	*Here*
4	Sa.	**New ●** • ☌♀☾ • Britain's King George III born, 1738 • Tides {10.8 12.2	*comes*
5	**B**	**3rd S. af. P.** • **Ramadan begins at sundown** • ☿ GR. ELONG. (24° WEST)	*the*
6	M.	D-Day, 1944 • ☾ RIDES HIGH • ♀ IN SUP. ☌ • Tides {12.2 10.8	*bride!*
7	Tu.	*Words are like eggs: When they are hatched, they have wings.* • Tides {12.0 10.6	*Thunder*
8	W.	Deadly tornado struck Baton Rouge, La., 1989 • {11.6 10.3	*clears*
9	Th.	**Orthodox Ascension** • Secretariat won Triple Crown, 1973 • Tides {11.1 10.0	*the*
10	Fr.	Canada Constitution Act passed, creating Upper and Lower Canada, 1791 • {10.5 9.8	*bleachers,*
11	Sa.	**St. Barnabas** • **Shavuot begins at sundown** • ☾ AT ☊ • ☌♃☾	*drowns out*
12	**B**	**4th S. af. P.** • Director Irwin Allen born, 1916 • {9.5 9.4	*graduation*
13	M.	☾ ON EQ. • Theologian Martin Luther wed Katharina von Bora, 1525 • {9.1 9.3	*speechers.*
14	Tu.	**St. Basil** • ♆ STAT. • *June damp and warm Does the farmer no harm.*	*Thrilling!*
15	W.	☾ AT APO. • Ark. admitted as 25th U.S. state, 1836 • {8.8 9.5	*Great*
16	Th.	Andrew Jackson Jr. issued patent for eye protectors for chickens, 1903 • Tides {8.8 9.7	*for*
17	Fr.	☌♂☾ • First U.S. mobile telephone commercial service inaugurated, St. Louis, Mo., 1946 • {8.8 9.9	*roto-*
18	Sa.	☌♄☾ • 3.47" rain in 1 hour, Atlanta, Ga., 1991 • {9.0 10.1	*tilling,*
19	**B**	**5th S. af. P.** • **Orthodox Pentecost** • **Father's Day**	*potato-*
20	M.	**Summer Solstice** • **Full Strawberry** ○ • ☾ RUNS LOW • Tides {9.2 —	*hilling,*
21	Tu.	☌♇☾ • *The beautiful is less what one sees than what one dreams.* • Tides {10.5 9.3	*and*
22	W.	**St. Alban** • 102°F, Vero Beach, Fla., 2009 • {10.6 9.5	*switchel-*
23	Th.	50-lb. 4-oz. red snapper caught, Gulf of Mexico, near La., 1996 • Tides {10.6 9.6	*swilling!*
24	Fr.	**Nativ. John the Baptist** • **Midsummer Day** • Painter Ferdinand Bol born, 1616	*Darkening*
25	Sa.	☌♆☾ • "Custer's Last Stand," Little Bighorn River, Mont., 1876 • Tides {10.5 9.9	*skies:*
26	**B**	**6th S. af. P.** • **Orthodox All Saints'** • ☾ AT ☋ • {10.4 10.1	*time*
27	M.	☾ ON EQ. • *The horse that you love draws more than four oxen.* • Tides {10.2 10.3	*for*
28	Tu.	**St. Irenaeus** • ☌♅☾ • Runner Terry Fox died, 1981 • {10.1 10.6	*strawberry-*
29	W.	**Sts. Peter & Paul** • San Francisco founded, 1776 • {9.9 10.9	*rhubarb*
30	Th.	♂ STAT. • London's Tower Bridge opened, 1894 • {9.9 11.2	*pies!*

We are all of us stars, and we deserve to twinkle. –Marilyn Monroe

Farmer's Calendar

■ All month, a bird in our woods has been driving me crazy. I call it the heeby-jeeby bird, because that's what its call sounds like to me: "heeby-jeeby, heeby-jeeby," or sometimes "heeby-jeeby-jeeby." I haven't seen it, so I can't look it up in bird books. Googling "bird that says 'heeby-jeeby'" wasn't helpful.

We had to drive to Connecticut for a commencement, so we decided to try listening to a CD of bird calls—perhaps we would hear it there. We hadn't counted on the dogs, who lounged in the back cargo area.

When they heard the recorded Canada geese, they stiffened. They know all about Canada geese, having chased and been chased by them. They started to thrash around, checking all the windows. Where were those geese? The recording moved on to the Wood Duck, the Gambel's Quail, the Greater Yellowlegs, none of which are familiar sounds around our house. False alarm: The dogs relaxed.

Then the Barred Owl started hooting: red alert! Wiggles spun in mad circles, scanning 360 degrees. Echo barked, she bayed, she squealed in excitement; she did her level best to hoot back. Fearing that some dog would crash through a window, we finally had to turn off the CD player.

We never did hear the heeby-jeeby bird.

C
A
L
E
N
D
A
R

SKY WATCH ☆ *Earth reaches aphelion, its annual point farthest from the Sun, on the 4th. Pluto comes nearest on the 5th, with an opposition on the 7th. However, each Pluto opposition is noticeably farther away than the previous year's, thanks to its highly elliptical orbit. After its 1989 closest approach, Pluto is decisively moving away, an exit that will continue until the 22nd century. Jupiter is now getting lower in the west at nightfall; its annual observation window is nearing its end. The waxing Moon passes above Mars on the 14th and above Saturn on the 15th; all are nearly due south at nightfall. Saturn is still amazing through backyard telescopes, while Mars is now rapidly shrinking.*

●	**New Moon**	4th day	7th hour	1st minute
◐	**First Quarter**	11th day	20th hour	52nd minute
○	**Full Moon**	19th day	18th hour	57th minute
◑	**Last Quarter**	26th day	19th hour	0 minute

All times are given in Eastern Daylight Time.

Get these pages with times set to your zip code at Almanac.com/Access.

Day of Year	Day of Month	Day of Week	☀ Rises h. m.	Rise Key	☀ Sets h. m.	Set Key	Length of Day h. m.	Sun Fast m.	Declination of Sun ° '	High Tide Times Boston		☾ Rises h. m.	Rise Key	☾ Sets h. m.	Set Key	☾ Astron. Place	☾ Age
183	1	Fr.	5:11	A	8:25	E	15 14	12	23 N. 02	9	9¼	2:53	B	5:23	E	TAU	27
184	2	Sa.	5:12	A	8:25	E	15 13	12	22 57	10	10¼	3:41	B	6:29	E	TAU	28
185	3	**B**	5:12	A	8:24	E	15 12	11	22 52	11	11¼	4:34	B	7:30	E	TAU	29
186	4	M.	5:13	A	8:24	E	15 11	11	22 47	11¾	—	5:33	B	8:24	E	GEM	0
187	5	Tu.	5:14	A	8:24	E	15 10	11	22 41	12	12¾	6:35	C	9:11	E	GEM	1
188	6	W.	5:14	A	8:23	E	15 09	11	22 35	12¾	1½	7:39	C	9:52	E	CAN	2
189	7	Th.	5:15	A	8:23	E	15 08	11	22 28	1¾	2¼	8:43	C	10:28	E	LEO	3
190	8	Fr.	5:16	A	8:23	E	15 07	11	22 21	2½	3	9:45	C	11:00	D	LEO	4
191	9	Sa.	5:16	A	8:22	E	15 06	10	22 14	3¼	4	10:45	D	11:29	D	LEO	5
192	10	**B**	5:17	A	8:22	E	15 05	10	22 06	4¼	4¾	11:44	D	11:58	C	VIR	6
193	11	M.	5:18	A	8:21	E	15 03	10	21 58	5	5½	12:41	D	—	–	VIR	7
194	12	Tu.	5:19	A	8:21	E	15 02	10	21 49	5¾	6¼	1:39	E	12:26	C	VIR	8
195	13	W.	5:19	A	8:20	E	15 01	10	21 41	6¾	7¼	2:35	E	12:56	C	VIR	9
196	14	Th.	5:20	A	8:20	E	15 00	10	21 31	7¾	8	3:32	E	1:27	B	LIB	10
197	15	Fr.	5:21	A	8:19	E	14 58	10	21 22	8½	8¾	4:28	E	2:02	B	LIB	11
198	16	Sa.	5:22	A	8:18	E	14 56	10	21 12	9½	9½	5:24	E	2:40	B	OPH	12
199	17	**B**	5:23	A	8:17	E	14 54	10	21 01	10¼	10½	6:17	E	3:24	B	OPH	13
200	18	M.	5:24	A	8:17	E	14 53	9	20 51	11	11	7:07	E	4:14	B	SAG	14
201	19	Tu.	5:25	A	8:16	E	14 51	9	20 40	11¾	11¾	7:54	E	5:09	B	SAG	15
202	20	W.	5:25	A	8:15	E	14 50	9	20 28	12½	—	8:37	E	6:09	C	CAP	16
203	21	Th.	5:26	A	8:14	E	14 48	9	20 17	12½	1¼	9:16	E	7:13	C	AQU	17
204	22	Fr.	5:27	A	8:13	E	14 46	9	20 04	1¼	1¾	9:53	D	8:19	C	AQU	18
205	23	Sa.	5:28	A	8:13	E	14 45	9	19 52	2	2½	10:27	D	9:27	D	AQU	19
206	24	**B**	5:29	A	8:12	E	14 43	9	19 39	2¾	3½	11:01	C	10:35	D	PSC	20
207	25	M.	5:30	B	8:11	E	14 41	9	19 26	3¾	4¼	11:36	C	11:44	D	CET	21
208	26	Tu.	5:31	B	8:10	E	14 39	9	19 13	4½	5	—	–	12:54	E	PSC	22
209	27	W.	5:32	B	8:09	E	14 37	9	18 59	5½	6	12:12	C	2:03	E	CET	23
210	28	Th.	5:33	B	8:08	E	14 35	9	18 45	6½	7	12:52	B	3:11	E	TAU	24
211	29	Fr.	5:34	B	8:07	E	14 33	9	18 31	7¾	8	1:36	B	4:17	E	TAU	25
212	30	Sa.	5:35	B	8:05	E	14 30	9	18 16	8¾	9	2:26	B	5:19	E	TAU	26
213	31	**B**	5:36	B	8:04	E	14 28	9	18 N. 01	9¾	10	3:21	B	6:14	E	GEM	27

Today the sun has steadfast been and clear.
No wind has marred the spell of hushful heat. –Philip Bourke Marston

Day of Month	Day of Week	Dates, Feasts, Fasts, Aspects, Tide Heights	Weather
1	Fr.	**Canada Day** • ☾ AT PERIG. • Cosmetics executive Estée Lauder born, 1908	*Reenact*
2	Sa.	Astrologer Nostradamus died, 1566 • Tides {10.1 / 11.7	*our*
3	**B**	**7th ☉. af. ℗.** • Dog days begin. • ☾ RIDES HIGH • Tides {10.2 / 11.8	*nation's*
4	M.	**Independence Day** • New ● • ☌♂☾ • ☌♂☽ • ⊕ AT APHELION	*battles.*
5	Tu.	Tennis pro Arthur Ashe won Wimbledon championship, 1975 • Tides {11.8 / 10.4	*Lightning*
6	W.	☿ IN SUP. ☌ Armadillos mate now. • Pirate Captain William Kidd seized, Boston, 1699	*flashes,*
7	Th.	♇ AT ☍ • Roosevelt Campobello International Park created, N.B., 1964 • {11.3 / 10.2	*thunder*
8	Fr.	☾ AT ☍ • First public reading of Declaration of Independence, Phila., Pa., 1776 • {10.8 / 10.0	*rattles.*
9	Sa.	☌♃☾ • 43°F, Williamstown, Mass., 1816 • Tides {10.3 / 9.8	*Too*
10	**B**	**8th ☉. af. ℗.** • ☾ ON EQ. • Cornscateous air is everywhere. • Tides {9.8 / 9.6	*cool*
11	M.	Wilfrid Laurier became Canadian prime minister, 1896 • Tides {9.3 / 9.4	*for*
12	Tu.	*Better bend the neck than bruise the forehead.* • Tides {8.9 / 9.3	*the*
13	W.	☾ AT APO. • First official cat show, Crystal Palace, London, 1871 • Tides {8.6 / 9.3	*pool;*
14	Th.	**Bastille Day** • ☌♂☾ • 113°F, Sac City, Iowa, 1936 • {8.5 / 9.4	*take*
15	Fr.	**St. Swithin** • Giant panda Lun Lun gave birth to twins, Zoo Atlanta, Ga., 2013 • Tides {8.5 / 9.6	*a*
16	Sa.	☌♂♀ • ☌♄☾ • 15–16: 22.22" rain in 24 hours, Altapass, N.C., 1916 • {8.6 / 9.8	*hike,*
17	**B**	**9th ☉. af. ℗.** • ☾ RUNS LOW • Spain transferred Fla. to U.S., 1821 • {8.8 / 10.1	*ride*
18	M.	☌♇☾ • 102°F, Fort Smith, N.W.T., 1941 • Tides {9.0 / 10.4	*a*
19	Tu.	**Full Buck** ○ • Surgeon Charles Horace Mayo born, 1865 • Tides {9.3 / 10.6	*bike!*
20	W.	Religious leader Anne Hutchinson baptized, 1591 • {9.6 / —	*Nights*
21	Th.	Black-eyed Susans in bloom now. • Tides {10.8 / 9.8	*are*
22	Fr.	**St. Mary Magdalene** • *A merry companion is music in a journey.* • {11.0 / 10.1	*dramatic,*
23	Sa.	☾ AT ☍ • ☌♅☾ • 8"-diameter, 1-lb. 15-oz. hailstone fell, Vivian, S.Dak., 2010	*operatic,*
24	**B**	**10th ☉. af. ℗.** • ☾ ON EQ. • Adult gypsy moths emerge.	*passionate*
25	M.	**St. James** • Walter Hunt granted patent for paper shirt collar, 1854 • Tides {10.6 / 10.6	*as*
26	Tu.	**St. Anne** • ☌♂☽ • Playwright George Bernard Shaw born, 1856 • {10.3 / 10.7	*Rossini!*
27	W.	☾ AT PERIG. • Grasshopper swarms ruined crops in Midwest this month, 1931 • Tides {10.0 / 10.8	*Stay*
28	Th.	Metric system became legal in U.S., 1866 • Tides {9.7 / 10.9	*ahead*
29	Fr.	**St. Martha** • ☿ STAT. • Britain's Prince Charles wed Lady Diana Spencer, 1981 • {9.6 / 10.9	*of*
30	Sa.	*When caught by the tempest, wherever it be, If it lightens and thunders, beware of a tree!* • Tides {9.6 / 11.1	*the*
31	**B**	**11th ☉. af. ℗.** • ☾ RIDES HIGH • Actor Dean Cain born, 1966	*zucchini!*

Farmer's Calendar

■ I can remember how much fun we had as children making up games once school was out. When adult intervention came along, in the form of Little League, I tried out and it was a complete disaster. It nearly destroyed my love of baseball. I was cut the first day. These days, nobody ever gets cut. I'm not sure which is worse.

Before Little League, we played a wonderfully democratic form of baseball we called work-up. There were only four players at bat, and everyone else played in the field. Whenever one of the batters made an out, he or she went out to play right field, and everyone else worked up (hence the name) one position: The right fielder moved to center, center fielder to left, left fielder to third base, third to shortstop, shortstop to second base, second to first base, first to pitcher, pitcher to catcher, and the catcher became a batter.

Work-up embodied economy, good sense, and fairness. You didn't need 18 players, and everyone got to play every position. Everyone batted at least once and, once you joined the batters, you never had long to wait before it was your turn to hit. There were no innings, and nobody kept score, because there were no teams. Everyone was just playing together. I wonder if anyone still plays work-up.

CALENDAR

C
A
L
E
N
D
A
R

SKY WATCH ☆ *Venus is now technically an evening star. With an unobstructed horizon, it can first be glimpsed in the western twilight on the 4th, 35 minutes after sunset. Look for the thin crescent Moon just to the left of Mercury, with Venus far to its lower right and Jupiter higher and to the left of them all. The Moon stands above fading Mars on the 11th. It sets by 1:00 A.M. to provide dark skies for the Perseid meteor shower, which peaks in the hours before dawn. This should be one of the better years for this most popular display of shooting stars. From the 19th to the 24th, Jupiter, Venus, and Mercury form a triangle very low in the western sky after sunset. Venus and Jupiter are extremely close together on the 27th.*

●	**New Moon**	2nd day	16th hour	45th minute
☽	**First Quarter**	10th day	14th hour	22nd minute
○	**Full Moon**	18th day	5th hour	27th minute
☾	**Last Quarter**	24th day	23rd hour	41st minute

All times are given in Eastern Daylight Time.

Get these pages with times set to your zip code at Almanac.com/Access.

Day of Year	Day of Month	Day of Week	Rises h. m.	Rise Key	Sets h. m.	Set Key	Length of Day h. m.	Sun Fast m.	Declination of Sun ° '	High Tide Times Boston		Rises h. m.	Rise Key	Sets h. m.	Set Key	Astron. Place	Age
214	1	M.	5:37	B	8:03	E	14 26	10	17 N.46	10¾	11	4:21	B	7:04	E	GEM	28
215	2	Tu.	5:38	B	8:02	E	14 24	10	17 31	11½	11¾	5:23	C	7:47	E	CAN	0
216	3	W.	5:39	B	8:01	E	14 22	10	17 15	12½	—	6:26	C	8:25	E	CAN	1
217	4	Th.	5:40	B	8:00	E	14 20	10	16 59	12½	1¼	7:29	C	8:59	D	LEO	2
218	5	Fr.	5:41	B	7:58	E	14 17	10	16 42	1¼	1¾	8:31	D	9:30	D	LEO	3
219	6	Sa.	5:42	B	7:57	E	14 15	10	16 26	2	2½	9:31	D	9:59	D	VIR	4
220	7	**B**	5:43	B	7:56	E	14 13	10	16 09	2¾	3¼	10:29	D	10:28	C	VIR	5
221	8	M.	5:44	B	7:54	E	14 10	10	15 52	3½	4	11:27	D	10:57	C	VIR	6
222	9	Tu.	5:45	B	7:53	E	14 08	10	15 34	4¼	4¾	12:24	E	11:27	C	VIR	7
223	10	W.	5:47	B	7:52	E	14 05	11	15 17	5¼	5½	1:21	E	—	C	LIB	8
224	11	Th.	5:48	B	7:50	E	14 02	11	14 59	6	6½	2:17	E	12:00	–	LIB	9
225	12	Fr.	5:49	B	7:49	D	14 00	11	14 41	7	7¼	3:12	E	12:37	B	SCO	10
226	13	Sa.	5:50	B	7:47	D	13 57	11	14 22	8	8¼	4:06	E	1:18	B	OPH	11
227	14	**B**	5:51	B	7:46	D	13 55	11	14 04	8¾	9	4:57	E	2:04	B	SAG	12
228	15	M.	5:52	B	7:45	D	13 53	11	13 45	9¾	9¾	5:46	E	2:56	B	SAG	13
229	16	Tu.	5:53	B	7:43	D	13 50	12	13 26	10½	10½	6:31	E	3:54	B	SAG	14
230	17	W.	5:54	B	7:42	D	13 48	12	13 07	11¼	11½	7:12	E	4:57	C	CAP	15
231	18	Th.	5:55	B	7:40	D	13 45	12	12 47	12	—	7:51	E	6:04	C	CAP	16
232	19	Fr.	5:56	B	7:38	D	13 42	12	12 27	12¼	12¾	8:27	D	7:12	D	AQU	17
233	20	Sa.	5:57	B	7:37	D	13 40	13	12 08	1	1½	9:02	D	8:23	D	AQU	18
234	21	**B**	5:58	B	7:35	D	13 37	13	11 48	1¾	2¼	9:37	C	9:33	D	CET	19
235	22	M.	5:59	B	7:34	D	13 35	13	11 27	2½	3	10:14	C	10:44	E	PSC	20
236	23	Tu.	6:00	B	7:32	D	13 32	13	11 07	3½	3¾	10:53	C	11:54	E	CET	21
237	24	W.	6:01	B	7:31	D	13 30	14	10 46	4¼	4¾	11:36	B	1:03	E	ARI	22
238	25	Th.	6:02	B	7:29	D	13 27	14	10 26	5¼	5¾	—	–	2:10	E	TAU	23
239	26	Fr.	6:03	B	7:27	D	13 24	14	10 05	6½	6¾	12:23	B	3:12	E	TAU	24
240	27	Sa.	6:05	B	7:26	D	13 21	15	9 44	7½	7¾	1:15	B	4:09	E	ORI	25
241	28	**B**	6:06	B	7:24	D	13 18	15	9 22	8½	8¾	2:12	B	4:59	E	GEM	26
242	29	M.	6:07	B	7:22	D	13 15	15	9 01	9½	9¾	3:12	C	5:44	E	CAN	27
243	30	Tu.	6:08	B	7:21	D	13 13	15	8 39	10½	10¾	4:14	C	6:23	E	CAN	28
244	31	W.	6:09	B	7:19	D	13 10	16	8 N.18	11¼	11½	5:17	C	6:58	D	LEO	29

AUGUST HATH 31 DAYS • 2016

Against the windows the storm comes dashing,
Through tattered foliage, the hail tears crashing. –James R. Lowell

Day of Month	Day of Week	Dates, Feasts, Fasts, Aspects, Tide Heights	Weather
1	M.	Lammas Day • *If the first week in August is unusually warm, the winter will be white and long.*	Thunder
2	Tu.	New ● • Cookies baked on vehicle's dashboard during heat wave, Bedford, N.H., 2006	muttering,
3	W.	Calvin Coolidge sworn in as U.S. president at 2:47 A.M. by father at Vermont homestead, 1923 • {10.1 / —	ideal
4	Th.	☌☿☾ • ☌♀☾ • Canada entered WWI, 1914 • {11.1 / 10.1	for
5	Fr.	☾ AT ☊ • ☌♃☾ • Astronaut Neil Armstrong born, 1930 • {10.9 / 10.1	basement
6	Sa.	**Transfiguration** • ☾ ON EQ. • G. Ederle swam Eng. Channel in 14 hrs., 31 min., 1926	puttering.
7	**B**	**12th S. af. P.** • Gray squirrels have second litters now. • {10.1 / 9.8	Roasting:
8	M.	**St. Dominic** • Explorer Matthew Henson born, 1866 • Tides {9.7 / 9.6	How
9	Tu.	☾ AT APO. • Deadly tornado, Wallingford, Conn., 1878	about
10	W.	**St. Lawrence** • *The horse thinks one thing and he that rides him another.* • {8.8 / 9.3	hosting a
11	Th.	**St. Clare** • Dog Days end. • ☌♂☾ • Tides {8.5 / 9.2	Perseids
12	Fr.	☌♄☾ • Isaac Singer received patent for continuous-stitch sewing machine, 1851	party,
13	Sa.	♄ STAT. • 3-yr.-old Jamie Gavin became youngest heart/lung transplant patient, 1985 • {8.3 / 9.4	smarty?
14	**B**	**13th S. af. P.** • ☾ RUNS LOW • FDR and Churchill signed Atlantic Charter, 1941	Electric
15	M.	**Assumption** • ☌♇☾ • French emperor Napoleon Bonaparte born, 1769 • {8.8 / 10.1	nights,
16	Tu.	☿ GR. ELONG. (27° EAST) • From 102,800', Joe Kittinger free-fell 4 min., 36 sec., N.Mex., 1960 • {9.2 / 10.5	then
17	W.	Cat Nights commence. • Frontiersman Davy Crockett born, 1786	not as
18	Th.	**Full Sturgeon** ○ • Ringo Starr joined The Beatles, 1962 • Tides {10.1 / —	warm—
19	Fr.	☌♆☾ • ☾ AT ☋ • "Bronze Fonz" statue unveiled, Milwaukee, Wis., 2008	watch
20	Sa.	☾ ON EQ. • Astronomer Sir Fred Hoyle died, 2001 • {11.3 / 10.8	out!
21	**B**	**14th S. af. P.** • ☾ AT PERIG. • Ragweed in bloom. • {11.3 / 11.1	Tropical
22	M.	☌♅☾ • Damaging frosts, New England to N.C., 1816 • Tides {11.1 / 11.2	storm!
23	Tu.	U.S. *Lunar Orbiter 1* took famed first photo of Earth from Moon's orbit, 1966 • {10.8 / 11.1	Delicious:
24	W.	**St. Bartholomew** • Quebec premier René Lévesque born, 1922 • Tides {10.4 / 11.0	just
25	Th.	☌♂♄ • U.S. National Park Service established, 1916 • Tides {9.9 / 10.8	right
26	Fr.	Hummingbirds migrate south. • Famed Krakatoa eruption began, Indonesia, 1883	for
27	Sa.	☾ RIDES HIGH • ☌☿♀ • ☌♀♃ • Tides {9.4 / 10.6	fooling
28	**B**	**15th S. af. P.** • John Herbert Chapman, father of Canadian Space Agency, born, 1921	fishes.
29	M.	**St. John the Baptist** • ☿ STAT. • Painter Frans Hals died, 1666	Showers
30	Tu.	Hotline between White House and Kremlin installed, 1963 • Tides {9.8 / 10.8	soften,
31	W.	*Arrogance is the obstruction of wisdom.* • Tides {10.0 / 10.7	often.

Farmer's Calendar

■ The fungus appeared suddenly in early August: shelf-like fruiting structures on an enormous dead ash tree that marked the boundary between our property and that of our neighbor to the south.

They seemed to appear overnight. One morning I looked out my kitchen window, and there they were. So I made a cup of coffee and walked into the woods to investigate. The color of the fungus was extraordinary: It glowed like hot coals. At first glance, it looked artificial, like a pile of discarded orange traffic cones. But how would they have gotten into our woods?

The bizarre organisms clustered thickly around the base of the tree and climbed its trunk, sprouting in the crotches of limbs 20 feet high. They looked like invaders from outer space in a 1950s horror film.

A little research revealed them to be *Laetiporus sulphureus*. It forms in late summer and weakens the tree so much that experts recommend taking it down immediately before it endangers people or structures. Indeed, broken limbs surrounded the trunk.

We won't miss the tree, and it's too far from our house to be a threat. What seemed most strange was how fast it all happened. This was not the decline and fall of the Roman Empire; it was breaking news.

SKY WATCH ☆ *Neptune comes closest to Earth on the 1st, with an opposition on the 2nd in Aquarius. A small telescope reveals its blue disk and its strange, backward-orbiting satellite, Triton. The Moon is to the upper left of Venus on the 3rd, above Saturn on the 8th, and to the upper left of Mars on the 9th, before passing to the left of Neptune on the 15th. Mars, still bright at magnitude –0.2, is increasing its eastward speed passing through Ophiuchus. The 22nd brings the equinox and autumn at 10:21 A.M. Look for Mercury's best morning star appearance from the 24th to the 30th. On the 29th, Mercury hovers above the crescent Moon.*

●	**New Moon**	1st day	5th hour	4th minute
◐	**First Quarter**	9th day	7th hour	50th minute
○	**Full Moon**	16th day	15th hour	5th minute
◑	**Last Quarter**	23rd day	5th hour	56th minute
●	**New Moon**	30th day	20th hour	12th minute

All times are given in Eastern Daylight Time.

Get these pages with times set to your zip code at Almanac.com/Access.

Day of Year	Day of Month	Day of Week	☼ Rises h. m.	Rise Key	☼ Sets h. m.	Set Key	Length of Day h. m.	Sun Fast m.	Declination of Sun °	'	High Tide Times Boston		☾ Rises h. m.	Rise Key	☾ Sets h. m.	Set Key	☾ Astron. Place	☾ Age
245	1	Th.	6:10	B	**7:17**	D	13 07	16	7	N. 56	**12**	—	6:18	C	**7:30**	D	LEO	0
246	2	Fr.	6:11	B	**7:16**	D	13 05	16	7	34	$12\frac{1}{4}$	**$12\frac{3}{4}$**	7:19	D	**8:00**	D	LEO	1
247	3	Sa.	6:12	B	**7:14**	D	13 02	17	7	12	1	**$1\frac{1}{4}$**	8:18	D	**8:28**	C	VIR	2
248	4	**B**	6:13	C	**7:12**	D	12 59	17	6	50	$1\frac{3}{4}$	**2**	9:16	D	**8:57**	C	VIR	3
249	5	M.	6:14	C	**7:11**	D	12 57	17	6	27	$2\frac{1}{4}$	**$2\frac{3}{4}$**	10:14	E	**9:27**	C	VIR	4
250	6	Tu.	6:15	C	**7:09**	D	12 54	18	6	05	3	**$3\frac{1}{4}$**	11:10	E	**9:59**	C	LIB	5
251	7	W.	6:16	C	**7:07**	D	12 51	18	5	43	$3\frac{3}{4}$	**4**	**12:06**	E	**10:34**	B	LIB	6
252	8	Th.	6:17	C	**7:05**	D	12 48	18	5	20	$4\frac{1}{2}$	**$4\frac{3}{4}$**	**1:01**	E	**11:12**	B	SCO	7
253	9	Fr.	6:18	C	**7:04**	D	12 46	19	4	57	$5\frac{1}{2}$	**$5\frac{3}{4}$**	**1:55**	E	**11:56**	B	OPH	8
254	10	Sa.	6:19	C	**7:02**	D	12 43	19	4	35	$6\frac{1}{4}$	**$6\frac{1}{2}$**	**2:47**	E	—	–	SAG	9
255	11	**B**	6:20	C	**7:00**	D	12 40	19	4	12	$7\frac{1}{4}$	**$7\frac{1}{2}$**	**3:36**	E	12:44	B	SAG	10
256	12	M.	6:21	C	**6:58**	D	12 37	20	3	49	$8\frac{1}{4}$	**$8\frac{1}{2}$**	**4:22**	E	1:39	B	SAG	11
257	13	Tu.	6:22	C	**6:57**	C	12 35	20	3	26	9	**$9\frac{1}{4}$**	**5:05**	E	2:39	C	CAP	12
258	14	W.	6:23	C	**6:55**	C	12 32	20	3	03	$9\frac{3}{4}$	**10**	**5:44**	E	3:43	C	AQU	13
259	15	Th.	6:25	C	**6:53**	C	12 28	21	2	40	$10\frac{3}{4}$	**11**	**6:22**	D	4:51	C	AQU	14
260	16	Fr.	6:26	C	**6:51**	C	12 25	21	2	17	$11\frac{1}{2}$	**$11\frac{3}{4}$**	**6:58**	D	6:02	D	AQU	15
261	17	Sa.	6:27	C	**6:49**	C	12 22	22	1	53	**$12\frac{1}{4}$**	—	**7:34**	C	7:14	D	PSC	16
262	18	**B**	6:28	C	**6:48**	C	12 20	22	1	30	$12\frac{1}{2}$	**1**	**8:11**	C	8:27	E	PSC	17
263	19	M.	6:29	C	**6:46**	C	12 17	22	1	07	$1\frac{1}{2}$	**$1\frac{3}{4}$**	**8:51**	C	9:40	E	PSC	18
264	20	Tu.	6:30	C	**6:44**	C	12 14	23	0	44	$2\frac{1}{4}$	**$2\frac{1}{2}$**	**9:33**	B	10:52	E	ARI	19
265	21	W.	6:31	C	**6:42**	C	12 11	23	0	N. 20	$3\frac{1}{4}$	**$3\frac{1}{2}$**	**10:20**	B	**12:01**	E	TAU	20
266	22	Th.	6:32	C	**6:41**	C	12 09	23	0	S. 02	4	**$4\frac{1}{2}$**	**11:12**	B	**1:06**	E	TAU	21
267	23	Fr.	6:33	C	**6:39**	C	12 06	24	0	25	5	**$5\frac{1}{2}$**	—	–	**2:05**	E	ORI	22
268	24	Sa.	6:34	C	**6:37**	C	12 03	24	0	49	$6\frac{1}{4}$	**$6\frac{1}{2}$**	12:07	B	**2:57**	E	GEM	23
269	25	**B**	6:35	C	**6:35**	C	12 00	24	1	12	$7\frac{1}{4}$	**$7\frac{1}{2}$**	1:06	B	**3:43**	E	GEM	24
270	26	M.	6:36	C	**6:34**	C	11 58	25	1	36	$8\frac{1}{4}$	**$8\frac{3}{4}$**	2:07	C	**4:23**	E	CAN	25
271	27	Tu.	6:37	C	**6:32**	C	11 55	25	1	59	$9\frac{1}{4}$	**$9\frac{1}{2}$**	3:08	C	**4:59**	E	LEO	26
272	28	W.	6:38	C	**6:30**	C	11 52	25	2	22	$10\frac{1}{4}$	**$10\frac{1}{2}$**	4:09	C	**5:31**	D	LEO	27
273	29	Th.	6:40	C	**6:28**	C	11 48	26	2	46	11	**$11\frac{1}{4}$**	5:10	D	**6:01**	D	LEO	28
274	30	Fr.	6:41	C	**6:27**	C	11 46	26	3	S. 09	$11\frac{1}{2}$	12	6:09	D	**6:30**	C	VIR	0

SEPTEMBER HATH 30 DAYS • 2016

And now the autumn season waits,
In mellowing forms of fruitage. –Stephen Henry Thayer

Day of Month	Day of Week	Dates, Feasts, Fasts, Aspects, Tide Heights	Weather
1	Th.	New ● • Eclipse ☉ • ☾ AT ☊ • Tides {10.1 / —	*Fine*
2	Fr.	☌☿☾ • ☌♃☾ • ♆ AT ☍ • Great Fire of London began, 1666 • {10.6 / 10.1	*for*
3	Sa.	☾ ON EQ. • ☌♀☾ • U.S./Great Britain signed Treaty of Paris, 1783 • {10.5 / 10.1	*Popsicles*
4	**B**	**16th S. af. P.** • Tornado, Minneapolis, Minn., 1941 • {10.2 / 10.0	*and*
5	M.	**Labor Day** • *Zeal without knowledge is fire without light.* • {9.9 / 9.9	*snow cones;*
6	Tu.	☾ AT APO. • Scientist John Dalton born, 1766 • {9.5 / 9.7	*beware*
7	W.	Destructive hailstorm, Calgary, Alta., 1991 • Tides {9.1 / 9.5	*of*
8	Th.	☌♄☾ • Original *Star Trek* series debuted on television, 1966 • Tides {8.8 / 9.3	*tropsical*
9	Fr.	☌♂☾ • Harland Sanders, Kentucky Fried Chicken founder, born, 1890 • {8.5 / 9.2	*cyclones!*
10	Sa.	☾ RUNS LOW • Cranberry bog harvest begins, Cape Cod, Mass. • Tides {8.3 / 9.2	*Batten*
11	**B**	**17th S. af. P.** • **Patriot Day** • ☌♇☾ • Tides {8.4 / 9.4	*hatches:*
12	M.	☿ IN INF. ☌ • Astronauts Jan Davis and Mark Lee first married couple to fly on same space mission, 1992	*showery*
13	Tu.	Psychiatrist Adolf Meyer born, 1866 • Tides {9.0 / 10.1	*patches.*
14	W.	**Holy Cross** • Boston Light, first lighthouse in North America, lit, 1716 • {9.5 / 10.6	*Cooler*
15	Th.	☾ AT ☋ • ☌♆☾ • Victoria Cross recipient Alexander Roberts Dunn born, 1833	*and*
16	Fr.	**Full Harvest** ○ • **Eclipse** ☾ • U.S. Great Seal used for for first time, 1782	*drier—*
17	Sa.	☾ ON EQ. • *A fault confessed is half redressed.* • {11.2 / —	*kindle*
18	**B**	**18th S. af. P.** • ☾ AT PERIG. • ☌⛢☾ • Tides {11.5 / 11.6	*an*
19	M.	Frogs' eggs fell from sky, Berlin, Conn., 2003 • {11.5 / 11.8	*evening*
20	Tu.	Elisha Otis sold his first elevator, 1853 • Tides {11.3 / 11.7	*fire.*
21	W.	**St. Matthew** • Ember Day • ☿ STAT. • Tides {10.8 / 11.5	*Orchard*
22	Th.	Harvest Home • **Autumnal Equinox** • *Much fog in autumn, much snow in winter.* • {10.4 / 11.1	*branches*
23	Fr.	Ember Day • ☾ RIDES HIGH • Planet Neptune discovered, 1846 • {9.9 / 10.7	*laden*
24	Sa.	Ember Day • Smoke from forest fires in Alta./B.C. made Sun appear blue/pink/purple, northeastern U.S., 1950	*bend*
25	**B**	**19th S. af. P.** • ♇ STAT. • Quebec premier Félix-Gabriel Marchand died, 1900	*under*
26	M.	☌♃☉ • Woodchucks hibernate now. • Tides {9.4 / 10.2	*the*
27	Tu.	**St. Vincent de Paul** • Rare waterspout seen, Long Island Sound, N.Y., 2006 • {9.6 / 10.2	*plunder*
28	W.	☾ AT ☊ • ☿ GR. ELONG. (18° WEST) • Writer Herman Melville died, 1891 • {9.8 / 10.3	*of*
29	Th.	**St. Michael** • ☌☿☾ • *OSO* 7 solar satellite launched, Cape Kennedy, Fla., 1971	*summer's*
30	Fr.	**St. Gregory the Illuminator** • **New** ● • ☾ ON EQ. • ☌♃☾	*end.*

Let difficulties know that you, too, are difficult. –Dr. Abdul Kalam

Farmer's Calendar

■ When May and I bought our piece of second-growth forest in 1978, we carved out a clearing for our house, a driveway and parking space, and a leach field. Now the forest is creeping back.

The last time the woods closed in, about 15 years ago, we had a notion of clearing a view of the Wapack Range, 10 miles away, and opening a slot that would allow a lance of sunrise to strike our bedroom window on the spring and fall equinoxes. It would be our private Stonehenge.

Then we realized that such a slot would have to be about a quarter-mile long and require constant trimming to be kept open. That sounded like too much work for the sake of feeling like a Druid two mornings a year. So we settled for pushing back the woods to let in more morning light.

Now it's time to do it again. But when? Weekends are already too hectic. My wife, who teaches, is in school for 10 to 14 hours every weekday, and I've promised not to use the chainsaw solo. Instead, I used our big clippers to take down the smallest saplings at ground level and lop off the tops of bigger ones. What's left is a strange spectacle: dozens of 4-foot-high sticks with no branches. It looks more like a modern art installation than Stonehenge. All it needs is a catalog.

C
A
L
E
N
D
A
R

SKY WATCH ☆ *The Moon passes above Venus on the 3rd, to the right of Saturn on the 5th, and above Mars on the 7th and 8th. Mars hits magnitude zero and races into Sagittarius. Mercury remains visible low in the predawn sky for the first 2 weeks of October. It forms a tight conjunction with returning Jupiter on the 11th. The pair of Mercury at magnitude –1 and Jupiter at –1.7 is gorgeous, although very low 40 minutes before sunrise. Uranus reaches opposition in Pisces on the 15th; seeing the Green Planet usually requires binoculars. After midnight early on the 19th, bright Aldebaran is occulted by the Moon, an event visible in the southern and eastern United States.*

◖	**First Quarter**	9th day	0 hour	33rd minute
○	**Full Moon**	16th day	0 hour	24th minute
◗	**Last Quarter**	22nd day	15th hour	14th minute
●	**New Moon**	30th day	13th hour	39th minute

All times are given in Eastern Daylight Time.

Get these pages with times set to your zip code at Almanac.com/Access.

Day of Year	Day of Month	Day of Week	☀ Rises h. m.	Rise Key	☀ Sets h. m.	Set Key	Length of Day h. m.	Sun Fast m.	Declination of Sun ° ′	High Tide Times Boston		☽ Rises h. m.	Rise Key	☽ Sets h. m.	Set Key	☽ Astron. Place	☽ Age
275	1	Sa.	6:42	C	**6:25**	C	11 43	26	3 s. 32	12¼	—		7:07	D	**6:59**	C	VIR	1
276	2	**B**	6:43	C	**6:23**	C	11 40	27	3 55	12½	**12¾**	8:05	E	**7:28**	C	VIR	2
277	3	M.	6:44	C	**6:21**	C	11 37	27	4 18	1¼	**1½**	9:02	E	**7:59**	C	VIR	3
278	4	Tu.	6:45	D	**6:20**	C	11 35	27	4 42	1¾	**2**	9:58	E	**8:33**	B	LIB	4
279	5	W.	6:46	D	**6:18**	C	11 32	28	5 05	2½	**2¾**	10:54	E	**9:09**	B	LIB	5
280	6	Th.	6:47	D	**6:16**	C	11 29	28	5 28	3¼	**3½**	11:48	E	**9:50**	B	OPH	6
281	7	Fr.	6:48	D	**6:15**	C	11 27	28	5 51	4	**4¼**	**12:39**	E	**10:36**	B	OPH	7
282	8	Sa.	6:50	D	**6:13**	C	11 23	28	6 13	4¾	**5**	**1:29**	E	**11:27**	B	SAG	8
283	9	**B**	6:51	D	**6:11**	C	11 20	29	6 36	5¾	**6**	**2:15**	E	—	–	SAG	9
284	10	M.	6:52	D	**6:10**	C	11 18	29	6 59	6½	**6¾**	**2:58**	E	12:23	C	SAG	10
285	11	Tu.	6:53	D	**6:08**	C	11 15	29	7 21	7½	**7¾**	**3:38**	E	**1:24**	C	CAP	11
286	12	W.	6:54	D	**6:06**	C	11 12	29	7 44	8½	**8¾**	**4:15**	D	**2:28**	C	CAP	12
287	13	Th.	6:55	D	**6:05**	B	11 10	30	8 06	9¼	**9½**	**4:51**	D	**3:37**	D	AQU	13
288	14	Fr.	6:56	D	**6:03**	B	11 07	30	8 29	10	**10½**	**5:27**	D	**4:48**	D	AQU	14
289	15	Sa.	6:58	D	**6:01**	B	11 03	30	8 51	11	**11¼**	**6:04**	C	**6:01**	E	CET	15
290	16	**B**	6:59	D	**6:00**	B	11 01	30	9 13	11¾	—	**6:43**	C	**7:15**	E	PSC	16
291	17	M.	7:00	D	**5:58**	B	10 58	31	9 35	12¼	**12½**	**7:25**	C	**8:30**	E	CET	17
292	18	Tu.	7:01	D	**5:57**	B	10 56	31	9 56	1	**1¼**	**8:12**	B	**9:44**	E	TAU	18
293	19	W.	7:02	D	**5:55**	B	10 53	31	10 18	2	**2¼**	**9:03**	B	**10:53**	E	TAU	19
294	20	Th.	7:03	D	**5:54**	B	10 51	31	10 39	2¾	**3**	**9:59**	B	**11:57**	E	TAU	20
295	21	Fr.	7:05	D	**5:52**	B	10 47	31	11 01	3¾	**4**	**10:59**	B	**12:54**	E	GEM	21
296	22	Sa.	7:06	D	**5:51**	B	10 45	31	11 22	4¾	**5**	—	–	**1:43**	E	GEM	22
297	23	**B**	7:07	D	**5:49**	B	10 42	32	11 43	6	**6¼**	12:00	C	**2:25**	E	CAN	23
298	24	M.	7:08	D	**5:48**	B	10 40	32	12 04	7	**7¼**	**1:02**	C	**3:02**	E	LEO	24
299	25	Tu.	7:09	D	**5:46**	B	10 37	32	12 24	8	**8¼**	**2:03**	C	**3:35**	D	LEO	25
300	26	W.	7:11	D	**5:45**	B	10 34	32	12 45	9	**9¼**	**3:03**	C	**4:05**	D	LEO	26
301	27	Th.	7:12	D	**5:44**	B	10 32	32	13 05	9¾	**10**	**4:02**	D	**4:34**	D	VIR	27
302	28	Fr.	7:13	D	**5:42**	B	10 29	32	13 25	10½	**10¾**	**5:01**	D	**5:02**	C	VIR	28
303	29	Sa.	7:14	D	**5:41**	B	10 27	32	13 45	11	**11½**	**5:58**	D	**5:31**	C	VIR	29
304	30	**B**	7:16	D	**5:39**	B	10 23	32	14 04	11¾	—	**6:55**	E	**6:01**	C	VIR	0
305	31	M.	7:17	D	**5:38**	B	10 21	32	14 s. 23	12¼	**12¼**	**7:52**	E	**6:33**	C	LIB	1

October hath 31 days • 2016

The white chrysanthemums and asters star
The frosty silence. –Alice Marland (Wellington) Rollins

Day of Month	Day of Week	Dates, Feasts, Fasts, Aspects, Tide Heights	Weather
1	Sa.	**First of Muharram begins at sundown** • Manufacturer William Boeing born, 1881 • Tides {10.2 —}	*A*
2	**B**	**20th S. af. P.** • **Rosh Hashanah begins at sundown** • {10.1 10.2}	*torrent,*
3	M.	☌♀☾ • "October Gale" hit southern New England, 1841 • Tides {9.9 10.1}	*we'll*
4	Tu.	**St. Francis of Assisi** • ☾ AT APO. • *Warm October, cold February.* • {9.6 10.0}	*warrant!*
5	W.	Pumpkin Flood, Susquehanna and Delaware Rivers, Pa., 1786 • Tides {9.3 9.8}	*Perfect*
6	Th.	☌♄☾ • Babe Ruth hit 3 home runs in World Series game, 1926 • Tides {9.0 9.6}	*clime*
7	Fr.	Georgia Tech defeated Cumberland University 222-0 in football, 1916 • Tides {8.8 9.4}	*for*
8	Sa.	☾ RUNS LOW • ☌♂☾ • ☌♇☾ • U.S. statesman John Hancock died, 1793	*foliage*
9	**B**	**21st S. af. P.** • Washington Monument opened to public, D.C., 1888	*time.*
10	M.	**Columbus Day (observed)** • **Thanksgiving Day (Canada)** • Tides {8.6 9.4}	*Savor*
11	Tu.	**Yom Kippur begins at sundown** • ☌☿♃ • First Lady Eleanor Roosevelt born, 1884	*every*
12	W.	*Who buys hath need of a hundred eyes; who sells, hath enough of one.* • Tides {9.4 10.1}	*tint*
13	Th.	☾ AT ☋ • ☌♆☾ • 14" snow, Buffalo, N.Y., 2006 • {10.0 10.6}	*and*
14	Fr.	☾ ON EQ. • German submarine U-69 sank SS *Caribou,* Nfld., 1942 • Tides {10.7 11.0}	*glow*
15	Sa.	☌♅☾ • ♅ AT ☍ • U.S. Department of Transportation created, 1966 • {11.4 11.4}	*in*
16	**B**	**Sukkoth begins at sundown** • **Full Hunter's** ○ • ☾ AT PERIG. • {11.9 —}	*the*
17	M.	**St. Ignatius of Antioch** • Ashrita Furman balanced 100 ice cream scoops on cone, 2013	*forest's*
18	Tu.	**St. Luke** • ☌♂♇ • St. Luke's little summer. • {11.4 12.3}	*fashion*
19	W.	2.5 earthquake, Littleton, Mass., 2007 • Tides {11.2 12.1}	*show:*
20	Th.	☾ RIDES HIGH • Oakland/Berkeley firestorm began, Calif., 1991 • Tides {10.8 11.7}	*maples,*
21	Fr.	Movie *My Fair Lady* premiered, 1964 • Tides {10.3 11.1}	*birches,*
22	Sa.	*No man is his craft's master the first day.* • {9.9 10.6}	*red*
23	**B**	**23rd S. af. P.** • Charlie Chaplin married Mildred Harris, 1918 • {9.6 10.1}	*barns,*
24	M.	**St. James of Jerusalem**[T] • First photos of Earth taken from space, 1946 • {9.4 9.9}	*white*
25	Tu.	☾ AT ☊ • Little brown bats hibernate now. • {9.5 9.7}	*churches.*
26	W.	After 8 years, Erie Canal completed, 1825 • Tides {9.6 9.7}	*Rain*
27	Th.	☾ ON EQ. • ☿ IN SUP. ☌ • –3°F, Jump River, Wis., 1976 • Tides {9.8 9.7}	*clouds*
28	Fr.	**Sts. Simon & Jude** • ☌♃☾ • Timber rattlesnakes move to winter dens. • {10.0 9.7}	*shade*
29	Sa.	Singer Fanny Brice born, 1891 • Publisher Joseph Pulitzer died, 1911 • {10.1 9.7}	*the*
30	**B**	**24th S. af. P.** • **New** ● • ☌☿☾ • ☌♀♄ • {10.2 —}	*grand*
31	M.	**All Hallows' Eve** • **Reformation Day** • ☾ AT APO. • Mt. Rushmore finished, 1941	*parade.*

Farmer's Calendar

■ One foggy morning, I took Wiggles and Echo out for our usual morning constitutional and, in the grass, I noticed dozens of handkerchief-size webs, as if the fog had landed on the ground and stuck there.

Later, I learned that the scraps of fog were the webs of funnel spiders. They got their name because they lurk in a funnel-shape hole in one corner of the web and dash out when they feel the vibrations of an insect walking across it.

Any funnel-shape holes in the webs escaped my eye, because our rambunctious dogs distracted me, keeping me from paying closer attention to the natural world. However, without the dogs, I wouldn't even be outdoors to observe the natural world. While I pondered this conundrum, the dogs studied the webs closely. Then Wiggy ate one.

I pulled the dogs away and we headed up the road, enjoying the fall colors that look much brighter against the fog. By the time we got back from our walk, the fog had lifted. This made the webs invisible—less appealing for me, but more effective for the spiders.

A serious naturalist would have sat down next to the webs and watched them carefully, through a magnifying glass, taking notes. But then again, a serious naturalist wouldn't have brought along the dogs.

SKY WATCH ☆ *The Moon floats above Saturn and Venus on the 2nd, 45 minutes after sunset. Returning Venus moves higher this month and will be widely noticed; it is no longer a challenge. The Moon stands high above Mars on the 6th, due south at nightfall. An extraordinary "Supermoon" occurs on the 14th as the Moon comes its nearest to Earth since January 26, 1948. For most people, this is the largest and brightest full Moon of their lives (page 112). The effect on the tides, especially on the 15th, will be dramatic. A bright waning gibbous Moon will spoil the medium-strength Leonid meteor shower on the 18th. On the 25th, the Moon dangles below returning Jupiter in its new home of Virgo. Jupiter rises at around 4:00 A.M.*

◐ **First Quarter**	7th day	14th hour	51st minute
○ **Full Moon**	14th day	8th hour	52nd minute
◑ **Last Quarter**	21st day	3rd hour	34th minute
● **New Moon**	29th day	7th hour	19th minute

After 2:00 A.M. on November 6, Eastern Standard Time is given.

Get these pages with times set to your zip code at Almanac.com/Access.

Day of Year	Day of Month	Day of Week	Rises h. m.	Rise Key	Sets h. m.	Set Key	Length of Day h. m.	Sun Fast m.	Declination of Sun ° ′	High Tide Times Boston		Rises h. m.	Rise Key	Sets h. m.	Set Key	Astron. Place	Age
306	1	Tu.	7:18	D	5:37	B	10 19	32	14 s. 43	12¾	1	8:48	E	7:08	B	LIB	2
307	2	W.	7:19	D	5:36	B	10 17	32	15 01	1½	1½	9:43	E	7:48	B	OPH	3
308	3	Th.	7:21	D	5:34	B	10 13	32	15 20	2	2¼	10:35	E	8:31	B	OPH	4
309	4	Fr.	7:22	D	5:33	B	10 11	32	15 38	2¾	3	11:25	E	9:20	B	SAG	5
310	5	Sa.	7:23	E	5:32	B	10 09	32	15 57	3½	3¾	12:12	E	10:13	B	SAG	6
311	6	**B**	6:24	E	4:31	B	10 07	32	16 14	3¼	3½	11:55	E	10:11	C	SAG	7
312	7	M.	6:26	E	4:30	B	10 04	32	16 32	4¼	4¼	12:35	E	11:12	C	CAP	8
313	8	Tu.	6:27	E	4:29	B	10 02	32	16 49	5	5¼	1:12	E	—	–	CAP	9
314	9	W.	6:28	E	4:28	B	10 00	32	17 06	6	6¼	1:47	D	12:16	C	AQU	10
315	10	Th.	6:29	E	4:27	B	9 58	32	17 23	6¾	7¼	2:21	D	1:24	D	AQU	11
316	11	Fr.	6:31	E	4:26	B	9 55	32	17 40	7¾	8¼	2:56	C	2:34	D	PSC	12
317	12	Sa.	6:32	E	4:25	B	9 53	32	17 56	8½	9	3:33	C	3:46	E	PSC	13
318	13	**B**	6:33	E	4:24	B	9 51	31	18 11	9½	10	4:13	C	5:01	E	PSC	14
319	14	M.	6:34	E	4:23	B	9 49	31	18 27	10¼	10¾	4:58	C	6:16	E	ARI	15
320	15	Tu.	6:36	E	4:22	B	9 46	31	18 42	11¼	11¾	5:48	B	7:30	E	TAU	16
321	16	W.	6:37	E	4:21	B	9 44	31	18 57	12	—	6:44	B	8:40	E	TAU	17
322	17	Th.	6:38	E	4:20	B	9 42	31	19 11	12¾	1	7:44	B	9:42	E	ORI	18
323	18	Fr.	6:39	E	4:19	B	9 40	30	19 26	1½	1¾	8:47	C	10:37	E	GEM	19
324	19	Sa.	6:40	E	4:19	B	9 39	30	19 39	2½	2¾	9:51	C	11:23	E	CAN	20
325	20	**B**	6:42	E	4:18	B	9 36	30	19 53	3½	3¾	10:54	C	12:03	E	CAN	21
326	21	M.	6:43	E	4:17	B	9 34	30	20 06	4½	4¾	11:56	D	12:38	D	LEO	22
327	22	Tu.	6:44	E	4:17	A	9 33	29	20 19	5½	5¾	—	–	1:09	D	LEO	23
328	23	W.	6:45	E	4:16	A	9 31	29	20 31	6½	6¾	12:56	D	1:38	D	LEO	24
329	24	Th.	6:46	E	4:15	A	9 29	29	20 43	7½	7¾	1:54	D	2:06	C	VIR	25
330	25	Fr.	6:48	E	4:15	A	9 27	29	20 55	8¼	8¾	2:52	D	2:34	C	VIR	26
331	26	Sa.	6:49	E	4:14	A	9 25	28	21 06	9	9½	3:49	E	3:04	C	VIR	27
332	27	**B**	6:50	E	4:14	A	9 24	28	21 17	9½	10	4:46	E	3:35	C	LIB	28
333	28	M.	6:51	E	4:13	A	9 22	28	21 27	10¼	10¾	5:42	E	4:09	B	LIB	29
334	29	Tu.	6:52	E	4:13	A	9 21	27	21 37	10¾	11½	6:38	E	4:47	B	SCO	0
335	30	W.	6:53	E	4:13	A	9 20	27	21 s. 46	11½	—	7:32	E	5:29	B	OPH	1

C A L E N D A R

NOVEMBER HATH 30 DAYS • 2016

The soft November days are here,
The aftermath of blossom's year. –Sara Louisa (Vickers) Oberholtzer

Day of Month	Day of Week	Dates, Feasts, Fasts, Aspects, Tide Heights	Weather
1	Tu.	**All Saints'** • Rainbow Bridge, connecting Niagara Falls of New York and Ontario, opened to public, 1941	*Fields*
2	W.	**All Souls'** • ☌♄☾ • *Sesame Street* character Cookie Monster born (no year)	*whitening,*
3	Th.	☌♀☾ • 96°F, Los Angeles, Calif., 1890 • {9.2 9.9	*cold*
4	Fr.	☾ RUNS LOW • Newscaster Walter Cronkite born, 1916 • Tides {9.0 9.8	*tightening:*
5	Sa.	Sadie Hawkins Day • ☌♇☾ • Actor Fred MacMurray died, 1991 • {8.8 9.6	*This*
6	**B**	**25th S. af. P.** • **Daylight Saving Time ends, 2:00 A.M.** • ☌♂☾ • {8.7 9.4	*is*
7	M.	Elston Howard won American League's Most Valuable Player award, 1963 • {8.7 9.4	*frightening!*
8	Tu.	**Election Day** • Black bears head to winter dens now. • Tides {8.9 9.5	*Lawns*
9	W.	☾ AT ☋ • ☌♆☾ • Maj. Robert White flew X-15 rocket plane at Mach 6.04, 1961	*are*
10	Th.	*The aurora, when very bright, indicates approaching storm.*	*lakes,*
11	Fr.	**St. Martin of Tours** • **Veterans Day** • ☾ ON EQ. • Tides {10.5 10.4	*floured*
12	Sa.	Indian Summer • ☌♅☾ • Ellis Island federal immigration station closed, N.Y./N.J., 1954	*with*
13	**B**	**26th S. af. P.** • Lobsters move to offshore waters now. • {11.8 11.1	*flakes.*
14	M.	**Full Beaver** ○ • ☾ AT PERIG. • Tides {12.2 11.2	*Miserable?*
15	Tu.	Elvis Presley's first movie, *Love Me Tender,* premiered, 1956 • Tides {12.5 11.2	*Worse!*
16	W.	Poet Louis-Honoré Fréchette born, 1839 • Tides {12.4 —	*It's*
17	Th.	**St. Hugh of Lincoln** • ☾ RIDES HIGH • {11.0 12.1	*blizzard-able!*
18	Fr.	**St. Hilda of Whitby** • Crab apples are ripe now. • Tides {10.7 11.7	*Everything*
19	Sa.	U.S. president James Garfield born, 1831 • {10.3 11.0	*squishes—*
20	**B**	**27th S. af. P.** • ♆ STAT. • J. Haven & C. Hettrich patented a whirligig (yo-yo), 1866	*even*
21	M.	☾ AT ☊ • Snowflakes fell in central Fla., 2006 • {9.6 9.9	*your*
22	Tu.	Entrepreneur Mary Kay Ash died, 2001 • Tides {9.4 9.4	*favorite*
23	W.	**St. Clement** • ☌☿♄ • *A feast is not made of mushrooms only.*	*Thanksgiving*
24	Th.	**Thanksgiving Day** • ☾ ON EQ. • ☌♀♇ • ☌♃☾ • {9.5 9.1	*dishes!*
25	Fr.	First YMCA in North America opened, Montreal, Que., 1851	*As*
26	Sa.	First lion exhibited in U.S., Boston, Mass., 1716 • {9.8 9.2	*the*
27	**B**	**1st S. of Advent** • ☾ AT APO. • Astronomer Anders Celsius born, 1701	*inches*
28	M.	Thomas Jefferson: ". . . the freezing of the ink on the point of my pen renders it difficult to write."	*accumulate,*
29	Tu.	**New** ● • *Better do it than wish it done.* • {10.2 9.2	*spirits*
30	W.	**St. Andrew** • ☌☿☾ • ☌♄☾ • Tides {10.2 —	*agloomulate.*

Sweet words butter no parsnips. –English proverb

Farmer's Calendar

■ The town moderator is responsible for running the elections. It's not a big chore. The town clerk, the supervisors of the checklist, and the ballot clerks do all the work; the moderator is a figurehead. In this town, I've been the figurehead for 12 years.

The moderator opens the polls at 8:00 A.M., stands at the checkout table, takes everyone's ballots from their hands (as state law requires), and puts them in the box.

The ballots are made of paper, and it's a wooden box, made in 1883, the same year that our Victorian town hall was built. The voters mark their ballots with pencils in little booths with red-white-and-blue curtains.

The polls close at 7:00 P.M. and we start counting the votes by hand. The only sounds are the shuffle of the ballots, the scratching of pencils, and the murmur of the clerks. We're usually finished by 10:00, although in a presidential election, we've stayed as late as 1:00 in the morning.

After announcing the results, I thank the workers for participating in this civic sacrament. That's when I get choked up; the weight of what we've been doing hits me hard. This is democracy—marking pieces of paper, putting them in a wooden box, and then counting them one by one.

C A L E N D A R

SKY WATCH ☆ *Venus finally makes its run to prominence, getting even higher and brighter as it meets the Moon on the 2nd and 3rd. Mercury lurks far lower as it starts a mediocre 3-week evening star apparition. Mars, just one-tenth as bright as it was in June, moves through Capricornus and into Aquarius, steadily sinking toward Venus. The solstice falls on the 21st at 5:44 A.M., inaugurating winter. On the predawn stage, the Moon floats above brilliant Jupiter early on the 22nd, with Virgo's famous blue star Spica just beneath them both after 3:00 A.M. Much more challenging is dim returning Saturn meeting a hair-thin Moon very low in morning twilight on the 27th.*

◑	**First Quarter**	7th day	4th hour	3rd minute
○	**Full Moon**	13th day	19th hour	6th minute
◐	**Last Quarter**	20th day	20th hour	56th minute
●	**New Moon**	29th day	1st hour	54th minute

All times are given in Eastern Standard Time.

Get these pages with times set to your zip code at Almanac.com/Access.

Day of Year	Day of Month	Day of Week	☼ Rises h. m.	Rise Key	☼ Sets h. m.	Set Key	Length of Day h. m.	Sun Fast m.	Declination of Sun ° ′	High Tide Times Boston		☾ Rises h. m.	Rise Key	☾ Sets h. m.	Set Key	☾ Astron. Place	☾ Age
336	1	Th.	6:54	E	4:12	A	9 18	26	21 s. 56	12	12¼	8:23	E	6:16	B	SAG	2
337	2	Fr.	6:55	E	4:12	A	9 17	26	22 04	12¾	12¾	9:11	E	7:08	B	SAG	3
338	3	Sa.	6:56	E	4:12	A	9 16	26	22 13	1½	1½	9:55	E	8:04	C	SAG	4
339	4	**B**	6:57	E	4:12	A	9 15	25	22 21	2	2¼	10:36	E	9:03	C	CAP	5
340	5	M.	6:58	E	4:12	A	9 14	25	22 28	2¾	3	11:13	E	10:05	C	AQU	6
341	6	Tu.	6:59	E	4:12	A	9 13	24	22 35	3½	3¾	11:48	D	11:09	C	AQU	7
342	7	W.	7:00	E	4:12	A	9 12	24	22 42	4½	4¾	**12:21**	D	—	–	AQU	8
343	8	Th.	7:01	E	4:12	A	9 11	24	22 48	5½	5¾	**12:54**	D	12:16	D	PSC	9
344	9	Fr.	7:02	E	4:12	A	9 10	23	22 53	6¼	6¾	**1:28**	C	1:24	D	CET	10
345	10	Sa.	7:03	E	4:12	A	9 09	23	22 59	7¼	7¾	**2:05**	C	2:35	E	PSC	11
346	11	**B**	7:04	E	4:12	A	9 08	22	23 03	8¼	8¾	**2:45**	C	3:48	E	ARI	12
347	12	M.	7:04	E	4:12	A	9 08	22	23 08	9	9¾	**3:31**	B	5:02	E	TAU	13
348	13	Tu.	7:05	E	4:12	A	9 07	21	23 12	10	10½	**4:24**	B	6:14	E	TAU	14
349	14	W.	7:06	E	4:12	A	9 06	21	23 15	10¾	11½	**5:23**	B	7:21	E	TAU	15
350	15	Th.	7:07	E	4:13	A	9 06	20	23 18	11¾	—	**6:26**	B	8:22	E	GEM	16
351	16	Fr.	7:07	E	4:13	A	9 06	20	23 20	12¼	12½	**7:32**	C	9:14	E	GEM	17
352	17	Sa.	7:08	E	4:13	A	9 05	19	23 22	1¼	1½	**8:38**	C	9:59	E	CAN	18
353	18	**B**	7:09	E	4:14	A	9 05	19	23 24	2¼	2¼	**9:43**	C	10:37	E	LEO	19
354	19	M.	7:09	E	4:14	A	9 05	18	23 25	3	3¼	**10:45**	D	11:11	D	LEO	20
355	20	Tu.	7:10	E	4:15	A	9 05	18	23 25	4	4¼	**11:45**	D	11:41	D	LEO	21
356	21	W.	7:10	E	4:15	A	9 05	17	23 26	4¾	5¼	—	–	**12:10**	D	VIR	22
357	22	Th.	7:11	E	4:16	A	9 05	17	23 25	5¾	6¼	12:44	D	**12:38**	C	VIR	23
358	23	Fr.	7:11	E	4:16	A	9 05	16	23 24	6¾	7¼	1:41	E	**1:07**	C	VIR	24
359	24	Sa.	7:12	E	4:17	A	9 05	16	23 23	7½	8	2:38	E	**1:37**	C	LIB	25
360	25	**B**	7:12	E	4:17	A	9 05	15	23 21	8¼	9	3:35	E	**2:10**	B	LIB	26
361	26	M.	7:12	E	4:18	A	9 06	15	23 19	9	9¾	4:31	E	**2:46**	B	LIB	27
362	27	Tu.	7:13	E	4:19	A	9 06	14	23 16	9¾	10¼	5:26	E	**3:27**	B	OPH	28
363	28	W.	7:13	E	4:19	A	9 06	14	23 13	10½	11	6:19	E	**4:12**	B	OPH	29
364	29	Th.	7:13	E	4:20	A	9 07	13	23 10	11	11¾	7:09	E	**5:03**	B	SAG	0
365	30	Fr.	7:13	E	4:21	A	9 08	13	23 05	11¾	—	7:55	E	**5:58**	B	SAG	1
366	31	Sa.	7:13	E	4:22	A	9 09	13	23 s. 01	12¼	12½	8:37	E	**6:57**	C	CAP	2

DECEMBER HATH 31 DAYS • 2016

Heart-warm against the stormy white,
The Rose of Joy burns warmer yet. –Thomas Gold Appleton

Day of Month	Day of Week	Dates, Feasts, Fasts, Aspects, Tide Heights	Weather
1	Th.	☾ RUNS LOW • First flight of helium-filled blimp (C-7), between Va. and D.C., 1921 • Tides {9.2 10.2	*Snow,*
2	Fr.	St. Viviana • ☌♇☾ • Former U.S. First Lady Jane Pierce died, 1863 • Tides {9.1 10.1	*then*
3	Sa.	☌♀☾ • Commonwealth Pacific Cable (COMPAC) opened, 1963 • Tides {9.1 10.0	*rain,*
4	**B**	**2nd S. of Advent** • Matisse's *Le Bateau* rehung after being upside down 47 days, MoMA, N.Y.C., 1961	*then*
5	M.	☌♂☾ • *A blustering night, a fair day.* • Tides {9.0 9.7	*temps*
6	Tu.	St. Nicholas • ☾ AT ☋ • ☌♆☾ • Winterberry fruit especially showy now.	*easing.*
7	W.	St. Ambrose • **Nat'l Pearl Harbor Remembrance Day** • Tides {9.3 9.6	*Déjà vu:*
8	Th.	☾ ON EQ. • After FDR's "a date which will live in infamy" speech, U.S. declared war on Japan, WWII, 1941	*one*
9	Fr.	☌♅☾ • Actor Kirk Douglas born, 1916 • Tides {10.1 9.8	*dump*
10	Sa.	St. Eulalia • ☌♄☉ • ☿ GR. ELONG. (21° EAST) • Tides {10.7 10.0	*or*
11	**B**	**3rd S. of Advent** • Ind. admitted to Union as 19th state, 1816 • {11.3 10.3	*two?*
12	M.	**Our Lady of Guadalupe** • ☾ AT PERIG. • George Grant received patent for improved golf tee, 1899	*Frosty's*
13	Tu.	St. Lucia • **Full Cold** ○ • *Love rules his kingdom without a sword.* • {12.1 10.7	*freezing!*
14	W.	Ember Day • Halcyon Days begin. • ☾ RIDES HIGH • Tides {12.3 10.8	*No*
15	Th.	U.S. Bill of Rights ratified, 1791 • Beware the Pogonip. • Tides {12.2 —	*relief*
16	Fr.	Ember Day • Beatrix Potter's *The Tale of Peter Rabbit* first published, 1901 • Tides {10.7 12.0	*to be*
17	Sa.	Ember Day • Bob Fisher made 2,371 basketball free throws in 1 hour, Centralia, Kans., 2011	*seen—*
18	**B**	**4th S. of Advent** • ☾ AT ☊ • Tides {10.2 10.9	*is*
19	M.	☿ STAT. • La. Purchase explorer Wm. Dunbar: ". . . the e[a]ves of our cabin hang with beautiful icicles," 1804	*that*
20	Tu.	$1 bachelor tax imposed, Mo., 1820 • Tides {9.6 9.6	*Santa*
21	W.	St. Thomas • **Winter Solstice** • ☾ ON EQ. • Vladimir Horowitz wed Wanda Toscanini, 1933	*riding*
22	Th.	☌♃☾ • Pirate Bluebeard died, 1440 • Tides {9.2 8.7	*on a*
23	Fr.	–50°F, Almont and Williston, N.Dak., 1983 • Tides {9.2 8.5	*snow*
24	Sa.	**Chanukah begins at sundown** • CONAD (later, NORAD) began to track Santa Claus, 1955	*machine?*
25	**B**	**Christmas** • ☾ AT APO. • Pansy blossoms picked, Manhattan, Mont., 1896	*Please:*
26	M.	St. Stephen • **Boxing Day (Canada)** • **First day of Kwanzaa** • Tides {9.7 8.7	*more*
27	Tu.	St. John • ☌♄☾ • *Man's best candle is his understanding.* • Tides {9.9 8.9	*green,*
28	W.	Holy Innocents • ☾ RUNS LOW • ☌☿☾ • ☿ IN INF. ☌ • {10.1 9.0	*less*
29	Th.	**New** ● • ☌♇☾ • ♅ STAT. • Chemist Charles Macintosh born, 1766	*spleen*
30	Fr.	1.3" snow, Las Vegas, Nev., 2003 • Tides {10.3 —	*in*
31	Sa.	St. Sylvester • Guy Lombardo and His Royal Canadians first played "Auld Lang Syne" at midnight, 1929	*'17!*

Farmer's Calendar

■ A few weeks before Christmas, I found a dead star-nosed mole near our pond. A little bigger than an ordinary mole, it has an uncanny star-shaped nose. Circling the tip are 22 hairless tentacles that serve as the mole's primary sensory organ.

Like other moles, it has weak eyesight, which is not much use belowground. Its nose, though, is covered with 25,000 sensory receptors called Eimer's organs, which make it six times more sensitive than the human hand. Underground, the tentacles whirl around, touching objects near the mole with astounding swiftness: 12 objects per second. In a quarter of a second, the mole can identify an object, decide if it's prey (worms, mostly), and eat it. Half the mole's brain is devoted to processing this information; it literally thinks with its nose.

This mole also hunts underwater by smell. Its stellar nostrils emit tiny bubbles—5 to 10 per second—that pick up scent molecules. These the mole inhales. Not until this was discovered did scientists believe that mammals could smell underwater.

I walked home that day contemplating the magnificent weirdness of nature and the Magi, those ancient astronomers who also found their way through the darkness by following a star.

Holidays and Observances

Jan. 1	New Year's Day
Jan. 18	**Martin Luther King Jr.'s Birthday** (*observed*)
Jan. 19	Robert E. Lee Day (*Fla., Ky.*)
Feb. 2	Groundhog Day
Feb. 9	Mardi Gras (*Baldwin & Mobile counties, Ala.; La.*)
Feb. 12	Abraham Lincoln's Birthday
Feb. 14	Valentine's Day
Feb. 15	**Washington's Birthday** (*observed*) Susan B. Anthony's Birthday (*Fla.*)
Feb. 29	Leap Day
Mar. 1	Town Meeting Day (*Vt.*)
Mar. 2	Texas Independence Day
Mar. 15	Andrew Jackson Day (*Tenn.*)
Mar. 17	St. Patrick's Day Evacuation Day (*Suffolk Co., Mass.*)
Mar. 28	Seward's Day (*Alaska*)
Apr. 2	Pascua Florida Day
Apr. 18	Patriots Day (*Maine, Mass.*)
Apr. 21	San Jacinto Day (*Tex.*)
Apr. 22	Earth Day
Apr. 29	National Arbor Day
May 5	Cinco de Mayo
May 8	Mother's Day Truman Day, traditional (*Mo.*)
May 21	Armed Forces Day
May 22	National Maritime Day
May 23	Victoria Day (*Canada*)
May 30	**Memorial Day**
June 5	World Environment Day
June 11	King Kamehameha I Day, traditional (*Hawaii*)
June 14	Flag Day
June 17	Bunker Hill Day (*Suffolk Co., Mass.*)
June 19	Father's Day Emancipation Day (*Tex.*)
June 20	West Virginia Day
July 1	Canada Day
July 4	**Independence Day**
July 25	Pioneer Day, observed (*Utah*)
Aug. 1	Colorado Day Civic Holiday (*parts of Canada*)
Aug. 16	Bennington Battle Day (*Vt.*)
Aug. 19	National Aviation Day
Aug. 26	Women's Equality Day
Sept. 5	**Labor Day**
Sept. 9	Admission Day (*Calif.*)
Sept. 11	Patriot Day Grandparents Day
Sept. 17	Constitution Day, traditional
Sept. 21	International Day of Peace
Oct. 3	Child Health Day
Oct. 9	Leif Eriksson Day
Oct. 10	**Columbus Day** (*observed*) Native Americans' Day (*S.Dak.*) Thanksgiving Day (*Canada*)
Oct. 18	Alaska Day
Oct. 24	United Nations Day
Oct. 28	Nevada Day
Oct. 31	Halloween
Nov. 4	Will Rogers Day (*Okla.*)
Nov. 8	Election Day
Nov. 11	**Veterans Day** Remembrance Day (*Canada*)
Nov. 19	Discovery of Puerto Rico Day
Nov. 24	**Thanksgiving Day**
Nov. 25	Acadian Day (*La.*)
Dec. 7	National Pearl Harbor Remembrance Day
Dec. 15	Bill of Rights Day
Dec. 17	Wright Brothers Day
Dec. 25	**Christmas Day**
Dec. 26	Boxing Day (*Canada*) First day of Kwanzaa

C
A
L
E
N
D
A
R

Love calendar lore? Find more at Almanac.com/Calendar.

Tidal Glossary

Apogean Tide: A monthly tide of decreased range that occurs when the Moon is at apogee (farthest from Earth).

Diurnal Tide: A tide with one high water and one low water in a tidal day of approximately 24 hours.

Mean Lower Low Water: The arithmetic mean of the lesser of a daily pair of low waters, observed over a specific 19-year cycle called the National Tidal Datum Epoch.

Neap Tide: A tide of decreased range that occurs twice a month, when the Moon is in quadrature (during its first and last quarters, when the Sun and the Moon are at right angles to each other relative to Earth).

Perigean Tide: A monthly tide of increased range that occurs when the Moon is at perigee (closest to Earth).

Semidiurnal Tide: A tide with one high water and one low water every half day. East Coast tides, for example, are semidiurnal, with two highs and two lows during a tidal day of approximately 24 hours.

Spring Tide: A tide of increased range that occurs at times of syzygy each month. Named not for the season of spring but from the German *springen* ("to leap up"), a spring tide also brings a lower low water.

Syzygy: The nearly straight-line configuration that occurs twice a month, when the Sun and the Moon are in conjunction (on the same side of Earth, at the new Moon) and when they are in opposition (on opposite sides of Earth, at the full Moon). In both cases, the gravitational effects of the Sun and the Moon reinforce each other, and tidal range is increased.

Vanishing Tide: A mixed tide of considerable inequality in the two highs and two lows, so that the lower high (or higher low) may appear to vanish. ∎

Glossary of Almanac Oddities

■ Many readers have expressed puzzlement over the rather obscure entries that appear on our **Right-Hand Calendar Pages, 125–151.** These "oddities" have long been fixtures in the Almanac, and we are pleased to provide some definitions. (Once explained, they may not seem so odd after all!)

–Beth Krommes

Ember Days: The four periods observed by some Christian denominations for prayer, fasting, and the ordination of clergy are called Ember Days. Specifically, these are the Wednesdays, Fridays, and Saturdays that occur in succession following (1) the First Sunday in Lent; (2) Whitsunday–Pentecost; (3) the Feast of the Holy Cross, September 14; and (4) the Feast of St. Lucia, December 13. The word *ember* is perhaps a corruption of the Latin *quatuor tempora,* "four times."

Folklore has it that the weather on each of the 3 days foretells the weather for the next 3 months; that is, in September, the first Ember Day, Wednesday, forecasts the weather for October; Friday predicts November; and Saturday foretells December.

Distaff Day (January 7): This was the first day after Epiphany (January 6), when women were expected to return to their spinning following the Christmas holiday. A distaff is the staff that women used for holding the flax or wool in spinning.

(Hence the term "distaff" refers to women's work or the maternal side of the family.)

Plough Monday (January): Traditionally, the first Monday after Epiphany was called Plough Monday because it was the day when men returned to their plough, or daily work, following the Christmas holiday. (Every few years, Plough Monday and Distaff Day fall on the same day.) It was customary at this time for farm laborers to draw a plough through the village, soliciting money for a "plough light," which was kept burning in the parish church all year. This traditional verse captures the spirit of it:

> *"Yule is come and Yule is gone,*
> *and we have feasted well;*
> *so Jack must to his flail again*
> *and Jenny to her wheel."*

Three Chilly Saints (May): Mamertus, Pancras, and Gervais were three early Christian saints. Because their feast days, on May 11, 12, and 13, respectively, are traditionally cold, they have come to be known as the Three Chilly Saints. An old French saying translates to: "St. Mamertus, St. Pancras, and St. Gervais do not pass without a frost."

Midsummer Day (June 24): To the farmer, this day is the midpoint of the growing season, halfway between planting and harvest. (Midsummer Eve is an occasion for festivity and celebrates fertility.) The Anglican church considered it a "Quarter Day," one of the four major divisions of the liturgical year. It also marks the feast day of St. John the Baptist.

Cornscateous Air (July): First used by early almanac makers, this term signifies warm, damp air. Though it signals ideal climatic conditions for growing corn, it poses a danger to those affected by asthma and other respiratory problems.

Dog Days (July 3–August 11): These 40 days are traditionally the year's hottest and unhealthiest. They once coincided with the year's heliacal (at sunrise) rising of the Dog Star, Sirius. Ancient folks thought that the "combined heat" of Sirius and the Sun caused summer's swelter.

Lammas Day (August 1): Derived from the Old English *hlaf maesse,* meaning "loaf mass," Lammas Day marked the beginning of the harvest. Traditionally, loaves of bread were baked from the first-ripened grain and brought to the churches to be consecrated. Eventually, "loaf mass" became "Lammas." In Scotland, Lammastide fairs became famous as the time when trial marriages could be made. These marriages could end after a year with no strings attached.

Cat Nights Begin (August 17): This term harks back to the days when people believed in witches. An Irish legend says that a witch could turn into a cat and regain herself eight times, but on the ninth time (August 17), she couldn't change back, hence the saying: "A cat has nine lives." Because August is a "yowly" time for cats, this may have initially prompted the speculation about witches on the prowl.

Harvest Home (September): In Europe and Britain, the conclusion of the harvest each autumn was marked by festivals of fun, feasting, and thanksgiving known as "Harvest Home." It was also a time to hold elections, pay workers, and collect rents. These festivals usually took place around the autumnal equinox.

Certain groups in the United States, particularly the Pennsylvania Dutch, have kept the tradition alive.

St. Luke's Little Summer (October): This is a spell of warm weather that occurs on or near St. Luke's feast day (October 18) and is sometimes called Indian summer.

Indian Summer (November): A period of warm weather following a cold spell or a hard frost, Indian summer can occur between St. Martin's Day (November 11) and November 20. Although there are differing dates for its occurrence, for more than 200 years the Almanac has adhered to the saying "If All Saints' (November 1) brings out winter, St. Martin's brings out Indian summer." The term may have come from early Native Americans, some of whom believed that the condition was caused by a warm wind sent from the court of their southwestern god, Cautantowwit.

Halcyon Days (December): This refers to about 2 weeks of calm weather that often follow the blustery winds of autumn's end. Ancient Greeks and Romans experienced this weather around the time of the winter solstice, when the halcyon, or kingfisher, was brooding in a nest floating on the sea. The bird was said to have charmed the wind and waves so that the waters were especially calm during this period.

Beware the Pogonip (December): The word *pogonip* refers to an uncommon occurrence—frozen fog. The word was coined by Native Americans to describe the frozen fogs of fine ice needles that occur in the mountain valleys of the western United States and Canada. According to their tradition, breathing the fog is injurious to the lungs. ∎

Best Fishing Days and Times

The best times to fish are when the fish are naturally most active. The Sun, Moon, tides, and weather all influence fish activity. For example, fish tend to feed more at sunrise and sunset, and also during a full Moon (when tides are higher than average). However, most of us go fishing when we can get the time off, not because it is the best time. But there *are* best times, according to fishing lore:

The Best Fishing Days for 2016, when the Moon is between new and full:

January 9–23
February 8–22
March 8–23
April 7–22
May 6–21
June 4–20
July 4–19
August 2–18
September 1–16, 30
October 1–16, 30, 31
November 1–14, 29, 30
December 1–13, 29–31

■ **One hour before and one hour after high tides, and one hour before and one hour after low tides. (The times of high tides for Boston are given on pages 124–150; also see pages 248–249. Inland, the times for high tides correspond with the times when the Moon is due south. Low tides are halfway between high tides.)**

■ During the "morning rise" (after sunup for a spell) and the "evening rise" (just before sundown and the hour or so after).

■ **During the rise and set of the Moon.**

■ When the barometer is steady or on the rise. (But even during stormy periods, the fish aren't going to give up feeding. The smart fisherman will find just the right bait.)

■ **When there is a hatch of flies—caddis flies or mayflies, commonly.**

■ When the breeze is from a westerly quarter, rather than from the north or east.

■ **When the water is still or slightly rippled, rather than during a wind.**

How to Estimate the Weight of a Fish

Measure the fish from the tip of its nose to the tip of its tail. Then measure its girth at the thickest portion of its midsection.

The weight of a fat-bodied fish (bass, salmon) = (length x girth x girth)/800

The weight of a slender fish (trout, northern pike) = (length x girth x girth)/900

Example: If a fish is 20 inches long and has a 12-inch girth, its estimated weight is (20 x 12 x 12)/900 = 2,880/900 = 3.2 pounds

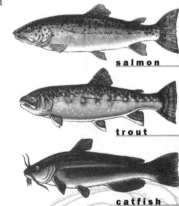

salmon

trout

catfish

156

Angling Advice for Anyone Anywhere

. . . and especially Mildred in Georgia

BY BOB SCAMMELL • ILLUSTRATIONS BY STEVEN NOBLE

IN MORE THAN 50 years of fishing and writing about it, I have received many propositions from readers that I take their kids fishing. I have done a considerable amount of that, but only if at least one parent also came along—because, as we know, fishing is about more than just fishing, bonding and learning being but two by-products. Many times I have taken kids and older folks together, from those who'd never held a fly rod to those who were able to get their first fly-caught fish in just 1 day.

None of this prepared me for the recent letter from Mildred in Georgia who wrote to the Almanac wanting to contact me for help with an angling problem. The letter absolutely enthralls everyone who reads it for varying reasons; with me, it first resonates because it is a real, pen-and-ink, handwritten letter.

"I am a poor fisher," Mildred wrote. "I can't catch a large fish. I see little children catching bigger fish than me. . . . I have a lot of lures and hooks, and when I was a child, my daddy would put my hooks on my fishing line. He's dead and gone now so I put them on myself, and I must be putting them on wrong."

Over the years, I have fished with and taught hundreds of kids, and with a few of them, it just didn't

Fishing is about
more than just fishing,
bonding and
learning being but
two by-products.

stick. It encourages me to hear that early fishing experiences can come back so strongly, as with Mildred.

Four decades ago, when I was fishing in Florida, I learned that Georgia, bordering to the north, then offered some of the best and most varied fishing in the USA. I'd love to head down and see if that fishing is still as great—for large- and small-mouth bass, bream, crappie, bluegill, catfish, walleye, trout in the Appalachian and Blue Ridge mountains to the north, sea bass and sea trout in the Atlantic salt, etc.—and I'd take Mildred with me.

Fine fishing, far away from home, is something that I have enjoyed enough times to have developed standard procedures that work for me and should work for anyone who yearns to catch a big fish.

■ **Find out all you can about the fishing available where you are going to fish.** Even though I'm not Georgia-bound, I have spent considerable time fishing around in a superb Web site befitting a state with 1.29 million resident anglers, that of Georgia's Department of Natural Resources, Wildlife Resources Division (www.georgiawildlife.org/fishing).

Other states and provinces have similar such resources. Anyone who wouldn't touch a computer with a 14-foot cane pole should think again.

Ironically, the iconic old cane pole remains a popular fishing rod in Georgia, especially for kids; could this be the secret of the local little children catching bigger fish than Mildred?

■ The next resort for Mildred is to do what I have done many times on fishing trips to many places in the world: **Go to the best tackle shop or sporting goods store in the area.** By all means, glance at the "Fishing Conditions" black or white board found in most shops; ignore the witticisms ("Great Yesterday: Too Late Tomorrow"); ask for tips, hints, and help; and buy some tackle and gear based on what you are being told.

Actually, no matter what I was told, I'd still buy a 14-foot cane pole, some bobbers, the bait *du jour,* and, for sure, if they had any, a couple of Calcasieu Pig Boat flies, created for largemouth bass by Louisiana fly-fishing great Tom Nixon.

■ In particular, **find out who the local fishing guides are.** If there are no guides, do what angling guru Lefty

> Ironically, the iconic old cane pole remains a popular fishing rod in Georgia, especially for kids; could this be the secret of the local little children catching bigger fish?

"There's days when even the guide can't catch fish."

Kreh has done so many times (once with me): **Find out who is the best fisherman in the area** and pick his brain—maybe even get him to take you fishing.

In my home province, real men do not use guides, but on my first trip to Montana, I hired a legendary West Yellowstone guide, the late Jim Danskin, who taught me more about fly-fishing on our first day than I had been able to teach myself in the previous decade. One tough day years later on challenging Henrys Fork in Idaho, Jim uttered this comforting truth: "Bob, there's days when even the guide can't catch fish."

■ **Do not ignore the near and familiar.** I have enjoyed fabulous fishing in rivers and streams that flow through population centers: Bow River, Crowsnest River, Pincher Creek, Red Deer River, all in Alberta, and Elk River in British Columbia. One of those wonderful-sounding "Hootchie-cootchie" southern rivers flows through Mildred's small city, and the latest Internet report I have says that it features good fishing for largemouth bass up to 6 pounds, catfish, bream, and crappie.

Catfish? It's a mercy I'm not going there, because I'd just have to try noodling (catching by hand) one of those; after all, I mastered guddling for trout on a 1987 trip to England.

One of the classic cliché covers of the golden age of outdoors magazines showed a cane pole kid having his huge trout weighed in the general store while an impeccably outfitted fly fisherman glowered in the background. Those children catching bigger fish than Mildred does are probably doing it close to home in the Hootchie-cootchie.

■ Our angling saint, Izaak Walton, counseled anglers to "study to be quiet." Mildred should study where and when those little children fish, and she should not be quiet. Give them a chance, and **kids love to demonstrate what they can do and how you, too, can catch a big fish.**

■ Mildred also asked for **a book suggestion.** My advice for her and everyone else is to try to obtain a second-hand copy of the best and most lavishly illustrated—but now out of print—general manual: *The Art of Freshwater Fishing* (Cy DeCosse Inc., 1985), by Dick Sternberg. You might be able to catch one on the Internet. ■

Distinguished outdoors writer and conservationist **Bob Scammell,** who writes from Red Deer, Alberta, was honored with a 2014 Canadian National Recreational Fisheries Award.

THE *Love* OF YOUR *Life*

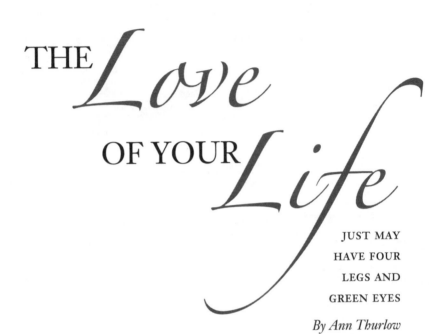

JUST MAY
HAVE FOUR
LEGS AND
GREEN EYES

By Ann Thurlow

The growth in the size and variety of pet stores confirms it: We love our animal friends. But have you ever looked into the deep eyes of your animal companion and thought, "Hey, do you love me back?"

Consider this: When Catherine O'Bryan and her husband moved to a remote island off the coast of British Columbia, they decided to take along a goat named Frisky for milk. What they hadn't counted on was Frisky falling in love . . . with Catherine's husband. So besotted was the poor animal that it took every opportunity to butt Catherine out of the way to get closer to the man of its dreams, more than once nearly sending her over a cliff.

Or how about this tale of love's sweet dream?

A cat in Massachusetts went nearly mad when its owner brought home a new husband. The cat spent every night in its hapless rival's face, howling. It refused to eat; it glared at the couple when they kissed.

Come to find out, a touch of the green-eyed monster is not all that uncommon in our four-legged friends.

Dr. Nicolas Dodman works at the Tufts University Animal Behavior Clinic and is a renowned expert on animal behavior. In his book *Dogs Behaving Badly*, he devotes a whole chapter to jealousy. He says that

Photos, clockwise from top left: Peter Samuels/Media Bakery; C. Quinnell; Brian Summers/Media Bakery; Martin Ragner/Media Bakery

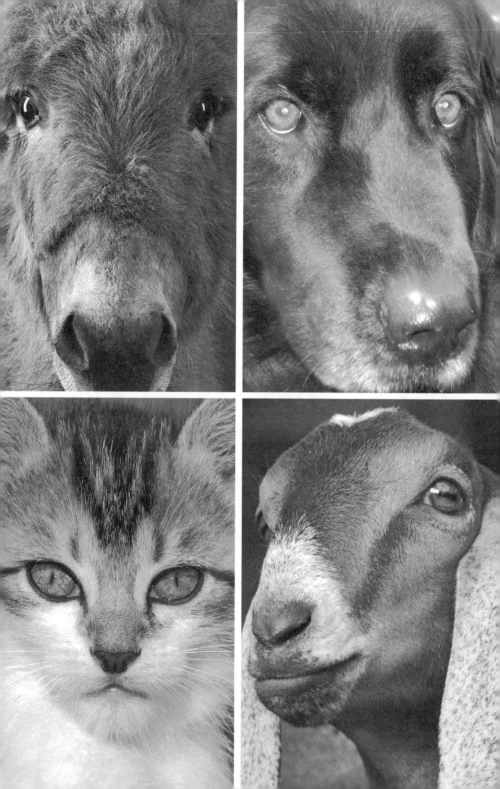

although some jealousy can be explained by an animal's desire to be leader of the pack, the real culprit is often the longing to be the one, the only one, for a human companion.

But can we call it "love"? Dr. Dodman thinks so. Despite the fact that some animal behaviorists disagree, Dodman believes strongly that animals are perfectly capable of forming loving attachments. He points out that animals are devoted to their offspring. He says that animals even fall in love with each other.

As an example: For 76 days, a bull moose visited a farm in Shrewsbury, Vermont, home of its beloved, a cow called Jessica. The moose nuzzled Jessica and pushed the other cows away so that Jessica could get at her food. The romance attracted a lot of attention and eventually became the subject of a children's book, *A Moose for Jessica*.

Little prairie voles are another example. They mate for life, the male spurns the attentions of other females, and the happy couple share baby-raising duties, groom each other, and cuddle for warmth.

In fact, prairie voles may offer an important clue about animal ardor. It seems that voles have an abundance of the hormone oxytocin. Scientists are starting to believe that animal and human bonding might have something to do with this hormone, which humans and other animals share.

It turns out that interacting with an animal can cause the release of oxytocin in both the petter and the petted. The hormone is responsible for feelings of bonding and well-being. It can also give relief from stress or even pain.

Prairie voles may offer an important clue about animal ardor.

When Jellybean and Mr. G were separated, Mr. G refused to eat.

Jellybean (left)
with Mr. G

D r. Anne Marie Carey sees the positive effects of human and animal bonding all the time. She works at the Atlantic Veterinary College in Charlottetown, Prince Edward Island. She says that animals in her care often respond better to treatment when their humans show up to pet them and encourage them.

"Really, I think that this is something beyond science," she says. "I can only describe it as love."

How else to explain a goat called Mr. G and its beloved, a donkey named Jellybean? The two spent all of their time together in Grass Valley, California. When they were separated, Mr. G went into such a funk that he refused to leave his corner of the barn or eat. The only solution? A joyous reunion.

I f you're looking for the most heartfelt examples of love and devotion, you need search no further than people and their dogs. Dogs have been domesticated for tens of thousands of

Even the most heartfelt of love stories can go bad when jealousy rears its head.

years. Although some dogs are trained to work, the majority of them live with people to provide companionship.

Some theorize that a dog's devotion is more to the contents of the food container than to the person who opens it. But any human who has been the happy recipient of doggie kisses would disagree. And they don't call it "puppy love" for nothing.

Tales of loyal dogs abound. There's Rin Tin Tin, of course. And Lassie. But there's also Willie, the Labrador retriever that saved its 6-year-old owner from a wolf attack in Alaska. Or Hachiko, the canine that became a legend in Japan when every day for 9 years it went to the train station where its

deceased master used to return home. And who can forget the Skye terrier known as Greyfriars Bobby that spent 14 years guarding the grave of its beloved owner? This love was immortalized in literature and movies and with a statue in Edinburgh, Scotland.

B ut as with Frisky the goat, even the most heartfelt of love stories can go bad when jealousy rears its head. Dog owners tell tales of dogs that push other dogs—or even other people—out of the way to claim their human's undivided attention.

A study done at the University of California found that dogs definitely tried to interfere when they thought that their owners were paying attention to another dog. The conclusion? The dogs were trying to protect what was, for them, an important social relationship. Maybe even someone they loved.

Dr. Dodman often treats this kind of jealous behavior in his own practice. He recommends family therapy to resolve the differences in a maladjusted *"ménagerie" à trois.*

If this doesn't work? "Seventy percent of people asked to choose between their spouse and their dog will choose the dog," he says. ∎

What did the lovestruck cat say to the man of her dreams?

O Romeow, Romeow, wherefore art thou Romeow?

Ann Thurlow, who writes from Charlottetown, PEI, is a regular contributor to the Almanac.

HOW CLEAN IS YOUR KITCHEN?

Discard everything you think you know—
and while you're at it, toss that old sponge, too!

BY CYNTHIA VAN HAZINGA

MOST COOKS believe they keep a clean kitchen. Before gathering this information, we certainly did. Now we're realizing that we may actually be encouraging toxic bacteria that make us vulnerable to food-borne illnesses! How about you? Take this quiz, test your knowledge, and face the dangers lurking in *your* kitchen.

Q. How hot should water be when washing hands?
a. 40°F
b. 75°F
c. 120°F
d. It doesn't matter.

A. d. Time spent washing, not water temperature, makes for clean hands. Scrub hands all over with soap for at least 20 seconds (the time it takes to hum "Happy Birthday" twice), then dry them, preferably with disposable towels.

Q. It's not necessary to wash fruit or vegetables if you're going to peel them. True or false?

A. False. While cutting, you can easily transfer bacteria from the peel or rind to the inside of your fruit and veggies. Wash all produce with clean running water (no soap).

Q. Rinse seafood, poultry, or other meat with cold water to eliminate any risk of bacteria like salmonella. True or false?

A. False. Potentially bacteria-laden juices in the rinse water that splashes onto your sink and counters pose the risk of food poisoning. Instead, cook the food at/to the proper temperature.

Q. How often should kitchen surfaces and implements (e.g., can openers) be washed?
a. every spring
b. once every month
c. once a week
d. every time you use them

A. d. Wash with soapy water and dry with paper towels. If you use cloth towels, wash them often in a hot cycle.

GOOD EGGS

Commercial eggs are washed before sale. Do not wash again, as this can increase the risk of cross-contamination, especially if the shell becomes cracked.

Q. Kitchen sponges are safe practically forever. True or false?

A. False. Bacteria thrive in moist environments, and a kitchen sponge probably has more bacteria in it than anything else in the house. Replace yours every 1 to 2 weeks. Between uses, squeeze it out and let it dry. Or, every 2 days, get the sponge soaking wet and microwave for 2 minutes to kill bacteria. Let dishrags dry between uses and wash them frequently. *(continued)*

Q. How cold should the interior of your refrigerator be?
a. 40°F
b. 45°F
c. 50°F

A. a. A constant 40°F or below slows, but does not stop, the growth of harmful bacteria. Avoid stuffing the refrigerator; allow for air to circulate.

Q. How long is cooked food safe in the refrigerator?
a. 1 to 2 days
b. 3 to 4 days
c. 5 to 6 days

A. b. As long as no bacteria have come into contact with the cooked leftovers, the food is safe for 3 to 4 days.

Q. To sanitize counters and cutting boards, use . . .
a. lemon juice and salt
b. dish detergent
c. 1 gallon of water with 1 tablespoon of bleach
d. 1 gallon of water with 1 cup of bleach

A. c. Bleach is toxic; an excess of it can be harmful. Using the milder solution (c), saturate surfaces and leave untouched for a few minutes. Rinse. Then dry with paper towels or air.

Q. Which cutting board is safer, wood or plastic?

A. Both are fine if cleaned thoroughly after each use, including edges as well as surfaces. Ideally, have one cutting board for meat/poultry and another for other foods.

Q. It is safe to store butter at room temperature. True or false?

A. True. Margarine, too. Butter may turn rancid in flavor after several days; leave out only what you will use within 1 or 2 days. Margarine may separate, but it's still safe.

Q. Perishable food kept at room temperature for more than 2 hours is not safe to eat. True or false?

A. True. Toss it after 2 hours. Bacteria grow rapidly in the "danger zone" (between 40° and 140°F). When the temperature is over 90°, toss unrefrigerated food after 1 hour.

Q. It is safe to thaw frozen food on the counter. True or false?

A. False. Thaw food in the refrigerator, under cold running water, or in a microwave, as directed. Food thawed on the counter could be in the "danger

THE UNTOUCHABLES

**Avoid putting raw meat, seafood, or eggs (raw or cooked)
in contact with other food. This is cross-contamination,
which can be hazardous to your health!**

zone" (between 40° and
140°F), enabling bacteria to
grow rapidly.

**Q. Hot foods should never
go directly into the refrigerator.
True or false?**

A. False. However, for quicker
cooling, divide a large quantity
into small, shallow container
portions.

**Q. Marinades contain acid,
which kills bacteria, so food
can be marinated on a kitchen
counter. True or false?**

A. False. Even in an acidic
marinade, bacteria can grow
rapidly at room temperature.
Marinate foods safely in the
refrigerator.

**Q. Food that falls on the floor
is safe to eat after . . .**
a. 5 seconds
b. 10 seconds
c. 1 minute
d. none of the above

A. d. Bacteria can be transferred
immediately upon contact.
Toss it.

**Q. If the power goes off, food
in a full refrigerator is safe
for how long?**
a. 4 hours
b. 8 hours
c. 12 hours
d. 16 hours

A. a. Also: Frozen food in a
full freezer is safe for 48 hours;
food in a half-full freezer is
safe for 24 hours.

**Q. Packaged food that is past
its "sell by" date should be
thrown out. True or false?**

A. False. "Sell by" dates are
used by retailers for inventory
control. "Use by" (or "best
by") dates usually refer to best
quality, not safety dates. While
some dates indicate freshness,
none reflect edibility or safety.

**Q. How long does canned
food last?**
a. 6 months
b. 1 year
c. 2 years
d. indefinitely

A. c. In general, canned food
stored at 75°F and below in a

cool, dry, dark place will last at least 2 years from the date of purchase. It retains its safety and nutritional value longer, but the food's quality (color and texture) may vary.

Q. Bulging or dented cans of food are unsafe. True or false?

A. True and false. A bulging can is unsafe. A dented can is safe, unless the dent is along the seam or it is leaking.

WASTE NOT!
Ninety percent of Americans occasionally discard good food because they mistakenly think that the "sell by," "best before," "use by," or "packed on" dates on food containers indicate safety.
It's all unnecessary waste! As far as food safety goes, the dates are meaningless.

Q. When a hamburger turns brown in the middle, it is cooked to a safe internal temperature. True or false?

A. False. Visual cues do not indicate that food is properly cooked. Use a food thermometer to be sure that ground meat is at least 160°F inside.

Q. Which kitchen tool might save your life?
a. cast-iron skillet
b. food thermometer
c. microwave
d. electric beater

A. b. As a general rule, cook poultry and stuffed meats to 165°F; ground meats to 160°F; and pork, lamb, veal, fish, and whole cuts of meat to 145°F in the thickest part. Heat cooked meats (e.g., hot dogs) until steaming hot. Food should be held at those temperatures for at least 15 seconds to kill any bacteria or pathogens.

Q. You can partially cook food and finish cooking it later. True or false?

A. False. Partial cooking increases the risk of bacterial growth.

Q. Leftovers are safe to eat until they smell bad. True or false?

A. False. Bacteria that cause food poisoning do not affect the look, smell, or taste of food. Heat leftovers to an internal temperature of 165°F. Never taste food to check for spoilage. ∎

After researching this piece, longtime contributor **Cynthia Van Hazinga** purchased a lifetime supply of sponges.

Table of Measures

APOTHECARIES'
1 scruple = 20 grains
1 dram = 3 scruples
1 ounce = 8 drams
1 pound = 12 ounces

AVOIRDUPOIS
1 ounce = 16 drams
1 pound = 16 ounces
1 hundredweight = 100 pounds
1 ton = 2,000 pounds
1 long ton = 2,240 pounds

LIQUID
4 gills = 1 pint
63 gallons = 1 hogshead
2 hogsheads = 1 pipe or butt
2 pipes = 1 tun

DRY
2 pints = 1 quart
4 quarts = 1 gallon
2 gallons = 1 peck
4 pecks = 1 bushel

LINEAR
1 hand = 4 inches
1 link = 7.92 inches

1 span = 9 inches
1 foot = 12 inches
1 yard = 3 feet
1 rod = 5$\frac{1}{2}$ yards
1 mile = 320 rods = 1,760 yards = 5,280 feet
1 international nautical mile = 6,076.1155 feet
1 knot = 1 nautical mile per hour
1 fathom = 2 yards = 6 feet
1 furlong = $\frac{1}{8}$ mile = 660 feet = 220 yards
1 league = 3 miles = 24 furlongs
1 chain = 100 links = 22 yards

SQUARE
1 square foot = 144 square inches
1 square yard = 9 square feet
1 square rod = 30$\frac{1}{4}$ square yards = 272$\frac{1}{4}$ square feet
1 acre = 160 square rods = 43,560 square feet
1 square mile = 640 acres = 102,400 square rods
1 square rod = 625 square links

1 square chain = 16 square rods
1 acre = 10 square chains

CUBIC
1 cubic foot = 1,728 cubic inches
1 cubic yard = 27 cubic feet
1 cord = 128 cubic feet
1 U.S. liquid gallon = 4 quarts = 231 cubic inches
1 imperial gallon = 1.20 U.S. gallons = 0.16 cubic foot
1 board foot = 144 cubic inches

KITCHEN
3 teaspoons = 1 tablespoon
16 tablespoons = 1 cup
1 cup = 8 ounces
2 cups = 1 pint
2 pints = 1 quart
4 quarts = 1 gallon

TO CONVERT CELSIUS AND FAHRENHEIT:
°C = (°F − 32)/1.8
°F = (°C × 1.8) + 32

Metric Conversions

LINEAR
1 inch = 2.54 centimeters
1 centimeter = 0.39 inch
1 meter = 39.37 inches
1 yard = 0.914 meter
1 mile = 1.61 kilometers
1 kilometer = 0.62 mile

SQUARE
1 square inch = 6.45 square centimeters
1 square yard = 0.84 square meter

1 square mile = 2.59 square kilometers
1 square kilometer = 0.386 square mile
1 acre = 0.40 hectare
1 hectare = 2.47 acres

CUBIC
1 cubic yard = 0.76 cubic meter
1 cubic meter = 1.31 cubic yards

HOUSEHOLD
$\frac{1}{2}$ teaspoon = 2 mL
1 teaspoon = 5 mL
1 tablespoon = 15 mL

$\frac{1}{4}$ cup = 60 mL
$\frac{1}{3}$ cup = 75 mL
$\frac{1}{2}$ cup = 125 mL
$\frac{2}{3}$ cup = 150 mL
$\frac{3}{4}$ cup = 175 mL
1 cup = 250 mL
1 liter = 1.057 U.S. liquid quarts
1 U.S. liquid quart = 0.946 liter
1 U.S. liquid gallon = 3.78 liters
1 gram = 0.035 ounce
1 ounce = 28.349 grams
1 kilogram = 2.2 pounds
1 pound = 0.45 kilogram

REUSE
RECYCLE
RENEW
REFRESH

A FEW OF OUR MORE THAN 900,000 FANS ON FACEBOOK SHARE THEIR COMMONSENSE AND, OCCASIONALLY, QUIRKY IDEAS FOR SAVING TIME, MONEY, AND SANITY.

GRATE APPEAL

I use my veg peeler to slice block cheese.
–*Vonda-Marie O.*

I always use my vegetable peelers to slice butter!
–*Tracey R.*

I use a cheese grater for cold butter when I make dumplings, biscuits, or piecrust.
–*Valerie E.*

I use a cheese grater on refrigerated butter for recipes that require "room temperature butter."
–*Michelle G.*

THE DAILY GRIND

When grinding hot peppers, I attach a regular-mouth quart- or pint-size mason jar directly to my bullet-type blender (fits perfectly). When done, I put a lid on the jar and store the peppers.
–*Lori F.*

I wash and dry eggshells and grind them with a mortar and pestle. These shells are great for cleaning out water bottles. I put in a few drops of soap and a spoonful of ground shells, fill halfway with water, then cap, shake, and swirl. The shells wash out easily.
–*Michelle G.*

I use coffee filters to dry-clean windows after I've sprayed them with a mix of 1 part alcohol to 2 parts water.
–*Sherri M.*

LAUNDRY LIST

I put dryer sheets into the pockets of my car doors. Smells great when the car gets hot from sitting out in the sun. One will last for a month or so.
–*Edward T.*

I wet down the car hood and use a dryer sheet to wipe off bugs.

–Lou T.-W.

Stuff dryer lint inside old toilet paper tubes and wrap with newspaper. Twist each end for free fire starters.

–Michelle G.

Use dryer lint covered in Vaseline for fire starters.

–Roxanne F.

I use an old dryer drum for my compost. I painted it and I love it.

–Heather F.

I used an old washer drum for a print washer in my dark room.

–Anonymous

I am using an old washer drum to house my worm farm!

–Richard K.

WHAT TO DO WITH LIDS

We used a black plastic coffee can lid as the center for a ceiling medallion on a chandelier. We stained the medallion dark mahogany, cut a hole in the center of the lid, and centered it in the medallion before we added the fixture. It blends in perfectly.

–Marianne B.

Put the lid of a big butter tub under your plunger to avoid drips and water stains on the floor.

–Penny J.

Put a butter container lid on top of your tea cup to keep it hot.

–Marie B.

CUTUPS

To make a gnat hat for gardening, I cut a doughnut out of a flattened cereal box, punch holes around half, and tie sections of kite string or ribbon to the holes.

–Kim C. K.

I use my pizza cutter to cut noodles.

–Ann B.

I use a pizza cutter to cut up pancakes quickly.

–Sarah P.

I use scissors to cut bacon (while it's still partially frozen) for fried bacon bits.

–Sandy O.

TOOL TIME

Butter knife = screwdriver!

–Nora O.

For touch-ups, I use an old soup ladle to dip a small amount of paint out of a 5-gallon bucket.

–Deborah S.

My dad uses a farrier's tool for cleaning out hooves to grasp old-fashioned storm windows and lower them for cleaning. He also uses an old, heavy-duty ice cream scoop as a lever to help him raise stuck windows.

–Regena L. M.

(continued)

STORE MORE

I use a plate draining rack to store all of my big glass lids, cake plates, and such vertically in my pantry. I use a letter holder for plastic lids and plates.
–Heather B.

Stuff plastic bags from the store into paper towel tubes.
–Teresa C.-G.

COOKING AND CLEANUP

I use a potato masher instead of a mixing hook to mix bread.
–Y. R.

Use a water glass for cutting biscuits.
–Joan M.

I use a clean mesh paint strainer to rinse quinoa.
–Elizabeth W.

I use cheap pillowcases to strain my fruit when making jellies.
–Monica C.

The inside of a sugar bag makes a great substitute for paper toweling when you fry something and need a grease "soaker upper."
–Martha C.

I use the plastic tops from soda bottles and milk containers to scrub dried food on pots and pans.
–Chris O. G.

Use an old credit card to scrape the top of a glass-top range.
–Marlene G.

OUTDOORS

We tie twine or dental floss around lint and hang it in trees for birds to use as nesting material.
–Libby G. M.

Put a bar of soap into a long sock. Tie to your spigot for easy hand-washing outdoors.
–Tammy L. P.

My husband punches holes in tuna cans and puts them under the feet of our lawn furniture to stop them from sinking into the ground.
–Marcia C.

HANDY-DANDIES

I use soda can rings to attach together the metal hangers of paired clothes. This saves closet space as well as lets my little one have complete and matched outfits.
–Kristi A. M.

When I get a few soap slivers, I add a few ingredients (scent, color, oatmeal, etc.) and put them into a plastic container that I have sprayed with cooking spray. I microwave it for a few seconds, stir, and microwave a few more seconds. New soap!
–Jessica H. ■

SANDALS, SOLES, AND SHOE-

WE PUT THEM ON EVERY morning and take them off every night. But what do we really know about shoes? Tromp through time and tradition to find out.

The bones in our feet are more delicate than those of human beings who lived 26,000 years ago. Paleontologists conclude that with the additional support shoes gave our feet, our foot bones became weaker. "The simple act of wearing shoes alters the structure of our feet," according to Elizabeth Semmelhack of the Bata Shoe Museum in Toronto.

In a Missouri cave, archaeologists found dozens of shoes made from the fibers of a tough plant called rattlesnake master. They are believed to be about 8,000 years old. No two are exactly alike. "It's human nature to make one pair a little more complex than others, to set it apart from someone else's," textile expert Jenna Tedrick Kuttruff told *National Geographic.*

Shoes make heroes of men. Ancient Romans toughened Greek sandals by adding metal tacks to the soles, and their legions conquered the known world. When Neil Armstrong took his famous "one small step for [a] man" onto the surface of the Moon, he was wearing $30,000 high-tech boots. (They're still there: To save weight for the return to Earth, the *Apollo* astronauts abandoned their shoes.)

In literature and folktales, shoes give wearers miraculous powers. Seven-league boots cover 21 miles with each stride; the ruby slippers that Dorothy wears in the film *The Wizard of Oz* (they are silver in the original L. Frank Baum book) take her home if she clicks the heels together and says, "There's no place like home"; a pair of glass slippers makes Cinderella a princess.

Shoes can cause pain and suffering. In Hans Christian Andersen's fairy tale "The Red Shoes," a vain girl has her feet cut off because of a pair of shoes with a life of their own. According to the American Academy of Orthopaedic Surgeons, nearly 7 million Americans saw a doctor

*A step-by-step examination of footwear
history, customs, and beliefs*

BY TIM CLARK

PERSTITIONS

for foot and toe pain in 2009, mostly due to ill-fitting shoes.

*Wear at the toe, live to see woe;
Wear at the side, live to be a bride;
Wear at the ball, live to spend all;
Wear at the heel, live to save a deal.*
–Old rhyme

Every culture on Earth has sayings like the one above. In 2008, I. Marc Carlson compiled hundreds of "shoe-perstitions."

HOW TO BE IN STEP WITH GOOD LUCK

■ In England, shoes are thrown after someone who is leaving on a journey. This is the origin of the modern custom of tying shoes to the back of a newlywed couple's car.

■ Also in England, a woman who wishes to conceive a child is told to try on the shoes of a woman who has just given birth.

■ African-American lore says that to drive away bad business, you should get a shoe from the oldest woman you can find, take it to your place of business, and burn it to a crisp.

■ In Poona, India, the victim of a curse can escape it by taking hold of an up-turned shoe.

■ English boatmen consider shoes taken from a dead man's feet to be especially lucky.

HOW TO BE A HEEL, OR HAVE BAD LUCK

■ In Bengal, India, if you leave shoes lying on their uppers, you will quarrel with someone that day.

■ In Germany, a woman who goes without shoes during the 6 weeks following childbirth causes her child to take a dangerous fall while learning to walk.

■ Hawaiians believe that to wear shoes in a house is to invite the devil to come in.

■ In the Ozark Mountains of the United

HUMAN HIST?RY IS THE HIST?RY ?F SH?ES

–Stebby Julionatan, Indonesian writer (b. 1983)

FOOTLOOSE FANS

Greek philosopher Socrates did it; John "Johnny Appleseed" Chapman did it; so did Abraham Lincoln as a boy, dancer Isadora Duncan, and Indian leader Mahatma Gandhi. Abebe Bikila of Ethiopia did it and won the Olympic Marathon on September 10, 1960, in record time.

They all did what folks have been doing for centuries: went barefoot. And it's a practice that thousands of people are taking in stride today. Barefoot hikers tread trails all over North America. Joggers run barefoot or in minimal footwear. In Europe, barefoot parks invite walkers onto man-made trails to feel textures such as those of moss, sand, and logs. Park routes can range from very short to more than 3 miles, and people of all ages participate.

Opponents of bare feet cite the risk of Achilles tendonitis or bone injury, among other possible ill effects.

Barefoot proponents claim heightened awareness of their surroundings, increased muscle strength, and overall comfort— not to mention never having to worry about "walking in someone else's shoes."

–Darren Richardson

States, it's bad luck to put the left shoe on first or to put shoes on a table or bed.

■ Jews in Minsk, Belarus, say that to walk in one shoe will cause a parent to die.

"Who are you?" said the stocking to the shoe.
Said the shoe to the stocking,
"How terribly shocking,
For such as you to say to a shoe,
'Who are you?'"
–Ange Fagnano

In many parts of the Middle East, it is an insult to reveal the soles of your shoes. Ancient Egyptians drew the faces of their enemies on the soles of their shoes so that they could walk on them. After the First Gulf War, a hotel in Baghdad featured a mosaic portraying President George H. W. Bush on the lobby floor for the same reason.

Some folk beliefs about shoes remain mysterious. For example, nobody knows why thousands of shoes, some dating back to Roman times, have been found hidden in walls, ceilings, floors, and fireplaces in Europe and North America.

"Why the shoe? It is the only garment we wear that retains the shape, the personality, the essence of the wearer," noted June Swann, an English shoe expert who started tracking concealed shoes in 1958, when she first learned of a pair of children's ankle boots that had been found in a thatched roof. Shoes were expensive, and, until recently in human history, they were repaired or reused far more often than replaced.

"I worried about that pair of boots for a long time," Swann told *National Geographic*. "What parent would let a child play on a thatched roof? Why would they allow a good pair of shoes to be left behind?"

She decided that shoes were not left behind by mistake after finding an adult shoe plastered into a wall in Devon, England. "It could not have been plastered over by accident," she said. "Obviously, care was involved."

Swann has never proven to her own satisfaction why people hid shoes in houses. She believes that it is superstition and that it might have been a charm against witches or evil spirits.

There is now a modern shoe mystery. All over the world, sneakers and running shoes can be found laced together and dangling from telephone and electric wires. Many reasons have been suggested, from bullying to gang signals or memorials to teens marking transitions in their lives such as graduation or sexual initiation. There's a custom among soldiers, it's said, of painting combat boots yellow or orange and tossing them over wires when leaving a post or the service itself.

It could also be what some call a "meme"—a practice that spreads in a society simply because others do it.

But June Swann has a simpler explanation: "We should remember the urge of ordinary people to leave a mark of their existence in the world." In one man's dusty old boot, hidden in a wall, she found a piece of wallpaper with a penciled inscription:

William Chapman
B 3d July 1828
this was don in 1876 ■

Tim Clark, who always puts on his left shoe first, has been writing about folklore for the Almanac for more than 30 years.

SOLE MATES

THEN . . .
In the 2nd century A.D., Greek writer and philosopher Plutarch related in his biographical *Lives* the story of a Roman who, in response to friends who demanded to know why he had divorced his wife without apparent cause, says, "No one of you can tell me where [my shoe] pinches my foot."

NOW . . .
At Kentucky's Murray State University, if two students fall in love and then marry, each nails a shoe to the "shoe tree" outside Pogue Library. They often return to nail a baby shoe to the tree, which has become little more than a tall stump.

10

Peculiar "Laws"
THAT EXPLAIN
Everything

OK, not *everything*. But these "laws,"
discovered by experts in many fields, shed
light on many of life's mysteries.

by Norm D. Bloom • Illustrations by Tim Robinson

CAMPBELL'S LAW

From: American social psychologist Donald T. Campbell (1976)

What it says: The more weight given to one element in a complex problem of social policy, the more likely that element will be corrupted.

What it means: When the consequences of failure are significant, people cheat.

Example: The use of high-stakes testing in U.S. schools has resulted in widespread cheating by the teachers and administrators who have the most to lose (such as their jobs) as a result of poor student performance.

DUNBAR'S NUMBER

From: English anthropologist Robin Dunbar (1992)

What it says: The size of the human brain limits the number of stable relationships that one human being can maintain to about 150.

What it means: A person can have about 150 good friends at one time.

Example: The number roughly matches the average size of villages, tribes, and military units all over the world.

③ THE DUNNING-KRUGER EFFECT

From: American social psychologists David Dunning and Justin Kruger (1999)

What it says: In Dunning's words, "If you're incompetent, you can't know you're incompetent."

What it means: Inept people overestimate their skills.

Example: Kruger and Dunning were inspired by a bank robber who knew that lemon juice can be used as "invisible ink" (the message can be read only after heating the paper). The thief rubbed it all over his face, believing it would make him invisible to security cameras.

④ THE BEN FRANKLIN EFFECT

From: *The Autobiography of Benjamin Franklin* (1791)

What it says: "He that has once done you a kindness will be more ready to do you another than he whom you yourself have obliged."

What it means: It's easier to make a friend by asking for a favor than by doing one.

Example: "Having heard that [another legislator] had in his library a certain very scarce and curious book, I wrote a note to him, expressing my desire of perusing that book, and requesting he would do me the favour of lending it to me for a few days. He sent it immediately, and I return'd it in about a week with another note, expressing strongly my sense of the favour. When we next met in the House, he spoke to me (which he had never done before), and with great civility; and he ever after manifested a readiness to serve me on all occasions."

5. HUMPHREY'S LAW

From: English psychologist George Humphrey (1923)

What it says: Paying too close attention to a normally automatic or unconscious activity hampers your ability to do it well.

What it means: Don't overthink things!

Example: Humphrey illustrated this with "The Centipede's Dilemma" by Katherine Craster (1871):

A centipede was happy—quite!
Until a toad in fun
Said, "Pray, which leg moves after which?"
This raised her doubts to such a pitch,
She fell exhausted in the ditch,
Not knowing how to run.

6. MARCHETTI'S CONSTANT

From: Italian physicist Cesare Marchetti (1994)

What it says: In all places throughout history, the average time that the average human being takes to travel to and from work each day is 1 hour, regardless of the form of transportation.

What it means: As roads and mass transit are improved, people will choose to live farther away from their jobs.

Example: A person who moves close to the workplace in order to give up a car (to walk, bike, or commute by other

means) will spend as much time getting to work as he or she did driving.

7. THE PARETO PRINCIPLE

From: Italian economist Vilfredo Pareto (1906)

What it says: 80 percent of the effect comes from 20 percent of the causes.

What it means: 80 percent of a company's sales come from 20 percent of the sales force; 80 percent of complaints come from 20 percent of customers; 80 percent of crimes are committed by 20 percent of criminals; and so forth.

Example: In 1992, the United Nations reported that the richest 20 percent of the world's population controlled 82.7 percent of the world's income.

8

SAYRE'S LAW

From: American political scientist Wallace Stanley Sayre (1973)

What it says: "Academic politics is the most vicious and bitter form of politics, because the stakes are so low."

What it means: The less important the issue, the more emotional the debate.

Example: In any New England town meeting, there is likely to be more impassioned debate over spending $100 than on spending $100,000.

9

STIGLER'S LAW OF EPONOMY

From: American statistics professor Stephen Stigler (1980)

What it says: No discovery is ever named after its discoverer.

What it means: The credit for important findings often goes to someone else.

Example: America is named after Amerigo Vespucci (not Christopher Columbus), and Stigler himself attributes Stigler's Law to sociologist Robert K. Merton.

10

THE ZEIGARNIK EFFECT

From: Russian psychologist Bluma Zeigarnik (1927)

What it says: We are more likely to remember incomplete or interrupted tasks than those that we have finished.

What it means: Cramming for a test is ineffective.

Example: Students studying for an exam remember the material better if they take breaks to do other things or study other subjects.

N. D. Bloom's personal law? "If a fact has no practical value, I know it. And vice versa."

Frosts and Growing Seasons

■ Dates given are normal averages for a light freeze; local weather and topography may cause considerable variations. The possibility of frost occurring after the spring dates and before the fall dates is 50 percent. The classification of freeze temperatures is usually based on their effect on plants. **Light freeze:** 29° to 32°F—tender plants killed. **Moderate freeze:** 25° to 28°F—widely destructive to most vegetation. **Severe freeze:** 24°F and colder—heavy damage to most plants. *–dates below courtesy of National Climatic Data Center*

State	City	Growing Season (days)	Last Spring Frost	First Fall Frost	State	City	Growing Season (days)	Last Spring Frost	First Fall Frost
AK	Juneau	148	May 8	Oct. 4	ND	Bismarck	129	May 14	Sept. 21
AL	Mobile	274	Feb. 28	Nov. 29	NE	Blair	167	Apr. 25	Oct. 10
AR	Pine Bluff	240	Mar. 16	Nov. 12	NE	North Platte	137	May 9	Sept. 24
AZ	Phoenix	*	*	*	NH	Concord	123	May 20	Sept. 21
AZ	Tucson	333	Jan. 19	Dec. 18	NJ	Newark	217	Apr. 3	Nov. 7
CA	Eureka	323	Jan. 27	Dec. 16	NM	Carlsbad	215	Mar. 31	Nov. 2
CA	Sacramento	297	Feb. 10	Dec. 4	NM	Los Alamos	149	May 11	Oct. 8
CA	San Francisco	*	*	*	NV	Las Vegas	283	Feb. 16	Nov. 27
CO	Denver	156	Apr. 30	Oct. 4	NY	Albany	153	May 2	Oct. 3
CT	Hartford	165	Apr. 26	Oct. 9	NY	Syracuse	167	Apr. 28	Oct. 13
DE	Wilmington	202	Apr. 10	Oct. 30	OH	Akron	192	Apr. 18	Oct. 28
FL	Miami	*	*	*	OH	Cincinnati	192	Apr. 13	Oct. 23
FL	Tallahassee	239	Mar. 22	Nov. 17	OK	Lawton	222	Mar. 29	Nov. 7
GA	Athens	227	Mar. 24	Nov. 7	OK	Tulsa	224	Mar. 27	Nov. 7
GA	Savannah	268	Mar. 1	Nov. 25	OR	Pendleton	187	Apr. 13	Oct. 18
IA	Atlantic	148	May 2	Sept. 28	OR	Portland	236	Mar. 23	Nov. 15
IA	Cedar Rapids	163	Apr. 25	Oct. 6	PA	Franklin	163	May 6	Oct. 17
ID	Boise	148	May 10	Oct. 6	PA	Williamsport	167	Apr. 30	Oct. 15
IL	Chicago	186	Apr. 20	Oct. 24	RI	Kingston	147	May 8	Oct. 3
IL	Springfield	182	Apr. 13	Oct. 13	SC	Charleston	260	Mar. 9	Nov. 25
IN	Indianapolis	181	Apr. 17	Oct. 16	SC	Columbia	213	Apr. 1	Nov. 1
IN	South Bend	175	Apr. 26	Oct. 19	SD	Rapid City	140	May 9	Sept. 27
KS	Topeka	174	Apr. 19	Oct. 11	TN	Memphis	235	Mar. 22	Nov. 13
KY	Lexington	192	Apr. 15	Oct. 25	TN	Nashville	204	Apr. 6	Oct. 28
LA	Monroe	256	Mar. 3	Nov. 15	TX	Amarillo	184	Apr. 18	Oct. 20
LA	New Orleans	302	Feb. 12	Dec. 11	TX	Denton	242	Mar. 18	Nov. 16
MA	Worcester	170	Apr. 26	Oct. 14	TX	San Antonio	270	Feb. 28	Nov. 25
MD	Baltimore	200	Apr. 11	Oct. 29	UT	Cedar City	132	May 21	Oct. 1
ME	Portland	156	May 2	Oct. 6	UT	Spanish Fork	167	May 1	Oct. 16
MI	Lansing	145	May 10	Oct. 3	VA	Norfolk	247	Mar. 20	Nov. 23
MI	Marquette	154	May 11	Oct. 13	VA	Richmond	206	Apr. 6	Oct. 30
MN	Duluth	124	May 21	Sept. 23	VT	Burlington	147	May 8	Oct. 3
MN	Willmar	153	Apr. 30	Oct. 1	WA	Seattle	251	Mar. 10	Nov. 17
MO	Jefferson City	187	Apr. 13	Oct. 18	WA	Spokane	153	May 2	Oct. 3
MS	Columbia	247	Mar. 13	Nov. 16	WI	Green Bay	150	May 6	Oct. 4
MS	Vicksburg	240	Mar. 20	Nov. 16	WI	Sparta	133	May 13	Sept. 24
MT	Fort Peck	140	May 8	Sept. 26	WV	Parkersburg	183	Apr. 21	Oct. 22
MT	Helena	121	May 19	Sept. 18	WY	Casper	119	May 22	Sept. 19
NC	Fayetteville	221	Mar. 28	Nov. 5					

Frosts do not occur every year.

How We Predict the Weather

We derive our weather forecasts from a secret formula that was devised by the founder of this Almanac, Robert B. Thomas, in 1792. Thomas believed that weather on Earth was influenced by sunspots, which are magnetic storms on the surface of the Sun.

Over the years, we have refined and enhanced this formula with state-of-the-art technology and modern scientific calculations. We employ three scientific disciplines to make our long-range predictions: solar science, the study of sunspots and other solar activity; climatology, the study of prevailing weather patterns; and meteorology, the study of the atmosphere. We predict weather trends and events by comparing solar patterns and historical weather conditions with current solar activity.

Our forecasts emphasize temperature and precipitation deviations from averages, or normals. These are based on 30-year statistical averages prepared by government meteorological agencies and updated every 10 years. The most-recent tabulations span the period 1981 through 2010.

The 16 regions of the contiguous states *(page 191)* are based primarily on climatology and how weather in each tends to differ based on a particular weather pattern. For example, while the average weather in Richmond, Virginia, and Boston, Massachusetts, is very different (although both are in Region 2), both areas tend to be affected by the same storms and high-pressure centers and have similar departures from normal weather.

We believe that nothing in the universe happens haphazardly, that there is a cause-and-effect pattern to all phenomena. However, although neither we nor any other forecasters have as yet gained sufficient insight into the mysteries of the universe to predict the weather with total accuracy, our results are almost always very close to our traditional claim of 80%.

WEATHER

How Accurate Was Our Forecast Last Winter?

We were correct in our forecast that "winter is expected to be another cold one in the eastern half to two-thirds of the nation, with above-normal temperatures, on average, in the West." We were also correct that "snowfall will be above normal in most of the Northeast." We disagreed with nearly all of the other forecasters by saying that the moderate to strong El Niño that they predicted would not develop and that, accordingly, most of California and the Southwest would have below-normal precipitation, with their drought worsening.

Our greatest errors were in underforecasting how far above normal California temperatures and Boston-area snowfall would be—although we did forecast both to be above normal.

As for our accuracy percentage, we were correct in our forecast temperature departure from normal in 17 of the 18 regions, as shown in the table below using one representative city from each region. In Region 12 (High Plains),

we forecast temperatures to be below normal in the north and above normal in the south, or normal overall. Since our representative city, Bismarck, is in the north and was below normal, while other cities in the region were above normal, a strong case could be made that our forecast was correct in this region, as well. We were correct in all 18 regions on our forecast of the direction of precipitation departure from normal and in 17 of the 18 regions on snowfall, missing only in Region 11 (Texas–Oklahoma). There we forecast below-normal snowfall, which was correct across the southern half of the region but incorrect in the north. With that, overall, our accuracy rate was 96.3%, well above our historical average rate of 80%.

The accuracy of our winter season temperature forecasts is shown in the table below, using a city selected from each region. On average, our temperature forecasts differed from actual conditions by 0.63 degrees F.

Region/ City	Nov.–Mar. Temp. Variations From Normal (degrees F)		Region/ City	Nov.–Mar. Temp. Variations From Normal (degrees F)	
	PREDICTED	ACTUAL		PREDICTED	ACTUAL
1. Caribou, ME	–2.8	–3.1	10. Topeka, KS	–1.0	–0.8
2. Richmond, VA	–2.6	–2.3	11. Oklahoma City, OK	–0.8	–1.3
3. Harrisburg, PA	–3.6	–4.2	12. Bismarck, ND	0.0	–0.2
4. Atlanta, GA	–3.2	–0.8	13. Pendleton, OR	+2.0	+2.3
5. Jacksonville, FL	–2.0	–0.7	14. El Paso, TX	–2.0	+1.8
6. Milwaukee, WI	–3.0	–3.1	15. Seattle, WA	+1.8	+3.0
7. Charleston, WV	–3.8	–3.6	16. Los Angeles, CA	+1.9	+3.7
8. Tupelo, MS	–3.0	–2.6	17. Nome, AK	+4.4	+4.8
9. Minneapolis, MN	–1.4	–1.5	18. Lihue, HI	+0.1	+0.1

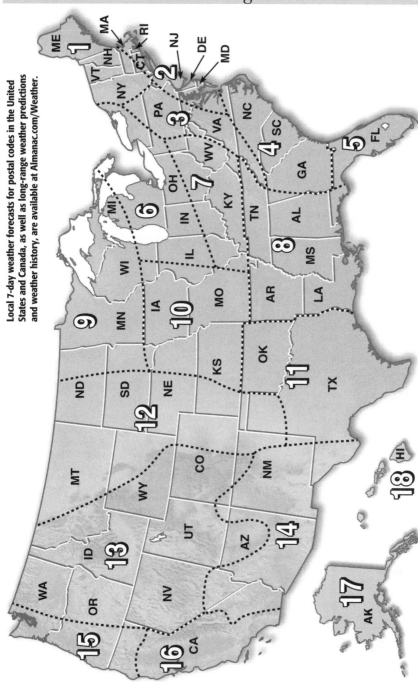

Local 7-day weather forecasts for postal codes in the United States and Canada, as well as long-range weather predictions and weather history, are available at Almanac.com/Weather.

WEATHER

Northeast

SUMMARY: Winter temperatures will be near normal across the north and a bit below normal, on average, in the south. Most of December and January will bring below-normal temperatures, with the coldest periods in early to mid- and late January. Precipitation will be slightly greater than normal, with snowfall below normal in the north but above normal elsewhere. The snowiest periods will be in early and mid-December, early to mid-January, late February, and early to mid-March.

April and May will be slightly cooler and drier than normal.

Summer will be slightly hotter and rainier than normal, with the hottest periods in mid- and late June, early July, early to mid-August, and late August. Watch for tropical storm threats from mid-August to mid-September.

September and October will be much warmer and slightly drier than normal.

NOV. 2015: Temp. 40° (2° above avg.); precip. 3" (0.5" below avg.). 1–2 Sunny, cold. 3–8 Rainy periods, mild. 9–12 Rain and snow showers. 13–16 Rainy periods, mild. 17–25 Showers, mild. 26–30 Snowy periods, cold.

DEC. 2015: Temp. 24° (4° below avg.); precip. 4" (1" above avg.). 1–3 Snowstorm. 4–9 Snow south, sunny north; cold. 10–14 Snowstorm, then snow showers, cold. 15–17 Snow, cold. 18–24 Snow showers, cold. 25–31 Snowstorm, then rain and snow showers, mild.

JAN. 2016: Temp. 19° (4° below avg.); precip. 2" (1" below avg.). 1–6 Snow showers, mild. 7–14 Snow, then flurries, very cold. 15–20 Periods of rain and snow, mild. 21–28 Snow showers, turning very cold. 29–31 Snow, then rain, mild.

FEB. 2016: Temp. 27° (4° above avg.); precip. 4.5" (2" above avg.). 1–7 Snow, then periods of rain and snow, mild. 8–15 Rain and snow showers, seasonable. 16–23 Snow, then rainy periods, mild. 24–29 Blizzard, then flurries, cold.

MAR. 2016: Temp. 34.5° (2° above avg. north, 1° below south); precip. 2.5" (0.5" below avg.). 1–6 Snow showers, cold. 7–10 Showers, mild. 11–21 Snowstorm, then sunny, cold. 22–31 Showers, seasonable.

APR. 2016: Temp. 44° (2° below avg.); precip. 2.5" (0.5" below avg.). 1–6 Snow, then sunny, turning warm. 7–10 Rain and snow showers,

cold. 11–13 Sunny, nice. 14–27 Showers, cool. 28–30 Sunny, warm.

MAY 2016: Temp. 56° (1° above avg.); precip. 2.5" (1" below avg.). 1–5 Sunny, warm. 6–10 Showers, then sunny, cool. 11–14 Sunny, warm. 15–20 Showers, cool. 21–31 Sunny, then a few showers, cool.

JUNE 2016: Temp. 66° (1° above avg.); precip. 3.5" (avg.). 1–7 Showers, then sunny, cool. 8–14 Scattered t-storms, turning hot. 15–22 Sunny, seasonable. 23–30 T-storms, hot, then sunny, cooler.

JULY 2016: Temp. 69° (1° below avg.); precip. 4.5" (0.5" above avg.). 1–5 Sunny, hot, then cool. 6–14 Scattered t-storms, cool. 15–27 Several t-storms, seasonable. 28–31 Sunny, cool.

AUG. 2016: Temp. 67° (1° above avg.); precip. 4.5" (0.5" above avg.). 1–4 A couple of t-storms, hot. 5–12 Sunny; cool, then hot. 13–19 T-storms, then sunny, cool. 20–22 Tropical storm threat. 23–28 Sunny, cool, then hot. 29–31 Showers, warm.

SEPT. 2016: Temp. 62° (3° above avg.); precip. 3.5" (0.5" below avg.). 1–5 Sunny, warm. 6–9 Tropical storm threat. 10–21 Showers, then sunny, chilly. 22–30 A few showers, mild.

OCT. 2016: Temp. 53° (5° above avg.); precip. 3.5" (avg.). 1–6 Heavy rain, then sunny, cool. 7–16 Sunny, nice. 17–25 Showers, then sunny, mild. 26–31 Showers, cool.

Caribou · Augusta · Burlington · Concord · Albany

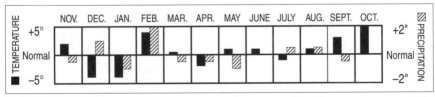

Atlantic Corridor

SUMMARY: Winter will be colder and snowier than normal in the north, with near-normal temperatures and below-normal snowfall in the south. The coldest period will be in mid-January, with cold weather also occurring in late December, most of January, mid-February, and early March. Precipitation will be slightly above normal, with the snowiest periods in mid- and late December, early to mid-January, and late March.

April and May will be slightly cooler than normal, with rainfall generally below normal.

Summer will be hotter and rainier than normal, with the hottest periods in late June, mid-July, and early and late August. The greatest tropical storm and hurricane threat is from early August to mid-September. September and October will be much warmer than normal, with above-normal rainfall.

Boston
Hartford
Providence
New York
Philadelphia
Baltimore
Atlantic City
Washington
Richmond

NOV. 2015: Temp. 48° (1° above avg.); pre-cip. 3" (0.5" below avg.). 1–2 Sunny, mild. 3–8 Rainy periods, turning chilly. 9–16 A few showers; mild north, cool south. 17–21 Sunny, cold, then mild. 22–26 Showers, then sunny, warm. 27–30 Wet snow north, rain south, then sunny, cold.

DEC. 2015: Temp. 37.5° (3° below avg. north, avg. south); precip. 4" (1" above avg.). 1–5 Snowy periods, cold north; showers, mild south. 6–9 Rain and snow showers, cold. 10–13 Rain to snow, then sunny, mild. 14–19 Heavy snow north, showers south. 20–23 Sunny, cold. 24–27 Snowstorm, then sunny, cold. 28–31 Rainy, mild.

JAN. 2016: Temp. 32° (3° below avg.); precip. 2.5" (1" below avg.). 1–5 Snow showers, cold. 6–14 Snow, then flurries, very cold. 15–19 Periods of rain and snow north, rain south; mild. 20–28 Snow showers, cold. 29–31 Heavy rain and snow.

FEB. 2016: Temp. 38° (4° above avg.); precip. 5" (2" above avg.). 1–5 Sunny, turning mild. 6–9 Heavy rain, then sunny, cold. 10–18 Flurries, cold north; showers, mild south. 19–23 Rain, then sunny, mild. 24–29 Periods of rain and snow.

MAR. 2016: Temp. 42° (2° below avg.); precip. 3" (1" below avg.). 1–3 Sunny, cold. 4–9 Snow, then showers north; a few showers south; turning mild. 10–16 Occasional rain and wet snow, chilly. 17–19 Sunny north, snow south; cold. 20–25 Sunny, mild. 26–29 Showers, turning cool. 30–31 Heavy rain coast, wet snow inland.

APR. 2016: Temp. 51° (1° below avg.); precip. 1.5" (2" below avg.). 1–6 Sunny, turning warm. 7–14 Showers north, sunny south; warm, then cooler. 15–23 A few showers north, sunny south; turning warm. 24–30 Scattered showers, cool.

MAY 2016: Temp. 62° (avg.); precip. 4" (avg. north, 2" above south). 1–3 Rainy periods, cool. 4–5 Sunny, warm. 6–11 Rainy periods, cool. 12–20 Scattered showers, turning warm. 21–23 Rainy, cool. 24–31 Scattered t-storms, turning hot.

JUNE 2016: Temp. 73° (2° above avg.); precip. 3" (0.5" below avg.). 1–4 Sunny, cooler. 5–13 T-storms, then sunny, turning warm. 14–24 A couple of t-storms, very warm. 25–30 Sunny, turning hot.

JULY 2016: Temp. 76° (avg.); precip. 5" (1" above avg.). 1–8 Scattered t-storms, turning cooler. 9–16 T-storms, then sunny, warm. 17–21 T-storms, then sunny, hot. 22–28 Scattered t-storms, locally heavy. 29–31 Sunny, warm.

AUG. 2016: Temp. 74° (1° above avg. north, 1° below south); precip. 5.5" (1.5" above avg.). 1–3 Sunny, hot. 4–10 Sunny, cool. 11–14 Tropical storm threat. 15–18 Sunny, cool. 19–21 Hurricane threat. 22–31 Sunny, turning hot.

SEPT. 2016: Temp. 70° (3° above avg.); precip. 4.5" (1" above avg.). 1–3 Sunny, turning cooler. 4–8 Tropical rains. 9–14 Scattered t-storms, warm. 15–22 Sunny; cool, then warm. 23–30 Scattered t-storms, turning cool.

OCT. 2016: Temp. 62° (6° above avg.): precip. 4.5" (1" above avg.). 1–10 Rain, then sunny, warm. 11–16 Showers, mild. 17–23 T-storms, then sunny, warm. 24–31 A few t-storms.

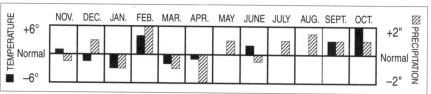

Appalachians

SUMMARY: Winter will be colder than normal, with precipitation slightly below normal. The coldest period will be in the middle part of January, with other cold periods in mid- and late December and early February. Snowfall will be near normal in Pennsylvania and above normal elsewhere in the region, with the snowiest periods in late December, mid- and late January, and early and mid-February.

April and May will have near-normal temperatures and be slightly rainier than usual.

Summer will be slightly cooler, with the hottest periods in mid-June and early and late August, and rainier than normal.

September and October will be much warmer than normal, with slightly above-normal rainfall.

NOV. 2015: Temp. 43° (1° below avg.); precip. 3.5" (avg.). 1–2 Sunny. 3–8 Rainy periods; warm, then cool. 9–11 Sunny, cold. 12–19 Rain, then flurries, cold. 20–27 A few showers, mild. 28–30 Snow showers, cold.

DEC. 2015: Temp. 35° (3° below avg. north, 1° above south); precip. 2.5" (0.5" below avg.). 1–3 Sunny, mild. 4–10 Periods of rain and snow north, showers south. 11–13 Sunny, mild. 14–19 Snow showers, cold. 20–23 Sunny, cold. 24–26 Snowstorm. 27–31 Rain, then sunny, cold.

JAN. 2016: Temp. 27° (3° below avg.); precip. 2.5" (0.5" below avg.). 1–5 Sunny; cold, then mild. 6–13 Snow showers, then flurries, very cold. 14–17 Periods of rain and snow. 18–26 Snow showers, very cold. 27–31 Rain and snow showers, turning quite mild.

FEB. 2016: Temp. 32° (2° above avg.); precip. 3.5" (1" above avg.). 1–4 Rain to snow, then sunny, cold. 5–7 Rain to snow. 8–10 Flurries, cold. 11–15 Rainy periods, mild. 16–22 Snow, then showers, mild. 23–29 Rain to snow, then sunny, cold.

MAR. 2016: Temp. 38° (2° below avg.); precip. 2.5" (0.5" below avg.). 1–5 Snow showers, cold north; showers, turning mild south. 6–9 Showers, mild. 10–17 Snowy periods north, showers south; chilly. 18–20 Wet snow, then sunny, cold. 21–29 A few showers, cool. 30–31 Rain and snow.

APR. 2016: Temp. 49° (1° below avg.); precip.

Elmira
Scranton
Harrisburg
Frederick
Roanoke
Asheville

1.5" (1" below avg.). 1–13 A couple of showers; cool, then warm. 14–25 Showers, cool. 26–30 Sunny, cool.

MAY 2016: Temp. 61° (1° above avg.); precip. 6" (2" above avg.). 1–4 Showers, cool. 5–13 Rain, then sunny, turning hot. 14–20 T-storms, then sunny, cool. 21–23 Rainy, cool. 24–28 Sunny, warm. 29–31 T-storms, hot.

JUNE 2016: Temp. 68° (1° above avg.); precip. 4.5" (0.5" above avg.). 1–5 Sunny north, t-storms south. 6–10 Rainy periods, cool. 11–25 Scattered t-storms, very warm. 26–30 Sunny, nice.

JULY 2016: Temp. 71° (2° below avg.); precip. 5.5" (2" above avg.). 1–8 T-storms, then sunny, cool. 9–16 T-storms, then sunny, cool. 17–21 T-storms, then sunny, cool. 22–28 Daily t-storms, humid. 29–31 Sunny north, t-storms south; cool.

AUG. 2016: Temp. 71° (avg.); precip. 2.5" (1" below avg.). 1–4 Sunny, hot. 5–9 T-storms, then sunny, cool. 10–16 Scattered t-storms, warm. 17–19 Sunny, cool. 20–26 T-storms, then sunny, cool. 27–31 Sunny, very warm.

SEPT. 2016: Temp. 67° (3° above avg.); precip. 3.5" (avg.). 1–3 Sunny, hot. 4–8 T-storms, then sunny, warm. 9–14 Scattered t-storms, warm. 15–18 Sunny, cool. 19–23 Showers, then sunny, warm. 24–30 Scattered showers, warm.

OCT. 2016: Temp. 58° (5° above avg.); precip. 4" (1" above avg.). 1–6 T-storms, then sunny, cool. 7–16 Sunny north, showers south; mild. 17–24 Rain, then sunny, warm. 25–31 Rain, then sunny, cool.

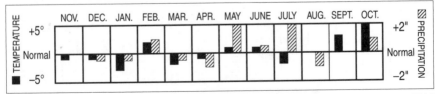

Southeast

SUMMARY: Winter will be colder and rainier than normal, with below-normal snowfall. The coldest period will be in mid-January, with other cold spells in early to mid- and late December, most of January, and early February. The snowiest periods will be in mid- to late December and early February, with icy periods in early and late January.

April and May will be slightly cooler than normal, with near-normal rainfall.

Summer will be cooler than normal, with the hottest period in mid-August, and rainier than normal. The greatest hurricane threats will be in early to mid-July and mid- to late September. The greatest threat of tropical storms will be in mid-August.

September and October will be much warmer than normal, with rainfall above normal in the north and below in the south.

NOV. 2015: Temp. 53° (2° below avg.); precip. 1.5" (1.5" below avg.). 1–2 Sunny, cool. 3–7 Rainy periods, mild. 8–15 Scattered showers, cool. 16–19 Sunny, cold. 20–27 Showers, then sunny, warm. 28–30 Showers, cool.

DEC. 2015: Temp. 48° (avg. north, 2° above south); precip. 4.5" (1" above avg.). 1–4 Sunny, turning mild. 5–11 Showers, then sunny, cold. 12–16 Rainy periods, mild. 17–21 Sunny, cool. 22–27 Rain to snow, then sunny, cold. 28–31 Rain, then sunny, cold.

JAN. 2016: Temp. 41.5° (3° below avg. north, avg. south); precip. 5" (0.5" above avg.). 1–6 Ice north, rain south, then sunny, mild. 7–14 Rain, then sunny, very cold. 15–22 Rain, then sunny, cold. 23–26 Rain, then sunny, very cold. 27–31 Ice to rain north, rainy periods south.

FEB. 2016: Temp. 47° (1° above avg.); precip. 6" (2" above avg.). 1–4 Rain, then sunny, cold. 5–9 Rain to snow, then sunny, cold. 10–15 Rain arriving, mild. 16–18 Sunny. 19–24 Rainy periods, mild. 25–29 Sunny, cold.

MAR. 2016: Temp. 52° (3° below avg.); precip. 4" (0.5" below avg.). 1–4 Showers, chilly. 5–8 Sunny, warm. 9–14 Sunny, cool. 15–21 Rain to snow, then sunny, cold. 22–31 Rainy periods, cool.

APR. 2016: Temp. 62° (1° below avg.); precip. 2.5" (0.5" below avg.). 1–13 Sunny, nice. 14–18 T-storms, then sunny, cool. 19–25 A few t-storms, cool. 26–30 Sunny, turning warm.

MAY 2016: Temp. 71° (avg.); precip. 4" (0.5" above avg.). 1–9 A few t-storms, cool. 10–13 Sunny, warm. 14–20 Scattered t-storms, warm. 21–24 T-storms, then sunny, cool. 25–31 Sunny, turning hot.

JUNE 2016: Temp. 78° (avg.); precip. 5" (0.5" above avg.). 1–4 Sunny, cool north; t-storms south. 5–12 A few t-storms; turning cool north, hot south. 13–19 Scattered t-storms. 20–27 T-storms, then sunny, cool. 28–30 Tropical storm threat.

JULY 2016: Temp. 81° (1° below avg.); precip. 5.5" (1" above avg.). 1–4 A few t-storms. 5–7 Sunny inland, hurricane threat coast. 8–12 Sunny north, t-storms south. 13–21 A few t-storms, cool. 22–31 P.M. t-storms, warm.

AUG. 2016: Temp. 79° (1° below avg.); precip. 7" (2" above avg.). 1–7 Sunny, cool. 8–11 Tropical storm threat. 12–14 Sunny, hot. 15–17 T-storms. 18–20 Tropical storm threat. 21–31 Isolated t-storms, warm.

SEPT. 2016: Temp. 76° (2° above avg.); precip. 4" (2" above avg. north, 3" below south). 1–5 Sunny, then t-storms, warm. 6–9 Sunny, nice. 10–15 Scattered t-storms, warm. 16–22 Sunny, warm. 23–25 Hurricane threat. 26–30 Sunny, warm.

OCT. 2016: Temp. 68° (4° above avg.); precip. 5" (1" above avg.). 1–6 Rain, then sunny, cool. 7–17 A few t-storms, warm. 18–22 Sunny, warm. 23–26 Showers, quite warm. 27–31 T-storms, then sunny, cool.

Raleigh

Columbia

Atlanta

Savannah

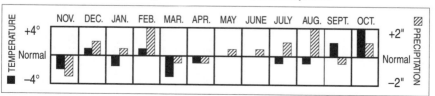

Florida

SUMMARY: Winter will be slightly milder and much drier than normal. The coldest temperatures will occur in mid- to late December, mid-January, and early February.

April and May will be hotter than normal, with below-normal rainfall.

Summer will be hotter than normal across most of the state, although slightly cooler than normal in the south. The hottest periods will be in early to mid-June, early to mid-July, and mid-August. Rainfall will be above normal, especially in the north, with hurricane threats in early July and early to mid-August.

September and October will be warmer than normal, with rainfall below normal in September and above normal in October.

W E A T H E R

NOV. 2015: Temp. 67° (2° below avg.); precip. 0.5" (2" below avg.). 1–8 Scattered t-storms, cool. 9–15 Sunny; chilly, then warm. 16–19 Showers, then sunny, cool. 20–30 Sunny; warm, then cool.

DEC. 2015: Temp. 66° (3° above avg.); precip. 2" (0.5" below avg.). 1–4 Sunny, warm. 5–10 Scattered showers, warm. 11–16 Sunny, warm. 17–26 A few showers north, sunny south; cool. 27–31 Showers, warm.

JAN. 2016: Temp. 62° (2° above avg.); precip. 1.5" (1" below avg.). 1–8 A few showers, cool north; sunny, warm south. 9–11 Sunny, cool. 12–14 T-storms, then sunny, cold. 15–19 Sunny, warm. 20–23 T-storms, then sunny, cool. 24–31 Scattered t-storms, mild.

FEB. 2016: Temp. 62° (1° above avg.); precip. 1.5" (1" below avg.). 1–6 Showers, cool. 7–13 Sunny, turning warm. 14–24 Scattered showers, warm. 25–29 Sunny, cool.

MAR. 2016: Temp. 65° (2° below avg.); precip. 2" (1" below avg.). 1–4 Sunny, cool. 5–9 Scattered t-storms, warm. 10–15 Sunny, cool. 16–31 A few t-storms, cool.

APR. 2016: Temp. 72° (1° above avg.); precip. 1.5" (1" below avg.). 1–14 Sunny, turning warm. 15–21 Scattered t-storms, warm. 22–28 T-storms, then sunny, cool. 29–30 Sunny, warm.

MAY 2016: Temp. 78° (1° above avg.); precip. 3" (1" below avg.). 1–4 Sunny, warm. 5–8 T-storms, warm. 9–17 Sunny, hot. 18–26 T-storms, then sunny, cool. 27–31 Scattered t-storms.

Jacksonville ⊙
Tampa ⊙
⊙ Orlando
Miami ⊙

JUNE 2016: Temp. 82° (1° above avg. north, 1° below south); precip. 8.5" (2" above avg.). 1–5 Scattered t-storms, cool. 6–14 A few t-storms north and central, sunny south; hot. 15–21 Scattered t-storms, seasonable. 22–30 A few t-storms, warm.

JULY 2016: Temp. 83° (1° above avg. north, 1° below south); precip. 6.5" (avg.). 1–3 Sunny. 4–6 Hurricane threat. 7–17 Scattered t-storms, hot and humid. 18–23 Isolated t-storms, seasonable. 24–31 Scattered t-storms, seasonable.

AUG. 2016: Temp. 83° (1° above avg.); precip. 10.5" (3" above avg.). 1–5 T-storms, humid. 6–11 Hurricane threat. 12–14 Sunny, hot. 15–18 A few t-storms, hot. 19–25 Daily t-storms; hot north and central, cool south. 26–31 A few t-storms, sultry.

SEPT. 2016: Temp. 81° (1° above avg.); precip. 3.5" (2" below avg.). 1–5 Daily t-storms, seasonable. 6–13 Isolated t-storms; cool, then hot. 14–17 T-storms, warm. 18–28 Sunny north, a few t-storms south and central; warm. 29–30 T-storms, hot.

OCT. 2016: Temp. 79° (4° above avg.); precip. 6" (2" above avg.). 1–5 T-storms, cool. 6–10 A few t-storms, warm. 11–17 Scattered t-storms, warm. 18–20 Sunny, warm. 21–31 A few t-storms, warm.

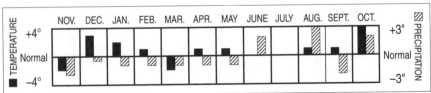

Lower Lakes

SUMMARY: Winter will be colder than normal, with below-normal precipitation and generally below-normal snowfall. The coldest periods will be in early to mid-December, late December, and early to mid- and mid- to late January and February. The snowiest periods will be in late November, December, mid-January, and early and late February.

April and May will be drier than normal, with temperatures below normal in the east and above normal in the west.

Summer will be hotter and slightly drier than normal, with the hottest periods in mid- and late June and mid- and late August.

September and October will be drier and much warmer than normal.

NOV. 2015: Temp. 41° (avg.); precip. 2" (0.5" below avg.). 1–2 Sunny, mild. 3–8 Rain to snow, turning cold. 9–11 Sunny. 12–15 Rain, then sunny, mild. 16–18 Snow squalls, cold. 19–26 Rainy periods, mild. 27–30 Lake snows, cold.

DEC. 2015: Temp. 31.5° (3° below avg. east, 2° above west); precip. 2.5" (0.5" below avg.). 1–3 Rain and snow showers. 4–8 Snowstorm, then flurries cold. 9–13 Snow east, rain west, then rain and snow showers, mild. 14–22 Lake snows and snow showers, cold. 23–26 Flurries, cold east; sunny, mild west. 27–31 Snowstorm, then flurries, cold.

JAN. 2016: Temp. 24° (3° below avg.); precip. 2" (0.5" below avg.). 1–7 Lake snows, cold east; sunny, mild west. 8–13 Lake snows, bitter cold. 14–18 Rain and snow showers, mild. 19–26 Lake snows, very cold. 27–31 Rain, then snow showers.

FEB. 2016: Temp. 29° (2° above avg.); precip. 3" (1" above avg.). 1–4 Snow, then turning mild. 5–9 Snowstorm, then flurries, cold. 10–20 Rainy periods, mild. 21–23 Sunny, cold. 24–29 Snowstorm, then rain and snow showers.

MAR. 2016: Temp. 35° (3° below avg.); precip. 1.5" (1.5" below avg.). 1–5 Snowy periods, cold. 6–8 Showers, warm. 9–20 Snowy periods, cold. 21–24 Flurries, cold east; sunny, warm west. 25–31 Rain and snow showers, then sunny, cool.

APR. 2016: Temp. 48° (2° below avg. east, 2° above west); precip. 2" (1.5" below avg.). 1–5 Snow, then sunny, warm east; sunny, warm west. 6–13 Rain, then sunny; cool east, warm west. 14–19 Showers east, sunny west; mild. 20–30 Showers, cool.

MAY 2016: Temp. 57.5° (0.5° below avg.); precip. 3" (0.5" below avg.). 1–5 A few showers, cool. 6–11 Sunny, very warm. 12–20 Showers, cool. 21–24 Sunny, nice. 25–31 Scattered t-storms, very warm.

JUNE 2016: Temp. 69° (3° above avg.); precip. 3" (0.5" below avg.). 1–3 Sunny, cool. 4–12 T-storms, then sunny, turning hot. 13–15 T-storms, then sunny, cool. 16–19 Scattered t-storms, warm. 20–24 A few t-storms, hot. 25–30 Scattered t-storms; cool, then hot.

JULY 2016: Temp. 69° (2° below avg.); precip. 4" (0.5" above avg.). 1–5 Sunny east west; turning cool. 6–14 Scattered t-storms, cool. 15–23 Isolated t-storms, cool. 24–27 Sunny, nice. 28–31 T-storms, then sunny, cool.

AUG. 2016: Temp. 71° (2° above avg.); precip. 3" (1" below avg.). 1–7 Scattered t-storms, warm. 8–12 Sunny; cool, then hot. 13–23 Daily t-storms east, isolated t-storms west; hot, then cool. 24–31 Sunny east, a few t-storms west; turning hot.

SEPT. 2016: Temp. 65° (3° above avg.); precip. 2.5" (1" below avg.). 1–3 Sunny, warm. 4–11 T-storms, then sunny, cool. 12–19 Showers, cool. 20–25 Sunny, quite warm. 26–30 Showers, turning cool.

OCT. 2016: Temp. 58° (6° above avg.); precip. 1.5" (1" below avg.). 1–5 Showers, cool. 6–14 Sunny, warm. 15–24 Showers, then sunny, warm. 25–31 Rain, then snow showers, turning cold.

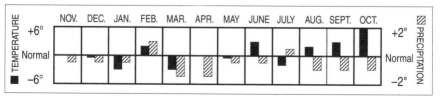

Ohio Valley

SUMMARY: Winter will be colder and slightly drier than normal, with above-normal snowfall. The coldest period will be in mid- to late January, with other cold spells in mid- and late December and early and late February. The snowiest periods will be in early to mid- and mid- to late December, February, and March.

April and May will be cooler and drier than normal.

Summer will be hotter than normal, with below-normal rainfall in the east and above normal in the west. The hottest periods will be in late June and early and late August.

September and October will be much warmer than normal, with the hottest period in early September, and will have near-normal rainfall.

NOV. 2015: Temp. 47° (1° above avg.); precip. 2.5" (1" below avg.). 1–2 Sunny, mild. 3–6 Rainy, mild. 7–11 Rain to snow, then sunny, cold. 12–15 Showers, mild. 16–19 Snow showers, cold. 20–27 A few showers, mild. 28–30 Snow showers, cold.

DEC. 2015: Temp. 36° (1° below avg.); precip. 4" (1" above avg.). 1–5 Sun, then rainy, mild. 6–12 Snow, then showers, mild. 13–16 Snow to rain. 17–23 Snow showers, cold. 24–25 Snowstorm. 26–31 Rain, then flurries, cold.

JAN. 2016: Temp. 31° (2° below avg.); precip. 2.5" (0.5" below avg.). 1–5 Sunny, turning mild. 6–14 Rain, then snow showers, cold. 15–18 Showers, mild. 19–26 Snow showers, turning bitterly cold. 27–31 Rainy periods, turning mild.

FEB. 2016: Temp. 35° (1° above avg.); precip. 4" (1" above avg.). 1–4 Snowstorm, then flurries, cold. 5–9 Snowstorm, then flurries, cold. 10–15 Rainy periods, mild. 16–22 Snow, then rainy periods, mild. 23–26 Snowstorm, then sunny, cold. 27–29 Rain to snow.

MAR. 2016: Temp. 42° (3° below avg.); precip. 3" (1" below avg.). 1–8 Snow, then showers, turning warm. 9–23 Snow showers, cold. 24–31 Rain, then sunny, cool.

APR. 2016: Temp. 54° (1° below avg.); precip. 2.5" (1" below avg.). 1–6 Isolated t-storms, mild. 7–13 Sunny, warm. 14–19 Showers, then sunny, cool. 20–27 Showers, cool. 28–30 Rainstorm.

MAY 2016: Temp. 63° (avg.); precip. 2.5" (2" below avg.). 1–9 A few showers, turning warm. 10–13 Sunny, warm. 14–22 A few showers, cool. 23–31 Scattered t-storms, turning very warm.

JUNE 2016: Temp. 74° (3° above avg.); precip. 3" (1" below avg.). 1–4 Sunny, nice. 5–11 T-storms, then sunny, cool. 12–17 T-storms, then sunny, very warm. 18–23 Scattered t-storms, hot. 24–30 Isolated t-storms, warm.

JULY 2016: Temp. 73° (2° below avg.); precip. 6" (2" above avg.). 1–7 T-storms, then sunny, nice. 8–15 T-storms, then sunny, cool. 16–31 Scattered t-storms, cool.

AUG. 2016: Temp. 74° (1° above avg.); precip. 4" (2" below avg. east, 2" above west). 1–2 Sunny, warm. 3–7 T-storms, then sunny, cool. 8–14 A few t-storms, warm. 15–23 Scattered t-storms, then sunny, cool. 24–31 Scattered t-storms, very warm.

SEPT. 2016: Temp. 70° (3° above avg.); precip. 3.5" (0.5" above avg.). 1–3 Sunny, hot. 4–13 A few t-storms, warm. 14–17 Sunny, cool. 18–28 Scattered t-storms, warm. 29–30 Showers, cool.

OCT. 2016: Temp. 62° (5° above avg.); precip. 2" (0.5" below avg.). 1–5 Showers, cool. 6–13 Isolated showers, warm. 14–17 Showers, mild. 18–24 Sunny, quite warm. 25–29 T-storms, then sunny, cool. 30–31 Snowy, cold.

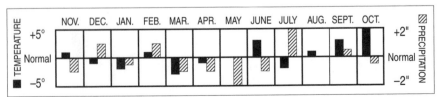

Deep South

SUMMARY: Winter will be drier than normal. The north will have below-normal temperatures and above-normal snowfall, while the south will have near-normal temperatures and no snowfall. The coldest periods will be in late November, mid- and late December, mid-January, and early February, with the greatest threats for snow in mid- to late December, early and late January, and early and mid- to late February.

April and May will be cooler and drier than normal.

Summer will be rainier and slightly cooler than normal, with the hottest periods in early June, mid-July, and early September. The greatest hurricane threats will be in mid- and late August and mid-September.

September and October will be much warmer than normal, with rainfall below normal in the north and above normal in the south.

W E A T H E R

NOV. 2015: Temp. 55.5° (2° above avg. north, 1° below south); precip. 3" (2" below avg.). 1–7 Rainy periods, cool. 8–10 Sunny, cold. 11–18 Rain, then sunny, very cold. 19–24 Sunny, turning warm. 25–30 Showers, then sunny, cold.

DEC. 2015: Temp. 49° (1° above avg.); precip. 5" (avg.). 1–3 Sunny, mild. 4–9 Rainy periods, cool. 10–15 Rainy periods north, sunny south; turning mild. 16–21 Rain, then sunny, cold. 22–24 Snow north, rain south. 25–31 Rain, then sunny, cold.

JAN. 2016: Temp. 46.5° (1° below avg. north, 4° above south); precip. 4" (1" below avg.). 1–5 Rain and snow, then sunny, mild. 6–13 Rain, then sunny, cold. 14–18 Rain, then sunny, mild. 19–23 Sunny; cold, then mild. 24–27 Snow north, rain south, then sunny, cold. 28–31 Rainy periods, cool.

FEB. 2016: Temp. 46° (1° below avg.); precip. 5" (avg.). 1–3 Snow, then sunny, very cold. 4–8 Rain, then sunny, cold. 9–15 Scattered t-storms, mild. 16–17 Sunny, cool. 18–22 Showers, mild. 23–26 Snow north, rain south; then sunny, cool. 27–29 Showers, cool.

MAR. 2016: Temp. 53° (3° below avg.); precip. 5" (1" below avg.). 1–2 Sunny, cold. 3–7 Rainy periods, turning warm. 8–10 Sunny, cool. 11–14 Rain, then sunny, cool. 15–20 Rain and snow showers north, rainy periods south; cool. 21–24 Rain, then sunny, cool. 25–31 Showers, cool.

APR. 2016: Temp. 64° (1° above avg.); precip. 3.5" (1" below avg.). 1–5 Sunny, nice.

6–14 Scattered t-storms, turning warm. 15–20 T-storms, then sunny, nice. 21–30 Scattered t-storms; cool, then warm.

MAY 2016: Temp. 69° (2° below avg.); precip. 4" (1" below avg.). 1–6 Isolated t-storms, turning cool. 7–15 Sunny, nice. 16–24 T-storms, then sunny, cool. 25–31 Scattered t-storms, warm.

JUNE 2016: Temp. 79° (1° above avg.); precip. 6" (1" above avg.). 1–8 Scattered t-storms, turning hot. 9–14 T-storms, warm. 15–19 Sunny north, t-storms south; hot. 20–30 A few t-storms, cool.

JULY 2016: Temp. 80° (1° below avg.); precip. 5.5" (3" above avg. north, 1" below south). 1–4 Sunny, hot north; t-storms south. 5–16 Scattered t-storms; hot, then cool. 17–25 Daily t-storms, cool. 26–31 T-storm, then sunny, warm.

AUG. 2016: Temp. 79° (1° below avg.); precip. 5.5" (1" below avg. north, 3" above south). 1–4 T-storms, warm. 5–9 Sunny north, t-storms south. 10–13 Hurricane threat. 14–19 Scattered t-storms, warm. 20–27 T-storms. 28–31 Hurricane threat, sunny elsewhere.

SEPT. 2016: Temp. 79° (3° above avg.); precip. 5.5" (1" below avg. north, 3" above south). 1–4 Sunny, hot north; t-storms south. 5–9 A few t-storms, hot and humid. 10–13 Hurricane threat. 14–21 Isolated t-storms, turning hot. 22–26 Sunny, hot. 27–30 T-storms, then sunny, cool.

OCT. 2016: Temp. 69° (4° above avg.); precip. 1.5" (1.5" below avg.). 1–7 Sunny; cool, then warm. 8–12 T-storms, then sunny, warm. 13–18 Scattered t-storms, warm. 19–25 Sunny, warm. 26–31 T-storms, then sunny, cool.

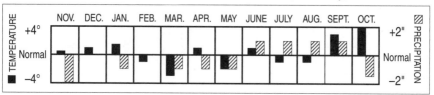

Upper Midwest

SUMMARY: Winter will be much colder than normal, on average, with above-normal precipitation. Snowfall will be near normal in most of the region but above normal in the east. Very cold weather will predominate from late December through early February, with the snowiest periods in late November, late January, and mid-March.

April and May will be slightly warmer and wetter than normal.

Summer will be hotter and drier than normal. The hottest periods will occur in late June and early and late August.

September and October will be much warmer and slightly rainier than normal in the east and rainier than normal, with near-normal temperatures, in the west.

NOV. 2015: Temp. 30° (1° above avg.); precip. 3" (1" above avg.). 1–4 Rainy periods, mild. 5–13 Snow showers; cold, then mild. 14–18 Snow, then flurries, cold. 19–23 Snow, then flurries, cold. 24–25 Rain and snow, mild. 26–30 Snowstorm, then flurries, cold.

DEC. 2015: Temp. 15.5° (1° above avg. east, 2° below west); precip. 1.5" (0.5" above avg.). 1–8 Snow showers, cold. 9–14 Snow showers; mild, then cold. 15–22 Lake snows east, flurries west; cold. 23–26 Snow showers, mild. 27–31 Lake snows east, flurries west; very cold.

JAN. 2016: Temp. 8° (5° below avg.); precip. 2" (1" above avg.). 1–10 Snowy periods, cold. 11–16 Lake snows east, flurries west; turning milder. 17–26 Snowy periods, very cold. 27–31 Snowstorm, then sunny, frigid.

FEB. 2016: Temp. 12° (avg.); precip. 1" (avg.). 1–6 Snow showers, very cold. 7–18 Snow showers, turning mild. 19–24 Snow, then flurries, cold. 25–29 Snow showers, cold.

MAR. 2016: Temp. 26.5° (4° below avg. east, 1° above avg.); precip. 1" (0.5" below avg.). 1–7 Snow showers, turning mild. 8–11 Snow, then sunny, cold. 12–18 Snow, then flurries, cold. 19–24 Snow, then showers, turning mild. 25–28 Snow showers, cold. 29–31 Sunny, mild.

APR. 2016: Temp. 44° (2° above avg.); precip. 1.5" (0.5" below avg.). 1–5 Showers, then sunny, mild. 6–14 A few showers, turning warm. 15–19 Sprinkles, cool. 20–26 Rain to snow, then sunny, cool. 27–30 Showers.

MAY 2016: Temp. 54° (1° below avg.); precip. 4" (1" above avg.). 1–3 Sunny, nice. 4–7 Showers, then sunny, warm. 8–11 Showers, warm. 12–18 Rain, then showers, cool. 19–22 Sunny, nice. 23–26 Showers, cool. 27–31 T-storms, warm.

JUNE 2016: Temp. 66° (3° above avg.); precip. 4" (avg.). 1–2 Sunny, very warm. 3–12 A few t-storms, warm. 13–19 Isolated t-storms, cool. 20–25 T-storms, then sunny, cool. 26–30 Scattered t-storms, warm.

JULY 2016: Temp. 64° (4° below avg.); precip. 3" (0.5" below avg.). 1–4 Sunny, turning cool. 5–15 Isolated t-storms, cool. 16–22 A few t-storms, cool. 23–31 Scattered t-storms, cool.

AUG. 2016: Temp. 69° (3° above avg.); precip. 3" (0.5" below avg.). 1–7 Scattered t-storms; hot, then cool. 8–10 Sunny, hot. 11–18 A few t-storms, turning cool. 19–22 Sunny, nice. 23–31 A few t-storms, turning hot.

SEPT. 2016: Temp. 58° (avg.); precip. 4" (1" above avg.). 1–6 T-storms, then sunny, nice. 7–11 Showers, then sunny, cool. 12–20 Rainy periods, then sunny, mild. 21–26 T-storms, warm. 27–30 Showers, turning cool.

OCT. 2016: Temp. 50° (6° above avg. east, avg. west); precip. 3" (0.5" below avg. east, 2" above west). 1–8 Showers, then sunny, cool. 9–18 Rain, then sunny, warm. 19–23 Rainy periods, mild. 24–31 Rain and snow showers, turning cold.

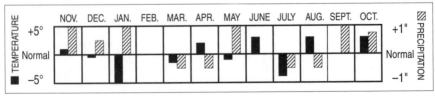

Get your local forecast at Almanac.com/Weather.

Heartland

SUMMARY: In winter, the northern part of the region will have above-normal temperatures, slightly below-normal precipitation, and near-normal snowfall, while the south will have near-normal temperatures, with below-normal precipitation and snowfall. The coldest periods will be in mid-November, late December, early and late January, and mid- and late February. The snowiest periods will be in early and late December, late January, late February, and mid-March.

April and May will be warmer and drier than normal.

Summer will be hotter and drier than normal, with drought a concern. The hottest periods will be in mid- and late June and early and mid- to late August.

September and October will be much milder than normal, with near-normal rainfall.

NOV. 2015: Temp. 45.5° (4° above avg. north, 1° above south); precip. 1.5" (1" below avg.). 1–7 Rainy periods, turning cool. 8–11 Sunny, mild. 12–17 Rain, then sunny, very cold. 18–26 Rain, then sunny, turning warm. 27–30 Sunny, cold.

DEC. 2015: Temp. 34° (2° above avg.); precip. 1.5" (1" above avg. north, 0.5" below south). 1–2 Sunny, mild. 3–7 Rain to snow, then sunny. 8–11 Rain to snow, then sunny, mild. 12–21 Rain and snow, then sunny, cold. 22–26 Rain and snow showers, turning mild. 27–31 Heavy snow north, rain south, then sunny, very cold.

JAN. 2016: Temp. 28° (1° below avg.); precip. 0.5" (0.5" below avg.). 1–4 Sunny, cold. 5–18 A few snow showers; cold, then mild. 19–26 Flurries, cold. 27–25 Sunny, turning quite mild. 26–31 Rain to snow, then sunny, very cold.

FEB. 2016: Temp. 30° (1° below avg.); precip. 1.5" (0.5" above avg. north, 0.5" below south). 1–4 Sunny, turning mild. 5–10 Snow, then sunny, mild. 11–17 Rain and snow, then sunny, cold. 18–25 Showers, mild; then flurries, cold. 26–29 Snow, then sunny, cold.

MAR. 2016: Temp. 43° (1° below avg.); precip. 1.5" (1" below avg.). 1–6 Rain and snow, then sunny, mild. 7–16 Showers, then flurries, cold. 17–22 Snow, then sunny, cool. 23–24 Sunny, warm. 25–31 Periods of rain and snow, cool.

APR. 2016: Temp. 57° (3° above avg.); precip. 2.5" (1" below avg.). 1–5 Sunny, warm. 6–13 Scattered t-storms; cool, then very warm. 14–24 A few t-storms, cool. 25–26 Sunny, cool. 27–30 Rainy, cool north; t-storms, warm south.

MAY 2016: Temp. 64° (avg.); precip. 4" (0.5" below avg.). 1–6 T-storms, then sunny, cool. 7–10 Sunny, warm. 11–17 Rainy periods, cool. 18–23 Sunny, cool. 24–31 Scattered t-storms, turning warm.

JUNE 2016: Temp. 75° (3° above avg.); precip. 3.5" (1" below avg.). 1–8 A few t-storms, warm. 9–12 Sunny, hot. 13–21 T-storms, then sunny, turning hot. 22–25 T-storms, then sunny, cool. 26–30 T-storms, turning hot.

JULY 2016: Temp. 74° (3° below avg.); precip. 3.5" (0.5" below avg.). 1–10 Scattered t-storms; cool north, hot south. 11–14 Sunny, cool. 15–20 T-storms, then sunny, cool. 21–24 T-storms, then sunny, cool. 25–31 T-storms, then sunny, cool.

AUG. 2016: Temp. 78° (3° above avg.); precip. 2" (1.5" below avg.). 1–3 Sunny, hot. 4–10 T-storms, then sunny, cool. 11–19 T-storms, then sunny, hot. 20–27 Sunny; cool, then hot. 28–31 T-storms, hot.

SEPT. 2016: Temp. 69° (2° above avg.); precip. 3" (1" below avg. north, avg. south). 1–7 Scattered showers, very warm. 8–13 Heavy rain south, showers north; cool. 14–18 Showers, cool. 19–24 Sunny, very warm. 25–30 T-storms, then sunny, nice.

OCT. 2016: Temp. 60° (4° above avg.); precip. 3.5" (2" above avg. north, 1" below south). 1–6 Showers, then sunny, cool. 7–11 Sunny, warm. 12–19 T-storms, then sunny, mild. 20–25 Rainy periods, mild. 26–31 Sunny, turning cold.

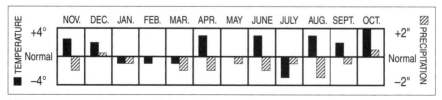

Texas–Oklahoma

SUMMARY: Winter will be much warmer and drier than normal, with below-normal snowfall. The coldest periods will be in early and late December, late January, and early February, while the snowiest periods across the north will occur in late December, early and late January, and mid- and late February.

April and May will be warmer and drier than normal, with drought a major concern.

Summer will be slightly rainier than normal, with near-normal temperatures. The hottest periods will be in early and late June, early July, and late August.

September and October will be warmer than normal, with near-normal rainfall in the north. Hurricanes in early and mid-September may help to ease the drought.

NOV. 2015: Temp. 59° (2° above avg.); precip. 1.5" (1.5" below avg.). 1–5 Sunny, cool. 6–10 T-storms, then sunny, cool. 11–17 Sunny; warm, then cool. 18–20 Sunny, warm. 21–30 Showers, then sunny, warm.

DEC. 2015: Temp. 56° (3° above avg.); precip. 1" (1.5" below avg.). 1–5 Sunny, turning cold. 6–11 Showers, then sunny, warm. 12–18 Showers, then sunny, warm. 19–27 Scattered t-storms, turning cold. 28–31 Flurries north, sprinkles south; cold.

JAN. 2016: Temp. 53° (2° above avg. north, 6° above south); precip. 0.5" (1.5" below avg.). 1–4 Showers, turning warm. 5–11 Flurries, cold north; sunny, warm south. 12–19 Sunny; cool, then warm. 20–29 A few showers, turning cooler. 30–31 Snow showers north, sunny south; cold.

FEB. 2016: Temp. 50.5° (2° below avg. north, 3° above south); precip. 1.5" (avg. north, 1" below south). 1–3 Sunny, cool. 4–10 Showers, then sunny, warm. 11–13 Showers, warm. 14–17 Rain to snow north; sunny, mild south. 18–22 Showers; cool north, warm south. 23–29 Snow north, rain south, then sunny, cool.

MAR. 2016: Temp. 60° (1° below avg. north, 3° above south); precip. 2" (2" below avg. north, 1" above south). 1–10 Sunny; cool, then warm. 11–13 Rain, then sunny, cool. 14–21 Sunny; cool, then warm north; warm south. 22–24 Sunny. 25–31 Sunny north, rainy south; cool.

APR. 2016: Temp. 69° (3° above avg.); precip. 1.5" (1.5" below avg.). 1–8 Sunny, warm. 9–15 Scattered t-storms, warm. 16–20 Sunny, warm.

21–30 A few showers, turning warm north; sunny, hot south.

MAY 2016: Temp. 73.5° (0.5° above avg.); precip. 4" (1" below avg.). 1–6 Scattered t-storms, turning cool. 7–10 Sunny, nice. 11–20 Scattered t-storms, warm. 21–31 Scattered t-storms north, sunny south; warm.

JUNE 2016: Temp. 80° (1° above avg.); precip. 3" (1" below avg.). 1–10 A few t-storms north, sunny south; hot. 11–15 Daily t-storms, warm. 16–19 Sunny, warm. 20–25 Scattered t-storms, warm. 26–30 Isolated t-storms, hot.

JULY 2016: Temp. 80° (1° below avg.); precip. 5" (2" above avg.). 1–11 Sunny, hot, isolated t-storms. 12–22 A few t-storms, cool north; isolated t-storms, hot south. 23–24 Sunny, cool. 25–31 Sunny north, heavy t-storms south; cool.

AUG. 2016: Temp. 81° (avg.); precip. 2.5" (avg.). 1–9 Scattered t-storms, cool. 10–13 Sunny, coastal t-storms, warm. 14–21 Sunny north, isolated t-storms south; warm. 22–31 Scattered t-storms, turning hot.

SEPT. 2016: Temp. 76° (avg.); precip. 6.5" (1" above avg. north, 5" above south). 1–6 Sunny, hot north; hurricane threat south. 7–9 Sunny north, t-storms south. 10–12 Hurricane threat. 13–15 Sunny, cool. 16–22 Scattered t-storms, warm. 23–30 Isolated t-storms, turning cooler.

OCT. 2016: Temp. 69° (2° above avg.); precip. 3" (1" below avg.). 1–8 Sunny north, a few t-storms south; cool. 9–13 T-storms, warm. 14–18 Sunny, nice. 19–25 A few t-storms north, sunny south; warm. 26–31 Sunny, turning cool.

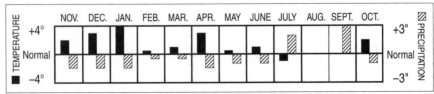

High Plains

SUMMARY: Winter will be colder than normal in the north, with above-normal temperatures in the south. The coldest periods will be in early and late December, early and late January, and mid- and late February. Precipitation will be slightly above normal, with above-normal snowfall in the east and below-normal snowfall elsewhere. The snowiest periods will be in early and late December, early and mid-January, early and mid-February, and mid-March.

April and May will be slightly drier than normal, with near-normal temperatures.

Summer will be slightly hotter and drier than normal, with the hottest periods in mid-June, early and late July, and mid-August.

September and October will be cooler than normal, with above-normal precipitation.

NOV. 2015: Temp. 40° (3° above avg.); precip. 1" (avg.). 1–7 Periods of rain and snow, turning cold. 8–10 Sunny, mild. 11–14 Periods of snow, cool. 15–20 Snow showers, cold. 21–30 Showers, then sunny, turning warm.

DEC. 2015: Temp. 25° (3° below avg.); precip. 0.5" (avg.). 1–4 Snowy periods, cold. 5–10 Snow showers north; sunny, mild south. 11–17 Snow showers, cold north; sunny, mild south. 18–23 Sunny, turning mild. 24–31 Snowy periods, turning very cold.

JAN. 2016: Temp. 28° (5° below avg. north, 5° above south); precip. 1" (0.5" above avg.). 1–8 Snowy periods, very cold north; sunny, mild south. 9–16 Rain and snow showers, mild north; sunny, warm south. 17–22 Snow, then sunny, turning quite mild. 23–31 Snowy periods, turning very cold.

FEB. 2016: Temp. 26° (2° below avg.); precip. 1" (0.5" above avg.). 1–10 Snow, then sunny, mild. 11–16 Flurries north, snowstorm south; turning cold. 17–29 Snow showers, cold.

MAR. 2016: Temp. 39° (avg.); precip. 0.5" (0.5" below avg.). 1–8 Rain and snow showers north, sunny south; mild. 9–17 Snowy periods, cold. 18–23 Rain and snow showers north, sunny south; mild. 24–27 Snow, then sunny, cold. 28–31 Showers, mild.

APR. 2016: Temp. 49° (1° above avg.); precip. 1.5" (0.5" below avg.). 1–6 Sunny; turning cold north, hot south. 7–14 Showers; mild, then cool. 15–17 Rain to snow. 18–22 Periods of rain and snow, cool north; sunny, mild south.

23–30 Scattered showers, mild.

MAY 2016: Temp. 57° (1° below avg.); precip. 2" (0.5" below avg.). 1–7 Scattered showers; warm north, cool south. 8–13 Showers, then sunny, cool. 14–17 Rainy, cool north; sunny, warm south. 18–21 Sunny, warm north; showers south. 22–26 Rainy, cool north; showers, hot south. 27–31 A few showers.

JUNE 2016: Temp. 68° (1° above avg.); precip. 2.5" (avg.). 1–12 Scattered t-storms, warm. 13–19 Scattered t-storms north, sunny south; very warm. 20–28 Scattered t-storms, cool. 29–30 Sunny; turning cool north, hot south.

JULY 2016: Temp. 70° (2° below avg.); precip. 1" (1" below avg.). 1–3 Sunny, hot. 4–10 Isolated t-storms; cool, then hot. 11–16 Isolated t-storms, cool. 17–23 Scattered t-storms, cool. 24–31 Sunny, hot north; a few t-storms, cool south.

AUG. 2016: Temp. 73° (2° above avg.); precip. 2" (avg.). 1–10 Sunny, hot north; a few t-storms, cool south. 11–20 Isolated t-storms; hot north, warm south. 21–31 Scattered t-storms, hot, then cool north; sunny, warm south.

SEPT. 2016: Temp. 59° (2° below avg.); precip. 2.5" (1" above avg.). 1–6 Sunny, warm. 7–16 Rainy periods, chilly. 17–22 Showers, cool north; sunny, warm south. 23–25 Rain and wet snow north, showers south. 26–30 Sunny, mild.

OCT. 2016: Temp. 47° (2° below avg.); precip. 1.5" (0.5" above avg.). 1–6 Sunny, nice. 7–11 Rain and snow, chilly. 12–18 Sunny, turning mild. 19–27 Snowstorm, then sunny, cold. 28–31 Flurries, cold.

Bismarck ◉
Billings ◉
Rapid City ◉
Cheyenne ◉
Denver ◉
Amarillo ◉

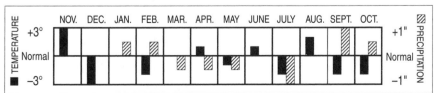

Intermountain

SUMMARY: Winter temperatures will be much above normal, with precipitation near normal in the north and below normal in the south. The coldest periods will be in mid- and late December, late January, and mid- and late February. Snowfall will be above normal near Reno but below normal elsewhere, with the snowiest periods in early and mid-December, early January, and mid- and late February.

April and May will be slightly cooler and wetter than normal.

Summer will be hotter than normal, with slightly above-normal rainfall. The hottest periods will be in mid-June, mid- and late July, and early August.

September and October will be much cooler than normal, with near-normal precipitation.

NOV. 2015: Temp. 43° (3° above avg.); precip. 2" (0.5" above avg.). 1–7 Showers, then sunny, cool. 8–12 Showers, mild. 13–16 Snow showers, cold. 17–21 Rain and snow north; sunny, mild south. 22–26 Periods of rain and snow, mild. 27–30 Rainy, mild north; snow south.

DEC. 2015: Temp. 31.5° (avg. north, 3° below south); precip. 1.5" (avg.). 1–5 Rain and snow showers north, snowstorm south. 6–10 Rain and snow showers, mild north; snowstorm central; sunny, cold south. 11–15 Snow showers, cold. 16–19 Sunny, cold. 20–24 Snow showers, mild. 25–31 Snow, then flurries, very cold.

JAN. 2016: Temp. 38° (6° above avg.); precip. 1" (0.5" below avg.). 1–4 Rain and snow showers north; sunny, cold south. 5–6 Snowstorm north and central, sunny south. 7–13 Rainy periods north, sunny south; quite mild. 14–25 A few rain and snow showers north, sunny south; mild. 26–31 Snow showers, turning cold.

FEB. 2016: Temp. 33° (1° below avg.); precip. 1" (0.5" below avg.). 1–9 A few showers north, sunny south; mild. 10–16 Rain and snow showers north; snowstorm, then flurries south; cold. 17–23 Snow showers, very cold. 24–29 Flurries north, snowstorm central, sunny south; cold.

MAR. 2016: Temp. 44° (1° above avg.); precip. 1.5" (0.5" above avg. north, 1" below south). 1–5 Rainy north, sunny south; mild. 6–12 Rain and snow showers, cold. 13–24 Showers north, sunny south; mild. 25–31 Sunny, warm.

APR. 2016: Temp. 49° (avg.); precip. 1" (avg.). 1–5 Rain, then sunny, cool north; sunny, warm south. 6–9 Sunny, mild. 10–14 Sunny north, rain to snow south. 15–21 Showers north, rain and

snow central, sunny south; cool. 22–27 Sunny, warm north and south; showers central. 28–30 Sunny, warm north; showers central; rain and snow south.

MAY 2016: Temp. 56° (1° below avg.); precip. 1.5" (0.5" above avg.). 1–3 Sunny; warm north, cool south. 4–12 Showers, then sunny, cool. 13–17 Showers, then sunny; warm north, cool south. 18–22 Rainy periods; warm north, cool south. 23–28 Rainy north, sunny south; cool. 29–31 Sunny.

JUNE 2016: Temp. 65° (1° below avg.); precip. 0.5" (avg.). 1–4 Rainy north, sunny south; cool. 5–15 A few showers north, sunny south; hot. 16–22 A couple of t-storms, cool. 23–30 Sunny, cool.

JULY 2016: Temp. 77° (4° above avg.); precip. 1" (0.5" above avg.). 1–6 T-storms, then sunny, cool north; sunny, hot south. 7–12 Sunny, hot north; t-storms, warm south. 13–26 Sunny north, scattered t-storms south; hot. 27–31 Isolated t-storms, hot.

AUG. 2016: Temp. 73° (1° above avg.); precip. 1.5" (0.5" above avg.). 1–4 Sunny, hot. 5–13 Sunny north, a few t-storms south; warm. 14–17 Scattered t-storms, cool. 18–26 A few t-storms; warm, then cool. 27–31 Sunny, cool.

SEPT. 2016: Temp. 59° (3° below avg.); precip. 1" (avg.). 1–6 Sunny, warm. 7–17 Scattered showers, cool. 18–22 Showers, cool. 23–25 Rain and snow, chilly. 26–30 Sunny, turning warm.

OCT. 2016: Temp. 47° (4° below avg.); precip. 1.5" (avg. north, 1" above south). 1–5 Sunny, nice. 6–8 Showers, north, sunny south. 9–16 Showers north; snow, then sunny. 17–19 Showers north, snow south. 20–22 Sunny north, snowstorm south. 23–31 Snow, then sunny, cold.

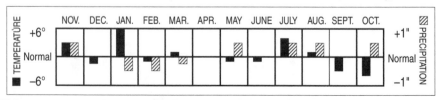

Desert Southwest

SUMMARY: Winter temperatures will be near to below normal in the east and below normal in the west. The coldest periods will be from mid-December into early January and in late January and mid-February. Precipitation and snowfall will be slightly below normal, with the snowiest periods in late December and late February.

April will be cooler and rainier than normal, followed by above-normal temperatures and near-normal rainfall in May.

Summer will be slightly drier than normal, with temperatures below normal in the east and above normal in the west. The hottest periods will be in mid-June, early and mid-July, and early and mid- to late August.

September and October will be much cooler and slightly rainier than normal.

NOV. 2015: Temp. 56° (1° above avg. east, 1° below west); precip. 0.5" (0.5" below avg.). 1–5 Sunny, mild. 6–18 Sunny, cool. 19–23 Showers, warm. 24–30 Sunny, seasonable.

DEC. 2015: Temp. 45° (3° below avg.); precip. 0.2" (0.3" below avg.). 1–2 A shower, warm. 3–6 Sunny, cool. 7–15 Scattered showers, cool. 16–24 Sunny, cold. 25–31 Rain and snow showers, then sunny, quite cold.

JAN. 2016: Temp. 50° (2° above avg.); precip. 0.2" (0.3" below avg.). 1–4 Sunny, cold. 5–16 Sunny, mild. 17–26 Showers, then sunny, mild. 27–31 Showers, then sunny, cold.

FEB. 2016: Temp. 48° (3° below avg.); precip. 0.2" (0.3" below avg.). 1–9 Sunny, mild. 10–21 Showers, then sunny, cold. 22–29 Rain and snow showers, then sunny, cold.

MAR. 2016: Temp. 60° (2° above avg.); precip. 0.5" (avg.). 1–5 Sunny, mild. 6–13 Showers, then sunny, cool. 14–24 Showers, then sunny, warm. 25–31 Showers, then sunny, cool.

APR. 2016: Temp. 62° (3° below avg.); precip. 1" (0.5" above avg.). 1–6 Sunny, warm. 7–14 Scattered showers, turning cool. 15–23 Showers, then sunny, cool. 24–30 Scattered showers, warm, then cool.

MAY 2016: Temp. 77° (3° above avg.); precip.

0.5" (avg.). 1–3 Sunny, cool. 4–9 Showers, then sunny, cool. 10–17 Sunny, cool. 18–22 Scattered t-storms, cool. 23–31 Sunny, cool.

JUNE 2016: Temp. 83° (avg.); precip. 0.5" (avg.). 1–7 Sunny, warm. 8–19 Isolated t-storms, warm east; sunny, hot west. 20–24 Sunny, warm. 25–30 Isolated t-storms, warm.

JULY 2016: Temp. 87.5° (2° below avg. east, 3° above west); precip. 1" (0.5" below avg.). 1–7 Sunny, hot. 8–12 Scattered t-storms, hot. 13–22 Isolated t-storms; cool east, hot west. 23–31 A couple of t-storms; cool east, hot west.

AUG. 2016: Temp. 84° (1° below avg.); precip. 1.5" (avg.). 1–8 Scattered t-storms, warm and humid. 9–16 Isolated t-storms, not as warm. 17–26 Scattered t-storms, hot. 27–31 Sunny, warm.

SEPT. 2016: Temp. 77° (2° below avg.); precip. 1" (avg.). 1–9 Scattered t-storms, then sunny, warm. 10–15 Scattered t-storms, then sunny, cool. 16–21 T-storms, then sunny, cool. 22–30 Scattered t-storms east, sunny west; cool, then warm.

OCT. 2016: Temp. 65° (3° below avg.); precip. 1.5" (0.5" above avg.). 1–8 Showers, turning warm east; sunny, warm west. 9–16 Showers, then sunny, cool. 17–31 Showers, then sunny, cool.

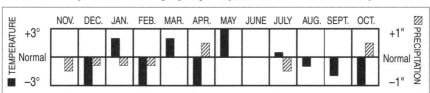

Pacific Northwest

SUMMARY: Winter will be cooler and rainier than normal, with above-normal snowfall. The stormiest periods will be throughout November and in early to mid- and mid- to late December, early January, and early March. The coldest periods will be in mid- and late December, late January, and mid- to late February, with the snowiest periods in mid-December, early to mid-January, and mid- to late February.

April and May will be cooler and slightly rainier than normal.

Summer will be warmer and rainier than normal, with the hottest temperatures in mid- and late July and early August.

September and October will be cooler than normal, with rainfall above normal in the north and near normal in the south.

NOV. 2015: Temp. 47° (avg.); precip. 8.5" (2" above avg.). 1–5 Rainy, mild. 6–7 Sunny. 8–14 Misty, turning cool. 15–19 Heavy rain. 20–22 Sunny, cool. 23–30 Rain, some heavy, turning mild.

DEC. 2015: Temp. 41° (2° below); precip. 6" (0.5" below avg.). 1–5 Periods of rain, cool. 6–9 Rainy, mild. 10–11 Sunny, cool. 12–18 Rain and snow, then sunny, cold. 19–23 Snow to heavy rain, turning mild. 24–29 Flurries, cold. 30–31 Rainy, cool.

JAN. 2016: Temp. 45° (2° above avg.); precip. 8" (2" above avg.). 1–3 Rainy, mild. 4–12 Snowstorm, then rain, heavy at times, turning mild. 13–19 Occasional rain; cool, then mild. 20–25 Sprinkles, mild. 26–31 Rain and wet snow, then sunny, cold.

FEB. 2016: Temp. 43° (1° below avg.); precip. 5" (avg.). 1–8 Rainy periods, mild. 9–16 Showers, cool. 17–25 Periods of rain and snow, cold. 26–29 Rainy, cool.

MAR. 2016: Temp. 46° (1° below avg.); precip. 5" (1" above avg.). 1–8 Rain, heavy at times, cool. 9–14 Sunny, cool days; cold nights. 15–23 Rainy periods, cool. 24–29 Showers, mild. 30–31 Rainy, cool.

APR. 2016: Temp. 49° (1° below avg.); precip. 3.5" (0.5" above avg.). 1–7 Heavy rain, then sunny, warm. 8–17 Showers, cool. 18–26 Sunny, turning warm. 27–30 Rain, then sunny, warm.

MAY 2016: Temp. 54° (1° below avg.); precip. 2" (avg.). 1–4 Sunny, turning hot. 5–13 Showers, cool. 14–16 Sunny, nice. 17–25 Showers, turning cool. 26–31 Showers, cool.

JUNE 2016: Temp. 58° (2° below avg.); precip. 2" (0.5" above avg.). 1–6 Occasional rain, cool. 7–15 A few showers; cool, then warm. 16–20 Rainy periods, cool. 21–27 Sunny; cool, then warmer. 28–30 Showers, cool.

JULY 2016: Temp. 68° (3° above avg.); precip. 0.2" (0.3" below avg.). 1–6 Showers, then sunny, cool. 7–15 Sunny, turning hot. 16–25 Isolated showers, warm. 26–31 Sunny, turning hot.

AUG. 2016: Temp. 67° (1° above avg.); precip. 2" (1" above avg.). 1–4 Sunny, hot. 5–12 Showers, then sunny, nice. 13–19 T-storms, then sunny, nice. 20–31 Rainy periods, cool.

SEPT. 2016: Temp. 60° (1° below avg.); precip. 1.5" (avg.). 1–8 Showers, then sunny, cool. 9–16 Sunny, nice. 17–23 Rainy periods, cool. 24–28 Sunny, turning warm. 29–30 Showers, mild.

OCT. 2016: Temp. 51° (3° below avg.); precip. 3.5" (1" above avg. north, avg. south). 1–5 Misty, mild. 6–10 Rainy periods, turning quite cool. 11–16 Rainy periods, some heavy; cool. 17–23 Showers, chilly. 24–31 Rainy periods, cool.

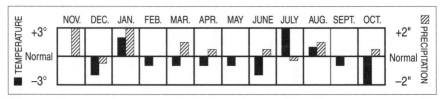

Pacific Southwest

SUMMARY: Although the early part of the winter season will feature above-normal rainfall, the drought will continue as rainy periods will diminish in the season's second half and precipitation will be below normal for the winter season as a whole, with below-normal mountain snows not helping to ease the drought. The stormiest periods will be in mid- to late November, early to mid-December, early January, and early March. Overall, temperatures will be slightly cooler than normal. The coldest period will be in late December, with other cold periods in early and late January and mid-February.

April and May will be cooler and slightly rainier than normal.

Summer will be hotter than normal, with near-normal rainfall. The hottest periods will be in early June, early to mid- and late July, and early and mid- to late August.

September and October will be slightly cooler than normal, with near-normal rainfall.

NOV. 2015: Temp. 60° (2° above avg.); precip. 3.5" (2" above avg.). 1–4 Showers north, sunny south. 5–16 Sunny; warm, then seasonable. 17–22 Stormy, heavy rains. 23–30 Rainy periods, mild.

DEC. 2015: Temp. 52° (2° below avg.); precip. 3" (1" above avg.). 1–5 Showers, then sunny, cool. 6–14 Rain, some heavy, cool. 15–17 Sunny, cool. 18–22 Rainy periods north, sunny south; cool. 23–24 Sunny. 25–31 Showers, then sunny, cold.

JAN. 2016: Temp. 53° (1° below avg.); precip. 1" (2" below avg.). 1–2 Sunny, cool. 3–7 Rainy periods, cool. 8–12 Showers north, sunny south; turning warm. 13–19 Showers, then sunny, cool. 20–23 Sunny; cool north, warm south. 24–31 Sunny, cool.

FEB. 2016: Temp. 53° (2° below avg.); precip. 1" (2" below avg.). 1–6 Sunny, mild. 7–15 A few showers, cool. 16–18 Sunny, cool. 19–29 Showers, then sunny, cool.

MAR. 2016: Temp. 58° (1° above avg.); precip. 1.5" (1" below avg.). 1–3 Sunny, cool. 4–7 Rainy, cool. 8–15 Sunny, seasonable. 16–20 Rainy periods north, sprinkles south. 21–28 Sunny, turning quite warm. 29–31 Showers, cool.

APR. 2016: Temp. 58° (2° below avg.); precip. 1.5" (0.5" above avg.). 1–5 Showers north, sunny south; seasonable. 6–14 Rainy periods, cool. 15–23 Showers, then sunny, cool. 24–30 Occasional rain, cool.

MAY 2016: Temp. 61.5° (2° below avg.); pre-

cip. 0.8" (0.3" above avg.). 1–9 Sunny, warm inland; A.M. clouds and sprinkles, P.M. sun coast. 10–16 Sunny, cool. 17–22 Showers, cool. 23–26 Sunny, cool. 27–31 Sunny, turning hot inland; A.M. clouds and sprinkles, P.M. sun coast.

JUNE 2016: Temp. 67° (1° below avg.); precip. 0.1" (avg.). 1–4 Sunny, cool inland; A.M. clouds and sprinkles, P.M. sun coast. 5–14 Sunny; hot inland, cool coast. 15–22 Sunny, turning cooler inland; A.M. clouds, P.M. sun coast. 23–30 Sunny, warm inland; A.M. clouds, P.M. sun, cool coast.

JULY 2016: Temp. 73° (2° above avg.); precip. 0" (avg.). 1–5 Sunny, cool. 6–13 Sunny, hot. 14–20 Showers, warm inland; A.M. clouds and sprinkles, P.M. sun coast. 21–27 Sunny inland; A.M. clouds and sprinkles, P.M. sun coast; turning hot. 28–31 Sunny, very warm.

AUG. 2016: Temp. 73° (2° above avg.); precip. 0.1" (avg.). 1–5 Sunny, cool. 6–11 Sunny; cool north, warm south. 12–17 Sunny inland; A.M. clouds and sprinkles, P.M. sun coast. 18–28 Sunny; cool inland, turning hot coast. 29–31 Isolated showers, warm.

SEPT. 2016: Temp. 72° (2° above avg.); precip. 0.2" (avg.). 1–8 Sunny, turning hot. 9–17 Showers, then sunny, cool. 18–25 Scattered showers, cool. 26–30 Sunny; cool north, turning hot south.

OCT. 2016: Temp. 62° (3° below avg.); precip. 0.5" (avg.). 1–7 Sunny; warm, then cool. 8–11 Sprinkles north, rain south; cool. 12–16 Sprinkles north, sunny south; cool. 17–22 Showers, then sunny, chilly. 23–31 Showers, then sunny, cool.

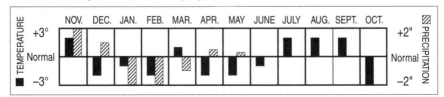

Alaska

SUMMARY: Winter season temperatures will be colder than normal in the north and above normal in the south, with the coldest temperatures in mid-January and late February N, early and mid-January and late February EC, mid-January and late February WC, and early January S. Precipitation will be near normal, with snowfall below normal SC and above normal EW. The snowiest periods will be in early to mid-November N+WC, mid-December EC, early to mid-November and late January SC, and late November, early December, mid-January, and late February P+A.

April and May will be slightly warmer than normal, with near-normal precipitation.

Summer will be cooler and a bit wetter than normal, with the hottest period in mid-June.

September and October will be drier than normal, with near-normal temperatures.

KEY: Panhandle (P), Aleutians (A), north (N), central (C), south (S), west-central (WC), east-central (EC), south-central (SC), elsewhere (EW).

NOV. 2015: Temp. 0° N, 34° S (2° below avg.); precip. 1.4" N, 4" S (1" above avg. N, 1" below S). 1–8 Clear, turning cold N; snow, then flurries, cold WC; flurries, mild EC; showers, mild S. 9–16 Snowstorm, then flurries N+C; snowy periods, cold S. 17–27 Snow, then flurries, cold. 28–30 Clear N+C, snowy S; cold.

DEC. 2015: Temp. –1° N, 37° S (6° above avg.); precip. 0.2" N, 5" S (avg.). 1–8 Flurries, cold N+C; snowy periods, mild S. 9–19 Snow showers, quite mild N+WC; snow, some heavy, mild EC; rain and snow, quite mild SC; clear, then rain and snow, mild P+A. 20–25 Snow showers N+C, snowy periods S; cold. 26–31 Snow showers, cold N; snow, then flurries, cold C; rain and snow, mild S.

JAN. 2016: Temp. –16° N, 25° S (4° below avg.); precip. 0.2" N, 5" S (avg.). 1–9 Flurries, turning mild N+WC; snow, then clear, bitter cold EC; clear, very cold S. 10–23 Flurries, very cold N+C; snowy periods, some heavy, cold S. 24–28 Snow showers, cold. 29–31 Flurries, cold N; snow, mild C; rain and snow, quite mild S.

FEB. 2016: Temp. –20° N, 33° S (6° below avg. N, 2° above S); precip. 0.2" N, 4" S (avg.). 1–9 Snow showers, turning cold N+C; periods of rain and snow, mild S. 10–15 Flurries, cold N+WC; flurries, mild C; rain and snow, mild S. 16–29 Snow showers, some heavy; very cold.

MAR. 2016: Temp. –14° N, 33° S (1° below avg.); precip. 0.5" N, 5" S (avg.). 1–8 Snow showers, cold N+C; rain and snow, then flurries S. 9–19 Flurries, mild N+C; snow showers, cold S. 20–31 Flurries N+C, periods of rain and snow S; cold.

APR. 2016: Temp. 2° N, 41° S (avg.); precip. 0.7" N, 3" S (avg.). 1–4 Snow showers, cold. 5–13 Rain and snow showers. 14–20 Flurries N, sunny C, showers S. 21–30 Flurries N, showers S; cool.

MAY 2016: Temp. 22° N, 48° EW (1° above avg.); precip. 0.6" N, 2.5" S (avg. N, 0.5" below S). 1–17 Flurries N+C, showers S; cool. 18–25 Showers, cool. 26–31 Showers, mild N+WC: sunny, turning warm EW.

JUNE 2016: Temp. 37° N, 53° EW (2° above avg. north, 2° below south); precip. 0.7" N, 2.5" S (avg. N, 0.5" below S). 1–4 Sunny, warm EC; showers, mild EW. 5–8 Showers, cool. 9–20 Sunny, warm N; showers, then sunny, hot C; showers, mild S. 21–30 A few showers, mild.

JULY 2016: Temp. 40° N, 55° EW (2° below avg.); precip. 2.2" N, 5" S (1" above avg.). 1–9 Rainy periods, turning cool. 10–13 Showers, warm. 14–24 A few showers, warm P+A; showers, cool EW. 25–31 Showers, cool.

AUG. 2016: Temp. 38° N, 54° EW (2° below avg.); precip. 1.2" N, 5" S (avg.). 1–5 Rain, then sunny, warm. 6–9 Sunny N, rain S. 10–19 Showers, cool. 20–31 Flurries N, showers S; cool.

SEPT. 2016: Temp. 32° N, 54° EW (avg.); precip. 1.1" N, 5" S (avg. north, 2" below south). 1–4 Flurries N, showers C+S; cool. 5–13 Snow showers N, a few showers C+S; mild. 14–20 Showers, mild N+C; sunny, cool S. 21–30 Snow showers, cold N+C; rainy periods, cool S.

OCT. 2016: Temp. 12° N, 43° S (avg.); precip. 0.1" N, 6.6" S (0.4" above avg.). 1–4 Snow showers N+C, showers S. 5–12 Snow showers N+C, rainy periods S. 13–19 Flurries N, periods of rain and snow EW. 20–23 Snow showers, mild N+C; rain and snow, cold S. 24–31 Flurries, turning cold N; snowy periods, cold EW.

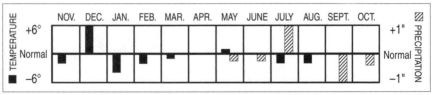

Hawaii

SUMMARY: Winter season temperatures will be below normal on the Big Island and Maui; near normal on Molokai, Oahu, Lanai, and Kahoolawe; and above normal on Kauai. The coolest periods will be in late December, early and mid-January, mid-February, and early March. Winter will be much rainier than normal, especially from November into mid-January.

April and May will be much rainier than normal, with temperatures close to normal.

Summer temperatures will be cooler than normal, on average, with slightly below-normal rainfall. The warmest period will be from the latter half of August into early September.

September and October temperatures will be slightly cooler than normal, with near-normal rainfall.

NOTE: Temperature and precipitation vary substantially based upon topography. The detailed forecast focuses on the Honolulu–Waikiki area and provides general trends elsewhere.

KEY: East (E), Central (C), West (W)

NOV. 2015: Temp. 77.5° (avg.); precip. 7.5" (5" above avg.). 1–3 T-storms, cool. 4–8 Showers, warm. 9–12 Sunny, nice C; a few t-storms, cool E+W. 13–18 A few t-storms, turning cool. 19–22 A few showers, warm C; t-storms, turning warm E+W. 23–30 Rainy periods and heavy t-storms, seasonable.

DEC. 2015: Temp. 75° (avg.); precip. 10.3" (7" above avg.). 1–4 T-storms, warm. 5–9 T-storms C, scattered showers E+W; warm. 10–24 Rainy with heavy t-storms C, scattered t-storms E+W; warm, then cool. 25–28 Sunny C+E, showers; cool. 29–31 T-storms, cool.

JAN. 2016: Temp. 73° (avg.); precip. 5.5" (3" above avg.). 1–4 Rainy periods, heavy E; cool. 5–9 Rain and heavy t-storms C+W, sunny E; turning warm. 10–14 Scattered showers C, a few t-storms E+W; cool. 15–18 Scattered showers, turning warm. 19–28 A few t-storms, cool. 29–31 Sunny, warm.

FEB. 2016: Temp. 73.5° (1° below avg. E, 2° above W); precip. 0.5" (1.5" below avg.). 1–6 Widely separated showers, warm. 7–14 Scattered showers, warm C+W; rainy periods, cool E. 15–17 T-storms, cool. 18–29 Scattered showers, warm C+W; daily t-storms, cool E.

MAR. 2016: Temp. 74° (2° below avg. E, 2° above W); precip. 4" (avg. E, 4" above W). 1–8 Daily showers, cool. 9–17 Scattered showers C+E, t-storms W; cool. 18–22 Heavy t-storms, then showers, warm. 23–31 Scattered t-storms; warm C+W, cool E.

APR. 2016: Temp. 75.5° (avg.); precip. 4.7" (10" above avg. E, 1" above C+W). 1–11 Iso- lated showers C+W, rain and t-storms E; sea- sonable. 12–18 Showers and t-storms; cool, then warm. 19–30 Brief showers C+W, a few t-storms E; cool E, warm W.

MAY 2016: Temp. 77.5° (1° below avg. E, 2° above W); precip. 0.2" (0.5" below avg.). 1–11 Iso- lated showers; cool, then warm. 12–31 Brief show- ers C+W, rainy periods E; cool C+E, warm W.

JUNE 2016: Temp. 79° (0.5° below avg.); pre- cip. 0.4" (avg.). 1–3 Scattered showers, cool. 4–7 Sunny, cool C+E; showers W. 8–16 Isolated showers C+E, scattered t-storms W. 17–30 Iso- lated showers C, scattered t-storms E+W; cool.

JULY 2016: Temp. 80.5 (0.5° below avg.); precip. 0.3" (0.2" below avg.). 1–5 Daily brief showers, cool C+W; scattered t-storms, warm E. 6–19 Scattered light showers, nice C+W; a few showers, warm E. 20–31 Daily showers, cool.

AUG. 2016: Temp. 81° (0.5° below avg.); pre- cip. 0.6" (avg.). 1–4 Sunny; cool C+W, hot E. 5–15 Daily showers; cool C, warm E+W. 16–31 Scattered showers, warm.

SEPT. 2016: Temp. 81° (0.5° below avg.); pre- cip. 0.8" (avg.). 1–7 A few showers, warm. 8–12 Showers; cool C+W, warm E. 13–18 A few t- storms, cool. 19–30 Daily light showers C+W, rain and t-storms E; seasonable.

OCT. 2016: Temp. 79.5° (0.5° below avg.); pre- cip. 2" (avg.). 1–9 Isolated showers, cool. 10–19 Daily showers, seasonable. 20–23 Showers and t-storms; cool C+W, warm E. 24–31 Isolated showers C+W, several showers E; cool.

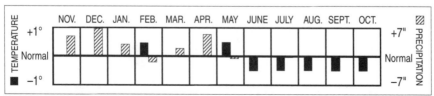

| | NOV. | DEC. | JAN. | FEB. | MAR. | APR. | MAY | JUNE | JULY | AUG. | SEPT. | OCT. | |

THE NORTHERN LIGHTS TOUR

The Old Farmer's Almanac Tours and Travel

We are excited to sponsor affordable travel tours to destinations that inspire wonder, knowledge, and discovery!

Only The Old Farmer's Almanac can bring you tours that are like stepping into the pages of its trusted and beloved publications!

We keep our tours small and personal, amazing and informative. Accompanied by experts in specific fields, we travel to some of the most fascinating places in the world to experience astronomical events such as grand auroral displays, as well as to locations that complement an existing hobby, passion, or profession—or inspire a new one.

Based on 20 years of experience in conducting such tours, we promise safe, comfortable journeys to exceptional destinations.

For details, visit Almanac.com/Tours or call 845-901-7049. BOOK NOW!

THE GLORIOUS GARDENS TOUR

Handy Tools on Almanac.com

ZIP to any link below and enter your zip code to get YOUR local info

Sun Rise or Set Calculator

Zip to Almanac.com/Astronomy

Hourly Weather Updates

Zip to Almanac.com/Weather

Planting & Harvesting Dates

Zip to Almanac.com/PlantingTable

Your Weather History

Zip to Almanac.com/WeatherHistory

Local Tide Calculator

Zip to Almanac.com/Tides

Your Moon Phase

Zip to Almanac.com/MoonPhase

ZIP to Almanac.com for everything under the Sun, including the Moon!

A HORSE
Is Not Just
A HORSE

Each breed has a different personality, skill set, and part in our history.

BY HEATHER SMITH THOMAS

Horses come in many sizes, shapes, and colors. This is because for centuries, horses have been selectively bred over many generations to have specific characteristics for defined purposes. The oldest breed is the "hot-blooded" Arabian, developed by desert tribes in Arabia and North Africa for speed and endurance over long distances. Almost all light riding horse breeds have some Arabian blood in their background. Draft breeds, descendants of large, strong "cold-blooded" horses of Europe and the British Isles and bred for their power and strength, were ridden by knights in armor. The Thoroughbred racehorse originated in England, where racing was the sport of kings, when hot-blooded horses from the Middle East were crossed with English and Irish mares of mixed breeding.

When early explorers and settlers from Spain, England, and France came to the New World, they brought their horses. In colonial America, several new breeds evolved as people selectively bred the

212

available bloodlines to produce better workhorses, carriage and buggy horses, and riding horses. Many of the best riding horses of that day were gaited (they did not trot). They were chosen for their smooth, ground-covering four-beat gaits that were more comfortable for a rider

Arabian

traveling long distances. Other bloodlines were selectively bred for working cattle. Before long, there were several distinctive American breeds.

MORGAN

The oldest American breed is the Morgan, the only breed ever descended from and named after a single horse. This sturdy little colt, originally named Figure, was acquired as payment for a debt by a Vermont singing teacher named Justin Morgan in 1791. Figure was rented to a farmer who used him to pull stumps, drag logs to clear land, plow, pull weight in contests, and race on the weekends. Later, the horse was renamed Justin Morgan after his owner, hence the breed name.

The accomplished colt passed his traits to all of his offspring and their descendants. During the 19th century, Morgans were used as coach and carriage horses, harness racers, and, during the Civil War, cavalry mounts.

Morgan bloodlines were instrumental in helping to create several other American breeds, including the standardbred, Tennessee Walker, and quarter horse. The dam of Dan Patch, world-famous pacing standardbred stallion in the early 1900s, was part Morgan.

Today, Morgans are desired for their good nature and versatility: They are

Morgan

strong enough to pull in harness yet light enough to be a riding horse that can excel in many roles.

STANDARDBRED

Colonial farmers sought fast horses and enjoyed informal contests to determine the fastest trotter. The standardbred dates

Standardbred

from this period. Its ancestors include the Norfolk Trotter from England, one of the earliest "road horses," which were bred for a fast trot while pulling a buggy, and a Thoroughbred stallion named Messenger, imported from England in 1788. By the mid–18th century, trotting races with small carts were held on official courses, and the standardbred was the preferred horsepower. The term "standardbred" was created to distinguish the harness racers that were bred to be able to trot or pace a mile to certain minimum time standards from the Thoroughbred racehorses, for which simply as much speed as possible was sought in breeding.

Today, the standardbred is bred for harness racing, and it is the fastest in that sport, either trotting (diagonal legs moving in unison) or pacing (same-side legs moving in unison). Heavier-bodied than a Thoroughbred, these horses tend to have a mellow temperament compared

with the more high-strung Thoroughbred. Standardbreds that are not quite fast enough to race are often used for riding or to pull buggies, such as those driven by the Amish.

AMERICAN SADDLE HORSE

With high-stepping gaits, this breed is one of the world's greatest show horses. Ancestors of this breed include riding horses of the late 1700s, with Morgan and Thoroughbred blood added as the breed developed. Many officers in the Civil War rode this fancy breed, which was originally called the Kentucky Saddler.

Show horses in this breed are bred and trained to perform five different gaits—the walk, the trot, the canter, the rack (a very fast four-beat gait often called a single-foot), and a slow gait. The slow gait can be a running walk; a fox-trot, which

American Saddle Horse

looks like the front legs are walking and hind legs are trotting; or the amble. The latter looks like a slow pace (lateral legs moving in unison) but is a four-beat gait.

TENNESSEE WALKER

Originally known as Plantation Walking Horses, Tennessee Walkers were bred with Morgan, standardbred, and Thoroughbred blood, in part for their

Tennessee Walker

fast, comfortable gaits during the late 1880s. Their unique four-beat running walk (8 to 10 mph) made them ideal for owners of large estates who needed a horse that could effortlessly cover a lot of miles with an easy gait that didn't jar or tire the rider. They also became a favorite of country doctors, circuit-riding preachers, and other riders who had many miles to travel. Today, this breed is used for showing and pleasure riding.

QUARTER HORSE

The most popular breed today descends from stout-bodied English cart horses that were crossed with English Thoroughbreds in colonial times. Later, these were crossed with Native American horses descended from Spanish horses with Arabian ancestry that were brought to the New World by the Conquistadors. The early quarter horse was bred to be a sprinter, and American colonists raced them on short tracks (often just a straight stretch of road). Pioneers rode quarter horses west, where they found a new role on ranches in outrunning and outmaneuvering wild cattle or holding one at the end of a rope.

This most popular horse is also one of the most versatile. The quarter horse is a sturdy, well-muscled riding horse capable of a tremendous burst of speed (up to 55 mph) for short distances; it is the fastest horse for a quarter of a mile, hence the name. These traits make it valuable

Quarter Horse

NEW BREEDS

When like-minded people get together to promote and perpetuate certain desired traits in their horses, a new breed is born and registries track them. Numerous other gaited breeds (not mentioned here) originated in North America, including the Missouri Fox Trotter, Spotted Mountain Horse, Kentucky Mountain Saddle Horse, Rocky Mountain Horse, Walking Horse, Walking Pony, and Racking Horse.

Some "new" breeds are offshoots of major breeds and focus on a unique trait that makes the new breed different. Registries have been created for half-breeds and crosses of certain breeds. There are also registries for color breeds such as buckskin and palomino and for mustangs and Native American horses.

Appaloosa

for short races, working cattle, and timed rodeo events such as calf roping and barrel racing.

APPALOOSA

Famous for unique coloring—a mostly white body, with dark spots overall or a dark body with a white "blanket" over the rump and spots in the blanket—the Appaloosa has European ancestry. Brought to the New World by Spanish explorers, some ended up with the Nez Percé tribe in the Northwest. The Nez Percé selectively bred Appaloosas for 200 years to perpetuate the color patterns. Later, settlers called the horses Palouse after the area surrounding the Palouse River in Washington and Idaho, and "a Palouse horse" eventually became "Appaloosa." These horses were scattered and lost after the Nez Percé as a tribe were subdued by federal troops in 1877. In the early 1900s, a dedicated man named Francis Haines began a search for speckled horses to save the breed. A registry was

formed in 1938, and in 1975, the Appaloosa was named Idaho's state horse. Today, it is one of the most popular breeds in the United States.

AMERICAN PAINT

Pinto, or two-color, horses exist in a variety of breeds, from gaited horses to ponies. The American Paint horse is a separate breed with its own registry, the result of crossing pintos with quarter horses and Thoroughbreds to create a stock horse body with spotted coloring. The Paint horse could be described as a two-color quarter horse. The Paint population in America today totals more than 1 million,

American Paint

TALK THE TALK

Cold-blooded: refers to draft horses and to pony breeds that do not have Arabian influence

Colt: young male horse

Crossbreed: a horse with two purebred parents of different breeds

Dam: mother of the horse

Filly: young female horse

Foal: young unweaned horse of either sex

Gelding: castrated male

Half-breed: a horse with one purebred parent

Hand: a unit of measurement equal to 4 inches

Hot-blooded: refers to Arabian and Thoroughbred horses and breeds with a high percentage of Arabian and Thoroughbred blood in their background

Mare: female horse at least 4 years old

Pony: any horse of less than 14½ hands (under 58 inches)

Purebred: a horse bred purely within the breed (not to be mistaken with the term "Thoroughbred," which is the name of a specific breed of racehorse)

Sire: father of the horse

Stallion: male horse at least 4 years old, sometimes called a stud

Stud book: record of the registered purebred animals in a breed

second in numbers only to the quarter horse. Pintos and Paints may display two color patterns called Tobiano (primarily white, with large round areas of color on the body) and Overo (jagged white splashes on a solid dark-colored coat).

CANADIAN HORSE

Ancestors of the Canadian Horse were brought from France to Quebec between 1665 and 1670. Being the only horses available to the colonists, they were used for everything—riding, farmwork, racing, and pulling wagons and buggies. By

Canadian Horse

the early 1800s, this versatile breed was pulling stagecoaches in New England. A few decades later, they served as cavalry horses in the Civil War. So many of these horses were exported from Canada that there was danger of the breed being lost. In 1886, a small group of breeders in Quebec formed a registry. Still, the breed dwindled. By 1976, there were fewer than 400, putting these horses on the Livestock Conservancy's rare and endangered list.

Today, as more people discover the versatility of this sturdy, energetic breed, its numbers have surpassed 6,000. ■

Heather Smith Thomas, a lifelong horse and cattle rancher, writes from Idaho, usually before dawn, when she attends to her horses.

Gestation and Mating Tables

		Proper Age or Weight for First Mating	Period of Fertility (yrs.)	Number of Females for One Male	Period of Gestation (days) AVERAGE	RANGE
CATTLE:	**Cow**	15–18 mos.[1]	10–14		283	279–290[2] 262–300[3]
	Bull	1 yr., well matured	10–12	50[4] / thousands[5]		
GOAT:	**Doe**	10 mos. or 85–90 lbs.	6		150	145–155
	Buck	well matured	5	30		
HORSE:	**Mare**	3 yrs.	10–12		336	310–370
	Stallion	3 yrs.	12–15	40–45[4] / record 252[5]		
PIG:	**Sow**	5–6 mos. or 250 lbs.	6		115	110–120
	Boar	250–300 lbs.	6	50[6] / 35–40[7]		
RABBIT:	**Doe**	6 mos.	5–6		31	30–32
	Buck	6 mos.	5–6	30		
SHEEP:	**Ewe**	1 yr. or 90 lbs.	6		147 / 151[8]	142–154
	Ram	12–14 mos., well matured	7	50–75[6] / 35–40[7]		
CAT:	**Queen**	12 mos.	6		63	60–68
	Tom	12 mos.	6	6–8		
DOG:	**Bitch**	16–18 mos.	8		63	58–67
	Male	12–16 mos.	8	8–10		

[1]Holstein and beef: 750 lbs.; Jersey: 500 lbs. [2]Beef; 8–10 days shorter for Angus. [3]Dairy. [4]Natural. [5]Artificial. [6]Hand-mated. [7]Pasture. [8]For fine wool breeds.

Incubation Period of Poultry (days)

Chicken.................................21
Duck.................................26–32
Goose...............................30–34
Guinea..............................26–28
Turkey................................28

Average Life Span of Animals in Captivity (years)

Cat (domestic) 14
Chicken (domestic) 8
Dog (domestic)........... 13
Duck (domestic)......... 10
Goat (domestic) 14

Goose (domestic) 20
Horse................ 22
Pig.................. 12
Rabbit 6
Turkey (domestic)........10

	Estral/Estrous Cycle (including heat period) AVERAGE	RANGE	Length of Estrus (heat) AVERAGE	RANGE	Usual Time of Ovulation	When Cycle Recurs If Not Bred
Cow	21 days	18–24 days	18 hours	10–24 hours	10–12 hours after end of estrus	21 days
Doe goat	21 days	18–24 days	2–3 days	1–4 days	Near end of estrus	21 days
Mare	21 days	10–37 days	5–6 days	2–11 days	24–48 hours before end of estrus	21 days
Sow	21 days	18–24 days	2–3 days	1–5 days	30–36 hours after start of estrus	21 days
Ewe	16½ days	14–19 days	30 hours	24–32 hours	12–24 hours before end of estrus	16½ days
Queen cat		15–21 days	3–4 days, if mated	9–10 days, in absence of male	24–56 hours after coitus	Pseudo-pregnancy
Bitch	24 days	16–30 days	7 days	5–9 days	1–3 days after first acceptance	Pseudo-pregnancy

MOOSE
Understood

Short takes on the world's tallest deer
BY SANDY NEWTON

VER THE PAST 100 years, *Alces alces*—"moose," to most North Americans—has slowly expanded its range across much of the northern half of the continent. Today, climate change and clashes with predators (humans included) are shifting this pattern, but moose still appear when we least expect them—astonishing, delighting, and sometimes scaring the wits out of us.

How well do you know this iconic symbol of northern wilderness?

Moose Family History

A. alces has Eurasian origins. It expanded into North America later on, arriving in what is now Alaska over the Bering land bridge. Because the beast had long been hunted out of existence in much of western Europe, explorers landing on our east coast thought that they were seeing a new

Clockwise from top: a cow bonds with her calf; moose can grow more than 8 feet tall; two bull moose clash during the rut; moose are the largest members of the deer family; moose can dive 18 feet under water.

creature. They borrowed Algonquian names—*mus, moosu*—meaning "eater of twigs" or "he who strips off bark" and called it "moose." Today, four of the mammal's eight subspecies live on our continent.

Tough Love

Moose do not form herds. They live alone for most of the year, searching out partners during the rut. The strongest moosely bond forms between cow and calf, which Mom abruptly severs after a new babe is born. Confused yearlings try

to reestablish good relations, but a few swift kicks set the record straight. However, moose can form a keen attachment to people if raised from infancy.

Yoo-Hoo!

To find a willing mate when the fall rut arrives, bull moose wander about wailing, snorting, and scraping trees with their antlers to advertise their presence. Cows have their own come-hither calls and also "talk" to their calves by snorting.

Bluff or Bigger Bull?

Bull moose often clash during the rut. When the game is on, they paw, charge, and spar in a head-to-head test of strength. The point is to drive the other bull off—not kill him—but injuries do occur. Two bulls can collide so hard that their antlers bend and interlock. This usually ends in starvation and death for both animals. Sometimes, a bull will back away from a contender, reading a bigger rack as a stronger foe.

FIVE SIGNS A MOOSE DOESN'T LIKE YOU

- It's heading toward you . . .
- grunting and stomping . . .
- throwing its head around . . .
- with its ears back . . .
- and the hairs on its back raised.

Moose Marks

Size: Moose are the largest members of the deer family. The Alaskan sub-species can grow more than 8 feet tall and top 1,800 pounds. The more southern its habitat, the smaller the moose, in general.

Agility & Grace: Moose look ungainly but move lightly and often silently. They lift their legs straight up, so that they can easily walk through muck and water and over fallen trees. Unlike other deer, they seldom jump, but they have been spotted on their hind legs to reach tender twigs.

Speed: Moose on the run can sustain a speed of almost 22 miles per hour and go even faster in short bursts.

Diving & Swimming: Moose have been seen pond diving down 18 feet to reach succulent plants. Calves learn to swim when only days old. With their hollow hair aiding buoyancy, adult moose will swim in salt or fresh water and can cover distances of 7½ miles or more.

Smelling & Hearing: Moose are exceptional at both. They can pivot their ears almost 360 degrees, and antlers help bulls to hear by focusing sound.

Sight: With eyes more on the side of their heads, moose don't see ahead clearly, but they easily detect motion and manage well in the dark.

Giddyap, Bullwinkle!

Big strong animals, moose—why not harness them? It has been tried. Siberians were known to ride moose that could outrun horses, so the invading Cossack forces of Ivan the Terrible (1580s) killed moose riders and outlawed moose taming. In the 1600s, Sweden's King Charles XI reportedly attempted to train a moose cavalry for winter deployment. It didn't take. In both Canada and Europe, moose have occasionally been trained to pull sleighs.

Moose Tonic

Traditional lore in several European locales said that medicine from a moose's hind foot would cure the "falling sickness"—epilepsy.

Yes, YOU!

You don't need to be a moose to look like a challenger. Hiker, hunter, car, train—if you look threatening to a bull or get between a cow and her calf, you may be charged. Unlike other deer, cows fight to defend their young instead of hiding them. They lash out with their front legs and kick with their powerful hind legs. It's no laughing matter.

Moose Defense

If you find yourself on the wrong side of an unhappy moose, keep your eye on it; hold up your hands, palms out; speak softly; and put something solid—tree, boulder, vehicle—between you and the moose ASAP. Some say that if you run, a moose won't chase you for long. If it knocks you down, curl up, play dead, and protect your head.

When Is a Moose Not a Moose?

When it's in Europe, where it's an elk! ■

Sandy Newton, a regular contributor to the Almanac, writes from Newfoundland, where moose occasionally mosey by her home.

IN DEFENSE OF COUNTRY

During Thomas Jefferson's tenure as U.S. ambassador to France (1784–89), Count Georges-Louis Leclerc Buffon, a renowned French natural historian, asserted that all plant and animal species (including humans) found in America were weak, feeble, and degenerate, due to pervasive cold and wet, swampy conditions.

To counter this disparaging claim, Jefferson presented Buffon with a panther skin and, later, mastodon bones—to no avail. Finally, he begged his colleagues—including Benjamin Franklin, George Washington, John Adams, and James Monroe—to send him a moose. Eventually, a 7-foot-tall stuffed ungulate from New Hampshire was shipped to France and delivered by Jefferson to Buffon, who died shortly thereafter.

Decades passed before Buffon's contentions were dismissed and people viewed America as a land of resources and opportunity.

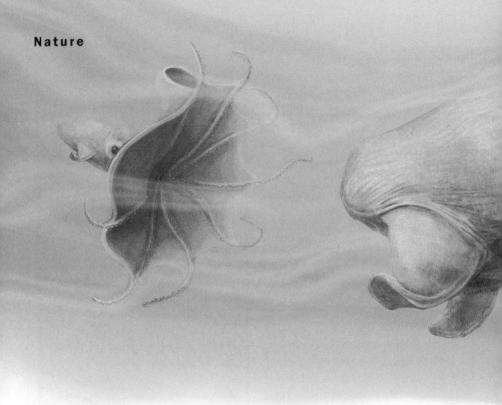

CREATURES

Or are their fear-inspiring

VAMPIRE SQUID

Famous deep-sea diver William Beebe described an encounter with this "terrible octopus, black as night, with ivory-white jaws and blood-red eyes" in his 1926 book *The Arcturus Adventure:*

"This came along, half swimming, half sidling, its eight cupped arms all joined together by an ebony web. In those icy, black depths, to be a small fish, and to come within reach of such sinister arms, to be enfolded by the living umbrella, and then drawn slowly, irrevocably toward the wide-open, gleaming beak, watched always by those cruel, lidless eyes, so frightfully like those of human beings, seemed, to my imagination, a much more awful fate than could ever befall, in our darkest night, any creature breathing air."

Pretty breathless prose for an animal that is only 6 inches long and "not even

By Tim Clark • Illustrations by Mesa Schumacher

The vampire squid's most remarkable feature is its huge eyes, proportionately larger than the eyes of any animal on Earth.

FROM HELL

names more bark than bite?

slightly dangerous to humans," according to researchers. In fact, the most recent studies prove that *Vampyroteuthis infernalis* doesn't hunt for prey at all. With the lowest metabolic rate of any cephalopod, it barely moves.

The vampire squid is a detritivore, surviving on flakes of organic matter that sink 3,000 feet into the cold, dark, oxygen-minimum layer where it lives. These particles go by the poetic name of "marine snow," but scientists Henk-Jan Hoving and Bruce Robison at the Monterey Bay Aquarium Research Institute say that it consists of "dead bodies, poop, and snot."

Like Bela Lugosi, the vampire squid can hide inside a dark cloak; it literally turns itself inside out, wrapping its dark mantle around its head while spraying phosphorescent particles from the tips of its tentacles and flashing the bioluminescent chromatophores in its skin, blinding and confusing predators in the lightless depths.

Its most remarkable feature is its huge eyes, proportionately larger than

The hellbender is an "indicator species": It can survive only in clean, well-oxygenated streams.

the eyes of any animal on Earth. Beebe called them "blood-red," but modern biologists say that, depending on the light source, these "cruel, lidless eyes" are a charming shade of blue.

HELLBENDERS

Weighing up to 5½ pounds and measuring as long as 30 inches, the hellbender is North America's largest salamander. It's no beauty, unless you like beady eyes and slimy skin (which may explain one of its nicknames—the "snot otter"). But "hellbender" seems overdone for a harmless animal that spends most of its life in hiding.

Cryptobranchus ("hidden gills") *alleganiensis* looks like something that might crawl out from under a rock, which is exactly where it lives in swift-flowing streams primarily in Missouri and Arkansas and from southern New York to northern Georgia. In fact, hellbenders need a stream with large, flat rocks under which to hide, and they may stay underneath the same rock for years, emerging only at dusk to feed for a few hours.

The hellbender is solitary except during mating season, and it's none too friendly even then. The male excavates a shallow nest under a rock or log in the streambed and waits for a female that he can drive into it. He won't let her leave until she's laid 150 to 200 eggs, which he sprays with his sperm. Then he chases her away and looks for another female. As many as 1,948 eggs have been found in one nest.

The male guards the nest for 45 to 75 days while the eggs incubate, waving his frills to ensure them a rich supply of oxygen. When the young hatch, he abandons them.

The hellbender has hardly changed in 160 million years. It has lungs, but only uses them for buoyancy, and its gills are lost after its first year. It breathes primarily through its skin, taking oxygen directly from the water. It has a rudder-like tail, but it doesn't swim; it walks on the streambed. Hence another nickname: the "walking catfish." Its eyesight is so poor that it hunts by smell. Like some fish, it also has a "lateral line," a sensory organ that detects movement.

It feeds primarily on crayfish and is preyed upon by fish, snakes, turtles, and other hellbenders, who cannibalize the eggs.

What good is it? The hellbender is an "indicator species": It can survive only in clean, well-oxygenated streams, which explains why pollution, disease, and dam building have reduced the hellbender population by an estimated 77 percent since the 1970s. Zoos in Nashville and St. Louis are the first to succeed in hatching hellbenders, so future generations of children may yet find them—and run screaming from the water.

DEVIL WORMS

When geomicrobiologist Tullis Onstott of Princeton University found minuscule worms living in a South African gold mine nearly a mile below the surface, he was so surprised that he called in a Belgian nematode specialist, Gaetan Borgonie, to confirm his findings. In 2011, they published their observations, naming the worms *Halicephalobus mephisto,* after Mephistopheles, the demonic spirit in Goethe's *Faust.* In Greek, the name means "he who loves not the light."

Mephisto is a new species that eats biofilms ("layers of gelatinous goo" on rocks) and requires only traces of oxygen. Although the worm is not more than half a millimeter long, Onstott

likened its discovery to finding Moby-Dick in Lake Ontario. It is the first multicellular organism to be found so far beneath the surface of Earth. Isotope dating of water in rock fractures where the species was found proved that the water was 3,000 to 12,000 years old and had been as warm as 118°F. No one suspected that life could be found in such a hot, oxygen-starved environment.

"I doubt this nematode sprang from Hell," commented evolutionary biologist

The devil worm is the first multicellular organism to be found so far beneath the surface of Earth.

Byron Adams of Brigham Young University. "It more likely evolved at Earth's surface, with the rest of the Nematoda."

With this discovery, "the deep subsurface of Mars looks very interesting," said Michael Meyer, lead scientist for NASA's Mars Exploration Program. "The universe might have many more habitats than we thought." ∎

The only creatures from hell that **Tim Clark** knows are his two rambunctious dogs, who live with him in Dublin, New Hampshire.

110 years ago, Typhoid Mary was . . .

THE MOST DANGEROUS WOMAN IN AMERICA

by Victor Parachin • Illustrations by Tim Robinson

F OR THE SUMMER of 1906, New York banker Charles Henry Warren arranged to rent the seasonal home of George Thompson in Oyster Bay, Long Island, New York, for his family. The Warrens hired maids and gardeners, as well as a cook named Mary Mallon.

On August 27, one of the Warren daughters fell desperately ill with typhoid fever. Soon, in rapid succession, Mrs. Warren, two maids, the gardener, and another Warren daughter fell victim. Of 11 people in the household that summer, six were stricken with a range of symptoms:

excruciating headache, fever, nausea, abdominal pain, diarrhea, and vomiting.

Fortunately, no one died. But Thompson faced financial disaster because his house could not be leased again until the source of the typhoid outbreak was uncovered. If none were found, his house would be burned to the ground, as was the custom, to destroy any remnant of disease.

Local health authorities were mystified. Initially, they thought that the outbreak was related to food, suspecting clams as the primary culprits. However, not all of those who became ill had eaten clams.

(continued)

230

Thompson hired George Soper, a New York City–area epidemiologist, to investigate further. Soper interviewed everyone who had been in residence during the outbreak. Only Mary Mallon was unavailable; she had departed the estate abruptly when the outbreak began to spread and left no forwarding address.

Ice Cream and Peaches

Soper had quickly concluded that everyone who contracted typhoid had consumed the homemade ice cream and fresh peaches prepared and served by Mallon. He wanted to talk with her.

Working with the employment agency that had placed Mallon and with others who knew her, Soper developed a

in Ithaca, New York, in 1903.

Although the evidence strongly indicated that Mallon was a carrier of *Salmonella typhosa,* the bacterium starter of typhoid fever, Soper needed clear scientific proof. He knew that typhoid fever was spread either by food and water contaminated by feces from an infected person or by direct contact with such a carrier. To gain definite evidence, he needed to get samples of her urine, stool, and blood.

In March 1907, Soper located Mallon. She was in good health and working as a cook for the Walter Bowen family in New York City. Soper first met up with Mallon in that home's kitchen. "I was as diplomatic as possible," he reported, "but

"SHE SEIZED A CARVING FORK AND ADVANCED IN MY DIRECTION . . . I FELT RATHER LUCKY TO ESCAPE."

profile: Mary Mallon had been born in Cookstown, Ireland, and at the age of 15 emigrated to the United States, where she found work as a domestic servant. She was tall, somewhat heavyset, yet strong and healthy, with fair hair and blue eyes. She was unmarried and had few friends.

Tracking her recent employment history, Soper discovered that previous typhoid outbreaks dotted her work record. In fact, he could connect her to outbreaks in the New York City area in 1897, 1901, 1902, and 1904, in addition to a second outbreak in 1906 that led to the death of a child. Soper's sleuthing also tied Mallon to a typhoid epidemic (1,400 cases)

I had to say that I suspected her of making people sick and that I wanted specimens of her urine, feces, and blood."

A Fork Like a Rapier

Mallon became enraged. "She seized a carving fork and advanced in my direction," Soper recalled. "I passed rapidly down the long narrow hall, through the tall iron gate . . . and so to the sidewalk. I felt rather lucky to escape."

Later, with an ambulance, five police officers, and the cooperation of the New York City Health Commissioner, Soper returned to the Bowen home. Mallon, he reported, greeted them with a "long

kitchen fork in her hand like a rapier." Lunging at Soper and the officers, she created enough fright and confusion to escape.

A 5-hour search of the neighborhood ensued. Finally, the group found Mallon hiding in a closet (others claim that it was an outhouse). One of those assisting Soper was New York City Health Department official Dr. S. Josephine Baker,

TYPHOID VS. EBOLA

■ Typhoid is transmitted through the ingestion of water or food contaminated by the feces of an infected person or through direct contact.

■ Ebola is transmitted through direct contact with one or more body fluids of an infected person or with a recently contaminated surface.

who described what happened when Mallon emerged from the closet:

"She came out fighting and swearing, both of which she could do with appalling efficiency and vigor. I made another effort to talk sensibly and asked her again to let me have the specimens, but it was of no use. By that time she was convinced that the law was wantonly persecuting her, when she had done nothing wrong. She knew that she had never had typhoid fever; she was maniacal in her integrity. There was nothing I could do but take her with us. The policemen lifted her into the ambulance and I literally sat on her all the way to the hospital; it was like being in a cage with an angry lion."

At the Willard Parker Hospital in New York, the required samples were taken. Typhoid bacilli were found in her stool and her gall bladder was found to be teeming with typhoid salmonella. After further interviews with Mallon, Soper concluded that she spread typhoid primarily as a result of her own poor bathroom hygiene because she didn't wash her hands and saw no need to do so. As a result, she transferred the bacteria she unknowingly carried from the bathroom to the kitchens where she prepared food.

By this time, Soper's investigation into Mallon had been reported in newspapers. In many sensational accounts, she was called "Typhoid Mary" and the "most dangerous woman in America." Although blamed for numerous typhoid outbreaks—3,467 cases were reported in New York City in 1906 alone—she was associated with just seven cases, all of them outside of the city.

Public outcry, combined with Mallon's reluctance to help health authorities, resulted in her being taken by force, without trial, and quarantined in a small cottage on the grounds of Riverside Hospital on North Brother Island. This was her home for 3 years.

On the Loose Again

Upon her release, she was given instructions never to work as a cook and ordered to report to the Department of Health every 3 months. When she failed to show up, the health department simply lost track of her.

Over the next 5 years, using an alias, Mallon found employment cooking for several families—and, each time, left

"SHE CAME OUT FIGHTING AND SWEARING, BOTH OF WHICH SHE COULD DO WITH APPALLING EFFICIENCY AND VIGOR."

typhoid in her wake.

The tide turned in 1915, when a serious typhoid epidemic—25 cases and two deaths—spread through the staff of New York's Sloan Hospital for Women, where only one hospital employee failed to report for work. Authorities soon identified the absent employee as Mallon and tracked her to Long Island, where she was again cooking for a family.

This time, when confronted by the authorities, Mallon offered no resistance. She was returned to North Brother Island, where she lived under close supervision and in isolation for more than a dozen years.

After suffering a paralyzing stroke, Mary Mallon died on November 11, 1938. A funeral mass for her at St. Luke's Roman Catholic Church in the Bronx was attended by three men, three women, and three children, whose identities were never revealed. She was buried by the Department of Health in St. Raymond's Cemetery, also in the Bronx, the following day. ■

Victor Parachin is a journalist and author of a dozen books.

PUT AWAY THE

SHOVEL!

Try these beds, and you will never dig a garden plot again.

By Doreen G. Howard • Illustrations by Kim Kurki

HAVE YOU given up on—or not attempted—vegetable gardening because of the work involved in creating a plot? Especially if you have only a sliver of yard, the edge of an asphalt driveway, or hard-packed ground that nurtures monster weeds?

Keyhole, straw bale, and cement block gardens may be the answer to your dilemma. These inexpensive "plots" let you grow in any spot, large or small. Plus, these are raised gardens, making it easier to reach and tend luscious tomatoes, fragrant basil, and even watermelons.

The Keyhole Garden

FIRST USED in Africa by missionaries to help natives grow food, keyhole gardens are highly productive. The round bed is about 6 feet in diameter. A pie slice cut out on the north side gives easy access to the center and thus forms the keyhole design. In the middle is a basket that distributes to the growing plants nutrients from compost, as well as kitchen and garden waste (and household "gray water," if desired). Soil in the bed is slightly sloped away from the center to aid water and nutrient distribution.

Rose Marie Nichols McGee, owner of Nichols Garden Nursery in Albany, Oregon, built a keyhole garden after learning about them. She said that it was easy to make and could be positioned even on a cement slab or driveway. Her garden is about 7 feet in diameter, and she stresses size: "Make sure that you can reach across it from the center basket."

TO MAKE A KEYHOLE GARDEN:

1. Measure a 6-foot-diameter circle to mark the wall. Notch the circle (like a wedge of pie) for access to the center.

2. Using the measured area to guide you, build the wall about 3 feet high, using rocks, metal edging, broken bricks, or any material that can support the weight of wet soil.

3. Use wire mesh to form a basket or tube about 1 foot in diameter and 4 feet high. Place it in the center of the circle.

4. Line the inside of the wall with cardboard.

5. Fill the bed with layers of compostable materials, wetting them as you go.

6. Top with a few inches of compost or potting soil, making sure that the mix slopes from the high point at the top of the center basket downward to the wall.

Nichols McGee filled her keyhole with garden soil, used potting soil, compost, and shredded leaves. You can use straw, wood ash, pieces of cardboard, and aged manure, too.

7. Fill the center basket with alternating layers of compostable material, along with layers of vegetable scraps and green weeds. These will provide moisture and nutrients.

8. Water the center basket and the garden only when the plants start to wilt; this will force plant roots toward the center basket for moisture and nutrients.

9. Feed the garden by adding vegetable scraps, lawn clippings, and other compostable matter to the center basket.

The Straw Bale Garden

AMANDA THOMSEN—author of the blog Kiss My Aster and a book (Storey Publishing, 2012) by the same name—of Palos Park, Illinois, used straw bales as decorations at a Halloween party and then to protect perennials over the winter. In the spring, she put her bales on the edge of her driveway, in hot, full-sun exposure, and used them as containers to grow strawberries, tomatoes, and squashes. Thomsen says that it was easy gardening, and her young daughter especially liked picking strawberries at eye level. In addition to the ease of use, Thomsen emphasizes location: You need to place straw bales where you want them and not move them. "I can not stress enough how heavy a wet straw bale is!"

"Straw bales aren't just the container,"

says Joel Karten, author of *Straw Bale Gardens* (Cool Springs Press, 2013). "They are also the growing media. As straw inside the bale decomposes, it provides nutrients for plants for the whole growing season. In the fall, you can toss what's left onto your compost heap."

The secret to a straw bale garden is to condition new bales for 12 to 18 days before planting. Here's how to do it.

FOR EACH BALE, YOU WILL NEED:

2¼ cups nitrogen-rich lawn fertilizer or 13½ cups balanced organic fertilizer (days 1–9)

1 cup of balanced (10–10–10) fertilizer or 3 cups organic fertilizer with phosphorus and potash (day 10)

Day 1: Lay the bale(s) with the strings parallel to the ground (for the largest planting area) on a porous surface, such as well-draining soil, or a hard surface off which water will run easily. (The bales should not sit in a puddle.) Sprinkle ½ cup of nitrogen-rich lawn fertilizer or 3 cups of balanced organic fertilizer evenly over the surface of each bale. Water thoroughly so that the fertilizer permeates the entire bale.

Day 2: Soak the bales again, preferably with warm water, until water runs out of the bottom. (Instead of taking warm water from a faucet, fill buckets with cold water and set them in the sun to warm.)

Day 3: Sprinkle each bale with ½ cup of lawn fertilizer or 3 cups of organic fertilizer. Soak with warm water.

Day 4: Soak with warm water again,

WHY YOU WANT STRAW— NOT HAY—BALES

When farmers harvest grains such as wheat, rye, or oats, they thresh, or shake, the grain seeds from the stalks, leaving behind dried stems. A baling machine gathers these stems into large round or small rectangular bales. These bales are true straw and the ones you want to use.

Hay bales are the entire grass stem, including grain seeds, which will sprout and grow when moistened. Hay is used as animal feed, usually. You want to avoid it.

Go to Strawbalemarket.com to find seed-free, healthy straw in your area.

until water runs out of the bale bottoms.

Day 5: Sprinkle with ½ cup of lawn fertilizer or 3 cups of organic fertilizer again and soak with warm water.

Day 6: Soak with warm water again. You should smell and see signs of decomposition.

Days 7, 8, and 9: Apply ¼ cup of lawn fertilizer or 1½ cups of organic fertilizer to each bale daily. Follow with warm water. Most of the growing medium is created during these days.

Day 10: Sprinkle with 1 cup of balanced (10–10–10) fertilizer or 3 cups of organic fertilizer with phosphorus and potash. Soak with warm water.

Day 11: Moisten bales with warm water.

Days 12 to 18: Set plants in the bales fed with lawn fertilizer, or . . .

Day 18: Set plants in the organically fertilized bales.

No other fertilizer is needed. Be sure to water the bales to keep the growing medium moist.

The Cement Block Garden

IBUILT MY first cement block garden when I lived on the Texas Gulf Coast, where the soil is gumbo clay (impossible to dig) and the water table is 3 inches below sea level. It was much easier to create fertile soil that drained than to accept flooding and the constant leaching of nutrients.

These easy beds were my salvation. They fit anywhere, provide an instant garden, and are very productive. I've found that 4x4-foot beds are easy to tend and yield a more than adequate harvest.

For a 4x4-foot bed that is one cement block high . . .

YOU WILL NEED:

14 cement blocks
2 bags (2 cu. ft. each) topsoil
1 bale (3 cu. ft.) peat moss
1 bag (2 to 3 cu. ft.) compost or composted cow manure
2-inch layer of shredded leaves or grass clippings

Line up two rows of cement blocks 4 feet apart. Then place blocks along the ends to make a square. You can make these beds as long, wide, and high as you like, but the bigger the garden is, the more soil ingredients you will need.

Mix the soil ingredients to create a homogeneous planting mix before adding to the garden. Water thoroughly.

Plant seeds and transplants immediately. Holes in cement blocks can be filled with the soil mix and planted with strawberries, herbs, or beneficial flowers such as nasturtiums and marigolds.

Multiply the ingredients to fill larger or additional beds. ■

Doreen G. Howard was a longtime contributor to *Old Farmer's Almanac* products. She also wrote a very popular gardening blog on our Web site, Almanac.com.

Gardening

Planting by the Moon's Phase

According to this age-old practice, cycles of the Moon affect plant growth.

■ Plant flowers and vegetables that bear crops above ground during the light, or waxing, of the Moon: from the day the Moon is new to the day it is full.

■ Plant flowering bulbs and vegetables that bear crops below ground during the dark, or waning, of the Moon: from the day after it is full to the day before it is new again.

The Moon Favorable columns give the best planting days based on the Moon's phases for 2016. (See the **Left-Hand Calendar Pages, 124–150,** for the exact days of the new and full Moons.) The Planting Dates columns give the safe periods for planting in areas that receive frost. See **Frosts and Growing Seasons, page 188,** for first/last frost dates and the average length of the growing season in your area.

Get local seed-sowing dates at Almanac.com/PlantingTable.

■ Aboveground crops are marked *.
■ (E) means early; (L) means late.
■ Map shades correspond to shades of date columns.

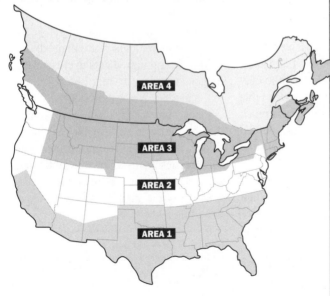

* Barley	
* Beans	(E)
	(L)
Beets	(E)
	(L)
* Broccoli plants	(E)
	(L)
* Brussels sprouts	
* Cabbage plants	
Carrots	(E)
	(L)
* Cauliflower plants	(E)
	(L)
* Celery plants	(E)
	(L)
* Collards	(E)
	(L)
* Corn, sweet	(E)
	(L)
* Cucumbers	
* Eggplant plants	
* Endive	(E)
	(L)
* Kale	(E)
	(L)
Leek plants	
* Lettuce	
* Muskmelons	
* Okra	
Onion sets	
* Parsley	
Parsnips	
* Peas	(E)
	(L)
* Pepper plants	
Potatoes	
* Pumpkins	
Radishes	(E)
	(L)
* Spinach	(E)
	(L)
* Squashes	
Sweet potatoes	
* Swiss chard	
* Tomato plants	
Turnips	(E)
	(L)
* Watermelons	
* Wheat, spring	
* Wheat, winter	

AREA 1		AREA 2		AREA 3		AREA 4	
Planting Dates	Moon Favorable	Planting Dates	Moon Favorable	Planting Dates	Moon Favorable	Planting Dates	Moon Favorable
2/15–29	2/15–22	3/15–4/7	3/20–23, 4/7	5/15–6/21	5/15–21, 6/4–20	6/1–30	6/4–20
3/15–4/7	3/15–23, 4/7	4/15–30	4/15–22	5/7–6/21	5/7–21, 6/4–20	5/30–6/15	6/4–15
8/7–31	8/7–18	7/1–21	7/4–19	6/15–7/15	6/15–20, 7/4–15	—	—
2/7–29	2/7, 2/23–29	3/15–4/3	3/24–4/3	5/1–15	5/1–5	5/25–6/10	5/25–6/3
9/1–30	9/17–29	8/15–31	8/19–31	7/15–8/15	7/20–8/1	6/15–7/8	6/21–7/3
2/15–3/15	2/15–22, 3/8–15	3/7–31	3/8–23	5/15–31	5/15–21	6/1–25	6/4–20
9/7–30	9/7–16, 9/30	8/1–20	8/2–18	6/15–7/7	6/15–20, 7/4–7	—	—
2/11–3/20	2/11–22, 3/8–20	3/7–4/15	3/8–23, 4/7–15	5/15–31	5/15–21	6/1–25	6/4–20
2/11–3/20	2/11–22, 3/8–20	3/7–4/15	3/8–23, 4/7–15	5/15–31	5/15–21	6/1–25	6/4–20
2/15–3/7	2/23–3/7	3/7–31	3/7, 3/24–31	5/15–31	5/22–31	5/25–6/10	5/25–6/3
8/1–9/7	8/1, 8/19–31	7/7–31	7/20–31	6/15–7/21	6/21–7/3, 7/20–21	6/15–7/8	6/21–7/3
2/15–3/7	2/15–22	3/15–4/7	3/15–23, 4/7	5/15–31	5/15–21	6/1–25	6/4–20
8/7–31	8/7–18	7/1–8/7	7/4–19, 8/2–7	6/15–7/21	6/15–20, 7/4–19	—	—
2/15–29	2/15–22	3/7–31	3/8–23	5/15–6/30	5/15–21, 6/4–20	6/1–30	6/4–20
9/15–30	9/15–16, 9/30	8/15–9/7	8/15–18, 9/1–7	7/15–8/15	7/15–19, 8/2–15	—	—
2/11–3/20	2/11–22, 3/8–20	3/7–4/7	3/8–23, 4/7	5/15–31	5/15–21	6/1–25	6/4–20
9/7–30	9/7–16, 9/30	8/15–31	8/15–18	7/1–8/7	7/4–19, 8/2–7	—	—
3/15–31	3/15–23	4/1–17	4/7–17	5/10–6/15	5/10–21, 6/4–15	5/30–6/20	6/4–20
8/7–31	8/7–18	7/7–21	7/7–19	6/15–30	6/15–20	—	—
3/7–4/7	3/8–23, 4/7–15	4/7–5/15	4/7–22, 5/6–15	5/7–6/20	5/7–21, 6/4–20	5/30–6/15	6/4–15
3/7–4/15	3/8–23, 4/7–15	4/7–5/15	4/7–22, 5/6–15	6/1–30	6/4–20	6/15–30	6/15–20
2/15–3/20	2/15–22, 3/8–20	4/7–5/15	4/7–22, 5/6–15	5/15–31	5/15–21	6/1–25	6/4–20
8/15–9/7	8/15–18, 9/1–7	7/15–8/15	7/15–19, 8/2–15	6/7–30	6/7–20	—	—
2/11–3/20	2/11–22, 3/8–20	3/7–4/7	3/8–23, 4/7	5/15–31	5/15–21	6/1–15	6/4–15
9/7–30	9/7–16, 9/30	8/15–31	8/15–18	7/1–8/7	7/4–19,8/2–7	6/25–7/15	7/4–15
2/15–4/15	2/23–3/7, 3/24–4/6	3/7–4/7	3/7, 3/24–4/6	5/15–31	5/22–31	6/1–25	6/1–3, 6/21–25
2/15–3/7	2/15–22	3/1–31	3/8–23	5/15–6/30	5/15–21, 6/4–20	6/1–30	6/4–20
3/15–4/7	3/15–23, 4/7	4/15–5/7	4/15–22, 5/6–7	5/15–6/30	5/15–21, 6/4–20	6/1–30	6/4–20
4/15–6/1	4/15–22, 5/6–21	5/25–6/15	6/4–15	6/15–7/10	6/15–20, 7/4–10	6/25–7/7	7/4–7
2/1–29	2/1–7, 2/23–29	3/1–31	3/1–7, 3/24–31	5/15–6/7	5/22–6/3	6/1–25	6/1–3, 6/21–25
2/20–3/15	2/20–22, 3/8–15	3/1–31	3/8–23	5/15–31	5/15–21	6/1–15	6/4–15
1/15–2/4	1/24–2/4	3/7–31	3/7, 3/24–31	4/1–30	4/1–6, 4/23–30	5/10–31	5/22–31
1/15–2/7	1/15–23	3/7–31	3/8–23	4/15–5/7	4/7–22, 5/6–7	5/15–31	5/15–21
9/15–30	9/15–16, 9/30	8/7–31	8/7–18	7/15–31	7/15–19	7/10–25	7/10–19
3/1–20	3/8–20	4/1–30	4/7–22	5/15–6/30	5/15–21, 6/4–20	6/1–30	6/4–20
2/10–29	2/23–29	4/1–30	4/1–6, 4/23–30	5/1–31	5/1–5, 5/22–31	6/1–25	6/1–3, 6/21–25
3/7–20	3/8–20	4/23–5/15	5/6–15	5/15–31	5/15–21	6/1–30	6/4–20
1/21–3/1	1/24–2/7, 2/23–3/1	3/7–31	3/7, 3/24–31	4/15–30	4/23–30	5/15–6/5	5/22–6/3
10/1–21	10/17–21	9/7–30	9/17–29	8/15–31	8/19–31	7/10–31	7/20–31
2/7–3/15	2/8–22, 3/8–15	3/15–4/20	3/15–23, 4/7–20	5/15–31	5/15–21	6/1–25	6/4–20
10/1–21	10/1–16	8/1–9/15	8/2–18, 9/1–15	7/17–9/7	7/17–19, 8/2–18, 9/1–7	7/20–8/5	8/2–5
3/15–4/15	3/15–23, 4/7–15	4/15–30	4/15–22	5/15–6/15	5/15–21, 6/4–15	6/1–30	6/4–20
3/23–4/6	3/24–4/6	4/21–5/9	4/23–5/5	5/15–6/15	5/22–6/3	6/1–30	6/1–3, 6/21–30
2/7–3/15	2/8–22, 3/8–15	3/15–4/15	3/15–23, 4/7–15	5/1–31	5/6–21	5/15–31	5/15–21
3/7–20	3/8–20	4/7–30	4/7–22	5/15–31	5/15–21	6/1–15	6/4–15
1/20–2/15	1/24–2/7	3/15–31	3/24–31	4/7–30	4/23–30	5/10–31	5/22–31
9/1–10/15	9/17–29	8/1–20	8/1, 8/19–20	7/1–8/15	7/1–3, 7/20–8/1	—	—
3/15–4/7	3/15–23, 4/7	4/15–5/7	4/15–22, 5/6–7	5/15–6/30	5/15–21, 6/4–20	6/1–30	6/4–20
2/15–29	2/15–22	3/1–20	3/8–20	4/7–30	4/7–22	5/15–6/10	5/15–21, 6/4–10
10/15–12/7	10/15–16, 10/30–11/4, 11/29–12/7	9/15–10/20	9/15–16, 9/30–10/16	8/11–9/15	8/11–18, 9/1–15	8/5–30	8/5–18

Secrets of the Zodiac

The Man of the Signs

Ancient astrologers believed that each astrological sign influenced a specific part of the body. The first sign of the zodiac—Aries—was attributed to the head, with the rest of the signs moving down the body, ending with Pisces at the feet.

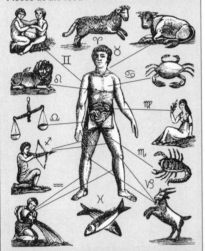

♈ Aries, head......**ARI** *Mar. 21–Apr. 20*
♉ Taurus, neck.....**TAU** *Apr. 21–May 20*
♊ Gemini, arms ... **GEM** *May 21–June 20*
♋ Cancer, breast....**CAN** *June 21–July 22*
♌ Leo, heart.......**LEO** *July 23–Aug. 22*
♍ Virgo, belly .....**VIR** *Aug. 23–Sept. 22*
♎ Libra, reins......**LIB** *Sept. 23–Oct. 22*
♏ Scorpio, secrets...**SCO** *Oct. 23–Nov. 22*
♐ Sagittarius, thighs .**SAG** *Nov. 23–Dec. 21*
♑ Capricorn, knees .**CAP** *Dec. 22–Jan. 19*
♒ Aquarius, legs .. **AQU** *Jan. 20–Feb. 19*
♓ Pisces, feet......**PSC** *Feb. 20–Mar. 20*

Astrology vs. Astronomy

■ **Astrology** is a tool we use to plan events according to the placements of the Sun, the Moon, and the planets in the 12 signs of the zodiac. In astrology, the planetary movements do not cause events; rather, they explain the path, or "flow," that events tend to follow. **Astronomy** is the study of the actual placement of the known planets and constellations. *(The placement of the planets in the signs of the zodiac is not the same astrologically and astronomically.)* The Moon's astrological place is given on **page 243**; its astronomical place is given in the **Left-Hand Calendar Pages, 124–150**.

The dates in the **Best Days** table, **page 244**, are based on the astrological passage of the Moon. However, consider all indicators before making any major decisions.

When Mercury Is Retrograde

■ Sometimes the other planets appear to be traveling backward through the zodiac; this is an illusion. We call this illusion *retrograde motion.*

Mercury's retrograde periods can cause our plans to go awry. However, this is an excellent time to reflect on the past. Intuition is high during these periods, and coincidences can be extraordinary.

When Mercury is retrograde, remain flexible, allow extra time for travel, and avoid signing contracts. Review projects and plans at these times, but wait until Mercury is direct again to make any final decisions.

In 2016, Mercury will be retrograde during January 5–25, April 28–May 22, August 30–September 22, and December 19–31.

–Celeste Longacre

Gardening by the Moon's Sign

Use the chart on the next page to find the best dates for the following garden tasks:

■ **Plant, transplant, and graft:** Cancer, Scorpio, or Pisces.

■ **Harvest:** Aries, Leo, Sagittarius, Gemini, or Aquarius.

■ **Build/fix fences or garden beds:** Capricorn.

■ **Control insect pests, plow, and weed:** Aries, Gemini, Leo, Sagittarius, or Aquarius.

■ **Prune:** Aries, Leo, or Sagittarius. During a waxing Moon, pruning encourages growth; during a waning Moon, it discourages growth.

Setting Eggs by the Moon's Sign

■ Chicks take about 21 days to hatch. Those born under a waxing Moon, in the fruitful signs of Cancer, Scorpio, and Pisces, are healthier and mature faster. To ensure that chicks are born during these times, determine the best days to "set eggs" (to place eggs in an incubator or under a hen). To calculate, find the three fruitful birth signs on the chart below. Use the **Left-Hand Calendar Pages, 124–150,** to find the dates of the new and full Moons.

Using only the fruitful dates between the new and full Moons, count back 21 days to find the best days to set eggs.

E X A M P L E :

The Moon is new on May 6 and full on May 21. Between these dates, on May 10 and 11, the Moon is in the sign of Cancer. To have chicks born on May 10, count back 21 days; set eggs on April 19.

	Nov.	Dec.	Jan.	Feb.	Mar.	Apr.	May	June	July	Aug.	Sept.	Oct.	Nov.	Dec.
1	CAN	LEO	LIB	SCO	SAG	CAP	PSC	ARI	GEM	CAN	VIR	LIB	SAG	CAP
2	LEO	VIR	LIB	SAG	SAG	AQU	PSC	TAU	GEM	LEO	VIR	LIB	SAG	CAP
3	LEO	VIR	LIB	SAG	CAP	AQU	PSC	TAU	CAN	LEO	LIB	SCO	SAG	CAP
4	LEO	VIR	SCO	SAG	CAP	PSC	ARI	GEM	CAN	VIR	LIB	SCO	CAP	AQU
5	VIR	LIB	SCO	CAP	AQU	PSC	ARI	GEM	CAN	VIR	SCO	SAG	CAP	AQU
6	VIR	LIB	SAG	CAP	AQU	ARI	TAU	CAN	LEO	VIR	SCO	SAG	AQU	PSC
7	LIB	SCO	SAG	AQU	AQU	ARI	TAU	CAN	LEO	LIB	SCO	SAG	AQU	PSC
8	LIB	SCO	CAP	AQU	PSC	TAU	GEM	LEO	VIR	LIB	SAG	CAP	AQU	ARI
9	LIB	SCO	CAP	PSC	PSC	TAU	GEM	LEO	VIR	SCO	SAG	CAP	PSC	ARI
10	SCO	SAG	CAP	PSC	ARI	GEM	CAN	VIR	LIB	SCO	CAP	AQU	PSC	TAU
11	SCO	SAG	AQU	ARI	ARI	GEM	CAN	VIR	LIB	SCO	CAP	AQU	ARI	TAU
12	SAG	CAP	AQU	ARI	TAU	CAN	LEO	VIR	LIB	SAG	CAP	PSC	ARI	GEM
13	SAG	CAP	PSC	TAU	TAU	CAN	LEO	LIB	SCO	SAG	AQU	PSC	TAU	GEM
14	SAG	AQU	PSC	TAU	GEM	LEO	VIR	LIB	SCO	CAP	AQU	ARI	TAU	CAN
15	CAP	AQU	ARI	GEM	GEM	LEO	VIR	SCO	SAG	CAP	PSC	ARI	GEM	CAN
16	CAP	AQU	ARI	GEM	CAN	LEO	VIR	SCO	SAG	AQU	PSC	TAU	GEM	LEO
17	AQU	PSC	TAU	GEM	CAN	VIR	LIB	SCO	SAG	AQU	ARI	TAU	CAN	LEO
18	AQU	PSC	TAU	CAN	LEO	VIR	LIB	SAG	CAP	AQU	ARI	GEM	CAN	LEO
19	PSC	ARI	GEM	CAN	LEO	LIB	SCO	SAG	CAP	PSC	TAU	GEM	LEO	VIR
20	PSC	ARI	GEM	LEO	VIR	LIB	SCO	CAP	AQU	PSC	TAU	GEM	LEO	VIR
21	ARI	TAU	CAN	LEO	VIR	LIB	SCO	CAP	AQU	ARI	GEM	CAN	VIR	LIB
22	ARI	TAU	CAN	VIR	VIR	SCO	SAG	CAP	PSC	ARI	GEM	CAN	VIR	LIB
23	TAU	GEM	CAN	VIR	LIB	SCO	SAG	AQU	PSC	TAU	CAN	LEO	VIR	SCO
24	TAU	GEM	LEO	VIR	LIB	SAG	CAP	AQU	ARI	TAU	CAN	LEO	LIB	SCO
25	TAU	CAN	LEO	LIB	LIB	SAG	CAP	PSC	ARI	GEM	LEO	VIR	LIB	SCO
26	GEM	CAN	VIR	LIB	SCO	SAG	AQU	PSC	ARI	GEM	LEO	VIR	SCO	SAG
27	GEM	LEO	VIR	SCO	SCO	CAP	AQU	ARI	TAU	CAN	LEO	LIB	SCO	SAG
28	CAN	LEO	LIB	SCO	SAG	CAP	AQU	ARI	TAU	CAN	VIR	LIB	SCO	CAP
29	CAN	LEO	LIB	SCO	SAG	AQU	PSC	TAU	GEM	LEO	VIR	LIB	SAG	CAP
30	LEO	VIR	LIB	–	CAP	AQU	PSC	TAU	GEM	LEO	LIB	SCO	SAG	CAP
31	–	VIR	SCO	–	CAP	–	ARI	–	CAN	VIR	–	SCO	–	AQU

The table title spans: **The Moon's Astrological Place, 2015–16**

Best Days for 2016

This chart is based on the Moon's sign and shows the best days each month for certain activities.

—Celeste Longacre

	JAN.	FEB.	MAR.	APR.	MAY	JUNE	JULY	AUG.	SEPT.	OCT.	NOV.	DEC.
Quit smoking	5, 27	1, 23, 28	27	5, 23	2, 30	3, 26, 30	23, 27, 31	19, 23, 28	20, 24, 29	17, 21, 26	18, 22, 27	15, 19, 24
Begin diet to lose weight	5, 27	1, 23, 28	27	5, 23	2, 30	3, 26, 30	23, 27, 31	19, 23, 28	20, 24, 29	17, 21, 26	18, 22, 27	15, 19, 24
Begin diet to gain weight	13, 18	10, 14, 18	12, 17	9, 13	10, 15	11, 16	9, 14	5, 10	6, 16	4, 13	10, 13	7, 11
Cut hair to encourage growth	17, 18	13, 14	12, 13	8, 9, 19, 20	17, 18	13, 14	10–12	7, 8	3, 4	2, 12, 13	9, 10, 13	6, 7
Cut hair to discourage growth	1–3, 28, 29	25, 26	24, 25	4, 5	29, 30	2, 3, 29, 30	22, 23, 27, 28	23, 24	19, 20	27–29	24, 25	21, 22
Have dental care	26, 27	23, 24	20–22	17, 18	14, 15	10–12	8, 9	5, 6, 31	1, 2, 28, 29	25, 26	21–23	19, 20
Start projects	11	9	10	8	7	6	5	3	2	2	30	30
End projects	9	7	8	6	5	4	3	1, 31	30	30	28	28
Go camping	6, 7	2, 3	1, 2, 28, 29	24–26	22, 23	18, 19	15–17	12, 13	8, 9	5–7	1–3, 29, 30	26, 27
Plant aboveground crops	13, 14, 21, 22	9, 10, 18, 19	16, 17	12, 13	19–21	15–17	5, 13, 14	9–11	6, 7	3, 4, 12, 13	9, 10	6, 7
Plant belowground crops	4, 5, 31	1, 27–29	26, 27	4, 5, 23	1–3, 29, 30	25, 26	3, 22, 23	1, 19, 20, 27, 28	23, 24	21, 22	17, 18, 26, 27	23–25
Destroy pests and weeds	15, 16	11, 12	10, 11	6, 7	4, 5, 31	1, 27, 28	24–26	21, 22	17, 18	14, 15	11, 12	8, 9
Graft or pollinate	21–23	18, 19	16, 17	12, 13	10, 11	6, 7	3, 4, 31	1, 27, 28	23, 24	21, 22	17, 18	14, 15
Prune to encourage growth	15, 16	11, 12, 20	18, 19	14–16	12, 13	8, 9	6, 7, 16, 17	12, 13	8, 9	5–7	1–3	8, 9
Prune to discourage growth	6, 7, 25	2–4	1, 2, 28, 29	6, 24–26	4, 5, 31	1, 27, 28	24–26	21, 22	25–27	23, 24	19, 20	16–18
Harvest above-ground crops	17, 18	13, 14	12, 13, 20	8, 9, 17, 18	7, 14–16	10–12	8, 9	4–6	1, 2	8, 9	4, 5	10, 11
Harvest below-ground crops	8, 26, 27	5, 6, 23, 24	3, 4, 30, 31	1, 27, 28	24, 25	2, 3, 29, 30	27, 28	23, 24	19, 20, 28, 29	25, 26	13, 22, 23	19, 20
Can, pickle, or make sauerkraut	4, 5, 31	1, 26, 27	26, 27	4, 5, 23	1–3, 29, 30	25, 26	3, 22, 23	19, 20, 27, 28	23, 24	21, 22	17, 18, 26–28	15, 23–25
Cut hay	15, 16	11, 12	10, 11	6, 7	4, 5, 31	1, 27, 28	24–26	21, 22	17, 18	14, 15	11, 12	8, 9
Begin logging	8–10	5, 6	3, 4, 30, 31	1, 27, 28	24, 25	20–22	18, 19	14, 15	10–12	8, 9	4, 5	1–3, 28–30
Set posts or pour concrete	8–10	5, 6	3, 4, 30, 31	1, 27, 28	24, 25	20–22	18, 19	14, 15	10–12	8, 9	4, 5	1–3, 28–30
Breed animals	4, 5, 31	1, 27–29	26, 27	22, 23	19–21	15–17	13, 14	9–11	5–7	3, 4, 30, 31	26–28	23–25
Wean animals or children	5, 27	1, 23, 28	27	5, 23	2, 30	3, 26, 30	23, 27, 31	19, 23, 28	20, 24, 29	17, 21, 26	18, 22, 27	15, 19, 24
Castrate animals	11, 12	7, 8	5–7	2, 3, 29, 30	26–28	23, 24	20, 21	17, 18	13, 14	10, 11	7, 8	4, 5, 31
Slaughter livestock	4, 5, 31	1, 27–29	26, 27	22, 23	19–21	15–17	13, 14	9–11	5–7	3, 4, 30, 31	26–28	23–25

See what to do when at Almanac.com/BestDays. **2016**

Maddening Mind~Manglers

FOOD FOUR THOUGHT

*Pairs abound in nature and the world.
Here we double your trouble. See if you can identify
the four items in these classifications:*

1. FDR's "Four Freedoms" _____

2. Canada's "Fundamental Freedoms" _____

3. honor cards in the game of bridge _____

4. ancient "elements" _____

5. zodiac signs that have human form _____

6. cycles of a 4-stroke internal combustion engine _____

7. horsemen of the Apocalypse _____

8. Galilean moons of Jupiter _____

9. colors in a 4-color process in photoengraving _____

10. stomach compartments of a cow _____

11. H's of the Four-H Club _____

12. the Fab Four _____

13. the Big Four (business) _____

14. in Canada, the Four Corners (geography) _____

15. in the U.S., the Four Corners (geography) _____

16. in Canada, the original members of the Confederation _____

Answers on page 271

Winners in the 2015 Essay Contest

My Best Car Story

First Prize: $250

When I was 9, I bought a packet of Batman stickers that came with pink bubble gum. Without thinking, and much to my father's chagrin, I pasted the stickers all over the glove compartment of our white Chevy Impala. The next year, my father traded in that car, Batman stickers and all.

Twenty years later, I was having a discussion with my husband about cars. He went on to regale me with the tale of his first car, a white Chevy Impala. He told me that it was a great car except that some kid had plastered Batman stickers all over the glove compartment! We have been together for over 30 years, and I don't believe in coincidence. It was fate.

–Lisa Behr, Castle Creek, New York

Second Prize: $150

In 1964, my brother, Paul, convinced his young, immensely popular high school English teacher, a Miss Maguire, to accept a ride to school with him after she informed the class that she would be absent because her car needed repairs. Paul asked our older brother if he could borrow his new car, a red-and-white 1957 Chevy Bel Air in mint condition. The car was backed into the carport and the keys were in the glove compartment when Paul arrived at our brother's house early that morning. Paul pulled the car out and headed up the hill to get Miss Maguire.

When they arrived at the school, he let Miss Maguire off at the curb. The sidewalk was full of students and teachers walking into the building. Paul drove to the parking lot, parked the car, and went into homeroom. By second period, the story was spreading throughout school. On the trunk of my brother's car was the spray-painted message "Just Married." This decoration had reduced the cost of the car, and my older brother had failed to mention this when he had told Paul about his new vehicle!

–Elle Dietemann, North Chatham, New York

Third Prize: $100

From the time I was 6 until I was 10, I had one of the grandest playthings a boy could have. Out by the barn was the frame of a Model T Ford. The wheels were gone, the motor had been removed, and the seats were missing their covers, exposing their coil springs. But the fenders and running boards were still there, and the steering wheel was intact with the gas and magneto control still in place. Hour after hour, I would sit on the seat and drive it. I would fill it with gas, check the tires that weren't there, turn the crank, jump in, and chug along. In my mind, I was a chauffeur, a racecar driver, or a bus driver. When cousins came to visit, I would take them for a ride and I might even let them drive. However, the only time the car ever moved an inch was when my older brothers carted it off to the scrap-metal pile that was collected for the WWII defense effort.

–Johnie Marion, Eastwood, Kentucky

Too Good to Leave Out

In June 1954, I worked at the local airport, the base for local crop dusters. I lived in a small town in Montana's wheat country and the airport was out of town, so my dad bought me a 1951 Studebaker to drive back and forth. The weather that summer was hot, sometimes reaching 100°F at the airport. My boss told me to park in the airplane hangar while the planes were out spraying, in order to keep the car cooler.

One hot day, a cocky young pilot known for his hotdogging landed and taxied his biplane duster while reclining in the second seat with his legs drooped over the front seat, steering the plane with his feet. In this way, he was blind to his front and directed the plane by memory. Unfortunately for me, his memory steered him straight for the hangar where my "Studie" was parked. I will never forget the "chop, chop, chop" sound as his propeller struck the trunk of my car or the difficulty of telling my father that my car had been hit by an airplane!

–Patti Bolstad, South Great Falls, Montana

At 88 years of age, I have owned many cars, but I will never forget my 1964 Lincoln. My wife and I traded this old gas and oil guzzler for a new, small Mercury. The salesman insisted that he keep the Lincoln to drive and loaned us a car for 2 days, until the Mercury was "detailed."

The next afternoon, that salesman was charged with murdering his wife, placing her body in the car trunk, and dumping her in a remote area. We were sure he premeditated the murder and wanted the Lincoln with the large trunk!

–P. H. Greene Jr., Knoxville, Tennessee ∎

Announcing the 2016 Essay Contest Topic: A New U.S. National Holiday We Need—and Why
See contest rules on page 271.

Tide Corrections

■ Many factors affect the times and heights of the tides: the shoreline, the time of the Moon's southing (crossing the meridian), and the Moon's phase. The High Tide column on the **Left-Hand Calendar Pages, 124–150,** lists the times of high tide at Commonwealth Pier in Boston Harbor. The heights of some of these tides, reckoned from Mean Lower Low Water, are given on the **Right-Hand Calendar Pages, 125–151.** Use the table below to calculate the approximate times and heights of high tide at the places shown. Apply the time difference to the times of high tide at Boston and the height difference to the heights at Boston. A tide calculator can be found at **Almanac.com/Tides.**

E X A M P L E :

The conversion of the times and heights of the tides at Boston to those at Cape Fear, North Carolina, is given below:

High tide at Boston	11:45 A.M.
Correction for Cape Fear	– 3 55
High tide at Cape Fear	7:50 A.M.
Tide height at Boston	11.6 ft.
Correction for Cape Fear	– 5.0 ft.
Tide height at Cape Fear	6.6 ft.

Estimations derived from this table are *not* meant to be used for navigation. *The Old Farmer's Almanac* accepts no responsibility for errors or any consequences ensuing from the use of this table.

Tidal Site	Difference: Time (h. m.)	Height (ft.)
Canada		
Alberton, PE	*–5 45	–7.5
Charlottetown, PE	*–0 45	–3.5
Halifax, NS	–3 23	–4.5
North Sydney, NS	–3 15	–6.5
Saint John, NB	+0 30	+15.0
St. John's, NL	–4 00	–6.5
Yarmouth, NS	–0 40	+3.0
Maine		
Bar Harbor	–0 34	+0.9
Belfast	–0 20	+0.4
Boothbay Harbor	–0 18	–0.8
Chebeague Island	–0 16	–0.6
Eastport	–0 28	+8.4
Kennebunkport	+0 04	–1.0
Machias	–0 28	+2.8
Monhegan Island	–0 25	–0.8
Old Orchard	0 00	–0.8
Portland	–0 12	–0.6
Rockland	–0 28	+0.1
Stonington	–0 30	+0.1
York	–0 09	–1.0
New Hampshire		
Hampton	+0 02	–1.3
Portsmouth	+0 11	–1.5
Rye Beach	–0 09	–0.9
Massachusetts		
Annisquam	–0 02	–1.1
Beverly Farms	0 00	–0.5

Tidal Site	Difference: Time (h. m.)	Height (ft.)
Cape Cod Canal		
East Entrance	–0 01	–0.8
West Entrance	–2 16	–5.9
Chatham Outer Coast	+0 30	–2.8
Inside	+1 54	**0.4
Cohasset	+0 02	–0.07
Cotuit Highlands	+1 15	**0.3
Dennis Port	+1 01	**0.4
Duxbury–Gurnet Point	+0 02	–0.3
Fall River	–3 03	–5.0
Gloucester	–0 03	–0.8
Hingham	+0 07	0.0
Hull	+0 03	–0.2
Hyannis Port	+1 01	**0.3
Magnolia–Manchester	–0 02	–0.7
Marblehead	–0 02	–0.4
Marion	–3 22	–5.4
Monument Beach	–3 08	–5.4
Nahant	–0 01	–0.5
Nantasket	+0 04	–0.1
Nantucket	+0 56	**0.3
Nauset Beach	+0 30	**0.6
New Bedford	–3 24	–5.7
Newburyport	+0 19	–1.8
Oak Bluffs	+0 30	**0.2
Onset–R.R. Bridge	–2 16	–5.9
Plymouth	+0 05	0.0
Provincetown	+0 14	–0.4
Revere Beach	–0 01	–0.3
Rockport	–0 08	–1.0
Salem	0 00	–0.5
Scituate	–0 05	–0.7

Tidal Site Difference:	Time (h. m.)	Height (ft.)	Tidal Site Difference:	Time (h. m.)	Height (ft.)
Wareham	−3 09	−5.3	Rehoboth Beach.	−3 37	−5.7
Wellfleet	+0 12	+0.5	Wilmington	+1 56	−3.8
West Falmouth.	−3 10	−5.4	**Maryland**		
Westport Harbor	−3 22	−6.4	Annapolis	+6 23	−8.5
Woods Hole			Baltimore.	+7 59	−8.3
Little Harbor	−2 50	**0.2	Cambridge.	+5 05	−7.8
Oceanographic			Havre de Grace	+11 21	−7.7
Institute	−3 07	**0.2	Point No Point	+2 28	−8.1
Rhode Island			Prince Frederick		
Bristol	−3 24	−5.3	Plum Point	+4 25	−8.5
Narragansett Pier	−3 42	−6.2	**Virginia**		
Newport.	−3 34	−5.9	Cape Charles	−2 20	−7.0
Point Judith	−3 41	−6.3	Hampton Roads	−2 02	−6.9
Providence.	−3 20	−4.8	Norfolk	−2 06	−6.6
Sakonnet	−3 44	−5.6	Virginia Beach.	−4 00	−6.0
Watch Hill	−2 50	−6.8	Yorktown.	−2 13	−7.0
Connecticut			**North Carolina**		
Bridgeport	+0 01	−2.6	Cape Fear.	−3 55	−5.0
Madison.	−0 22	−2.3	Cape Lookout	−4 28	−5.7
New Haven	−0 11	−3.2	Currituck	−4 10	−5.8
New London	−1 54	−6.7	Hatteras		
Norwalk	+0 01	−2.2	Inlet.	−4 03	−7.4
Old Lyme			Kitty Hawk	−4 14	−6.2
Highway Bridge	−0 30	−6.2	Ocean	−4 26	−6.0
Stamford	+0 01	−2.2	**South Carolina**		
Stonington	−2 27	−6.6	Charleston	−3 22	−4.3
New York			Georgetown.	−1 48	**0.36
Coney Island	−3 33	−4.9	Hilton Head	−3 22	−2.9
Fire Island Light	−2 43	**0.1	Myrtle Beach.	−3 49	−4.4
Long Beach	−3 11	−5.7	St. Helena		
Montauk Harbor	−2 19	−7.4	Harbor Entrance	−3 15	−3.4
New York City–Battery . .	−2 43	−5.0	**Georgia**		
Oyster Bay.	+0 04	−1.8	Jekyll Island.	−3 46	−2.9
Port Chester.	−0 09	−2.2	St. Simon's Island	−2 50	−2.9
Port Washington	−0 01	−2.1	Savannah Beach		
Sag Harbor.	−0 55	−6.8	River Entrance	−3 14	−5.5
Southampton			Tybee Light.	−3 22	−2.7
Shinnecock Inlet	−4 20	**0.2	**Florida**		
Willets Point	0 00	−2.3	Cape Canaveral	−3 59	−6.0
New Jersey			Daytona Beach.	−3 28	−5.3
Asbury Park.	−4 04	−5.3	Fort Lauderdale	−2 50	−7.2
Atlantic City	−3 56	−5.5	Fort Pierce Inlet	−3 32	−6.9
Bay Head–Sea Girt	−4 04	−5.3	Jacksonville		
Beach Haven	−1 43	**0.24	Railroad Bridge.	−6 55	**0.1
Cape May	−3 28	−5.3	Miami Harbor Entrance . .	−3 18	−7.0
Ocean City.	−3 06	−5.9	St. Augustine	−2 55	−4.9
Sandy Hook.	−3 30	−5.0			
Seaside Park	−4 03	−5.4			
Pennsylvania					
Philadelphia.	+2 40	−3.5			
Delaware					
Cape Henlopen	−2 48	−5.3			

Varies widely; accurate only to within 1½ hours. Consult local tide tables for precise times and heights.

**Where the difference in the Height column is so marked, the height at Boston should be multiplied by this ratio.*

Time Corrections

■ Astronomical data for Boston is given on **pages 104, 108–109**, and **124–150**. Use the Key Letter shown to the right of each time on those pages with this table to find the number of minutes that you must add to or subtract from Boston time to get the correct time for your city. (Because of complex calculations for different locales, times are approximate.) For more information on the use of Key Letters and this table, **see How to Use This Almanac, page 120.**

Get times simply and specifically: Download astronomical times calculated for your zip code and presented like a Left-Hand Calendar Page at **Almanac.com/Access.**

TIME ZONES: Codes represent *standard time.* Atlantic is −1, Eastern is 0, Central is 1, Mountain is 2, Pacific is 3, Alaska is 4, and Hawaii-Aleutian is 5.

State	City	North Latitude °	North Latitude ′	West Longitude °	West Longitude ′	Time Zone Code	A (min.)	B (min.)	C (min.)	D (min.)	E (min.)
AK	Anchorage	61	10	149	59	4	−46	+27	+71	+122	+171
AK	Cordova	60	33	145	45	4	−55	+13	+55	+103	+149
AK	Fairbanks	64	48	147	51	4	−127	+2	+61	+131	+205
AK	Juneau	58	18	134	25	4	−76	−23	+10	+49	+86
AK	Ketchikan	55	21	131	39	4	−62	−25	0	+29	+56
AK	Kodiak	57	47	152	24	4	0	+49	+82	+120	+154
AL	Birmingham	33	31	86	49	1	+30	+15	+3	−10	−20
AL	Decatur	34	36	86	59	1	+27	+14	+4	−7	−17
AL	Mobile	30	42	88	3	1	+42	+23	+8	−8	−22
AL	Montgomery	32	23	86	19	1	+31	+14	+1	−13	−25
AR	Fort Smith	35	23	94	25	1	+55	+43	+33	+22	+14
AR	Little Rock	34	45	92	17	1	+48	+35	+25	+13	+4
AR	Texarkana	33	26	94	3	1	+59	+44	+32	+18	+8
AZ	Flagstaff	35	12	111	39	2	+64	+52	+42	+31	+22
AZ	Phoenix	33	27	112	4	2	+71	+56	+44	+30	+20
AZ	Tucson	32	13	110	58	2	+70	+53	+40	+24	+12
AZ	Yuma	32	43	114	37	2	+83	+67	+54	+40	+28
CA	Bakersfield	35	23	119	1	3	+33	+21	+12	+1	−7
CA	Barstow	34	54	117	1	3	+27	+14	+4	−7	−16
CA	Fresno	36	44	119	47	3	+32	+22	+15	+6	0
CA	Los Angeles–Pasadena–Santa Monica	34	3	118	14	3	+34	+20	+9	−3	−13
CA	Palm Springs	33	49	116	32	3	+28	+13	+1	−12	−22
CA	Redding	40	35	122	24	3	+31	+27	+25	+22	+19
CA	Sacramento	38	35	121	30	3	+34	+27	+21	+15	+10
CA	San Diego	32	43	117	9	3	+33	+17	+4	−9	−21
CA	San Francisco–Oakland–San Jose	37	47	122	25	3	+40	+31	+25	+18	+12
CO	Craig	40	31	107	33	2	+32	+28	+25	+22	+20
CO	Denver–Boulder	39	44	104	59	2	+24	+19	+15	+11	+7
CO	Grand Junction	39	4	108	33	2	+40	+34	+29	+24	+20
CO	Pueblo	38	16	104	37	2	+27	+20	+14	+7	+2
CO	Trinidad	37	10	104	31	2	+30	+21	+13	+5	0
CT	Bridgeport	41	11	73	11	0	+12	+10	+8	+6	+4
CT	Hartford–New Britain	41	46	72	41	0	+8	+7	+6	+5	+4
CT	New Haven	41	18	72	56	0	+11	+8	+7	+5	+4
CT	New London	41	22	72	6	0	+7	+5	+4	+2	+1
CT	Norwalk–Stamford	41	7	73	22	0	+13	+10	+9	+7	+5
CT	Waterbury–Meriden	41	33	73	3	0	+10	+9	+7	+6	+5
DC	Washington	38	54	77	1	0	+35	+28	+23	+18	+13
DE	Wilmington	39	45	75	33	0	+26	+21	+18	+13	+10

State	City	North Latitude °		West Longitude °		Time Zone Code	A (min.)	B (min.)	C (min.)	D (min.)	E (min.)
FL	Fort Myers	26	38	81	52	0	+87	+63	+44	+21	+4
FL	Jacksonville	30	20	81	40	0	+77	+58	+43	+25	+11
FL	Miami	25	47	80	12	0	+88	+57	+37	+14	−3
FL	Orlando	28	32	81	22	0	+80	+59	+42	+22	+6
FL	Pensacola	30	25	87	13	1	+39	+20	+5	−12	−26
FL	St. Petersburg	27	46	82	39	0	+87	+65	+47	+26	+10
FL	Tallahassee	30	27	84	17	0	+87	+68	+53	+35	+22
FL	Tampa	27	57	82	27	0	+86	+64	+46	+25	+9
FL	West Palm Beach	26	43	80	3	0	+79	+55	+36	+14	−2
GA	Atlanta	33	45	84	24	0	+79	+65	+53	+40	+30
GA	Augusta	33	28	81	58	0	+70	+55	+44	+30	+19
GA	Macon	32	50	83	38	0	+79	+63	+50	+36	+24
GA	Savannah	32	5	81	6	0	+70	+54	+40	+25	+13
HI	Hilo	19	44	155	5	5	+94	+62	+37	+7	−15
HI	Honolulu	21	18	157	52	5	+102	+72	+48	+19	−1
HI	Lanai City	20	50	156	55	5	+99	+69	+44	+15	−6
HI	Lihue	21	59	159	23	5	+107	+77	+54	+26	+5
IA	Davenport	41	32	90	35	1	+20	+19	+17	+16	+15
IA	Des Moines	41	35	93	37	1	+32	+31	+30	+28	+27
IA	Dubuque	42	30	90	41	1	+17	+18	+18	+18	+18
IA	Waterloo	42	30	92	20	1	+24	+24	+24	+25	+25
ID	Boise	43	37	116	12	2	+55	+58	+60	+62	+64
ID	Lewiston	46	25	117	1	3	−12	−3	+2	+10	+17
ID	Pocatello	42	52	112	27	2	+43	+44	+45	+46	+46
IL	Cairo	37	0	89	11	1	+29	+20	+12	+4	−2
IL	Chicago–Oak Park	41	52	87	38	1	+7	+6	+6	+5	+4
IL	Danville	40	8	87	37	1	+13	+9	+6	+2	0
IL	Decatur	39	51	88	57	1	+19	+15	+11	+7	+4
IL	Peoria	40	42	89	36	1	+19	+16	+14	+11	+9
IL	Springfield	39	48	89	39	1	+22	+18	+14	+10	+6
IN	Fort Wayne	41	4	85	9	0	+60	+58	+56	+54	+52
IN	Gary	41	36	87	20	1	+7	+6	+4	+3	+2
IN	Indianapolis	39	46	86	10	0	+69	+64	+60	+56	+52
IN	Muncie	40	12	85	23	0	+64	+60	+57	+53	+50
IN	South Bend	41	41	86	15	0	+62	+61	+60	+59	+58
IN	Terre Haute	39	28	87	24	0	+74	+69	+65	+60	+56
KS	Fort Scott	37	50	94	42	1	+49	+41	+34	+27	+21
KS	Liberal	37	3	100	55	1	+76	+66	+59	+51	+44
KS	Oakley	39	8	100	51	1	+69	+63	+59	+53	+49
KS	Salina	38	50	97	37	1	+57	+51	+46	+40	+35
KS	Topeka	39	3	95	40	1	+49	+43	+38	+32	+28
KS	Wichita	37	42	97	20	1	+60	+51	+45	+37	+31
KY	Lexington–Frankfort	38	3	84	30	0	+67	+59	+53	+46	+41
KY	Louisville	38	15	85	46	0	+72	+64	+58	+52	+46
LA	Alexandria	31	18	92	27	1	+58	+40	+26	+9	−3
LA	Baton Rouge	30	27	91	11	1	+55	+36	+21	+3	−10
LA	Lake Charles	30	14	93	13	1	+64	+44	+29	+11	−2
LA	Monroe	32	30	92	7	1	+53	+37	+24	+9	−1
LA	New Orleans	29	57	90	4	1	+52	+32	+16	−1	−15
LA	Shreveport	32	31	93	45	1	+60	+44	+31	+16	+4
MA	Brockton	42	5	71	1	0	0	0	0	0	−1
MA	Fall River–New Bedford	41	42	71	9	0	+2	+1	0	0	−1
MA	Lawrence–Lowell	42	42	71	10	0	0	0	0	0	+1
MA	Pittsfield	42	27	73	15	0	+8	+8	+8	+8	+8
MA	Springfield–Holyoke	42	6	72	36	0	+6	+6	+6	+5	+5
MA	Worcester	42	16	71	48	0	+3	+2	+2	+2	+2

(continued)

Time Corrections

State	City	North Latitude °	North Latitude ′	West Longitude °	West Longitude ′	Time Zone Code	A (min.)	B (min.)	C (min.)	D (min.)	E (min.)
MD	Baltimore	39	17	76	37	0	+32	+26	+22	+17	+13
MD	Hagerstown	39	39	77	43	0	+35	+30	+26	+22	+18
MD	Salisbury	38	22	75	36	0	+31	+23	+18	+11	+6
ME	Augusta	44	19	69	46	0	−12	−8	−5	−1	0
ME	Bangor	44	48	68	46	0	−18	−13	−9	−5	−1
ME	Eastport	44	54	67	0	0	−26	−20	−16	−11	−8
ME	Ellsworth	44	33	68	25	0	−18	−14	−10	−6	−3
ME	Portland	43	40	70	15	0	−8	−5	−3	−1	0
ME	Presque Isle	46	41	68	1	0	−29	−19	−12	−4	+2
MI	Cheboygan	45	39	84	29	0	+40	+47	+53	+59	+64
MI	Detroit–Dearborn	42	20	83	3	0	+47	+47	+47	+47	+47
MI	Flint	43	1	83	41	0	+47	+49	+50	+51	+52
MI	Ironwood	46	27	90	9	1	0	+9	+15	+23	+29
MI	Jackson	42	15	84	24	0	+53	+53	+53	+52	+52
MI	Kalamazoo	42	17	85	35	0	+58	+57	+57	+57	+57
MI	Lansing	42	44	84	33	0	+52	+53	+53	+54	+54
MI	St. Joseph	42	5	86	26	0	+61	+61	+60	+60	+59
MI	Traverse City	44	46	85	38	0	+49	+54	+57	+62	+65
MN	Albert Lea	43	39	93	22	1	+24	+26	+28	+31	+33
MN	Bemidji	47	28	94	53	1	+14	+26	+34	+44	+52
MN	Duluth	46	47	92	6	1	+6	+16	+23	+31	+38
MN	Minneapolis–St. Paul	44	59	93	16	1	+18	+24	+28	+33	+37
MN	Ortonville	45	19	96	27	1	+30	+36	+40	+46	+51
MO	Jefferson City	38	34	92	10	1	+36	+29	+24	+18	+13
MO	Joplin	37	6	94	30	1	+50	+41	+33	+25	+18
MO	Kansas City	39	1	94	20	1	+44	+37	+33	+27	+23
MO	Poplar Bluff	36	46	90	24	1	+35	+25	+17	+8	+1
MO	St. Joseph	39	46	94	50	1	+43	+38	+35	+30	+27
MO	St. Louis	38	37	90	12	1	+28	+21	+16	+10	+5
MO	Springfield	37	13	93	18	1	+45	+36	+29	+20	+14
MS	Biloxi	30	24	88	53	1	+46	+27	+11	−5	−19
MS	Jackson	32	18	90	11	1	+46	+30	+17	+1	−10
MS	Meridian	32	22	88	42	1	+40	+24	+11	−4	−15
MS	Tupelo	34	16	88	34	1	+35	+21	+10	−2	−11
MT	Billings	45	47	108	30	2	+16	+23	+29	+35	+40
MT	Butte	46	1	112	32	2	+31	+39	+45	+52	+57
MT	Glasgow	48	12	106	38	2	−1	+11	+21	+32	+42
MT	Great Falls	47	30	111	17	2	+20	+31	+39	+49	+58
MT	Helena	46	36	112	2	2	+27	+36	+43	+51	+57
MT	Miles City	46	25	105	51	2	+3	+11	+18	+26	+32
NC	Asheville	35	36	82	33	0	+67	+55	+46	+35	+27
NC	Charlotte	35	14	80	51	0	+61	+49	+39	+28	+19
NC	Durham	36	0	78	55	0	+51	+40	+31	+21	+13
NC	Greensboro	36	4	79	47	0	+54	+43	+35	+25	+17
NC	Raleigh	35	47	78	38	0	+51	+39	+30	+20	+12
NC	Wilmington	34	14	77	55	0	+52	+38	+27	+15	+5
ND	Bismarck	46	48	100	47	1	+41	+50	+58	+66	+73
ND	Fargo	46	53	96	47	1	+24	+34	+42	+50	+57
ND	Grand Forks	47	55	97	3	1	+21	+33	+43	+53	+62
ND	Minot	48	14	101	18	1	+36	+50	+59	+71	+81
ND	Williston	48	9	103	37	1	+46	+59	+69	+80	+90
NE	Grand Island	40	55	98	21	1	+53	+51	+49	+46	+44
NE	Lincoln	40	49	96	41	1	+47	+44	+42	+39	+37
NE	North Platte	41	8	100	46	1	+62	+60	+58	+56	+54
NE	Omaha	41	16	95	56	1	+43	+40	+39	+37	+36
NH	Berlin	44	28	71	11	0	−7	−3	0	+3	+7
NH	Keene	42	56	72	17	0	+2	+3	+4	+5	+6

State	City	North Latitude °	North Latitude '	West Longitude °	West Longitude '	Time Zone Code	Key Letters A (min.)	B (min.)	C (min.)	D (min.)	E (min.)
NH	Manchester–Concord	42	59	71	28	0	0	0	+1	+2	+3
NH	Portsmouth	43	5	70	45	0	−4	−2	−1	0	0
NJ	Atlantic City	39	22	74	26	0	+23	+17	+13	+8	+4
NJ	Camden	39	57	75	7	0	+24	+19	+16	+12	+9
NJ	Cape May	38	56	74	56	0	+26	+20	+15	+9	+5
NJ	Newark–East Orange	40	44	74	10	0	+17	+14	+12	+9	+7
NJ	Paterson	40	55	74	10	0	+17	+14	+12	+9	+7
NJ	Trenton	40	13	74	46	0	+21	+17	+14	+11	+8
NM	Albuquerque	35	5	106	39	2	+45	+32	+22	+11	+2
NM	Gallup	35	32	108	45	2	+52	+40	+31	+20	+11
NM	Las Cruces	32	19	106	47	2	+53	+36	+23	+8	−3
NM	Roswell	33	24	104	32	2	+41	+26	+14	0	−10
NM	Santa Fe	35	41	105	56	2	+40	+28	+19	+9	0
NV	Carson City–Reno	39	10	119	46	3	+25	+19	+14	+9	+5
NV	Elko	40	50	115	46	3	+3	0	−1	−3	−5
NV	Las Vegas	36	10	115	9	3	+16	+4	−3	−13	−20
NY	Albany	42	39	73	45	0	+9	+10	+10	+11	+11
NY	Binghamton	42	6	75	55	0	+20	+19	+19	+18	+18
NY	Buffalo	42	53	78	52	0	+29	+30	+30	+31	+32
NY	New York	40	45	74	0	0	+17	+14	+11	+9	+6
NY	Ogdensburg	44	42	75	30	0	+8	+13	+17	+21	+25
NY	Syracuse	43	3	76	9	0	+17	+19	+20	+21	+22
OH	Akron	41	5	81	31	0	+46	+43	+41	+39	+37
OH	Canton	40	48	81	23	0	+46	+43	+41	+38	+36
OH	Cincinnati–Hamilton	39	6	84	31	0	+64	+58	+53	+48	+44
OH	Cleveland–Lakewood	41	30	81	42	0	+45	+43	+42	+40	+39
OH	Columbus	39	57	83	1	0	+55	+51	+47	+43	+40
OH	Dayton	39	45	84	10	0	+61	+56	+52	+48	+44
OH	Toledo	41	39	83	33	0	+52	+50	+49	+48	+47
OH	Youngstown	41	6	80	39	0	+42	+40	+38	+36	+34
OK	Oklahoma City	35	28	97	31	1	+67	+55	+46	+35	+26
OK	Tulsa	36	9	95	60	1	+59	+48	+40	+30	+22
OR	Eugene	44	3	123	6	3	+21	+24	+27	+30	+33
OR	Pendleton	45	40	118	47	3	−1	+4	+10	+16	+21
OR	Portland	45	31	122	41	3	+14	+20	+25	+31	+36
OR	Salem	44	57	123	1	3	+17	+23	+27	+31	+35
PA	Allentown–Bethlehem	40	36	75	28	0	+23	+20	+17	+14	+12
PA	Erie	42	7	80	5	0	+36	+36	+35	+35	+35
PA	Harrisburg	40	16	76	53	0	+30	+26	+23	+19	+16
PA	Lancaster	40	2	76	18	0	+28	+24	+20	+17	+13
PA	Philadelphia–Chester	39	57	75	9	0	+24	+19	+16	+12	+9
PA	Pittsburgh–McKeesport	40	26	80	0	0	+42	+38	+35	+32	+29
PA	Reading	40	20	75	56	0	+26	+22	+19	+16	+13
PA	Scranton–Wilkes-Barre	41	25	75	40	0	+21	+19	+18	+16	+15
PA	York	39	58	76	43	0	+30	+26	+22	+18	+15
RI	Providence	41	50	71	25	0	+3	+2	+1	0	0
SC	Charleston	32	47	79	56	0	+64	+48	+36	+21	+10
SC	Columbia	34	0	81	2	0	+65	+51	+40	+27	+17
SC	Spartanburg	34	56	81	57	0	+66	+53	+43	+32	+23
SD	Aberdeen	45	28	98	29	1	+37	+44	+49	+54	+59
SD	Pierre	44	22	100	21	1	+49	+53	+56	+60	+63
SD	Rapid City	44	5	103	14	2	+2	+5	+8	+11	+13
SD	Sioux Falls	43	33	96	44	1	+38	+40	+42	+44	+46
TN	Chattanooga	35	3	85	19	0	+79	+67	+57	+45	+36
TN	Knoxville	35	58	83	55	0	+71	+60	+51	+41	+33
TN	Memphis	35	9	90	3	1	+38	+26	+16	+5	−3
TN	Nashville	36	10	86	47	1	+22	+11	+3	−6	−14

(continued)

Time Corrections

State/ Province	City	North Latitude °	North Latitude '	West Longitude °	West Longitude '	Time Zone Code	A (min.)	B (min.)	C (min.)	D (min.)	E (min.)
TX	Amarillo	35	12	101	50	1	+85	+73	+63	+52	+43
TX	Austin	30	16	97	45	1	+82	+62	+47	+29	+15
TX	Beaumont	30	5	94	6	1	+67	+48	+32	+14	0
TX	Brownsville	25	54	97	30	1	+91	+66	+46	+23	+5
TX	Corpus Christi	27	48	97	24	1	+86	+64	+46	+25	+9
TX	Dallas–Fort Worth	32	47	96	48	1	+71	+55	+43	+28	+17
TX	El Paso	31	45	106	29	2	+53	+35	+22	+6	–6
TX	Galveston	29	18	94	48	1	+72	+52	+35	+16	+1
TX	Houston	29	45	95	22	1	+73	+53	+37	+19	+5
TX	McAllen	26	12	98	14	1	+93	+69	+49	+26	+9
TX	San Antonio	29	25	98	30	1	+87	+66	+50	+31	+16
UT	Kanab	37	3	112	32	2	+62	+53	+46	+37	+30
UT	Moab	38	35	109	33	2	+46	+39	+33	+27	+22
UT	Ogden	41	13	111	58	2	+47	+45	+43	+41	+40
UT	Salt Lake City	40	45	111	53	2	+48	+45	+43	+40	+38
UT	Vernal	40	27	109	32	2	+40	+36	+33	+30	+28
VA	Charlottesville	38	2	78	30	0	+43	+35	+29	+22	+17
VA	Danville	36	36	79	23	0	+51	+41	+33	+24	+17
VA	Norfolk	36	51	76	17	0	+38	+28	+21	+12	+5
VA	Richmond	37	32	77	26	0	+41	+32	+25	+17	+11
VA	Roanoke	37	16	79	57	0	+51	+42	+35	+27	+21
VA	Winchester	39	11	78	10	0	+38	+33	+28	+23	+19
VT	Brattleboro	42	51	72	34	0	+4	+5	+5	+6	+7
VT	Burlington	44	29	73	13	0	0	+4	+8	+12	+15
VT	Rutland	43	37	72	58	0	+2	+5	+7	+9	+11
VT	St. Johnsbury	44	25	72	1	0	–4	0	+3	+7	+10
WA	Bellingham	48	45	122	29	3	0	+13	+24	+37	+47
WA	Seattle–Tacoma–Olympia	47	37	122	20	3	+3	+15	+24	+34	+42
WA	Spokane	47	40	117	24	3	–16	–4	+4	+14	+23
WA	Walla Walla	46	4	118	20	3	–5	+2	+8	+15	+21
WI	Eau Claire	44	49	91	30	1	+12	+17	+21	+25	+29
WI	Green Bay	44	31	88	0	1	0	+3	+7	+11	+14
WI	La Crosse	43	48	91	15	1	+15	+18	+20	+22	+25
WI	Madison	43	4	89	23	1	+10	+11	+12	+14	+15
WI	Milwaukee	43	2	87	54	1	+4	+6	+7	+8	+9
WI	Oshkosh	44	1	88	33	1	+3	+6	+9	+12	+15
WI	Wausau	44	58	89	38	1	+4	+9	+13	+18	+22
WV	Charleston	38	21	81	38	0	+55	+48	+42	+35	+30
WV	Parkersburg	39	16	81	34	0	+52	+46	+42	+36	+32
WY	Casper	42	51	106	19	2	+19	+19	+20	+21	+22
WY	Cheyenne	41	8	104	49	2	+19	+16	+14	+12	+11
WY	Sheridan	44	48	106	58	2	+14	+19	+23	+27	+31
CANADA											
AB	Calgary	51	5	114	5	2	+13	+35	+50	+68	+84
AB	Edmonton	53	34	113	25	2	–3	+26	+47	+72	+93
BC	Vancouver	49	13	123	6	3	0	+15	+26	+40	+52
MB	Winnipeg	49	53	97	10	1	+12	+30	+43	+58	+71
NB	Saint John	45	16	66	3	–1	+28	+34	+39	+44	+49
NS	Halifax	44	38	63	35	–1	+21	+26	+29	+33	+37
NS	Sydney	46	10	60	10	–1	+1	+9	+15	+23	+28
ON	Ottawa	45	25	75	43	0	+6	+13	+18	+23	+28
ON	Peterborough	44	18	78	19	0	+21	+25	+28	+32	+35
ON	Thunder Bay	48	27	89	12	0	+47	+61	+71	+83	+93
ON	Toronto	43	39	79	23	0	+28	+30	+32	+35	+37
QC	Montreal	45	28	73	39	0	–1	+4	+9	+15	+20
SK	Saskatoon	52	10	106	40	1	+37	+63	+80	+101	+119

General Store Classifieds

For advertising information, contact Bernie Gallagher, 203-263-7171.

Classifieds

BEAUTY & HEALTH

**FREE ESSENTIAL OILS GUIDE
& NATURAL PRODUCTS CATALOG**
170 pure essential oils. Large selection of
blends, liniments, creams, rubs,
cosmetics, diffusers, and supplies.
1-800-308-6284
www.AromaTherapeutix.com/fa

BEER & WINE MAKING

FREE ILLUSTRATED CATALOG
Fast service. Since 1967.
Kraus, PO Box 7850-YB,
Independence MO 64054
1-800-841-7404
www.eckraus.com/offers/fd.asp

BUILDING

BUILD UNDERGROUND
houses/shelters/greenhouses dirt-cheap!
Live protected. Slash energy costs. "Brilliant
breakthrough thinking"–*Countryside Magazine*
Featured on HGTV. 1-800-328-8790.
www.undergroundhousing.com

BUSINESS OPPORTUNITIES

$500 WEEKLY ASSEMBLING PRODUCTS
from home. For free information, send SASE:
Home Assembly-FA, PO Box 450, New Britain CT
06050-0450.

CATALOGS/PUBLICATIONS/BOOKS

FREE! 40 OCCULT SECRETS
for gaining money and love
you can use immediately!
Plus our Super Catalog!
Neuman, PO Box 1157,
Saint George UT 84771

FREE BOOKLETS: Life, immortality, soul,
pollution crisis, Judgment Day, restitution. Sample
magazine. Bible Standard (OF), 1156 St. Matthews
Rd., Chester Springs PA 19425. Visit our Web site:
www.biblestandard.com.

FREE BOOKLET: Pro-and-con assessment of Jeho-
vah's Witnesses teachings. Bible Standard (OFA),
1156 St. Matthews Rd., Chester Springs PA 19425.
www.biblestandard.com.

CRAFTS

TANDY LEATHER
We have a free 188-page Buyers' Guide
full of supplies for the leather craftsman.
Saddle and tack hardware,
leather, tools, and more
farm and ranch essentials.
Tandy Leather Factory,
Dept. 15FA, 1900 SE Loop 820,
Ft. Worth TX 76140
www.tandyleatherfactory.com

FARM & GARDEN

GOJI PLANTS
Grow your own super-food, nutrient-tested.
Hardy in Zones 3–10.
Bareroot plants and dried leaves.
Phoenix Tears Nursery,
435-753-3656
www.phoenixtearsnursey.com

OPEN-POLLINATED CORN SEED
Silage, grain, wildlife. 75-85-87-90-95-100-114-
120-day. Open-pollinated Cinderella pumpkin,
popcorn, sweet corn seed. Green Haven,
607-566-9253
www.openpollinated.com

**NEPTUNE'S HARVEST
ORGANIC FERTILIZERS**
Extremely effective. Commercially proven.
Outperform chemicals. Wholesale/retail/farm.
Catalog.
1-800-259-4769
www.neptunesharvest.com

FRUIT TREES

ANTIQUE APPLE TREES. 100+ varieties!
Catalog, $3. Urban Homestead, 818-B Cumber-
land St., Bristol VA 24201. Visit our Web site:
www.OldVaApples.com.

GREENHOUSES

EXTEND YOUR GROWING SEASON BY 3–4
MONTHS! Easy-to-assemble greenhouse kits
starting at $349. Call us today for your FREE
brochure or visit online to see everything. Hoop
House, Mashpee, MA. Call our toll-free number
800-760-5192, or visit us online at our Web site:
www.hoophouse.com.

HEALTH AIDS

WHO'S SLEEPING WITH YOU TONIGHT?

Nontoxic Kleen Green stops bed bugs, scabies, lice, and mites fast! Safe for children and pets. Fast, confidential shipping.

1-800-807-9350

www.kleengreen.com

HOME PRODUCTS

GET FREE SHIPPING!

Streak-free cleaning cloth and frog with purchase of any nonchemical Wonder Laundry Balls. Use discount code FAR16 at checkout.

mysticwondersinc.com

MUSIC/RECORDS/TAPES/CDS

ACCORDIONS, CONCERTINAS,

button boxes, Rolands. Buy, sell, trade, repair, tune. Catalogs, $5. Castiglione, PO Box 40, Warren MI 48090
586-755-6050

www.castiglioneaccordions.com

OLD PHONOGRAPH RECORDS

OLD PHONOGRAPH RECORDS WANTED

Buying blues, jazz, rock, and country! 78s, 45s, and LPs from 1920s–1960s. Paying as high as $12,000 for certain blues 78-rpm records! Will come to you! John, "The Record Man":

1-800-955-1326

PERSONALS

ASIAN BRIDES!

Pen pals, romance overseas! Color brochure: Box 4601-OFA, Thousand Oaks, CA 91359
805-493-8040

www.pacisl.com

DIAL-A-MATE. Live talk and voice personals. 10,000 singles call every day! Try it free! 18+. 800-234-5558.

IT'S FREE! Ladies, talk to local guys. It's new, fun, and exciting! 18+. 800-485-4047.

SLIPCOVERS

CUSTOM AND READY SLIPCOVERS

For furniture, daybeds, chairs, futons, ottomans, fabrics, cushions, pet covers. All shapes. Made in USA!
1-888-405-4758

www.slipcovershop.com

SPIRITUAL ADVICE

FATIMA

Voted number one psychic in service completion. Certified karma healing & life coach.
38 years of experience. Proven positive results in life's path. Dreams—good luck—customize—telepathy Fatima helps where others have failed

1-844-532-8462
Visit us: psychicfatimahealer.com

EMMA, FREE PSYCHIC READING! Solves problems. Removes evil. Permanent results! Call now, 817-298-0316.

FEEL THERE'S TOO MUCH JEALOUSY around you? Can't sleep? Feel like darkness has been put upon you? Call now to rebuke all evil and get the help you really need. Stop living in the devil's shadow and start living the way God wanted you to. Call: 770-624-9144.

SUPERIOR PSYCHIC. Destroys evil and restores relationships. Never failed, permanent results. Free psychic reading. 817-298-0316.

GOD'S MESSENGER, SISTER ANN. Religious holy worker. Reunites lovers forever. Clears stumbling blocks. Stops rootwork! Solves problems. Never fails! 47 years same location: Fayetteville, NC. 910-864-3981.

MISS BELLA, SPIRITUALIST. Helps with love, health, money. Removes bad luck. One free reading. 219-779-4474.

SPIRITUAL HEALERS

SISTER AVA, MIRACLE HEALER. Removes bad luck. Helps in love, marriage, health. Call now: 843-813-6425.

ATTENTION: BISHOP, spiritual healer, solves all problems. Love, happiness, health, luck. Call today: 843-291-0782.

Classifieds

LOVE SPECIALIST
Tired of Loved Ones Leaving?
Let me guide you to your true Soul-Mate.
404-709-1840

REV. JACKSON, VOODOO HEALER. Guaranteed to remove cross conditions, bad luck, sickness. 252-469-6420.

DO YOU WANT LUCK, LOVE, MONEY?
With spiritual cleansing,
you can achieve your goals in life.
Call for your free Tarot card reading today!
811 Saluda St., Rockhill SC 29730
803-371-7711

NEED HELP FAST? Spiritualist Leza cures all evil spells. Reunites lovers; potions; luck. Opelika, AL. 229-630-5386 or 334-745-0866.

BROTHER ROY
Spiritual Root Worker
Healing oils, health, luck.
Success guaranteed.
Call: **912-262-6897** or **912-264-3259**

MISS ANNIE, SPIRITUALIST. Reunites lovers. Removes bad luck. Helps with all problems. One free reading: 219-677-3380.

PROFESSOR OF ASTRONOMY
JOE BLACK
Helps in all matters.
Change your Life Now!
Call: **615-477-6031**

MS. HARRIS, New Orleans queen of voodoo love. Removes bad luck. Specializing in reuniting the separated. Call: 601-301-0022. Visit online: www.psychicdoraharris.com

REV. EVETTE
answers all questions, solves life's problems.
Need help desperately? Does what others claim!
Call immediately, 100% guaranteed!
PO Box 80322, Chattanooga TN 37414
423-894-6699

PSYCHIC SPIRITUAL ADVISOR
Melinda Walters helps all problems of life.
Stops divorce, reunites separated,
removes evil influences. Guaranteed results.
www.realpsychiclove.com
214-799-8513

MOTHER KENNEDY: Call 916-889-1998
Helps all problems; $20.00 fee
Letters answered with
Miracle Power Package.
Send to: 2120 Marconi Ave.,
Sacramento CA 95821

STEAM MODEL TOYS

WORKING STEAM ENGINES!
Stationary engines, steam tractors, rollers, trains, and accessories. Great discounts!
Catalog: $6.95, refundable.
Yesteryear Toys & Books Inc.,
Box 537, Alexandria Bay NY 13607
1-800-481-1353 www.yesteryeartoys.com

WANTED TO BUY

BUYING OLD hi-fi mono or stereo audio tube amplifiers, speakers, turntables, studio microphones, Western Electric/Bell System vacuum tubes, and radio station equipment. Call: 203-272-6030. Email: Larry2942@cox.net.

The Old Farmer's Almanac consistently reaches a proven, responsive audience and is known for delivering readers who are active buyers. The 2017 edition closes on May 2, 2016. Ad opportunities are also available in *The Old Farmer's Almanac Garden Guide*, which closes on January 8, 2016.

For ad information or rates, please contact Bernie Gallagher by email at OFAads@aol.com; by phone at 203-263-7171; by fax at 203-263-7174; or by mail at The Old Farmer's Almanac, PO Box 959, Woodbury CT 06798.

Index to Advertisers

The Old Farmer's Almanac Products

Anecdotes & Pleasantries

*A sampling from the hundreds of letters, clippings,
articles, and emails sent to us by Almanac readers from all over
the United States and Canada during the past year.*

Global Warming and Chickens

*Do you like your chicken
a little bitter?*

–courtesy of R. L., Montreal, Quebec,
from *The Guardian* newspaper

Researchers at the University of Delaware, with funds from the U.S. Department of Agriculture, are developing hardier chickens that can cope with extreme heat, such as might occur from climate change. In extreme heat, chickens pant, like dogs. This changes the chemical balance of their blood, which gives the meat a bitter taste.

How Happy Is a Clam?

–courtesy of T. C., Dublin, New Hampshire

We will probably never know exactly what makes a clam happy, but people usually list a long life and true love among their hopes. Thus, by human standards, a clam has good reason to be happy, because according to Ida Thompson of Princeton University, the clam is the foxy grandpa of the invertebrate kingdom. Thompson has determined that the bands you find on a clamshell correspond to the rings found in a tree trunk and can be used to determine the clam's age. By this method, she has discovered that clams live as long as 150 years (assuming that they are not made into chowder), show no signs of aging (other than adding bands), and remain sexually active throughout their lives. In fact, Thompson is uncertain whether clams ever die of old age.

So how happy is a clam? Answer: REAL happy.

76 Beavers Forced to Skydive. Seriously.

–courtesy of K. V., Norton, Massachusetts, from *Scientific American*

Not to be outdone by the "Screaming Eagles" of the U.S. Army's 101st Airborne Division, it turns out that the Idaho Fish and Game Department in the late 1940s had 76 of its own airborne "Screaming Beavers"—or at least that's what they might be called.

Because of increased residential development in some prime beaver territory, IF&G needed to relocate the crafty castors to more pristine pastures where they could do their dam thing in peace and thus provide environmental benefits such as improved wildlife habitats and flood protection. The problem was that the animals don't travel well by pack mule, so parachuting was proposed. Special boxes were built—heavy enough to deploy the parachute, easy enough to open once down—and #1 Test Beaver "Geronimo" made a number of jumps to help whittle down the design options.

Eventually, 76 bombs-away beavers were dropped, with only one not making it: A daredevil, wing-walker type (who knew?) somehow managed to get out in mid-descent and climb on top of the box, but for some reason it bailed out early 75 feet above the ground. The 75 survivors (of both sexes) managed to do just fine, though, and IF&G's beaver kits had the desired result of producing even more beaver kits (of the flat-tail type), whose progeny have lived happily ever after in the beautiful Idaho wilderness.

Jokes. Just Jokes.

We never knew these had a name.
–courtesy of M.C.F., Shaker Heights, Ohio

A paraprosdokian, derived from a Greek word that means beyond expectation, is a type of wordplay in which a "straight" line or phrase is set off by a humorous or dramatic conclusion. Here are a few.

■ When fish are in schools, they sometimes take debate.

■ Acupuncture is a jab well done. That's the point of it.

■ A will is a dead giveaway.

■ I stayed up all night to see where the Sun went. Then it dawned on me.

■ They told me that I had type A blood, but it was a type O.

■ I'm reading a book about antigravity. I can't put it down.

■ I tried to catch some fog. I missed.

■ I used to be a banker, but then I lost interest.

■ Those who get too big for their britches will be exposed in the end.

(continued)

How to Get Yourself Made Into a Stew

....

–courtesy of M.H.B., Jacksonville, Vermont, from Channel3000.com

....

It seems that Jimmy the Groundhog, star of Sun Prairie, Wisconsin's 2015 Groundhog Day celebration, bit the ear of Mayor Jonathan Freund prior to whispering to him his prognostication about the possible prolongation of winter. Apparently this led to some confusion about Jimmy's jabbering, which was interpreted by the mayor to be at some odds with what that day's sky conditions normally would have indicated.

This cloudy situation was cleared up, we think, but we hope that Jimmy will allow us to observe that such behavior, if it had continued, would not seem to be in concert with a long life expectancy and in fact might lead to getting into a real stew—in both the figurative and literal senses.

Fortunately, Jimmy may have avoided a fricasseed future by subsequently having been released into the wild. Nonetheless, he remains the object of a groundswell of goodwill from across the continent for having done what a lot of us would like to do: take a real bite out of a real politician.

The Wisdom of an Old-Timer

....

Probably need to be an old-timer ...

–courtesy of J. D., Topsfield, Massachusetts

....

A farmer was explaining the philosophical differences between two local churches to a new member of the community. He did so with his corncob pipe, pointing the stem at each building. "That one there says there ain't no hell." Shifting his feet slightly, he continued, "That one says the hell there ain't."

Two World Records to Note

....

Or are we maybe running out of world records to celebrate?

–courtesy of J. B., Bainbridge Island, Washington, via Reuters and C. W., Indianapolis, Indiana, via the *Chicago Tribune*

....

RECORD #1: A 51-foot-high peanut butter–and–jelly sandwich created by some California kids.

RECORD #2: The world's tallest cow. She was a Holstein from Orangeville, Illinois; stood 6 feet 4.8 inches tall; and was named Blosom.

Going for a Walk in the Woods?

First off, know your bear poop.
–courtesy of A. L., Kalispell, Montana

In light of the rising frequency of human–grizzly bear conflicts, the Montana Department of Fish and Game has advised hikers, hunters, and fishermen to take extra precautions and keep alert for bears while in the field. They advise that outdoorsmen wear noisy little bells on their clothing so as not to startle the bears that aren't expecting them. Outdoorsmen are also advised to carry pepper spray with them in case of an encounter with a bear.

It's a good idea, too, to watch out for fresh signs of bear activity. Outdoorsmen should recognize the difference between black bear and grizzly bear poop. Black bear poop is smaller and contains a lot of berry seeds and squirrel fur. Grizzly bear poop has little bells in it and smells like pepper spray.

12 New Proverbs

Out of the mouths of babes . . .
–courtesy of J. S., New Canaan, Connecticut

A first grade teacher gave each of the 6-year-old students in her class the first half of a well-known proverb and asked them to complete it. Their submissions give new meanings to these familiar adages.

■ Strike while the . . . bug is close.

■ It's always darkest before . . . Daylight Saving Time.

■ Don't bite the hand that . . . looks dirty.

■ A penny saved is . . . not much.

■ Don't put off till tomorrow . . . what you put on to go to bed.

■ Laugh and the whole world laughs with you, cry and . . . you have to blow your nose.

■ Where there's smoke, there's . . . pollution.

■ Never underestimate the power of . . . termites.

■ No news is . . . impossible.

■ A miss is as good as a . . . mister.

■ Better late than . . . pregnant.

■ An idle mind is . . . the best way to relax. *(continued)*

Rules for Teachers in 1911

....

*Think teachers have it
tough today? Well . . .*

–courtesy of J. O'B., Hartford, Connecticut
....

- You will not marry during the term of your contract.
- You are not to keep company with men.
- You must be home between the hours of 8:00 P.M. and 6:00 A.M. unless at a school function.
- You may not loiter downtown in any of the ice cream stores.
- You may not ride in carriages or automobiles with any man except your father or brother.
- You may not travel beyond the city limits unless you have permission of the chairman of the school board.
- You may not smoke cigarettes.
- You may not dress in bright colors.

- You may under no circumstances dye your hair.
- You must wear at least two petticoats.
- Your dresses may not be shorter than 2 inches above the ankles.

- To keep the classroom neat and clean, you must sweep the floor once a day; scrub the floor with hot, soapy water once a week; clean the blackboards once a day; and start the fire at 7:00 A.M. to have the school warm by 8:00 A.M., when the scholars arrive.

Advice to a Child on Dental Hygiene

....

–courtesy of L. H.
....

Brush your teeth
In your youth,
Or when you're old,
You'll brush your tooth. ■

ANSWERS TO MADDENING MIND-MANGLERS (FROM PAGE 245):

1. freedom of speech and expression, of worship, from want, and from fear

2. freedom of conscience and religion; of thought, belief, opinion, and expression (including freedom of speech and of the press); of peaceful assembly; of association

3. ace, king, queen, jack

4. earth, air, fire, water

5. Aquarius, Gemini, Sagittarius, Virgo

6. intake, compression, power, exhaust

7. war, famine, pestilence, death

8. Callisto, Europa, Ganymede, Io

9. cyan, magenta, yellow, black

10. rumen, reticulum, omasum, abomasum

11. head, heart, hands, health

12. John Lennon, Paul McCartney, George Harrison, Ringo Starr

13. accounting firms Deloitte Touche Tohmatsu (Deloitte), PricewaterhouseCoopers (PwC), Ernst & Young, and Klyveld Peat Marwick Goerdeler (KPMG)

14. where Manitoba, Saskatchewan, the Northwest Territories, and Nunavut meet

15. where Arizona, Colorado, New Mexico, and Utah meet

16. New Brunswick, Nova Scotia, Ontario, and Quebec

ESSAY AND RECIPE CONTEST RULES

Cash prizes (first, $250; second, $150; third, $100) will be awarded for the best essays in 200 words or less on the subject "A New U.S. National Holiday We Need—and Why" and the best recipes in the category "Savory Pies." Entries must be yours, original, and unpublished. Amateur cooks only, please. One recipe per person. All entries become the property of Yankee Publishing, which reserves all rights to the material. The deadline for entries is Friday, January 29, 2016. Enter at Almanac.com/EssayContest or Almanac.com/RecipeContest or label "Essay Contest" or "Recipe Contest" and mail to The Old Farmer's Almanac, P.O. Box 520, Dublin, NH 03444. Include your name, mailing address, and email address. Winners will appear in *The 2017 Old Farmer's Almanac* and on Almanac.com.

Why Diet? Try Vinegar!
Eat and lose pounds the healthy way.

If you want to lose weight and keep it off -- hate dieting and are tired of taking pills, buying costly diet foods or gimmick "fast loss" plans that don't work-- *you'll love the easy Vinegar way to lose all the pounds you want to lose. And keep them off!*

Today, the natural Vinegar weight loss plan is a reality after years of research by noted vinegar authority Emily Thacker. Her just published book "Vinegar Anniversary" will help you attain your ideal weight the healthiest and most enjoyable way ever.

You'll never again have to count calories. Or go hungry. Or go to expensive diet salons. Or buy pills, drugs.

You'll eat foods you like and get a trimmer, slimmer figure-- free of fat and flab-- as the pounds fade away.

To prove that you can eat great and feel great while losing ugly, unhealthy pounds the natural Vinegar way, you're invited to try the program for up to 3 months on a *"You Must Be Satisfied Trial."*

Let your bathroom scale decide if the plan works for you. You must be satisfied. You never risk one cent. Guaranteed.

What's the secret? Modern research combined with nature's golden elixir.

Since ancient times apple cider vinegar has been used in folk remedies to help control weight and speed-up the metabolism to burn fat. And to also aid overall good health.

Now-- for the first time-- Emily has combined the latest scientific findings and all the weight loss benefits of vinegar into a program with lifetime benefits-- to melt away pounds for health and beauty.

If you like food and hate dieting, you'll love losing pounds and inches the Vinegar way.

Suddenly your body will be energized with new vigor and zest as you combine nature's most powerful, nutritional foods with vinegar to trim away pounds while helping the body to heal itself.

You'll feel and look years younger shed-ding unhealthy pounds that make one look older than their age.

According to her findings, staying trim and fit the Vinegar way also provides preventive health care against the curses of mankind-- cancer, heart disease, diabetes, high cholesterol and blood pressure and other maladies.

In fact, the book's program is so complete that it also helps you:
- Learn secrets of ageless beauty and glowing skin
- Help build the immune system, to fight arthritis and disease
- Speed the metabolism to use natural thermogenesis to burn fat

PLUS so much more that you simply must use the book's easy Vinegar way to lose all the weight you want to lose--and enjoy all its other benefits-- before deciding if you want to keep it.

To Lose Pounds and Enjoy a 90-Day No-Risk Trial... Do This Now To Get Your Personal Copy of the Book:

Simply write "Vinegar Anniversary" on a piece of paper and send it with your check or money order of only $12.95 plus $3.98 shipping and handling (total of $16.93, OH residents please add 6.5% sales tax) to: James Direct Inc., Dept. VA2703, 500 S. Prospect Ave., Box 980, Hartville, Ohio 44632.

You can charge to your VISA, MasterCard, Discover or American Express by mail. Be sure to include your card number, expiration date and signature.

Remember: You're protected by the publisher's 90-Day Money Back Guarantee if you are not delighted.

WANT TO SAVE MORE? Do a favor for a relative or friend and get 2 books for the low introductory price of $20 postpaid. You save $13.86.

Special Bonus - Act promptly to also receive "The Very Best Old-Time Remedies" booklet absolutely FREE. Supplies are limited so order now.   ©2015 JDI VA188S03

http://www.jamesdirect.com

A Reference Compendium

REFERENCE

PHASES OF THE MOON

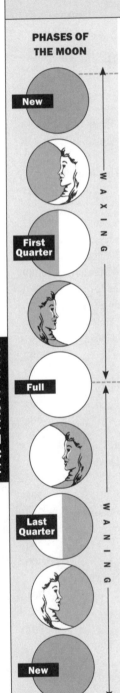

New

First Quarter

Full

Last Quarter

New

WAXING

WANING

When Will the Moon Rise Today?

A lunar puzzle involves the timing of moonrise. If you enjoy the out-of-doors and the wonders of nature, you may wish to commit to memory the following gem:

The new Moon always rises near sunrise;

The first quarter, near noon;

The full Moon always rises near sunset;

The last quarter, near midnight.

Moonrise occurs about 50 minutes later each day.

Full Moon Names

NAME	MONTH	VARIATIONS
Full Wolf Moon	January	Full Old Moon
Full Snow Moon	February	Full Hunger Moon
Full Worm Moon	March	Full Crow Moon Full Crust Moon Full Sugar Moon Full Sap Moon
Full Pink Moon	April	Full Sprouting Grass Moon Full Egg Moon Full Fish Moon
Full Flower Moon	May	Full Corn Planting Moon Full Milk Moon
Full Strawberry Moon	June	Full Rose Moon Full Hot Moon
Full Buck Moon	July	Full Thunder Moon Full Hay Moon
Full Sturgeon Moon	August	Full Red Moon Full Green Corn Moon
Full Harvest Moon*	September	Full Corn Moon Full Barley Moon
Full Hunter's Moon	October	Full Travel Moon Full Dying Grass Moon
Full Beaver Moon	November	Full Frost Moon
Full Cold Moon	December	Full Long Nights Moon

The Harvest Moon is always the full Moon closest to the autumnal equinox. If the Harvest Moon occurs in October, the September full Moon is usually called the Corn Moon.

The Origin of Full Moon Names

Historically, the Native Americans who lived in the area that is now the northern and eastern United States kept track of the seasons by giving a distinctive name to each recurring full Moon. This name was applied to the entire month in which it occurred. These names, and some variations, were used by the Algonquin tribes from New England to Lake Superior.

Meanings of Full Moon Names

January's full Moon was called the **Wolf Moon** because it appeared when wolves howled in hunger outside the villages.

February's full Moon was called the **Snow Moon** because it was a time of heavy snow. It was also called the **Hunger Moon** because hunting was difficult and hunger often resulted.

March's full Moon was called the **Worm Moon** because, as the Sun increasingly warmed the soil, earthworms became active and their castings (excrement) began to appear.

April's full Moon was called the **Pink Moon** because it heralded the appearance of the moss pink, or wild ground phlox—one of the first spring flowers.

May's full Moon was called the **Flower Moon** because blossoms were abundant everywhere at this time.

June's full Moon was called the **Strawberry Moon** because it appeared when the strawberry harvest took place.

July's full Moon was called the **Buck Moon** because it arrived when male deer started growing new antlers.

August's full Moon was called the **Sturgeon Moon** because this large fish, which is found in the Great Lakes and Lake Champlain, was caught easily at this time.

September's full Moon was called the **Corn Moon** because this was the time to harvest corn.

The **Harvest Moon** is the full Moon that occurs closest to the autumnal equinox. It can occur in either September or October. At this time, crops such as corn, pumpkins, squash, and wild rice are ready for gathering.

October's full Moon was called the **Hunter's Moon** because this was the time to hunt in preparation for winter.

November's full Moon was called the **Beaver Moon** because it was the time to set beaver traps, before the waters froze over.

December's full Moon was called the **Cold Moon**. It was also called the **Long Nights Moon** because nights at this time of year were the longest.

R
E
F
E
R
E
N
C
E

The Origin of Month Names

January. For the Roman god Janus, protector of gates and doorways. Janus is depicted with two faces, one looking into the past, the other into the future.

February. From the Latin *februa*, "to cleanse." The Roman Februalia was a month of purification and atonement.

March. For the Roman god of war, Mars. This was the time of year to resume military campaigns that had been interrupted by winter.

April. From the Latin *aperio*, "to open (bud)," because plants begin to grow now.

May. For the Roman goddess Maia, who oversaw the growth of plants. Also from the Latin *maiores*, "elders," who were celebrated now.

June. For the Roman goddess Juno, patroness of marriage and the well-being of women. Also from the Latin *juvenis*, "young people."

July. To honor Roman dictator Julius Caesar (100 B.C.–44 B.C.). In 46 B.C., with the help of Sosigenes, he developed the Julian calendar, the precursor to the Gregorian calendar we use today.

August. To honor the first Roman emperor (and grandnephew of Julius Caesar), Augustus Caesar (63 B.C.–A.D. 14).

September. From the Latin *septem*, "seven," because this was the seventh month of the early Roman calendar.

October. From the Latin *octo*, "eight," because this was the eighth month of the early Roman calendar.

November. From the Latin *novem*, "nine," because this was the ninth month of the early Roman calendar.

December. From the Latin *decem*, "ten," because this was the tenth month of the early Roman calendar.

Easter Dates (2016–19)

Christian churches that follow the Gregorian calendar celebrate Easter on the first Sunday after the paschal full Moon on or just after the vernal equinox.

YEAR	EASTER
2016	March 27
2017	April 16
2018	April 1
2019	April 21

The Julian calendar is used by some churches, including many Eastern Orthodox. The dates below are Julian calendar dates for Easter converted to Gregorian dates.

YEAR	EASTER
2016	May 1
2017	April 16
2018	April 8
2019	April 28

Friggatriskaidekaphobia Trivia

Here are a few facts about Friday the 13th:

- In the 14 possible configurations for the annual calendar (see any perpetual calendar), the occurrence of Friday the 13th is this:

  6 of 14 years have one Friday the 13th.
  6 of 14 years have two Fridays the 13th.
  2 of 14 years have three Fridays the 13th.

- No year is without one Friday the 13th, and no year has more than three.

- Months that have a Friday the 13th begin on a Sunday.

- 2016 has a Friday the 13th in May.

The Origin of Day Names

The days of the week were named by ancient Romans with the Latin words for the Sun, the Moon, and the five known planets. These names have survived in European languages, but English names also reflect Anglo-Saxon and Norse influences.

English	Latin	French	Italian	Spanish	Anglo-Saxon and Norse
Sunday	dies Solis (Sol's day)	dimanche	domenica	domingo	Sunnandaeg (Sun's day)
		from the Latin for "Lord's day"			
Monday	dies Lunae (Luna's day)	lundi	lunedì	lunes	Monandaeg (Moon's day)
Tuesday	dies Martis (Mars's day)	mardi	martedì	martes	Tiwesdaeg (Tiw's day)
Wednesday	dies Mercurii (Mercury's day)	mercredi	mercoledì	miércoles	Wodnesdaeg (Woden's day)
Thursday	dies Jovis (Jupiter's day)	jeudi	giovedì	jueves	Thursdaeg (Thor's day)
Friday	dies Veneris (Venus's day)	vendredi	venerdì	viernes	Frigedaeg (Frigga's day)
Saturday	dies Saturni (Saturn's day)	samedi	sabato	sábado	Saeterndaeg (Saturn's day)
		from the Latin for "Sabbath"			

How to Find the Day of the Week for Any Given Date

To compute the day of the week for any given date as far back as the mid–18th century, proceed as follows:

Add the last two digits of the year to one-quarter of the last two digits (discard any remainder), the day of the month, and the month key from the key box below. Divide the sum by 7; the remainder is the day of the week (1 is Sunday, 2 is Monday, and so on). If there is no remainder, the day is Saturday. If you're searching for a weekday prior to 1900, add 2 to the sum before dividing; prior to 1800, add 4. The formula doesn't work for days prior to 1753. From 2000 through 2099, subtract 1 from the sum before dividing.

Example:

The Dayton Flood was on March 25, 1913.

Last two digits of year:	13
One-quarter of these two digits:	3
Given day of month:	25
Key number for March:	4
Sum:	45

45 ÷ 7 = 6, with a remainder of 3. The flood took place on Tuesday, the third day of the week.

KEY	
January	1
leap year	0
February	4
leap year	3
March	4
April	0
May	2
June	5
July	0
August	3
September	6
October	1
November	4
December	6

R E F E R E N C E

Animal Signs of the Chinese Zodiac

The animal designations of the Chinese zodiac follow a 12-year cycle and are always used in the same sequence. The Chinese year of 354 days begins 3 to 7 weeks into the western 365-day year, so the animal designation changes at that time, rather than on January 1. **See page 123** for the exact date of the start of the Chinese New Year.

RAT

Ambitious and sincere, you can be generous with your money. Compatible with the dragon and the monkey. Your opposite is the horse.

1924	1936	1948
1960	1972	1984
1996	2008	2020

OX OR BUFFALO

A leader, you are bright, patient, and cheerful. Compatible with the snake and the rooster. Your opposite is the sheep.

1925	1937	1949
1961	1973	1985
1997	2009	2021

TIGER

Forthright and sensitive, you possess great courage. Compatible with the horse and the dog. Your opposite is the monkey.

1926	1938	1950
1962	1974	1986
1998	2010	2022

RABBIT OR HARE

Talented and affectionate, you are a seeker of tranquility. Compatible with the sheep and the pig. Your opposite is the rooster.

1927	1939	1951
1963	1975	1987
1999	2011	2023

DRAGON

Robust and passionate, your life is filled with complexity. Compatible with the monkey and the rat. Your opposite is the dog.

1928	1940	1952
1964	1976	1988
2000	2012	2024

SNAKE

Strong-willed and intense, you display great wisdom. Compatible with the rooster and the ox. Your opposite is the pig.

1929	1941	1953
1965	1977	1989
2001	2013	2025

HORSE

Physically attractive and popular, you like the company of others. Compatible with the tiger and the dog. Your opposite is the rat.

1930	1942	1954
1966	1978	1990
2002	2014	2026

SHEEP OR GOAT

Aesthetic and stylish, you enjoy being a private person. Compatible with the pig and the rabbit. Your opposite is the ox.

1931	1943	1955
1967	1979	1991
2003	2015	2027

MONKEY

Persuasive, skillful, and intelligent, you strive to excel. Compatible with the dragon and the rat. Your opposite is the tiger.

1932	1944	1956
1968	1980	1992
2004	2016	2028

ROOSTER OR COCK

Seeking wisdom and truth, you have a pioneering spirit. Compatible with the snake and the ox. Your opposite is the rabbit.

1933	1945	1957
1969	1981	1993
2005	2017	2029

DOG

Generous and loyal, you have the ability to work well with others. Compatible with the horse and the tiger. Your opposite is the dragon.

1934	1946	1958
1970	1982	1994
2006	2018	2030

PIG OR BOAR

Gallant and noble, your friends will remain at your side. Compatible with the rabbit and the sheep. Your opposite is the snake.

1935	1947	1959
1971	1983	1995
2007	2019	2031

REFERENCE

A Table Foretelling the Weather Through All the Lunations of Each Year, or Forever

This table is the result of many years of actual observation and shows what sort of weather will probably follow the Moon's entrance into any of its quarters. For example, the table shows that the week following January 31, 2016, will be fair and frosty, because the Moon enters the last quarter that day at 10:29 P.M. EST. (See the **Left-Hand Calendar Pages, 124–150,** for Moon phases.)

EDITOR'S NOTE: Although the data in this table is taken into consideration in the yearlong process of compiling the annual long-range weather forecasts for *The Old Farmer's Almanac*, we rely far more on our projections of solar activity.

TIME OF CHANGE	SUMMER	WINTER
Midnight to 2 A.M.	Fair	Hard frost, unless wind is south or west
2 A.M. to 4 A.M.	Cold, with frequent showers	Snow and stormy
4 A.M. to 6 A.M.	Rain	Rain
6 A.M. to 8 A.M.	Wind and rain	Stormy
8 A.M. to 10 A.M.	Changeable	Cold rain if wind is west; snow, if east
10 A.M. to noon	Frequent showers	Cold with high winds
Noon to 2 P.M.	Very rainy	Snow or rain
2 P.M. to 4 P.M.	Changeable	Fair and mild
4 P.M. to 6 P.M.	Fair	Fair
6 P.M. to 10 P.M.	Fair if wind is northwest; rain if wind is south or southwest	Fair and frosty if wind is north or northeast; rain or snow if wind is south or southwest
10 P.M. to midnight	Fair	Fair and frosty

This table was created more than 180 years ago by Dr. Herschell for the Boston Courier; *it first appeared in* The Old Farmer's Almanac *in 1834.*

Safe Ice Thickness*

ICE THICKNESS	PERMISSIBLE LOAD	ICE THICKNESS	PERMISSIBLE LOAD
3 inches	Single person on foot	12 inches	Heavy truck (8-ton gross)
4 inches	Group in single file	15 inches	10 tons
7½ inches	Passenger car (2-ton gross)	20 inches	25 tons
8 inches	Light truck (2½-ton gross)	30 inches	70 tons
10 inches	Medium truck (3½-ton gross)	36 inches	110 tons

***Solid, clear, blue/black pond and lake ice**
Slush ice has only half the strength of blue ice. The strength value of river ice is 15 percent less.

Heat Index °F (°C)

TEMP. °F (°C)	RELATIVE HUMIDITY (%)								
	40	45	50	55	60	65	70	75	80
100 (38)	109 (43)	114 (46)	118 (48)	124 (51)	129 (54)	136 (58)			
98 (37)	105 (41)	109 (43)	113 (45)	117 (47)	123 (51)	128 (53)	134 (57)		
96 (36)	101 (38)	104 (40)	108 (42)	112 (44)	116 (47)	121 (49)	126 (52)	132 (56)	
94 (34)	97 (36)	100 (38)	103 (39)	106 (41)	110 (43)	114 (46)	119 (48)	124 (51)	129 (54)
92 (33)	94 (34)	96 (36)	99 (37)	101 (38)	105 (41)	108 (42)	112 (44)	116 (47)	121 (49)
90 (32)	91 (33)	93 (34)	95 (35)	97 (36)	100 (38)	103 (39)	106 (41)	109 (43)	113 (45)
88 (31)	88 (31)	89 (32)	91 (33)	93 (34)	95 (35)	98 (37)	100 (38)	103 (39)	106 (41)
86 (30)	85 (29)	87 (31)	88 (31)	89 (32)	91 (33)	93 (34)	95 (35)	97 (36)	100 (38)
84 (29)	83 (28)	84 (29)	85 (29)	86 (30)	88 (31)	89 (32)	90 (32)	92 (33)	94 (34)
82 (28)	81 (27)	82 (28)	83 (28)	84 (29)	84 (29)	85 (29)	86 (30)	88 (31)	89 (32)
80 (27)	80 (27)	80 (27)	81 (27)	81 (27)	82 (28)	82 (28)	83 (28)	84 (29)	84 (29)

EXAMPLE: *When the temperature is 88°F (31°C) and the relative humidity is 60 percent, the heat index, or how hot it feels, is 95°F (35°C).*

The UV Index for Measuring Ultraviolet Radiation Risk

The U.S. National Weather Service's daily forecasts of ultraviolet levels use these numbers for various exposure levels:

UV Index Number	Exposure Level	Time to Burn	Actions to Take
0, 1, 2	Minimal	60 minutes	Apply SPF 15 sunscreen
3, 4	Low	45 minutes	Apply SPF 15 sunscreen; wear a hat
5, 6	Moderate	30 minutes	Apply SPF 15 sunscreen; wear a hat
7, 8, 9	High	15–25 minutes	Apply SPF 15 to 30 sunscreen; wear a hat and sunglasses; limit midday exposure
10 or higher	Very high	10 minutes	Apply SPF 30 sunscreen; wear a hat, sunglasses, and protective clothing; limit midday exposure

"Time to Burn" and "Actions to Take" apply to people with fair skin that sometimes tans but usually burns. People with lighter skin need to be more cautious. People with darker skin may be able to tolerate more exposure.

85	90	95	100
135 (57)			
126 (52)	131 (55)		
117 (47)	122 (50)	127 (53)	132 (56)
110 (43)	113 (45)	117 (47)	121 (49)
102 (39)	105 (41)	108 (42)	112 (44)
96 (36)	98 (37)	100 (38)	103 (39)
90 (32)	91 (33)	93 (34)	95 (35)
85 (29)	86 (30)	86 (30)	87 (31)

What Are Cooling/Heating Degree Days?

Each degree of a day's average temperature above 65°F is considered one cooling degree day, an attempt to measure the need for air-conditioning. If the average of the day's high and low temperatures is 75°, that's ten cooling degree days.

Similarly, each degree of a day's average temperature below 65° is considered one heating degree and is an attempt to measure the need for fuel consumption. For example, a day with temperatures ranging from 60° to 40° results in an average of 50°, or 15 degrees less than 65°. Hence, that day would be credited as 15 heating degree days.

How to Measure Hail

The **Torro Hailstorm Intensity Scale** was introduced by Jonathan Webb of Oxford, England, in 1986 as a means of categorizing hailstorms. The name derives from the private and mostly British research body named the TORnado and storm Research Organisation.

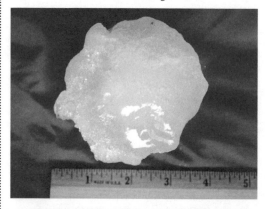

INTENSITY/DESCRIPTION OF HAIL DAMAGE

H0 True hail of pea size causes no damage

H1 Leaves and flower petals are punctured and torn

H2 Leaves are stripped from trees and plants

H3 Panes of glass are broken; auto bodies are dented

H4 Some house windows are broken; small tree branches are broken off; birds are killed

H5 Many windows are smashed; small animals are injured; large tree branches are broken off

H6 Shingle roofs are breached; metal roofs are scored; wooden window frames are broken away

H7 Roofs are shattered to expose rafters; autos are seriously damaged

H8 Shingle and tile roofs are destroyed; small tree trunks are split; people are seriously injured

H9 Concrete roofs are broken; large tree trunks are split and knocked down; people are at risk of fatal injuries

H10 Brick houses are damaged; people are at risk of fatal injuries

REFERENCE

Weather

How to Measure Wind Speed

The **Beaufort Wind Force Scale** is a common way of estimating wind speed. It was developed in 1805 by Admiral Sir Francis Beaufort of the British Navy to measure wind at sea. We can also use it to measure wind on land.

Admiral Beaufort arranged the numbers 0 to 12 to indicate the strength of the wind from calm, force 0, to hurricane, force 12. Here's a scale adapted to land.

"Used Mostly at Sea but of Help to All Who Are Interested in the Weather"

Beaufort Force	Description	When You See or Feel This Effect	Wind Speed (mph)	(km/h)
0	Calm	Smoke goes straight up	less than 1	less than 2
1	Light air	Wind direction is shown by smoke drift but not by wind vane	1–3	2–5
2	Light breeze	Wind is felt on the face; leaves rustle; wind vanes move	4–7	6–11
3	Gentle breeze	Leaves and small twigs move steadily; wind extends small flags straight out	8–12	12–19
4	Moderate breeze	Wind raises dust and loose paper; small branches move	13–18	20–29
5	Fresh breeze	Small trees sway; waves form on lakes	19–24	30–39
6	Strong breeze	Large branches move; wires whistle; umbrellas are difficult to use	25–31	40–50
7	Moderate gale	Whole trees are in motion; walking against the wind is difficult	32–38	51–61
8	Fresh gale	Twigs break from trees; walking against the wind is very difficult	39–46	62–74
9	Strong gale	Buildings suffer minimal damage; roof shingles are removed	47–54	75–87
10	Whole gale	Trees are uprooted	55–63	88–101
11	Violent storm	Widespread damage	64–72	102–116
12	Hurricane	Widespread destruction	73+	117+

R E F E R E N C E

RETIRED ATLANTIC HURRICANE NAMES

These storms have been some of the most destructive and costly.

NAME	YEAR	NAME	YEAR	NAME	YEAR
Charley	2004	Wilma	2005	Paloma	2008
Ivan	2004	Dean	2007	Igor	2010
Dennis	2005	Felix	2007	Tomas	2010
Katrina	2005	Noel	2007	Irene	2011
Rita	2005	Gustav	2008	Sandy	2012
Stan	2005	Ike	2008	Ingrid	2013

Atlantic Tropical (and Subtropical) Storm Names for 2016			Eastern North-Pacific Tropical (and Subtropical) Storm Names for 2016		
Alex	Ian	Richard	Agatha	Ivette	Roslyn
Bonnie	Julia	Shary	Blas	Javier	Seymour
Colin	Karl	Tobias	Celia	Kay	Tina
Danielle	Lisa	Virginie	Darby	Lester	Virgil
Earl	Matthew	Walter	Estelle	Madeline	Winifred
Fiona	Nicole		Frank	Newton	Xavier
Gaston	Otto		Georgette	Orlene	Yolanda
Hermine	Paula		Howard	Paine	Zeke

How to Measure Hurricane Strength

The **Saffir-Simpson Hurricane Wind Scale** assigns a rating from 1 to 5 based on a hurricane's intensity. It is used to give an estimate of the potential property damage from a hurricane landfall. Wind speed is the determining factor in the scale, as storm surge values are highly dependent on the slope of the continental shelf in the landfall region. Wind speeds are measured at a height of 33 feet (10 meters) using a 1-minute average.

CATEGORY ONE. Average wind: 74–95 mph. Significant damage to mobile homes. Some damage to roofing and siding of well-built frame homes. Large tree branches snap and shallow-rooted trees may topple. Power outages may last a few to several days.

CATEGORY TWO. Average wind: 96–110 mph. Mobile homes may be destroyed. Major roof and siding damage to frame homes. Many shallow-rooted trees snap or topple, blocking roads. Widespread power outages could last from several days to weeks. Potable water may be scarce.

CATEGORY THREE. Average wind: 111–129 mph. Most mobile homes destroyed. Frame homes may sustain major roof damage. Many trees snap or topple, blocking numerous roads. Electricity and water may be unavailable for several days to weeks.

CATEGORY FOUR. Average wind: 130–156 mph. Mobile homes destroyed. Frame homes severely damaged or destroyed. Windborne debris may penetrate protected windows. Most trees snap or topple. Residential areas isolated by fallen trees and power poles. Most of the area uninhabitable for weeks to months.

CATEGORY FIVE. Average wind: 157+ mph. Most homes destroyed. Nearly all windows blown out of high-rises. Most of the area uninhabitable for weeks to months.

REFERENCE

How to Measure a Tornado

The original **Fujita Scale** (or F Scale) was developed by Dr. Theodore Fujita to classify tornadoes based on wind damage. All tornadoes, and other severe local windstorms, were assigned a number according to the most intense damage caused by the storm. An enhanced F (EF) scale was implemented in the United States on February 1, 2007. The EF scale uses 3-second gust estimates based on a more detailed system for assessing damage, taking into account different building materials.

F SCALE		EF SCALE (U.S.)
F0 • 40–72 mph (64–116 km/h)	light damage	EF0 • 65–85 mph (105–137 km/h)
F1 • 73–112 mph (117–180 km/h)	moderate damage	EF1 • 86–110 mph (138–178 km/h)
F2 • 113–157 mph (181–253 km/h)	considerable damage	EF2 • 111–135 mph (179–218 km/h)
F3 • 158–207 mph (254–332 km/h)	severe damage	EF3 • 136–165 mph (219–266 km/h)
F4 • 208–260 mph (333–419 km/h)	devastating damage	EF4 • 166–200 mph (267–322 km/h)
F5 • 261–318 mph (420–512 km/h)	incredible damage	EF5 • over 200 mph (over 322 km/h)

Wind/Barometer Table

Barometer (Reduced to Sea Level)	Wind Direction	Character of Weather Indicated
30.00 to 30.20, and steady	westerly	Fair, with slight changes in temperature, for one to two days
30.00 to 30.20, and rising rapidly	westerly	Fair, followed within two days by warmer and rain
30.00 to 30.20, and falling rapidly	south to east	Warmer, and rain within 24 hours
30.20 or above, and falling rapidly	south to east	Warmer, and rain within 36 hours
30.20 or above, and falling rapidly	west to north	Cold and clear, quickly followed by warmer and rain
30.20 or above, and steady	variable	No early change
30.00 or below, and falling slowly	south to east	Rain within 18 hours that will continue a day or two
30.00 or below, and falling rapidly	southeast to northeast	Rain, with high wind, followed within two days by clearing, colder
30.00 or below, and rising	south to west	Clearing and colder within 12 hours
29.80 or below, and falling rapidly	south to east	Severe storm of wind and rain imminent; in winter, snow or cold wave within 24 hours
29.80 or below, and falling rapidly	east to north	Severe northeast gales and heavy rain or snow, followed in winter by cold wave
29.80 or below, and rising rapidly	going to west	Clearing and colder

NOTE: *A barometer should be adjusted to show equivalent sea-level pressure for the altitude at which it is to be used. A change of 100 feet in elevation will cause a decrease of ¹/₁₀ inch in the reading.*

Windchill Table

As wind speed increases, your body loses heat more rapidly, making the air feel colder than it really is. The combination of cold temperature and high wind can create a cooling effect so severe that exposed flesh can freeze.

	Calm	35	30	25	20	15	10	5	0	–5	–10	–15	–20	–25	–30	–35
	5	31	25	19	13	7	1	–5	–11	–16	–22	–28	–34	–40	–46	–52
	10	27	21	15	9	3	–4	–10	–16	–22	–28	–35	–41	–47	–53	–59
	15	25	19	13	6	0	–7	–13	–19	–26	–32	–39	–45	–51	–58	–64
	20	24	17	11	4	–2	–9	–15	–22	–29	–35	–42	–48	–55	–61	–68
WIND SPEED (mph)	25	23	16	9	3	–4	–11	–17	–24	–31	–37	–44	–51	–58	–64	–71
	30	22	15	8	1	–5	–12	–19	–26	–33	–39	–46	–53	–60	–67	–73
	35	21	14	7	0	–7	–14	–21	–27	–34	–41	–48	–55	–62	–69	–76
	40	20	13	6	–1	–8	–15	–22	–29	–36	–43	–50	–57	–64	–71	–78
	45	19	12	5	–2	–9	–16	–23	–30	–37	–44	–51	–58	–65	–72	–79
	50	19	12	4	–3	–10	–17	–24	–31	–38	–45	–52	–60	–67	–74	–81
	55	18	11	4	–3	–11	–18	–25	–32	–39	–46	–54	–61	–68	–75	–82
	60	17	10	3	–4	–11	–19	–26	–33	–40	–48	–55	–62	–69	–76	–84

TEMPERATURE (°F)

Frostbite occurs in ▢ **30 minutes** ▢ **10 minutes** ▢ **5 minutes**

EXAMPLE: *When the temperature is 15°F and the wind speed is 30 miles per hour, the windchill, or how cold it feels, is –5°F. For a Celsius version of this table, visit Almanac.com/WindchillCelsius.* —courtesy National Weather Service

How to Measure Earthquakes

In 1979, seismologists developed a measurement of earthquake size called **Moment Magnitude**. It is more accurate than the previously used Richter scale, which is precise only for earthquakes of a certain size and at a certain distance from a seismometer. All earthquakes can now be compared on the same scale.

MAGNITUDE	EFFECT
Less than 3	Micro
3–3.9	Minor
4–4.9	Light
5–5.9	Moderate
6–6.9	Strong
7–7.9	Major
8 or more	Great

R
E
F
E
R
E
N
C
E

A Gardener's Worst Phobias

Name of Fear	Object Feared
Alliumphobia	Garlic
Anthophobia	Flowers
Apiphobia	Bees
Arachnophobia	Spiders
Batonophobia	Plants
Bufonophobia	Toads
Dendrophobia	Trees
Entomophobia	Insects
Lachanophobia	Vegetables
Melissophobia	Bees
Mottephobia	Moths
Myrmecophobia	Ants
Ornithophobia	Birds
Ranidaphobia	Frogs
Rupophobia	Dirt
Scoleciphobia	Worms
Spheksophobia	Wasps

Herbs to Plant in Lawns

Choose plants that suit your soil and your climate. All of these can withstand mowing and considerable foot traffic.

Ajuga or bugleweed (*Ajuga reptans*)
Corsican mint (*Mentha requienii*)
Dwarf cinquefoil (*Potentilla tabernaemontani*)
English pennyroyal (*Mentha pulegium*)
Green Irish moss (*Sagina subulata*)
Pearly everlasting (*Anaphalis margaritacea*)
Roman chamomile (*Chamaemelum nobile*)
Rupturewort (*Herniaria glabra*)
Speedwell (*Veronica officinalis*)
Stonecrop (*Sedum ternatum*)
Sweet violets (*Viola odorata* or *V. tricolor*)
Thyme (*Thymus serpyllum*)
White clover (*Trifolium repens*)
Wild strawberries (*Fragaria virginiana*)
Wintergreen or partridgeberry (*Mitchella repens*)

Lawn-Growing Tips

■ Test your soil: The pH balance should be 7.0 or more; 6.2 to 6.7 puts your lawn at risk for fungal diseases. If the pH is too low, correct it with liming, best done in the fall.

■ The best time to apply fertilizer is just before it rains.

■ If you put lime and fertilizer on your lawn, spread half of it as you walk north to south, the other half as you walk east to west to cut down on missed areas.

■ Any feeding of lawns in the fall should be done with a low-nitrogen, slow-acting fertilizer.

■ In areas of your lawn where tree roots compete with the grass, apply some extra fertilizer to benefit both.

■ Moss and sorrel in lawns usually means poor soil, poor aeration or drainage, or excessive acidity.

■ Control weeds by promoting healthy lawn growth with natural fertilizers in spring and early fall.

■ Raise the level of your lawn-mower blades during the hot summer days. Taller grass resists drought better than short.

■ You can reduce mowing time by redesigning your lawn, reducing sharp corners and adding sweeping curves.

■ During a drought, let the grass grow longer between mowings and reduce fertilizer.

■ Water your lawn early in the morning or in the evening.

Flowers and Herbs That Attract Butterflies

Allium . . . . *Allium*
Aster . . . . *Aster*
Bee balm . . . . *Monarda*
Butterfly bush . . . . *Buddleia*
Catmint . . . . *Nepeta*
Clove pink . . . . *Dianthus*
Cornflower . . . . *Centaurea*
Creeping thyme . . . . . . *Thymus serpyllum*
Daylily . . . . *Hemerocallis*
Dill . . . . *Anethum graveolens*
False indigo . . . . *Baptisia*
Fleabane . . . . *Erigeron*
Floss flower . . . . *Ageratum*
Globe thistle . . . . *Echinops*
Goldenrod . . . . *Solidago*
Helen's flower . . . . *Helenium*
Hollyhock . . . . *Alcea*
Honeysuckle . . . . *Lonicera*
Lavender . . . . *Lavandula*
Lilac . . . . *Syringa*
Lupine . . . . *Lupinus*
Lychnis . . . . *Lychnis*

Mallow . . . . *Malva*
Mealycup sage . . . . *Salvia farinacea*
Milkweed . . . . *Asclepias*
Mint . . . . *Mentha*
Oregano . . . . *Origanum vulgare*
Pansy . . . . *Viola*
Parsley . . . . *Petroselinum crispum*
Phlox . . . . *Phlox*
Privet . . . . *Ligustrum*
Purple coneflower . . *Echinacea purpurea*
Rock cress . . . . *Arabis*
Sea holly . . . . *Eryngium*
Shasta daisy . . . . *Chrysanthemum*
Snapdragon . . . . *Antirrhinum*
Stonecrop . . . . *Sedum*
Sweet alyssum . . . . *Lobularia*
Sweet marjoram . . . . *Origanum majorana*
Sweet rocket . . . . *Hesperis*
Tickseed . . . . *Coreopsis*
Verbena . . . . *Verbena*
Zinnia . . . . *Zinnia*

Flowers* That Attract Hummingbirds

Beard tongue . . . . *Penstemon*
Bee balm . . . . *Monarda*
Butterfly bush . . . . *Buddleia*
Catmint . . . . *Nepeta*
Clove pink . . . . *Dianthus*
Columbine . . . . *Aquilegia*
Coral bells . . . . *Heuchera*
Daylily . . . . *Hemerocallis*
Desert candle . . . . *Yucca*
Flag iris . . . . *Iris*
Flowering tobacco . . . . . . *Nicotiana alata*
Foxglove . . . . *Digitalis*
Larkspur . . . . *Delphinium*
Lily . . . . *Lilium*
Lupine . . . . *Lupinus*
Petunia . . . . *Petunia*
Pincushion flower . . . . *Scabiosa*
Red-hot poker . . . . *Kniphofia*
Scarlet sage . . . . *Salvia splendens*

Soapwort . . . . *Saponaria*
Summer phlox . . . . *Phlox paniculata*
Trumpet honeysuckle . . . . *Lonicera sempervirens*
Verbena . . . . *Verbena*
Weigela . . . . *Weigela*

＊NOTE: Choose varieties in red and orange shades, if available.

REFERENCE

pH Preferences of Trees, Shrubs, Flowers, and Vegetables

An accurate soil test will indicate your soil pH and will specify the amount of lime or sulfur that is needed to bring it up or down to the appropriate level. A pH of 6.5 is just about right for most home gardens, since most plants thrive in the 6.0 to 7.0 (slightly acidic to neutral) range. Some plants (azaleas, blueberries) prefer more strongly acidic soil in the 4.0 to 6.0 range, while a few (asparagus, plums) do best in soil that is neutral to slightly alkaline. Acidic, or sour, soil (below 7.0) is counteracted by applying finely ground limestone, and alkaline, or sweet, soil (above 7.0) is treated with ground sulfur.

Common Name	Optimum pH Range	Common Name	Optimum pH Range	Common Name	Optimum pH Range
Trees and Shrubs		Bee balm	6.0–7.5	Sunflower	6.0–7.5
Apple	5.0–6.5	Begonia	5.5–7.0	Tulip	6.0–7.0
Azalea	4.5–6.0	Black-eyed Susan	5.5–7.0	Zinnia	5.5–7.0
Beautybush	6.0–7.5	Bleeding heart	6.0–7.5		
Birch	5.0–6.5	Canna	6.0–8.0	**Vegetables**	
Blackberry	5.0–6.0	Carnation	6.0–7.0	Asparagus	6.0–8.0
Blueberry	4.0–5.0	Chrysanthemum	6.0–7.5	Bean	6.0–7.5
Boxwood	6.0–7.5	Clematis	5.5–7.0	Beet	6.0–7.5
Cherry, sour	6.0–7.0	Coleus	6.0–7.0	Broccoli	6.0–7.0
Crab apple	6.0–7.5	Coneflower, purple	5.0–7.5	Brussels sprout	6.0–7.5
Dogwood	5.0–7.0	Cosmos	5.0–8.0	Cabbage	6.0–7.5
Fir, balsam	5.0–6.0	Crocus	6.0–8.0	Carrot	5.5–7.0
Hemlock	5.0–6.0	Daffodil	6.0–6.5	Cauliflower	5.5–7.5
Hydrangea, blue-flowered	4.0–5.0	Dahlia	6.0–7.5	Celery	5.8–7.0
		Daisy, Shasta	6.0–8.0	Chive	6.0–7.0
Hydrangea, pink-flowered	6.0–7.0	Daylily	6.0–8.0	Collard	6.5–7.5
Juniper	5.0–6.0	Delphinium	6.0–7.5	Corn	5.5–7.0
Laurel, mountain	4.5–6.0	Foxglove	6.0–7.5	Cucumber	5.5–7.0
Lemon	6.0–7.5	Geranium	6.0–8.0	Eggplant	6.0–7.0
Lilac	6.0–7.5	Gladiolus	5.0–7.0	Garlic	5.5–8.0
Maple, sugar	6.0–7.5	Hibiscus	6.0–8.0	Kale	6.0–7.5
Oak, white	5.0–6.5	Hollyhock	6.0–8.0	Leek	6.0–8.0
Orange	6.0–7.5	Hyacinth	6.5–7.5	Lettuce	6.0–7.0
Peach	6.0–7.0	Iris, blue flag	5.0–7.5	Okra	6.0–7.0
Pear	6.0–7.5	Lily-of-the-valley	4.5–6.0	Onion	6.0–7.0
Pecan	6.4–8.0	Lupine	5.0–6.5	Pea	6.0–7.5
Plum	6.0–8.0	Marigold	5.5–7.5	Pepper, sweet	5.5–7.0
Raspberry, red	5.5–7.0	Morning glory	6.0–7.5	Potato	4.8–6.5
Rhododendron	4.5–6.0	Narcissus, trumpet	5.5–6.5	Pumpkin	5.5–7.5
Willow	6.0–8.0	Nasturtium	5.5–7.5	Radish	6.0–7.0
		Pansy	5.5–6.5	Spinach	6.0–7.5
Flowers		Peony	6.0–7.5	Squash, crookneck	6.0–7.5
Alyssum	6.0–7.5	Petunia	6.0–7.5	Squash, Hubbard	5.5–7.0
Aster, New England	6.0–8.0	Phlox, summer	6.0–8.0	Swiss chard	6.0–7.0
Baby's breath	6.0–7.0	Poppy, oriental	6.0–7.5	Tomato	5.5–7.5
Bachelor's button	6.0–7.5	Rose, hybrid tea	5.5–7.0	Watermelon	5.5–6.5
		Rose, rugosa	6.0–7.0		
		Snapdragon	5.5–7.0		

Produce Weights and Measures

VEGETABLES

Asparagus: 1 pound = 3 cups chopped

Beans (string): 1 pound = 4 cups chopped

Beets: 1 pound (5 medium) = 2½ cups chopped

Broccoli: 1 pound = 6 cups chopped

Cabbage: 1 pound = 4½ cups shredded

Carrots: 1 pound = 3½ cups sliced or grated

Celery: 1 pound = 4 cups chopped

Cucumbers: 1 pound (2 medium) = 4 cups sliced

Eggplant: 1 pound = 4 cups chopped = 2 cups cooked

Garlic: 1 clove = 1 teaspoon chopped

Leeks: 1 pound = 4 cups chopped = 2 cups cooked

Mushrooms: 1 pound = 5 to 6 cups sliced = 2 cups cooked

Onions: 1 pound = 4 cups sliced = 2 cups cooked

Parsnips: 1 pound = 1½ cups cooked, puréed

Peas: 1 pound whole = 1 to 1½ cups shelled

Potatoes: 1 pound (3 medium) sliced = 2 cups mashed

Pumpkin: 1 pound = 4 cups chopped = 2 cups cooked and drained

Spinach: 1 pound = ¾ to 1 cup cooked

Squashes (summer): 1 pound = 4 cups grated = 2 cups sliced and cooked

Squashes (winter): 2 pounds = 2½ cups cooked, puréed

Sweet potatoes: 1 pound = 4 cups grated = 1 cup cooked, puréed

Swiss chard: 1 pound = 5 to 6 cups packed leaves = 1 to 1½ cups cooked

Tomatoes: 1 pound (3 or 4 medium) = 1½ cups seeded pulp

Turnips: 1 pound = 4 cups chopped = 2 cups cooked, mashed

FRUIT

Apples: 1 pound (3 or 4 medium) = 3 cups sliced

Bananas: 1 pound (3 or 4 medium) = 1¾ cups mashed

Berries: 1 quart = 3½ cups

Dates: 1 pound = 2½ cups pitted

Lemon: 1 whole = 1 to 3 tablespoons juice; 1 to 1½ teaspoons grated rind

Lime: 1 whole = 1½ to 2 tablespoons juice

Orange: 1 medium = 6 to 8 tablespoons juice; 2 to 3 tablespoons grated rind

Peaches: 1 pound (4 medium) = 3 cups sliced

Pears: 1 pound (4 medium) = 2 cups sliced

Rhubarb: 1 pound = 2 cups cooked

Sowing Vegetable Seeds

Sow or plant in cool weather	Beets, broccoli, brussels sprouts, cabbage, lettuce, onions, parsley, peas, radishes, spinach, Swiss chard, turnips
Sow or plant in warm weather	Beans, carrots, corn, cucumbers, eggplant, melons, okra, peppers, squashes, tomatoes
Sow or plant for one crop per season	Corn, eggplant, leeks, melons, peppers, potatoes, spinach (New Zealand), squashes, tomatoes
Resow for additional crops	Beans, beets, cabbage, carrots, kohlrabi, lettuce, radishes, rutabagas, spinach, turnips

A Beginner's Vegetable Garden

The vegetables suggested below are common, easy-to-grow crops. Make 11 rows, 10 feet long, with at least 18 inches between them. Ideally, the rows should run north and south to take full advantage of the sun. This garden, planted as suggested, can feed a family of four for one summer, with a little extra for canning and freezing or giving away.

ROW
1. Zucchini (4 plants)
2. Tomatoes (5 plants, staked)
3. Peppers (6 plants)
4. Cabbage

ROW
5. Bush beans
6. Lettuce
7. Beets
8. Carrots
9. Swiss chard
10. Radishes
11. Marigolds (to discourage rabbits!)

Traditional Planting Times

■ Plant **corn** when elm leaves are the size of a squirrel's ear, when oak leaves are the size of a mouse's ear, when apple blossoms begin to fall, or when the dogwoods are in full bloom.

■ Plant **lettuce, spinach, peas,** and other cool-weather vegetables when the lilacs show their first leaves or when daffodils begin to bloom.

■ Plant **tomatoes** and **peppers** when dogwoods are in peak bloom or when daylilies start to bloom.

■ Plant **cucumbers** and **squashes** when lilac flowers fade.

■ Plant **perennials** when maple leaves begin to unfurl.

■ Plant **morning glories** when maple trees have full-size leaves.

■ Plant **pansies, snapdragons,** and other hardy annuals after the aspen and chokecherry trees leaf out.

■ Plant **beets** and **carrots** when dandelions are blooming.

R
E
F
E
R
E
N
C
E

When to . . .

	. . . FERTILIZE	. . . WATER
Beans	After heavy bloom and set of pods	Regularly, from start of pod to set
Beets	At time of planting	Only during drought conditions
Broccoli	3 weeks after transplanting	Only during drought conditions
Brussels sprouts	3 weeks after transplanting	At transplanting
Cabbage	3 weeks after transplanting	2 to 3 weeks before harvest
Carrots	In the fall for the following spring	Only during drought conditions
Cauliflower	3 weeks after transplanting	Once, 3 weeks before harvest
Celery	At time of transplanting	Once a week
Corn	When 8 to 10 inches tall, and when first silk appears	When tassels appear and cobs start to swell
Cucumbers	1 week after bloom, and 3 weeks later	Frequently, especially when fruits form
Lettuce	2 to 3 weeks after transplanting	Once a week
Melons	1 week after bloom, and again 3 weeks later	Once a week
Onion sets	When bulbs begin to swell, and when plants are 1 foot tall	Only during drought conditions
Parsnips	1 year before planting	Only during drought conditions
Peas	After heavy bloom and set of pods	Regularly, from start of pod to set
Peppers	After first fruit-set	Once a week
Potato tubers	At bloom time or time of second hilling	Regularly, when tubers start to form
Pumpkins	Just before vines start to run, when plants are about 1 foot tall	Only during drought conditions
Radishes	Before spring planting	Once a week
Spinach	When plants are one-third grown	Once a week
Squashes, summer	Just before vines start to run, when plants are about 1 foot tall	Only during drought conditions
Squashes, winter	Just before vines start to run, when plants are about 1 foot tall	Only during drought conditions
Tomatoes	2 weeks before, and after first picking	Twice a week

How to Grow Herbs

HERB	START SEEDS INDOORS (weeks before last spring frost)	START SEEDS OUTDOORS (weeks before/after last spring frost)	HEIGHT/ SPREAD (inches)	SOIL	LIGHT**
Basil*	6–8	Anytime after	12–24/12	Rich, moist	○
Borage*	Not recommended	Anytime after	12–36/12	Rich, well-drained, dry	○
Chervil	Not recommended	3–4 before	12–24/8	Rich, moist	◑
Chives	8–10	3–4 before	12–18/18	Rich, moist	○
Cilantro/ coriander	Not recommended	Anytime after	12–36/6	Light	○◑
Dill	Not recommended	4–5 before	36–48/12	Rich	○
Fennel	4–6	Anytime after	48–80/18	Rich	○
Lavender, English*	8–12	1–2 before	18–36/24	Moderately fertile, well-drained	○
Lavender, French	Not recommended	Not recommended	18–36/24	Moderately fertile, well-drained	○
Lemon balm*	6–10	2–3 before	12–24/18	Rich, well-drained	○◑
Lovage*	6–8	2–3 before	36–72/36	Fertile, sandy	○◑
Mint	Not recommended	Not recommended	12–24/18	Rich, moist	◑
Oregano*	6–10	Anytime after	12–24/18	Poor	○
Parsley*	10–12	3–4 before	18–24/6–8	Medium-rich	◑
Rosemary*	8–10	Anytime after	48–72/48	Not too acid	○
Sage	6–10	1–2 before	12–48/30	Well-drained	○
Sorrel	6–10	2–3 after	20–48/12–14	Rich, organic	○
Summer savory	4–6	Anytime after	4–15/6	Medium rich	○
Sweet cicely	6–8	2–3 after	36–72/36	Moderately fertile, well-drained	○◑
Tarragon, French	Not recommended	Not recommended	24–36/12	Well-drained	○◑
Thyme, common*	6–10	2–3 before	2–12/7–12	Fertile, well-drained	○◑

*Recommend minimum soil temperature of 70°F to germinate

** ○ full sun ◑ partial shade

R E F E R E N C E

Annual
Annual, biennial
Annual, biennial
Perennial
Annual
Annual
Annual
Perennial
Tender perennial
Perennial
Perennial
Perennial
Tender perennial
Biennial
Tender perennial
Perennial
Perennial
Annual
Perennial
Perennial
Perennial

Drying Herbs

Before drying, remove any dead or diseased leaves or stems. Wash under cool water, shake off excess water, and put on a towel to dry completely. Air drying preserves an herb's essential oils; use for sturdy herbs. A microwave dries herbs more quickly, so mold is less likely to develop; use for moist, tender herbs.

■ **Hanging Method:** Gather four to six stems of fresh herbs in a bunch and tie with string, leaving a loop for hanging. Or, use a rubber band with a paper clip attached to it. Hang the herbs in a warm, well-ventilated area, out of direct sunlight, until dry. For herbs that have full seed heads, such as dill or coriander, use a paper bag. Punch holes in the bag for ventilation, label it, and put the herb bunch into the bag before you tie a string around the top of the bag. The average drying time is 1 to 3 weeks.

■ **Microwave Method:** This is better for small quantities, such as a cup or two at a time. Arrange a single layer of herbs between two paper towels and put them in the microwave for 1 to 2 minutes on high power. Let the leaves cool. If they are not dry, reheat for 30 seconds and check again. Repeat as needed. Let cool. Do not overcook, or the herbs will lose their flavor.

Storing Herbs and Spices

■ **Fresh herbs:** Dill and parsley will keep for about 2 weeks with stems immersed in a glass of water tented with a plastic bag. Most other fresh herbs (and greens) will keep for short periods unwashed and refrigerated in tightly sealed plastic bags with just enough moisture to prevent wilting. For longer storage, use moisture- and gas-permeable paper and cellophane. Plastic cuts off oxygen to the plants and promotes spoilage.

■ **Spices and dried herbs:** Store in a cool, dry place.

Cooking With Herbs

■ **Bouquet garni** is usually made with bay leaves, thyme, and parsley tied with string or wrapped in cheesecloth. Use to flavor casseroles and soups. Remove after cooking.

■ **Fines herbes** use equal amounts of fresh parsley, tarragon, chives, and chervil chopped fine. Commonly used in French cooking, they make a fine omelet or add zest to soups and sauces. Add to salads and butter sauces, or sprinkle on noodles, soups, and stews.

How to Grow Bulbs

	COMMON NAME	LATIN NAME	HARDINESS ZONE	SOIL	LIGHT*	SPACING (inches)
SPRING-PLANTED BULBS	**Allium**	*Allium*	3–10	Well-drained/moist	○	12
	Begonia, tuberous	*Begonia*	10–11	Well-drained/moist	◑●	12–15
	Blazing star/ gayfeather	*Liatris*	7–10	Well-drained	○	6
	Caladium	*Caladium*	10–11	Well-drained/moist	◑●	8–12
	Calla lily	*Zantedeschia*	8–10	Well-drained/moist	○◑	8–24
	Canna	*Canna*	8–11	Well-drained/moist	○	12–24
	Cyclamen	*Cyclamen*	7–9	Well-drained/moist	◑	4
	Dahlia	*Dahlia*	9–11	Well-drained/fertile	○	12–36
	Daylily	*Hemerocallis*	3–10	Adaptable to most soils	○◑	12–24
	Freesia	*Freesia*	9–11	Well-drained/moist/sandy	○◑	2–4
	Garden gloxinia	*Incarvillea*	4–8	Well-drained/moist	○	12
	Gladiolus	*Gladiolus*	4–11	Well-drained/fertile	○◑	4–9
	Iris	*Iris*	3–10	Well-drained/sandy	○	3–6
	Lily, Asiatic/Oriental	*Lilium*	3–8	Well-drained	○◑	8–12
	Peacock flower	*Tigridia*	8–10	Well-drained	○	5–6
	Shamrock/sorrel	*Oxalis*	5–9	Well-drained	○◑	4–6
	Windflower	*Anemone*	3–9	Well-drained/moist	○◑	3–6
FALL-PLANTED BULBS	**Bluebell**	*Hyacinthoides*	4–9	Well-drained/fertile	○◑	4
	Christmas rose/ hellebore	*Helleborus*	4–8	Neutral–alkaline	○◑	18
	Crocus	*Crocus*	3–8	Well-drained/moist/fertile	○◑	4
	Daffodil	*Narcissus*	3–10	Well-drained/moist/fertile	○◑	6
	Fritillary	*Fritillaria*	3–9	Well-drained/sandy	○◑	3
	Glory of the snow	*Chionodoxa*	3–9	Well-drained/moist	○◑	3
	Grape hyacinth	*Muscari*	4–10	Well-drained/moist/fertile	○◑	3–4
	Iris, bearded	*Iris*	3–9	Well-drained	○◑	4
	Iris, Siberian	*Iris*	4–9	Well-drained	○◑	4
	Ornamental onion	*Allium*	3–10	Well-drained/moist/fertile	○	12
	Snowdrop	*Galanthus*	3–9	Well-drained/moist/fertile	○◑	3
	Snowflake	*Leucojum*	5–9	Well-drained/moist/sandy	○◑	4
	Spring starflower	*Ipheion uniflorum*	6–9	Well-drained loam	○◑	3–6
	Star of Bethlehem	*Ornithogalum*	5–10	Well-drained/moist	○◑	2–5
	Striped squill	*Puschkinia scilloides*	3–9	Well-drained	○◑	6
	Tulip	*Tulipa*	4–8	Well-drained/fertile	○◑	3–6
	Winter aconite	*Eranthis*	4–9	Well-drained/moist/fertile	○◑	3

REFERENCE

	* ○ full sun	◑ partial shade	● full shade

DEPTH (inches)	BLOOMING SEASON	HEIGHT (inches)	NOTES
3–4	Spring to summer	6–60	Usually pest-free; a great cut flower
1–2	Summer to fall	8–18	North of Zone 10, lift in fall
4	Summer to fall	8–20	An excellent flower for drying; north of Zone 7, plant in spring, lift in fall
2	Summer	8–24	North of Zone 10, plant in spring, lift in fall
1–4	Summer	24–36	Fragrant; north of Zone 8, plant in spring, lift in fall
Level	Summer	18–60	North of Zone 8, plant in spring, lift in fall
1–2	Spring to fall	3–12	Naturalizes well in warm areas; north of Zone 7, lift in fall
4–6	Late summer	12–60	North of Zone 9, lift in fall
2	Summer	12–36	Mulch in winter in Zones 3 to 6
2	Summer	12–24	Fragrant; can be grown outdoors in warm climates
3–4	Summer	6–20	Does well in woodland settings
3–6	Early summer to early fall	12–80	North of Zone 10, lift in fall
4	Spring to late summer	3–72	Divide and replant rhizomes every two to five years
4–6	Early summer	36	Fragrant; self-sows; requires excellent drainage
4	Summer	18–24	North of Zone 8, lift in fall
2	Summer	2–12	Plant in confined area to control
2	Early summer	3–18	North of Zone 6, lift in fall
3–4	Spring	8–20	Excellent for borders, rock gardens and naturalizing
1–2	Spring	12	Hardy, but requires shelter from strong, cold winds
3	Early spring	5	Naturalizes well in grass
6	Early spring	14–24	Plant under shrubs or in a border
3	Midspring	6–30	Different species can be planted in rock gardens, woodland gardens, or borders
3	Spring	4–10	Self-sows easily; plant in rock gardens, raised beds, or under shrubs
2–3	Late winter to spring	6–12	Use as a border plant or in wildflower and rock gardens; self-sows easily
4	Early spring to early summer	3–48	Naturalizes well; a good cut flower
4	Early spring to midsummer	18–48	An excellent cut flower
3–4	Late spring to early summer	6–60	Usually pest-free; a great cut flower
3	Spring	6–12	Best when clustered and planted in an area that will not dry out in summer
4	Spring	6–18	Naturalizes well
3	Spring	4–6	Fragrant; naturalizes easily
4	Spring to summer	6–24	North of Zone 5, plant in spring, lift in fall
3	Spring	4–6	Naturalizes easily; makes an attractive edging
4–6	Early to late spring	8–30	Excellent for borders, rock gardens, and naturalizing
2–3	Late winter to spring	2–4	Self-sows and naturalizes easily

R
E
F
E
R
E
N
C
E

Substitutions for Common Ingredients

ITEM	QUANTITY	SUBSTITUTION
Baking powder	1 teaspoon	¼ teaspoon baking soda plus ¼ teaspoon cornstarch plus ½ teaspoon cream of tartar
Buttermilk	1 cup	1 tablespoon lemon juice or vinegar plus milk to equal 1 cup; or 1 cup plain yogurt
Chocolate, unsweetened	1 ounce	3 tablespoons cocoa plus 1 tablespoon unsalted butter, shortening, or vegetable oil
Cracker crumbs	¾ cup	1 cup dry bread crumbs; or 1 tablespoon quick-cooking oats (for thickening)
Cream, heavy	1 cup	¾ cup milk plus ⅓ cup melted unsalted butter (this will not whip)
Cream, light	1 cup	⅞ cup milk plus 3 tablespoons melted, unsalted butter
Cream, sour	1 cup	⅞ cup buttermilk or plain yogurt plus 3 tablespoons melted, unsalted butter
Cream, whipping	1 cup	⅔ cup well-chilled evaporated milk, whipped; or 1 cup nonfat dry milk powder whipped with 1 cup ice water
Egg	1 whole	2 yolks plus 1 tablespoon cold water; or 3 tablespoons vegetable oil plus 1 tablespoon water (for baking); or 2 to 3 tablespoons mayonnaise (for cakes)
Egg white	1 white	2 teaspoons meringue powder plus 3 tablespoons water, combined
Flour, all-purpose	1 cup	1 cup plus 3 tablespoons cake flour (not advised for cookies or quick breads); or 1 cup self-rising flour (omit baking powder and salt from recipe)
Flour, cake	1 cup	1 cup minus 3 tablespoons sifted all-purpose flour plus 3 tablespoons cornstarch
Flour, self-rising	1 cup	1 cup all-purpose flour plus 1½ teaspoons baking powder plus ¼ teaspoon salt
Herbs, dried	1 teaspoon	1 tablespoon fresh, minced and packed
Honey	1 cup	1¼ cups sugar plus ½ cup liquid called for in recipe (such as water or oil)
Ketchup	1 cup	1 cup tomato sauce plus ¼ cup sugar plus 3 tablespoons apple-cider vinegar plus ½ teaspoon salt plus pinch of ground cloves combined; or 1 cup chili sauce
Lemon juice	1 teaspoon	½ teaspoon vinegar
Mayonnaise	1 cup	1 cup sour cream or plain yogurt; or 1 cup cottage cheese (puréed)
Milk, skim	1 cup	⅓ cup instant nonfat dry milk plus ¾ cup water

R
E
F
E
R
E
N
C
E

ITEM	QUANTITY	SUBSTITUTION
Milk, to sour	1 cup	1 tablespoon vinegar or lemon juice plus milk to equal 1 cup. Stir and let stand 5 minutes.
Milk, whole	1 cup	½ cup evaporated whole milk plus ½ cup water; or ¾ cup 2 percent milk plus ¼ cup half-and-half
Molasses	1 cup	1 cup honey or dark corn syrup
Mustard, dry	1 teaspoon	1 tablespoon prepared mustard less 1 teaspoon liquid from recipe
Oat bran	1 cup	1 cup wheat bran or rice bran or wheat germ
Oats, old-fashioned (rolled)	1 cup	1 cup steel-cut Irish or Scotch oats
Quinoa	1 cup	1 cup millet or couscous (whole wheat cooks faster) or bulgur
Sugar, dark-brown	1 cup	1 cup light-brown sugar, packed; or 1 cup granulated sugar plus 2 to 3 tablespoons molasses
Sugar, granulated	1 cup	1 cup firmly packed brown sugar; or 1¾ cups confectioners' sugar (makes baked goods less crisp); or 1 cup superfine sugar
Sugar, light-brown	1 cup	1 cup granulated sugar plus 1 to 2 tablespoons molasses; or ½ cup dark-brown sugar plus ½ cup granulated sugar
Sweetened condensed milk	1 can (14 oz.)	1 cup evaporated milk plus 1¼ cups granulated sugar. Combine and heat until sugar dissolves.
Vanilla bean	1-inch bean	1 teaspoon vanilla extract
Vinegar, apple-cider	—	malt, white-wine, or rice vinegar
Vinegar, balsamic	1 tablespoon	1 tablespoon red- or white-wine vinegar plus ½ teaspoon sugar
Vinegar, red-wine	—	white-wine, sherry, champagne, or balsamic vinegar
Vinegar, rice	—	apple-cider, champagne, or white-wine vinegar
Vinegar, white-wine	—	apple-cider, champagne, fruit (raspberry), rice, or red-wine vinegar
Yeast	1 cake (⅗ oz.)	1 package (¼ ounce) or 1 scant tablespoon active dried yeast
Yogurt, plain	1 cup	1 cup sour cream (thicker; less tart) or buttermilk (thinner; use in baking, dressings, sauces)

R
E
F
E
R
E
N
C
E

Types of Fat

One way to minimize your total blood cholesterol is to manage the amount and types of fat in your diet. Aim for monounsaturated and polyunsaturated fats; avoid saturated and trans fats.

■ **Monounsaturated fat** lowers LDL (bad cholesterol) and may raise HDL (good cholesterol) or leave it unchanged; found in almonds, avocados, canola oil, cashews, olive oil, peanut oil, and peanuts.

■ **Polyunsaturated fat** lowers LDL and may lower HDL; includes omega-3 and omega-6 fatty acids; found in corn oil, cottonseed oil, fish such as salmon and tuna, safflower oil, sesame seeds, soybeans, and sunflower oil.

■ **Saturated fat** raises both LDL and HDL; found in chocolate, cocoa butter, coconut oil, dairy products (milk, butter, cheese, ice cream), egg yolks, palm oil, and red meat.

■ **Trans fat** raises LDL and lowers HDL; a type of fat common in many processed foods, such as most margarines (especially stick), vegetable shortening, partially hydrogenated vegetable oil, many commercial fried foods (doughnuts, french fries), and commercial baked goods (cookies, crackers, cakes).

Calorie-Burning Comparisons

If you hustle through your chores to get to the fitness center, relax. You're getting a great workout already. The left-hand column lists "chore" exercises, the middle column shows the number of calories burned per minute per pound of body weight, and the right-hand column lists comparable "recreational" exercises. For example, a 150-pound person forking straw bales burns 9.45 calories per minute, the same workout he or she would get playing basketball.

Chopping with an ax, fast	0.135	Skiing, cross country, uphill
Climbing hills, with 44-pound load	0.066	Swimming, crawl, fast
Digging trenches	0.065	Skiing, cross country, steady walk
Forking straw bales	0.063	Basketball
Chopping down trees	0.060	Football
Climbing hills, with 9-pound load	0.058	Swimming, crawl, slow
Sawing by hand	0.055	Skiing, cross country, moderate
Mowing lawns	0.051	Horseback riding, trotting
Scrubbing floors	0.049	Tennis
Shoveling coal	0.049	Aerobic dance, medium
Hoeing	0.041	Weight training, circuit training
Stacking firewood	0.040	Weight lifting, free weights
Shoveling grain	0.038	Golf
Painting houses	0.035	Walking, normal pace, asphalt road
Weeding	0.033	Table tennis
Shopping for food	0.028	Cycling, 5.5 mph
Mopping floors	0.028	Fishing
Washing windows	0.026	Croquet
Raking	0.025	Dancing, ballroom
Driving a tractor	0.016	Drawing, standing position

Freezer Storage Time

(freezer temperature 0°F or colder)

PRODUCT	MONTHS IN FREEZER
Fresh meat	
Beef	6 to 12
Lamb	6 to 9
Veal	6 to 9
Pork	4 to 6
Ground beef, veal, lamb, pork	3 to 4
Frankfurters	1 to 2
Sausage, fresh pork	1 to 2
Ready-to-serve luncheon meats	Not recommended
Fresh poultry	
Chicken, turkey (whole)	12
Chicken, turkey (pieces)	6 to 9
Cornish game hen, game birds	6 to 9
Giblets	3 to 4
Cooked poultry	
Breaded, fried	4
Pieces, plain	4
Pieces covered with broth, gravy	6
Fresh fruit (prepared for freezing)	
All fruit except those listed below	10 to 12
Avocados, bananas, plantains	3
Lemons, limes, oranges	4 to 6
Fresh vegetables (prepared for freezing)	
Beans, beets, bok choy, broccoli, brussels sprouts, cabbage, carrots, cauliflower, celery, corn, greens, kohlrabi, leeks, mushrooms, okra, onions, peas, peppers, soybeans, spinach, summer squashes	10 to 12
Asparagus, rutabagas, turnips	8 to 10
Artichokes, eggplant	6 to 8
Tomatoes (overripe or sliced)	2
Bamboo shoots, cucumbers, endive, lettuce, radishes, watercress	Not recommended
Cheese (except those listed below)	6
Cottage cheese, cream cheese, feta, goat, fresh mozzarella, Neufchâtel, Parmesan, processed cheese (opened)	Not recommended

PRODUCT	MONTHS IN FREEZER
Dairy products	
Margarine (not diet)	12
Butter	6 to 9
Cream, half-and-half	4
Milk	3
Ice cream	1 to 2

Freezing Hints

For meals, remember that a quart container holds four servings, and a pint container holds two servings.

To prevent sticking, spread the food to be frozen (berries, hamburgers, cookies, etc.) on a cookie sheet and freeze until solid. Then place in plastic bags and freeze.

Label foods for easy identification. Write the name of the food, number of servings, and date of freezing on containers or bags.

Freeze foods as quickly as possible by placing them directly against the sides of the freezer.

Arrange freezer into sections for each food category.

If power is interrupted, or if the freezer is not operating normally, do not open the freezer door. Food in a loaded freezer will usually stay frozen for 2 days if the freezer door remains closed during that time period.

R
E
F
E
R
E
N
C
E

Plastics

In your quest to go green, use this guide to use and sort plastic. The number, usually found with a triangle symbol on a container, indicates the type of resin used to produce the plastic. Call **1-800-CLEANUP** for recycling information in your state.

PETE

Number 1 • *PETE or PET (polyethylene terephthalate)*

IS USED IN . . . . microwavable food trays; salad dressing, soft drink, water, and juice bottles

STATUS . . . . hard to clean; absorbs bacteria and flavors; avoid reusing

IS RECYCLED TO MAKE. . . carpet, furniture, new containers, Polar fleece

HDPE

Number 2 • *HDPE (high-density polyethylene)*

IS USED IN . . . . household cleaner and shampoo bottles, milk jugs, yogurt tubs

STATUS . . . . transmits no known chemicals into food

IS RECYCLED TO MAKE. . . detergent bottles, fencing, floor tiles, pens

V

Number 3 • *V or PVC (vinyl)*

IS USED IN . . . . cooking oil bottles, clear food packaging, mouthwash bottles

STATUS . . . . .is believed to contain phalates that interfere with hormonal development; avoid

IS RECYCLED TO MAKE. . . cables, mudflaps, paneling, roadway gutters

Number 4 • *LDPE (low-density polyethylene)*

IS USED IN . . . . bread and shopping bags, carpet, clothing, furniture

STATUS . . . . transmits no known chemicals into food

LDPE

IS RECYCLED TO MAKE. . . envelopes, floor tiles, lumber, trash-can liners

PP

Number 5 • *PP (polypropylene)*

IS USED IN. . . . . ketchup bottles, medicine and syrup bottles, drinking straws

STATUS . . . . transmits no known chemicals into food

IS RECYCLED TO MAKE. . . battery cables, brooms, ice scrapers, rakes

PS

Number 6 • *PS (polystyrene)*

IS USED IN . . . . disposable cups and plates, egg cartons, take-out containers

STATUS . . . . is believed to leach styrene, a possible human carcinogen, into food; avoid

IS RECYCLED TO MAKE. . . foam packaging, insulation, light switchplates, rulers

OTHER

Number 7 • *Other (miscellaneous)*

IS USED IN . . . . 3- and 5-gallon water jugs, nylon, some food containers

STATUS . . . . contains bisphenol A, which has been linked to heart disease and obesity; avoid

IS RECYCLED TO MAKE. . . custom-made products

R
E
F
E
R
E
N
C
E

How Much Do You Need?

WALLPAPER

Before choosing your wallpaper, keep in mind that wallpaper with little or no pattern to match at the seams and the ceiling will be the easiest to apply, thus resulting in the least amount of wasted wallpaper. If you choose a patterned wallpaper, a small repeating pattern will result in less waste than a large repeating pattern. And a pattern that is aligned horizontally (matching on each column of paper) will waste less than one that drops or alternates its pattern (matching on every other column).

To determine the amount of wall space you're covering:

■ Measure the length of each wall, add these figures together, and multiply by the height of the walls to get the area (square footage) of the room's walls.

■ Calculate the square footage of each door, window, and other opening in the room. Add these figures together and subtract the total from the area of the room's walls.

■ Take that figure and multiply by 1.15, to account for a waste rate of about 15 percent in your wallpaper project. You'll end up with a target amount to purchase when you shop.

■ Wallpaper is sold in single, double, and triple rolls. Coverage can vary, so be sure to refer to the roll's label for the proper square footage. (The average coverage for a double roll, for example, is 56 square feet.) After choosing a paper, divide the coverage figure (from the label) into the total square footage of the walls of the room you're papering. Round the answer up to the nearest whole number. This is the number of rolls you need to buy.

■ Save leftover wallpaper rolls, carefully wrapped to keep clean.

INTERIOR PAINT

Estimate your room size and paint needs before you go to the store. Running out of a custom color halfway through the job could mean disaster. For the sake of the following exercise, assume that you have a 10x15-foot room with an 8-foot ceiling. The room has two doors and two windows.

For Walls

Measure the total distance (perimeter) around the room:

(10 ft. + 15 ft.) x 2 = 50 ft.

Multiply the perimeter by the ceiling height to get the total wall area:

50 ft. x 8 ft. = 400 sq. ft.

Doors are usually 21 square feet (there are two in this exercise):

21 sq. ft. x 2 = 42 sq. ft.

Windows average 15 square feet (there are two in this exercise):

15 sq. ft. x 2 = 30 sq. ft.

Take the total wall area and subtract the area for the doors and windows to get the wall surface to be painted:

> **400 sq. ft. (wall area)**
> **– 42 sq. ft. (doors)**
> **– 30 sq. ft. (windows)**
> _____
> **328 sq. ft.**

As a rule of thumb, one gallon of quality paint will usually cover 400 square feet. One quart will cover 100 square feet. Because you need to cover 328 square feet in this example, one gallon will be adequate to give one coat of paint to the walls. (Coverage will be affected by the porosity and texture of the surface. In addition, bright colors may require a minimum of two coats.)

Metric Conversion

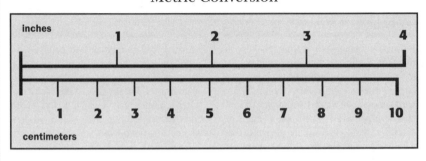

U.S. measure	x this number	= metric equivalent	metric measure	x this number	= U.S. equivalent
inch	2.54	centimeter	0.39	inch
foot	30.48	centimeter	0.033	foot
yard	0.91	meter	1.09	yard
mile	1.61	kilometer	0.62	mile
square inch	6.45	square centimeter	0.15	square inch
square foot	0.09	square meter	10.76	square foot
square yard	0.8	square meter	1.2	square yard
square mile	0.84	square kilometer	0.39	square mile
acre	0.4	hectare	2.47	acre
ounce	28.0	gram	0.035	ounce
pound	0.45	kilogram	2.2	pound
short ton (2,000 pounds)	0.91	metric ton	1.10	short ton
ounce	30.0	milliliter	0.034	ounce
pint	0.47	liter	2.1	pint
quart	0.95	liter	1.06	quart
gallon	3.8	liter	0.26	gallon

If you know the U.S. measurement and want to convert it to metric, multiply it by the number in the left shaded column (example: 1 inch equals 2.54 centimeters). If you know the metric measurement, multiply it by the number in the right shaded column (example: 2 meters equals 2.18 yards).

Where Do You Fit in Your Family Tree?

Technically it's known as consanguinity; that is, the quality or state of being related by blood or descended from a common ancestor. These relationships are shown below for the genealogy of six generations of one family. *–family tree information courtesy Frederick H. Rohles*

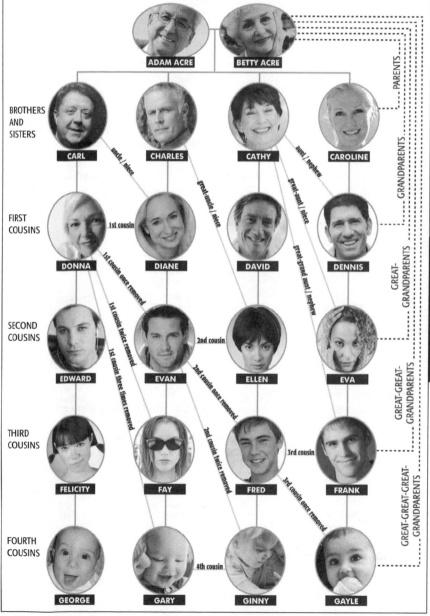

R
E
F
E
R
E
N
C
E

The Golden Rule

(It's true in all faiths.)

Brahmanism:
This is the sum of duty: Do naught unto others which would cause you pain if done to you.

Mahabharata 5:1517

Buddhism:
Hurt not others in ways that you yourself would find hurtful.

Udana-Varga 5:18

Christianity:
All things whatsoever ye would that men should do to you, do ye even so to them; for this is the law and the prophets.

Matthew 7:12

Confucianism:
Surely it is the maxim of loving-kindness: Do not unto others what you would not have them do unto you.

Analects 15:23

Islam:
No one of you is a believer until he desires for his brother that which he desires for himself.

Sunnah

Judaism:
What is hateful to you, do not to your fellow man. That is the entire Law; all the rest is commentary.

Talmud, Shabbat 31a

Taoism:
Regard your neighbor's gain as your own gain and your neighbor's loss as your own loss.

T'ai Shang Kan Ying P'ien

Zoroastrianism:
That nature alone is good which refrains from doing unto another whatsoever is not good for itself.

Dadistan-i-dinik 94:5

—courtesy Elizabeth Pool

Famous Last Words

Waiting, are they? Waiting, are they? Well—let 'em wait.
(To an attending doctor who attempted to comfort him by saying, "General, I fear the angels are waiting for you.")
–Ethan Allen, American Revolutionary general, d. February 12, 1789

A dying man can do nothing easy.
–Benjamin Franklin, American statesman, d. April 17, 1790

Now I shall go to sleep. Good night.
–Lord George Byron, English writer, d. April 19, 1824

Is it the Fourth?
–Thomas Jefferson, 3rd U.S. president, d. July 4, 1826

Thomas Jefferson—still survives . . .
(Actually, Jefferson had died earlier that same day.)
–John Adams, 2nd U.S. president, d. July 4, 1826

Friends, applaud. The comedy is finished.
–Ludwig van Beethoven, German-Austrian composer, d. March 26, 1827

Moose . . . Indian . . .
–Henry David Thoreau, American writer, d. May 6, 1862

Go on, get out—last words are for fools who haven't said enough.
(To his housekeeper, who urged him to tell her his last words so she could write them down for posterity.)
–Karl Marx, German political philosopher, d. March 14, 1883

Is it not meningitis?
–Louisa M. Alcott, American writer, d. March 6, 1888

How were the receipts today at Madison Square Garden?
–P. T. Barnum, American entrepreneur, d. April 7, 1891

Turn up the lights, I don't want to go home in the dark.
–O. Henry (William Sidney Porter), American writer, d. June 4, 1910

Get my swan costume ready.
–Anna Pavlova, Russian ballerina, d. January 23, 1931

Is everybody happy? I want everybody to be happy. I know I'm happy.
–Ethel Barrymore, American actress, d. June 18, 1959

I'm bored with it all.
(Before slipping into a coma. He died 9 days later.)
–Winston Churchill, English statesman, d. January 24, 1965

You be good. You'll be in tomorrow. I love you.
–Alex, highly intelligent African Gray parrot, d. September 6, 2007